CRITICAL WHITENESS PRAXIS IN HIGHER EDUCATION

CRITICAL WHITENESS PRAXIS IN HIGHER EDUCATION

Considerations for the Pursuit of Racial Justice on Campus

Edited by Zak Foste and Tenisha L. Tevis

Foreword by Tracy Davis

STERLING, VIRGINIA

Published by Stylus Publishing, LLC.
22883 Quicksilver Drive
Sterling, Virginia 20166-2019

Library of Congress Cataloging-in-Publication-Data
The CIP data for this title is pending.

13-digit ISBN: 978-1-64267-268-8 (cloth)
13-digit ISBN: 978-1-64267-269-5 (paperback)
13-digit ISBN: 978-1-64267-270-1 (library networkable e-edition)
13-digit ISBN: 978-1-64267-271-8 (consumer e-edition)

Printed in the United States of America

All first editions printed on acid free paper
that meets the American National Standards Institute
Z39-48 Standard.

First Edition, 2022

To Allie and Max

—Zak

To my family

—Tenisha

CONTENTS

FOREWORD ix
Tracy Davis

ACKNOWLEDGMENTS xv

1 ON THE ENORMITY OF WHITENESS IN HIGHER EDUCATION 1
Zak Foste and Tenisha L. Tevis

PART ONE: THEORETICAL FOUNDATIONS

2 TOWARD DEFINITIONS OF WHITENESS AND CRITICAL WHITENESS STUDIES
Disruption and Response-ability 21
Moira L. Ozias and Penny A. Pasque

3 WHITE NORMATIVITY
Tracing Historical and Contemporary (Re)Productions of Whiteness in Higher Education 48
Lauren N. Irwin

4 WHITE RACIAL IGNORANCE
White Lies and Inverted Epistemologies 70
Chris Corces-Zimmerman and Tonia Guida

5 RELINQUISHING WHITE INNOCENCE
Slaying a Defender of White Supremacy 90
Douglas H. Lee, Ellie Ash-Balá, Anton Ward-Zanotto, James Black, and OiYan A. Poon

PART TWO: PRACTICAL CONSIDERATIONS

6 EPISTEMIC ASPHYXIATION
Whiteness, Academic Publishing, and the Suffocation of Black Knowledge Production 115
Wilson Kwamogi Okello

7 DEAR WHITE PEOPLE
Black Women Students' Perspective 135
Kenyona N. Walker and Lori D. Patton

8 HOW WHITENESS WERQS IN LGBTQ CENTERS 155
Alex C. Lange, Antonio Duran, and Romeo Jackson

9 INTERROGATING WHITENESS IN SORORITY AND FRATERNITY LIFE 172
Cameron C. Beatty and Crystal E. Garcia

10 THE PERMEATION OF WHITENESS IN STUDENT LEADERSHIP ORGANIZATIONS 188
Brittany M. Williams, Bryan K. Hotchkins, and Meg E. Evans

11 POSSIBILITIES AND FORECLOSURES
Exploring the Relationship Between Whiteness and Anti-Blackness in Higher Education 205
Tenisha L. Tevis and Natasha Croom

12 THE WHITE RACIAL ENGAGEMENT MODEL
Unlearning the Oppressive Conditioning of Whiteness 224
Melvin A. Whitehead, Erin Weston, and Meg E. Evans

13 WHITENESS AND THE ERASURE OF INDIGENOUS PERSPECTIVES IN HIGHER EDUCATION 245
Jameson D. Lopez and Felisia Tagaban Gaskin

14 STARTING FROM THE MARGINS
Reflections on Challenging Whiteness in Higher Education 256
Zak Foste and Melvin A. Whitehead

EDITORS AND CONTRIBUTORS 273

INDEX 281

FOREWORD

One warm summer afternoon several colleagues and I were sitting in a gazebo overlooking the Illinois River. We were discussing the movie *I Am Not Your Negro* (Peck, 2016) after watching it together like we often do during our retreats. I recall saying that while it delivered a clearly powerful story of racism in America, we need to always view oppression through an intersectional lens. My friend and mentor, JQ Adams, who has taught me more about race than anyone else in my life, challenged that it was important to focus on a particular form of racism—the anti-Blackness that was centered in the film. I insisted that, again, while I agree we needed to dive into race, there were other systematic forms of oppression at play. JQ said something like, "Why do you always want to avoid the discussion of race"? I defended myself saying something like, "What do you mean . . . I've led on-campus book discussions on *White Privilege, How to be an Anti-Racist,* and *Between the World and Me.*" Adams countered sternly, "Yes, and you keep wanting to change the subject." I actually teared up and felt attacked, but by someone whose love I don't actually question. I was confused, so I just sat and reflected over the next few hours. What I discovered is that my defensiveness and fear was tethered to my ideological development within and through whiteness. As Ahmed (2007) and others describe in their scholarship, my lens on race was functioning deeply in the background and thereby keeping my "racial" positionality, thinking and behaviors out of my immediate consciousness.

I was, more specifically, experiencing what Whitehead et al. (chapter 12, this volume) describe as denial and white liberalism in their white racial engagement model. At the same time I claimed I was simply adding the dimension of intersectionality to the discussion I was also actively avoiding the saliency of race in the film due to race-based stress and discomfort I would feel if we focused on anti-Blackness. In addition, my unarticulated white liberalism led me to redirect the conversation away from facing my participation in and benefits from embedded racism. After all, I was a "good person" (see chapter 5, this volume, regarding white innocence) who wanted my performative activism to extricate me from responsibility in participating in systematic white supremacy. My view, in reflection, was whitewashed (Compton-Lilly et al., 2021) and I had to scrape, sand, and do some repairing to be conscious of how whiteness operated in me. I still have to do this in my effort to remain conscious. I've had to accept that like fish in water, I am surrounded by whiteness. I can't seem to shake its influence, so I try to be as conscious as possible, work to stay unfinished, and sometimes fail. While my whiteness is too often invisible to me, it is much too familiar to the many BIPOC including my mentor who challenged me. In fact, understanding and negotiating whiteness not only influences opportunities for success, but also can have life or death consequences.

The initial power of *Critical Whiteness Praxis in Higher Education* is this complex centering of whiteness in order to uncover its presence and interrogate its salience in both people's lives and institutional systems. As Baldwin wrote in 1962, "Not everything that is faced can be changed. But nothing can be changed until it is faced" (p. 38). There is significant evidence that we are still not effectively facing racism in this country, much less disrupting it or effectively addressing its disparate and violent impacts (Bonilla-Silva, 2018; Cabrera, 2014; Kendi, 2017; Mustaffa 2017). It's notable that placing whiteness under scrutiny will unleash the same confusions and reactions that serve to keep various forms of oppression in place. For example, some will read whiteness as so-called "white" people. While "white" people certainly benefit from systematic whiteness, conflating people with systems will continue to undermine progress toward equity. The authors in this book do an excellent job nuancing and centering whiteness not to reify what is already normatively privileged, but as a necessary step toward interrogation and unmasking. I have done similar work using men and masculinities as subjects of scrutiny in the field of higher education and student affairs. Some in the academy have assumed that centering masculinity would only bolster men's position in the patriarchy. While this is an initially reasonable perspective, the nature of systematic oppression is that it becomes so deeply embedded that it becomes unseen to those who are conferred with agency and rationalized through processes like hegemony (Brookfield, 2005), common-sense folklore (Gramsci, 1971), and neoliberalism (Giroux, 2015). Thus, while whiteness, like other forms of oppression results in blatant conscious discrimination, it also functions through unconscious mindsets and discriminatory practices that presumes covert but widespread white cultural norms (Flagg, 1993).

Foste and Tevis have gathered a wealth of talented scholars who depose whiteness from its densely normative, opaque status and place it under the critical analysis necessary to challenge white supremacy and other forms of racial oppression. By using a critical approach, whiteness is placed in the foreground so that a framework for both what whiteness means as a system and how it gets sold as a pervasive ideology through power, hegemony, and other discursive practices can be understood. Moreover, like other critical theories, a critical whiteness framework seeks to move us beyond interrogation and abstractions toward explicit political outcomes that improve the human condition. The authors of this insightful text provoke a call to praxis that seeks liberation, challenges practices that serve as barriers to inclusion, and promotes moving beyond neoliberal performances that obstruct equity. In Friere's articulation of praxis, he argues, "It is not enough for people to come together in dialogue in order to gain knowledge of their social reality. They must act together upon their environment in order critically to reflect upon their reality and so transform it through further action and critical reflection" (Friere Institute, 2020, para. 2).

What does it mean to relinquish white innocence? What are the various ways that our policies and practices in higher education are immersed in whiteness? How is whiteness both different from and similar to other forms of oppression, and how do these intersect to reinforce a matrix of subjugation? How do unique histories and contexts influence critical similarities and differences regarding racism and particular forms of racism, for example, anti-Blackness and anti-Indigeneity. These and other questions are addressed in this book. But rather than simply another intellectual exercise that leaves those who engage with it feeling like they understand (which is, in an ironic twist, itself an insidious barrier to progress), Foste, Tevis, and the contributors disrupt and challenge us to enact a critical whiteness praxis that will require us to go beyond reductionist strategies for change that make us feel good. A critical unveiling, however, causes some to enact their pain through unconscious countertransference or distancing judgment that also inhibits real change. As hooks (1994) argues, many who see their behaviors as resistance to domination are ultimately motivated by self-interest seeking "simply for an end to what we feel is hurting us" (p. 290). While understandable and valid, such motivation can leave the systematic intact. A more powerful response, according to hooks, is to shift our motivation from focusing on our own suffering toward the care and concern for others made possible through a "love ethic" (p. 290). When we see that we are all impacted by whiteness and how it limits both individual choice and human connection, we can more powerfully transform ourselves and the systems of oppression that sell division, othering and oppression.

In fact, I believe that even "white" people are harmed by racism like men are harmed by sexism. My friend Alan Berkowitz refers to these as the disadvantages of the advantages. I am not saying that the impact of such institutional oppression is equally dispensed—those who are targeted receive radically disproportionate and overt aggression. What I and others believe is that the very act of othering causes a fundamental rupture that simultaneously secures privilege and severs one's connection to the common good.

Another way of viewing this is that unconsciously living in a community that confers agency to some and delivers violence to others on the basis of socially constructed characteristics like race is being complicit in that oppression. Chapters 2 and 14 describe the human costs for those who uncritically accept violence-inducing ideologies of separation. For example, Ozias and Pasque (chapter 2) cite Matias and Mackey (2016) who argue that "loyalty to whiteness pulls one's soul *away* from humanity" (p. 34).

The hope offered in this book is that by adding to our understanding of how whiteness operates to stabilize racial oppression we begin to transform the conditions that too often keep the historical violence and contemporary material consequences hidden from consciousness and public discourse. The recent fear unleashed and lies spread about critical race theory is a testament to both the power of critical perspectives to disrupt oppression and fear that embedded whiteness perpetrates to keep systematic benefits in place. The path forward reminds me of my colleague and friend Rachel Wagner's question that she sometimes asks: "What does liberation look like?" While my answer continues to unfold, my lived experience is that when I engage in the frameworks like those offered in this insightful text I sometimes feel confusion, excitement, anger, guilt, and other emotions. I also know that these are signals that I still have work to do. The path toward liberation looks to me like having the courage to engage in both deep self-reflection and learning engagement with others. It looks sometimes quite chaotic, painful, and distancing. The other side of such a process, however, can be connecting and fertile grounds for building a common humanity toward equity and justice. This book puts us on such a path.

—Tracy Davis
Western Illinois University

References

Ahmed, S. (2007). A phenomenology of whiteness. *Feminist Theory, 8*(2), 149–168. https://doi.org/10.1177/1464700107078139

Baldwin, J. (1962, January 14). As much truth as one can bear. *The New York Times*, BR, BR38.

Bonilla-Silva, E. (2018). *Racism without racists: Color-blind racism and the persistence of racial inequality in America* (5th ed.). Rowman & Littlefield.

Brookfield, S. D. (2005). *The power of critical theory: Liberating adult learning and teaching*. Jossey-Bass.

Cabrera, N. L. (2014). Exposing whiteness in higher education: White male college students minimizing racism, claiming victimization, and recreating

White supremacy. *Race Ethnicity and Education, 17*(1), 30–55. https://doi.org/10.1080/13613324.2012.725040

Compton-Lilly, C., Ellison, T. L., Perry, K. H. & Smagorinsky P. (Eds.). (2021). *Whitewashed critical perspectives: Restoring the edge to edgy ideas.* Taylor & Francis.

Ellison, T. L. (2021). "Stop whitewashing our stories": Using counter-stories to dismantle racist and deficit perspectives in BIPOC narratives. In C. Compton-Lilly, T. L. Ellison, K. H. Perry & P. Smagorinsky (Eds.), *Whitewashed critical perspectives: Restoring the edge to edgy ideas* (pp. 86–103). Taylor & Francis.

Flagg, B. J. (1992). Was blind, but now I see: White race consciousness and the requirement of discriminatory intent, *Michigan Law Review, 91*, 953–1017. https://repository.law.umich.edu/mlr/vol91/iss5/5

Friere Institute. (2022). *Praxis/reflection.*

Giroux, H. A. (2015). Democracy in crisis, the specter of authoritarianism, and the future of higher education. *Journal of Critical Scholarship on Higher Education and Student Affairs, 1*(1), 101–113. https://ecommons.luc.edu/jcshesa/vol1/iss1/7/

Gramsci, A. (1971). *Selections from the prison notebooks* (Quentin Hoare & Geoffrey Nowell Smith, Eds. & Trans.). International Publishers.

hooks, b. (1994). *Outlaw culture.* Routledge.

Kendi, I. X. (2017). *Stamped from the beginning: The definitive history of racist ideas in America.* Bold Type Books.

Matias, C. E., & Mackey, J. (2016). Breakin' down whiteness in antiracist teaching: Introducing critical whiteness pedagogy. *The Urban Review, 48*, 119. https://doi.org/10.1007/s11256-015-0344-7

Mustaffa, J. B. (2017). Mapping violence, naming life: A history of anti-Black oppression in the higher education system. *International Journal of Qualitative Studies in Education, 30*(8), 711–727. https://doi.org/10.1080/09518398.2017.1350299

Peck, R. (Director). (2016). *I am not your negro* [Film]. Magnolia Pictures.

Wilder, C. S. (2013). *Ebony & ivy: Race, slavery, and the troubled history of America's universities.* Bloomsbury Press.

ACKNOWLEDGMENTS

We are both indebted to numerous individuals who have supported us throughout this journey. We are both incredibly thankful to chapter contributors for believing in this project and buying into our vision. This book project spanned both the trials of COVID-19 and the heightened racial unrest resulting from racial terror and anti-Blackness across the United States. We are deeply grateful that the chapter contributors shared their thinking and labor with us for this text during incredibly difficult and taxing times, both personally and professionally.

Zak is thankful to friends, family, and colleagues who supported his thinking throughout this journey. He is thankful for his wife, who was pregnant with their first child during much of this process; she continually reminds him of what is important in life. Zak is especially thankful for his doctoral advisor, Susan R. Jones, who encouraged him to take up this project when he was most unsure of it. He also wishes to express gratitude for Melvin Whitehead, who graciously agreed to coauthor the final chapter of this book. Melvin's thinking, writing, and friendship has pushed his ways of engaging in antiracist work in ways too numerous to count. And finally, Zak would like to extend a special thank you to Tenisha Tevis for collaborating on this book. To see this book come to fruition is so special and to have guided its direction with such an amazing scholar and friend is the highlight of my career. While I could mention the many ways in which you are an accomplished teacher, researcher, and advocate for racial justice, I will simply say that the academy could use more Tenisha Tevises. I am better because of our friendship and collaboration.

Tenisha would like to thank her family, friends, and colleagues who have been patient, gracious, and supportive along this journey. She extends a thank you to her mentors and peers (you all know who you are) who have been invested in her success and scholarly trajectory. Tenisha would like to offer a special thank you to her chapter coauthor Natasha Croom whose writing, thinking, and musings inspired and shaped her along the way. Lastly, she would like to thank her coeditor Zak Foste for his insightfulness, friendship, unwavering commitment to racial justice, and for sharing this platform with her. I am honored to be part of your life professionally as well as personally and I am most grateful that you are in mine. We defied the "rules" in developing this project to do what we wanted to do, and I am so glad we did so. Thank you for these things and all that is to come.

I

ON THE ENORMITY OF WHITENESS IN HIGHER EDUCATION

Zak Foste and Tenisha L. Tevis

We began working on this project in February of 2020. As we embarked on a book dedicated to interrogating the historical and contemporary manifestations of whiteness in higher education, we knew our efforts would not exist in a vacuum. Although we did not know the specifics, at what moment or in what manner, we knew that we would be reminded of the enormity of whiteness in everyday life and its suffocating effects on Communities of Color. Amy Cooper calling the police on Christian Cooper as he bird-watched on Memorial Day weekend. *The enormity of whiteness.* Ahmaud Arbery, George Floyd, and Breonna Taylor taken from this world at the hands of white racial violence and terror, a reminder of how easily white supremacy discards the humanity and dignity of Black life. *The enormity of whiteness.* Anti-Asian rhetoric that fueled anti-Asian violence in the wake of COVID-19. A violence so normalized many felt comfortable enacting these deeds in broad daylight. *The enormity of whiteness.* A white St. Louis couple becomes famous for brandishing firearms at Black Lives Matter activists. *The enormity of whiteness*. The disproportionate impact of COVID-19 on Communities of Color. *The enormity of whiteness.* Reckoning with racist mascots in Cleveland and Washington DC. *The enormity of whiteness.* And on January 6th, a brutal culmination of festering white rage that descended on the U.S. Capitol building to "stop the steal" of a supposedly illegitimate president elected, due in large part, to a Black vote some are so eager to suppress. The enormity of whiteness, indeed.

Although each of these instances occurred beyond the confines of higher education, our historically white colleges and universities (HWCUs) are often a microcosm of the United States. And they, too, reflect the enormity of whiteness. A litany of higher education scholarship has long made clear that Students of Color experience the university environment qualitatively differently than their white peers (Harper & Hurtado, 2007; George Mwangi et al., 2018). As Caroline Turner (1994) once explained, Students of Color often feel like a guest in someone else's home at HWCUs. If we were to extend her analogy, we might consider how the very foundation of the home is one built on a racial ideology of whiteness and that it is white people who are entitled to comfort, affirmation, and belonging in such spaces. It is white people who see pictures of themselves on the walls and interact with peers, faculty, and administrators who share common cultural references and experiences, and an institutional history that reflects their own. Although whiteness is not a static category, and contains a diversity of experiences with regard to gender, sexuality, ability, social class and so forth, it is unlikely white students will feel unwelcome at HWCUs because of their race. Conversely, whiteness positions People of Color as provisional, tenuous members of the campus community. One need look no further than the experience of Lolade Siyonbola, a Black woman graduate student at Yale who fell asleep in a residence hall lounge only to have the police called on her by a white student (Wootson, 2018). Whiteness positioned her as an outsider within her own campus. She was, in effect, a Black body in what Elijah Anderson (2015) has described as the white space. Further, when Students, Faculty, and Staff of Color are embraced by the institution, it is often in tokenizing and dehumanizing ways—as commodities or forms of racial capital (Leong, 2013) that serve the institution's interest.

And although one might hope that at this particular historical moment, where anti-Blackness and other forms of racial oppression have been thrust into the national conversation, that our colleges and universities might be transformed in ways that rectify racial injustices rather than perpetuate them. Instead, many HWCUs continue to maintain racial dominance through policies, behaviors, and practices. Even more troubling, at this same historical moment, conservative state legislatures are attempting to take away the very tools necessary to make sense of deeply entrenched racial inequities. At the time of this writing numerous states have banned, or are in the process of debating a ban, on the teaching of critical race theory (Dutton, 2021). Similar objections have been hurled toward the 1619 Project, an undertaking aimed at more accurately capturing the history of white racial violence, genocide, wealth accumulation, and their lasting impacts. Such moves aimed at restricting this knowledge follow a predictable pattern: Obfuscate any part of the historical record that might expose the terror and violence inflicted in the name of whiteness (Glaude, 2020), thereby mystifying the consequences of such actions and any understanding of today's inequitable outcomes. It is, as Baldwin described, the big lie (Glaude, 2020). The cycle continues.

So why this book? Why now? Critical whiteness studies (CWS), as a field of scholarship in higher education and student affairs, has grown in recent years (Cabrera, 2014; Cabrera et al., 2016; Gusa, 2010; Foste, 2019, Foste & Irwin, 2020; Irwin & Foste, 2021; Linley, 2017; Tapia-Fuselier & Irwin, 2019; Tevis, 2020; Weaver et al., 2021; Whitehead, 2021). CWS seeks to dislodge whiteness from its normative, taken-for-granted status. Further, such an approach explicitly names how whiteness is a central, underlying element to the maintenance and reproduction of racial oppression (Matias et al., 2014; Owen, 2007). As Matias et al. (2014) explained, "According to CWS, whiteness is the underlying mechanism that maintains a racist system, and not acknowledging whiteness contributes to the permanence of race and racism" (p. 291). Similarly, Applebaum (2010) noted that the origins of CWS lie in desires to expose white people to the devastating consequences of whiteness, which, although invisible to whites, are all too familiar for People of Color:

> Critical whiteness studies begin with the acknowledgement that whiteness and its concomitant privileges tend to remain invisible to most white people. . . . From this perspective, racism is essentially a white problem. Whiteness is mainly invisible to those who benefit from it. For those who don't, whiteness is often blatantly and painfully ubiquitous. (p. 9)

Within higher education and student affairs scholars have examined whiteness in a variety of ways. It is important to note that not all scholars explicitly ground this work in a critical whiteness approach. Although many do employ a CWS lens, others draw on approaches such as critical race theory (see Stewart, 2019) to name and challenge whiteness. Early work on the nature of whiteness examined the contexts and conditions that promote the development of white racial allies (Reason & Evans, 2007; Reason et al., 2005). Others have examined the ways in which white students make meaning of their racial identities and how the college environment might move students to more antiracist ways of knowing (Cabrera, 2012; Foste & Jones, 2020; Linder, 2015; Robbins, 2016; Whitehead, 2021). A smaller subset of studies have examined white faculty and administrators' racial attitudes and commitment to racial justice (Patton & Bondi, 2015; Tevis, 2020). Others have gone beyond the level of the individual to explore the ways in which whiteness infuses the campus climate broadly (Cabrera et al., 2016; Gusa, 2010) and particular campus environments such as academic spaces (Bondi, 2012; Linley, 2017; Matias & Mackey, 2016; Nishi, 2021), community service-learning (Irwin & Foste, 2021; Mitchell et al., 2012), leadership programs (Tapia-Fuselier & Irwin, 2019; Weaver et al., 2021), and university housing (Foste, 2021). Recent work has also offered insights into the process of doing critical whiteness research (Cabrera, 2016; Corces-Zimmerman & Guida, 2019; Foste, 2020).

In our own conversations, however, we continually reflected on the need to bridge the gap between important theoretical contributions offered by whiteness scholarship broadly and CWS work in particular, and the immediate need to implement such ideas in everyday practice. In short, we wanted a way to translate theoretical concepts into practice in ways that might advance racial justice on our campuses. In this book we argue for a critical whiteness praxis that disrupts the normative, taken-for-granted status of whiteness in postsecondary contexts. In the rest of this chapter, we outline what such work might look like.

Before proceeding, however, we wish to make two points that we believe offer important context for what is to follow. First, we want to clarify what this book is and what it is not. Although this book endeavors to name and challenge whiteness in higher education, it is not a book primarily concerned with white people or white people's racial identity development. Numerous resources exist on this topic (see Brookfield & Hess, 2021). Rather, this book is focused largely on the effects, or the consequences, of whiteness in the lives of Students, Faculty, and Staff of Color and how those who work in higher education and student affairs might disrupt such patterns. Such an approach is grounded in the belief that "whiteness in the United States can be understood largely through the social consequences it provides for those who are considered to be non-white" (McLaren, 1998, p. 66). In turn, many of the accounts in this book powerfully illuminate the material consequences of whiteness in the lives of Faculty, Staff, and Students of Color.

To the extent that white readers come to this book seeking strategies for development, we hope our white readers sit with the accounts offered by our authors with humility and uncertainty in what one does not know. Indeed, a defining effect of whiteness in the lives of white people is a distorted sense of history, of the racial world, and the confidence to all too easily ignore, delegitimize, or outright dismiss the experiences and knowledge of Black, Indigenous, and People of Color (BIPOC). As Thompson and Watson (2016) noted, "Rather than stay present to feel the pain of brutalized bodies and psyches, and then act from that knowledge, most white people deny, justify, and then reproduce the very violence that was the source of their own dis-ease" (p. 236). In this spirit, we ask our white readers to avoid temptations to flee and instead stay present in the accounts shared in this text. Chapter authors in this book have labored to reveal the numerous ways in which whiteness is deeply embedded in HWCUs.

Second, we want to acknowledge the potential dangers of critical whiteness work in colonizing race-based scholarship, theorizing, and practice among People of Color (Leonardo, 2013). We have noticed an uptick in this work, particularly at conferences in the field of higher education and student affairs. The possibilities of this body of work excite us, but we also recognize and understand the trepidation and concern among Scholars and Practitioners of Color who fear this work may simply take up too much space or that it might recenter white experiences. As Leonardo (2013) noted, "The fear is that race scholarship will become another White-dominated field of knowledge. A chorus of 'They've done it to us again!' from people of color may be a reasonable response" (p. 98). In this vein, we believe it is absolutely necessary to make clear that a commitment to critical whiteness work must always be grounded in a commitment to addressing and dismantling white supremacy, anti-Blackness, anti-Indigeneity, and other forms of racial oppression. It is not difficult to imagine how this line of work could quickly devolve into narcissistic recentering of white people. Thus, it is our hope that the ideas, concepts, and suggestions made in this book enter into a conversation with a long list of scholarship, largely driven by Scholars of Color, to challenge white supremacy and promote racial equity in higher education.

The Effects of Whiteness

It has been our experience in higher education and student affairs that too often discussions of whiteness are often reduced to individual white people and white racial identity. These are important conversations, to be sure. Those who work in higher education and student affairs contexts have often relied on the works of racial identity theorists to explore the ways in which white people come to name and understand themselves as racial beings. This body of scholarship (Hardiman & Keehn, 2012; Helms, 2008) has been useful in arming practitioners with frameworks for promoting more antiracist ways of knowing and being among white students. Yet an exclusive focus on white identity development can lead to an overly individualistic approach where the central focus is on becoming, or worse yet merely appearing, less racist. But our institutions will not be transformed by incremental increases in white people's racial awareness or one-off diversity training (Patton & Haynes, 2020). As such, we concur with education scholar Zeus Leonardo (2009), who reminded us that we should not reduce whiteness to individual white people alone, because in doing so we fail to recognize how whiteness functions as a racial ideology grounded in histories of anti-Blackness, anti-Indigeneity, and settler colonialism. Or, as Peter McLaren (1998) explained, whiteness represents a "sociohistorical form of consciousness, given birth at the nexus of capitalism, colonial rule, and the emergent relationships among dominant and subordinate groups" (p. 66). In short, we fail to recognize the enormity of whiteness when we reduce the concept to individual white people and matters of increased racial consciousness.

Instead, we encourage readers to think about how whiteness functions ideologically, structurally, institutionally, and epistemically to produce inequitable outcomes across the educational landscape. Today whiteness permeates every corner, every fiber of higher education. To think about whiteness exclusively in terms of white people fails to acknowledge the deeply relational nature of whiteness (Morrison, 1992; Rodriguez, 1998; Yancy, 2018). Historically whiteness has functioned to produce a center/margin, universal/particular dynamic (Perry, 2001; Rodriguez, 1998), wherein whiteness represents the unnamed, unmarked location, the "yardstick with which others are compared" (Rodriguez, 1998, p. 44). Much of this is missed when we reduce whiteness to identity alone.

One of the many ways in which whiteness operates in higher education, and a central concern of this book, is by drawing boundaries that demarcate insiders and outsiders, those who belong and those who do not. Those who are assumed natural occupants of our classrooms, laboratories, student organizations, and student centers, and those who are, as Puwar (2004) explained, bodies out of place in the white imagination. When Nikole Hannah Jones was initially denied tenure at the University of North Carolina Chapel Hill, she, along with the knowledge that emanates from her standpoint as a Black woman in a white supremacist society (Collins, 2002), were rendered outsiders. When a white student decided to call the police on Siyonbola for sleeping in the common lounge while studying, Siynobla and other Black students on campus were reminded of their provisional, outsider status. When the SAE chapter at the University of Oklahoma was caught on tape singing a song riddled with racial slurs and anti-Black sentiments, joyfully proclaiming they would never let a Black man join SAE, Black students across OU were again made aware of their troubled and tenuous relationship to the institution in Norman, Oklahoma. And when a white parent called the police on two Native American teenage brothers, Lloyd and Thomas Gray, during a campus tour at Colorado State University, the young men who had driven 7 hours to preview the institution were sent a clear message about what they might expect should they decide to enroll.

Our Journeys to This Book

Our own journey collaborating on this project reminded us daily of the ways in which we are differentially situated in relationship to whiteness, both in higher education and beyond. We often dialogued about these divergent relationships throughout this process. Zak, as a white man from a predominantly white, racially insulated community in central Illinois, came to this work because of his own developmental journey attempting to unlearn the insidious conditioning of whiteness. Through high school and college, he operated from the assumption that unlearning the conditioning of a white supremacist world required consuming as much content as possible. In this regard, Zak reduced the unlearning of deeply entrenched ways of knowing to content knowledge alone. He enrolled in African American studies courses and, midway through his time at Western Illinois University, declared a second major in sociology. These experiences, coupled with his time as a resident assistant in campus housing, were critical in pushing him to rethink so much of what he had learned in his racially insulated town of approximately 6,000 people. Zak was pushed to think how whiteness was understood to be raceless and normative and challenged to rethink supposed historical truths about the morally virtuous arc of U.S. history.

Yet this exclusive focus on his personal transformation was problematic for multiple reasons. First, it assumed that he could consume enough material about race, whiteness, and white privilege in such a way that would eventually produce some sense of personal transformation or an expanded racial consciousness. Early on this led to a detached, depersonalized understanding of racism and white supremacy and, as such, he rarely if ever considered his complicity in such systems. Second, by focusing on content knowledge and coursework, he tended to intellectualize (Watt, 2007) matters of racism and white supremacy that are, in fact, anything but academic or abstract in the lives of BIPOC communities. This initial entry point into the work often influenced his early writings and teaching on the matter. Notably his own undergraduate experience, focused on personal transformation and an enlarged white consciousness, meant that he entered conversations from a white vantage point. That is, he operated from what Whitehead et al. (2021) described as the flawed "whiteness-as-invisible analytic" (p. 2) that presumes whiteness is invisible and unnamed to everyone. In doing so, he centered the learning of white students at the expense of People of Color by focusing more on the development of increased white racial consciousness at the expense of racial liberation. As such, much of his own thinking about this project has been grounded in reflections on how, as a white person, he has come to this work. Throughout this process he is continually reminded of George Yancy's (2018) words that, "as a white person, you never clearly come to a place of 'arrival'—where such a place suggests a static noun—as a '*nonracist* white'" (p. 80).

Tenisha, as a Black cisgender woman, has always been reminded of her social position and lack of proximity to power with racist statements like "go back to Africa!" and/or the ever-*harmless* jokes by "friends" about slavery. To mitigate the discomfort of those in her social sphere, both directly and indirectly, rather than her own, and attempt to garner some semblance of safety, she consciously adorns herself in whiteness. How does one do that? Specifically, how does a Black woman *put on* whiteness? Answers to these questions begin, briefly, with the understanding that most elements of social life were once constructed for and the property of white people (Harris, 1993), evidenced by "whites only" policies and signs that once governed most public spaces, from schools and colleges to restaurants. Hence, whether traveling or going for a run, which are just a couple of activities often viewed as being owned by white people, she puts on what some would deem expensive leggings (worn by an elite female clientele), college/university gear, and of course brand name running shoes. When spoken to in mixed company she makes sure to speak with clear pronunciation. And more often than not, she refrains from calling out racist or insensitive commentary that is often passed as friendly banter. These very visible gestures and intentional actions on her part are, for some, invisible and yet instinctively interpreted as belonging in the space, which she then perceives will keep her safe. This behavior of putting on whiteness was carried into the workplace as well. To mitigate the discomfort of others, at the expense of her own, as well as the assumptions made by her colleagues, she once again engaged in what seemed to be a natural exercise, but to no avail. Although it would have been fitting to come to the study of whiteness solely through her personal experiences, it was her professional experiences in higher education as a practitioner and faculty member that truly piqued her interest in this area of study.

As a scholar-practitioner, Tenisha would describe herself as having been "dry-clean only"—pressed shirts and slacks, business attire pencil skirts, and brand name loafers, heels, and accessories. Once again, she made sure to speak with clear pronunciation, attended meetings on time, touted where she earned her degree (at the advice of her dean at the time), and took on a high service load. Quite often, she worked long hours to demonstrate a strong work ethic and an unwavering commitment to the institution. Yet these efforts could not prevent the barrage of gendered-racism (Essed, 1991) aimed at her and her leadership. Tenisha had been described, by her mostly white colleagues, who happen to also be men, as "viscerally angry," "hostile," and "hard to work with." She was often circumvented in her role regardless of her accomplishments and her ability to work across divisions. As she continued to navigate deficit narratives and experienced blatant displacement, it was clear that gendered-racism was an influential force; however, the ascension of some at her demise and the allowance of others to refuse to work with her also made it clear that another force was simultaneously at play—whiteness. Specifically, the institution is organized and functions around the preponderance of white leadership, and within that white privilege, but a particular brand of entitlement that dismisses any harm to the community brought on by racialized events. Hence, Tenisha found it fitting to explore the ways in which identity, and relatedly how systems such as racism and whiteness, influences leadership in an attempt to disrupt dominant ideologies and biased institutional practices. Having learned about racism and whiteness *the hard way*, it does beg the question the level of preparedness to lead, teach, and/or conduct research, had she been given the opportunity to learn of these systems more formally. Although higher education programs are more inclined to teach about whiteness, including a great willingness to adopt books like this one in student development and leadership courses, Tenisha wishes she had been afforded these opportunities within her own academic and professional training.

Toward a Critical Whiteness Praxis

Whiteness is most powerful when it remains universalized as the human experience, when white attitudes and beliefs are rendered raceless, and when the sources of racial inequities are presumed the result of personal failure rather than inequitable systems that serve white interests. We intentionally use the language of praxis to highlight the need for both reflection and action (Freire, 2005). Most commonly, *praxis* is referred to as theory in action. Within the context of this edited book, it is a transformative approach that would allow for a disrupting of whiteness and enable a substantive pursuit of social justice within higher education. We liken this to the liberation Freire described in *Pedagogy of the Oppressed*. He explained that liberation—a freedom from, in this instance, suppressive and oppressive behaviors and practices, is not by chance but gained through praxis; the very fight for it. He further expressed "the oppressed must confront reality critically, simultaneously objectifying and acting upon that reality" (p. 52). Because whiteness, again, has been deemed invisible to most white folks, yet it is quite visible to those who have been *othered* by it; for this reason it is reality. Therefore, there is a need to acknowledge and address the presence of whiteness, and the consequences thereof, as a reality within the functions of higher education. As recommended by Freire, we as scholars and contributors to this text come together beyond merely an intellectual exercise (i.e., offer theory) and through "serious reflection" seek to inform practice by speaking to the various ways whiteness shows up on college campuses, to then incite transformational action (i.e., praxis).

Critical whiteness praxis requires a sort of racial literacy to recognize how whiteness functions to underwrite racist, hostile, and unwelcoming campuses *and* the ability to use these tools in everyday life to advance campus environments that promote equitable learning spaces. It should be noted that this type of work necessitates a shift from the all-too-common diversity discourses that dominate campus life and prize the celebration of difference without any accompanying structural critiques (Bell & Hartmann, 2007; Berrey, 2015; Warikoo & De Novais, 2015) without any accompanying structural critiques. A critical whiteness praxis then requires an attention to, and disruption of, the normative nature of whiteness on campus, the contexts and conditions that induce white racial ignorance, and individually and institutionally produced desires for white racial innocence. In short, then, a critical whiteness praxis considers the following questions:

1. How is whiteness rendered normative and raceless on campus? And how does whiteness position Faculty, Staff, and Students of Color—their bodies, experiences, knowledge, and histories—in relation to the white normative center?
2. How does whiteness induce a state of racial ignorance among both white individuals and white institutions? What are the consequences of such ignorance, both at the level of the individual and the institution?
3. How does whiteness encourage white individuals and institutions to maintain a sense of innocence, to remain so certain of their goodness, in effect detaching themselves from systems and structures? Why are desires for innocence so strong?

We believe these questions offer an important starting place to interrogate the ways in which whiteness draws boundaries, marks People of Color as outsiders, and continually reproduces structural advantages that benefit white people in higher education. Further, it requires that faculty, staff, practitioners, and students alike name not only the ways in which whiteness operates but its devastating effects as well. These questions direct us to how whiteness is marked as the universal, raceless representation of humanity; the contexts and environments that produce and maintain a collective not knowing of the racial past and present; and the prioritization of white racial innocence over meaningful institutional transformation. To this end, each of these three concepts are explored in the first half of the book and taken up by many of the authors in the second half of the text.

Overview of the Book

It is our hope that this book is of use to a variety of audiences. First and foremost, this text is intended to speak to those who work in HWCUs and desire to cultivate more inclusive, equitable, and affirming campus environments. Although whiteness permeates higher education broadly, it is particularly pervasive at historically white institutions. This is so given the founding of these institutions as white-only spaces (Arendale, 2011); the preponderance of white faculty, staff, and students (National Center for Education Statistics [NCES], 2020, 2021); low representation of Students of Color (NCES, 2021), and lack of racial and ethnic diversity among faculty, staff, and leadership (Dedman, 2019; Espinosa et al., 2019). The very notion of praxis then calls for the bridging of theory and practice, of reflection and action (Freire, 2005). As such, we hope this book speaks to campus administrators, staff, and faculty who desire to both name and disrupt whiteness in campus life. We also believe this book may be useful for scholars who desire to critically interrogate whiteness in educational research. This book offers both theoretical grounding in the study of whiteness and numerous examples of how whiteness manifests in particular campus spaces. We hope the ideas offered by chapter contributors spark further dialogue and inspiration for research that aims to disrupt whiteness in higher education.

In order to advance a critical whiteness praxis, we have organized this book into two sections. Authors in the first section of the book introduce key theoretical ideas and concepts that readers may find useful in naming and disrupting whiteness on campus. Authors in the second half of the book draw on many of these ideas to interrogate the ways in which whiteness functions in higher education and student affairs contexts. We are immensely thankful to the contributors who have shared their work with us on the pages that follow. These contributors wrote these chapters during the rise of the COVID-19 pandemic and the racial uprising in the summer of 2020 following anti-Black violence across the United States. For our authors, particularly our Authors of Color, the effects of whiteness are anything but abstract or academic. Here we offer a brief overview of the chapters in each section.

In chapter 2 Moira L. Ozias and Penny A. Pasque provide an introduction to the field of critical whiteness studies and invite readers to think about the various ways in which whiteness has been defined and understood in theorizing and scholarship. Their writing serves as a useful primer to the broader landscape of critical whiteness work. Chapter 3, written by

Lauren N. Irwin, explores white normativity and how the normalization of whiteness is central to the reproduction of racial inequities in higher education. In chapter 4 Chris Corces-Zimmerman and Tonia Guida examine notions of white racial ignorance. Notably, they encourage deeper consideration for how racial ignorance is a socially supported form of not knowing (Mills, 1997). Their writing challenges educators to think not only about *what* white students, faculty, and staff know about race but more importantly *how* it is they come to know. Finally, chapter 5, authored by Douglas H. Lee, Ellie Ash-Bala, Anton Ward-Zanotto, James Black, and OiYan A. Poon, provides an overview of white racial innocence and how desires for racial innocence interfere with meaningful progress toward racial justice in postsecondary education. Taken together, these chapters provide an important theoretical foundation for analyzing, naming, and disrupting whiteness in higher education and student affairs. Additionally, they represent the theoretical concepts that contributed to our own understanding of a critical whiteness praxis.

The second half of this book examines the tangible manifestations of whiteness across university life. In chapter 6, Wilson Kwamogi Okello introduces the notion of epistemic asphyxiation to illuminate how whiteness limits what constitutes knowledge and who is understood to be a knower in academic spaces. Okello examines the tenure denials of Ashley Woodson at the University of Missouri and Paul Harris at the University of Virginia to document how whiteness inflicts a sense of epistemic asphyxiation on Black scholars. In chapter 7 Kenyona N. Walker and Lori D. Patton write to white faculty and administrators to illuminate the lived experiences of Black women in academic and cocurricular spaces. Using the format of "Dear White People," they present a series of letters that challenge white faculty and administrators to value the experiential knowledge of Black women students. Chapter 8, authored by Alex C. Lange, Antonio Duran, and Romeo Jackson, considers how whiteness permeates LGBTQ centers. Their writing calls attention to how programs and practices center the needs and experiences of white students, in turn pushing LGBTQ Students of Color to the margins. In chapter 9, Cameron C. Beatty and Crystal E. Garcia begin a generative conversation about the implicit and explicit ways in which whiteness functions in sorority and fraternity life. In particular, they explore how white normativity and white racial ignorance operate in such spaces.

In chapter 10 Brittany M. Williams, Bryan K. Hotchkins, and Meg E. Evans examine how whiteness is maintained and reproduced in student leadership organizations. Their writing examines how student leadership and whiteness are frequently synonymous, requiring critical attention to who is naturally understood to be a leader on campus. Chapter 11, authored by Tenisha L. Tevis and Natasha Croom, offers readers a critical interrogation of the linkage between whiteness and anti-Blackness. Their writing invites readers to consider the historical relationship between whiteness and anti-Black ways of knowing and being. Although a majority of chapters in the text attend to the material consequences of whiteness in the lives of People of Color, Melvin A. Whitehead, Erin Weston, and Meg E. Evans offer readers ways to think about engaging white undergraduates in unlearning the oppressive conditioning of whiteness. In Chapter 12 they provide readers a conceptual model to guide programs and interventions designed to engage white students on matters of race and racism. Chapter 13, authored by Jameson D. Lopez and Felisia J. Tagaban, considers how whiteness works to erase Indigenous perspectives in higher education. Their writing focuses on how institutions of higher education might support Indigenous data sovereignty and the funding of Indigenous initiatives. Finally, in chapter 14 Zak Foste and Melvin A. Whitehead offer practical suggestions to challenge whiteness on campus. Their chapter is grounded in hooks's (1990, 1992) notion of starting from the margins and whiteness as a form of terror in the Black imagination, and as such, encourages readers to enter such work from the vantage point of the pain and terror inflicted in the name of whiteness.

Concluding Thoughts

The fingerprints of whiteness are visible across higher education. For a majority of white people, such patterns are largely invisible. For People of Color, they are often painfully obvious. The chapters that follow require us to confront the enormity of whiteness to, as Baldwin explained, bear witness (Glaude, 2020). Our goal is not to frame white people or historically white institutions as irredeemable and inherently destined to reproduce whiteness. As we mentioned at the outset of this chapter, we do not find it productive to reduce whiteness to white people alone. As Leonardo (2009) noted, although white people are the beneficiaries of systemic racial power relations, "in this journey we give up hope in whiteness as an oppressive racial epistemology but retain hope in white people as concrete subjects in the struggle against racial oppression" (p. 109). And although white people and white institutions benefit from systemic power arrangements that privilege whiteness, they can make decisions about how they will live and exist in relation to whiteness (Leonardo, 2009). To this end, we seek to tell a more truthful story about our institutions in hope for more equitable, inclusive, and affirming possibilities in higher education.

References

Anderson, E. (2015). The white space. *Sociology of Race and Ethnicity, 1*(1), 10–21. https://doi.org/10.1177/2332649214561306

Applebaum, B. (2010). *Being white, being good: White complicity, white moral responsibility, and social justice pedagogy.* Lexington Books.

Arendale, D. R. (2011). Then and now: The early years of developmental education. *Research and Teaching in Developmental Education, 27*(2), 58–76.

Bell, J. M., & Hartmann, D. (2007). Diversity in everyday discourse: The cultural ambiguities and consequences of "happy talk." *American Sociological Review, 72*(6), 895–914. https://doi.org/10.1177%2F000312240707200603

Berrey, E. C. (2015). *The enigma of diversity: The language of race and the limits of racial justice.* University of Chicago Press.

Bondi, S. (2012). Students and institutions protecting Whiteness as property: A critical race theory analysis of student affairs preparation. *Journal of Student Affairs Research and Practice, 49*(4), 397–414. https://doi.org/10.1515/jsarp-2012-6381

Brookfield, S. D., & Hess, M. E. (2021). *Becoming a white antiracist: A practical guide for educators, leaders, and activists.* Stylus.

Cabrera, N. L. (2012). Working through whiteness: White, male college students challenging racism. *The Review of Higher Education, 35*(3), 375–401. https://doi.org/10.1353/rhe.2012.0020

Cabrera, N. L. (2014). Exposing whiteness in higher education: White male college students minimizing racism, claiming victimization, and recreating white supremacy. *Race Ethnicity and Education, 17*(1), 30–55. https://doi.org/10.1080/13613324.2012.725040

Cabrera, N. L. (2016). When racism and masculinity collide: Some methodological considerations from a man of colour studying Whiteness. *Whiteness and Education, 1*(1), 15–25. https://doi.org/10.1080/13613324.2015.1122662

Cabrera, N. L., Watson, J. S., & Franklin, J. D. (2016). Racial arrested development: A critical whiteness analysis of the campus ecology. *Journal of College Student Development, 57*(2), 119–134. http://doi.org/10.1353/csd.2016.0014

Collins, P. H. (2002). *Black feminist thought: Knowledge, consciousness, and the politics of empowerment.* Routledge.

Corces-Zimmerman, C., & Guida, T. F. (2019). Toward a critical whiteness methodology: Challenging whiteness through qualitative research. In J. Huisman & M. Tight (Eds.), *Theory and method in higher education research* (pp. 91–109). Emerald.

Dedman, B. (2019, March 7). *College students are more diverse than ever. Faculty and administrators are not.* Association of American Colleges & Universities. https://www.aacu.org/aacu-news/newsletter/2019/march/facts-figures

Dutton, J. (2021, June 11). Critical race theory is banned in these states. *Newsweek.* https://www.newsweek.com/critical-race-theory-banned-these-states-1599712

Espinosa, L. L., Turk, J. M., Taylor, M., & Chessman, H. M. (2019). *Race and ethnicity in higher education: A status report.* American Council on Education.

Essed, P. (1991). *Understanding everyday racism: An interdisciplinary theory* (Vol. 2). SAGE.

Foste, Z. (2019). Reproducing Whiteness: How white students justify the campus racial status quo. *Journal of Student Affairs Research and Practice, 56*(3), 241–253. https://doi.org/10.1080/19496591.2019.1576530

Foste, Z. (2020). Remaining vigilant: Reflexive considerations for white researchers studying whiteness. *Whiteness and Education, 5*(2), 131–146. https://doi.org/10.1080/23793406.2020.1738264

Foste, Z. (2021). "Oh, that's the white dorm": The racialization of university housing and the policing of racial boundaries. *Journal of College Student Development, 62*(2), 169–185. http://doi.org/10.1353/csd.2021.0015

Foste, Z., & Irwin, L. (2020). Applying critical whiteness studies in college student development theory and research. *Journal of College Student Development, 61*(4), 439–455. http://doi.org/10.1353/csd.2020.0050

Foste, Z., & Jones, S. R. (2020). Narrating whiteness: A qualitative exploration of how white college students construct and give meaning to their racial location. *Journal of College Student Development, 61*(2), 171–188. http://doi.org/10.1353/csd.2020.0016

Freire, P. (2005). *Pedagogy of the oppressed* (30th anniversary ed; M. Bergman Ramos, Trans.). Bloomsbury.

George Mwangi, C. A., Thelamour, B., Ezeofor, I., & Carpenter, A. (2018). "Black elephant in the room": Black students contextualizing campus racial climate within U.S. racial climate. *Journal of College Student Development, 59*(4), 456–474. https://doi.org/10.1353/csd.2018.0042

Glaude, E. (2020). *Begin again: James Baldwin's America and its urgent lessons for our own.* Penguin Random House.

Gusa, D. L. (2010). White institutional presence: The impact of whiteness on campus climate. *Harvard Educational Review, 80*(4), 464–490. https://doi.org/10.17763/haer.80.4.p5j483825u110002

Hardiman, R., & Keehn, M. (2012). White identity development revisited: Listening to white students. In C. L. Wijeyesinghe & B. W. Jackson III (Eds.), *New perspectives on racial identity development: Integrating emerging frameworks* (2nd ed., pp. 121–137). NYU Press.

Harper, S. R., & Hurtado, S. (2007). Nine themes in campus racial climates and implications for institutional transformation. In S. R. Harper & L. D. Patton (Eds.). *Responding to the Realities of Race on Campus.* (New Directions for Student Services, no. 120, pp. 7–24). Jossey-Bass. https://doi.org/10.1002/ss.254

Harris, C. I. (1993). Whiteness as property. *Harvard Law Review, 106*(8), 1707–1791. https://doi.org/1341787

Helms, J. E. (2008). *A race is a nice thing to have: A guide to being a white person or understanding the white persons in your life* (2nd ed.). Microtraining Associates.

hooks, b. (1990). *Yearning: Race, gender, and cultural studies.* South End Press.

hooks, b. (1992). Representing whiteness in the Black imagination. In L. Grossberg, C. Nelson, & P. Treichler (Eds.), *Cultural studies* (pp. 338–346). Routledge.

Irwin, L. N., & Foste, Z. (2021). Service-learning and racial capitalism: On the commodification of People of Color for white advancement. *The Review of Higher Education, 44*(4), 419–446. http://doi.org/10.1353/rhe.2021.0008

Leonardo, Z. (2009). *Race, whiteness, and education.* Routledge.

Leonardo, Z. (2013). *Race frameworks: A multidimensional theory of racism and education.* Teachers College Press.

Leong, N. (2013). Racial capitalism. *Harvard Law Review, 126*(8), 2151–2226.

Linder, C. (2015). Navigating guilt, shame, and fear of appearing racist: A conceptual model of antiracist white feminist identity development. *Journal of College Student Development, 56*(6), 535–550. https://doi.org/10.1353/csd.2015.0057

Linley, J. L. (2017). Teaching to deconstruct whiteness in higher education. *Whiteness and Education, 2*(1), 48–59. https://doi.org/10.1080/23793406.2017.1362943

Matias, C. E., & Mackey, J. (2016). Breakin' down whiteness in antiracist teaching: Introducing critical whiteness pedagogy. *The Urban Review, 48*(1), 32–50. https://doi.org/10.1007/s11256-015-0344-7

Matias, C. E., Viesca, K. M., Garrison-Wade, D. F., Tandon, M., & Galindo, R. (2014). "What is critical whiteness doing in OUR nice field like critical race theory?" Applying CRT and CWS to understand the white imaginations of white teacher candidates. *Equity & Excellence in Education, 47*(3), 289–304. https://doi.org/10.1080/10665684.2014.933692

McLaren, P. (1998). Whiteness is . . .: The struggle for postcolonial hybridity. In J. L. Kincheloe, S. R. Steinberg, N. M. Rodriguez, & R. E. Chennault (Eds.), *White reign: Deploying Whiteness in America* (pp. 63–76). St. Martin's.

Mills, C. W. (1997). *The racial contract.* Cornell University Press.

Mitchell, T. D., Donahue, D. M., & Young-Law, C. (2012). Service learning as a pedagogy of whiteness. *Equity & Excellence in Education, 45*(4), 612–629. https://doi.org/10.1080/10665684.2012.715534

Morrison, T. (1992). *Playing in the dark: Whiteness and the literary imagination.* Vintage.

National Center for Education Statistics. (2020). *Characteristics of postsecondary faculty.* U.S. Department of Education. https://nces.ed.gov/programs/coe/indicator/csc

National Center for Education Statistics. (2021). *Characteristics of postsecondary students.* U.S. Department of Education. https://nces.ed.gov/programs/coe/indicator/csb

Nishi, N. W. (2021, May 20). White hoarders: A portrait of whiteness and resource allocation in college algebra. *The Journal of Higher Education.* Advance online publication. https://doi.org/10.1080/00221546.2021.1914495

Owen, D. S. (2007). Towards a critical theory of whiteness. *Philosophy & Social Criticism, 33*(2), 203–222. https://doi.org/10.1177%2F0191453707074139

Patton, L. D., & Bondi, S. (2015). Nice white men or social justice allies?: Using critical race theory to examine how white male faculty and administrators engage in ally work. *Race Ethnicity and Education, 18*(4), 488–514. https://doi.org/10.1080/13613324.2014.1000289

Patton, L. D., & Haynes, C. (2020). Dear White people: Reimagining whiteness in the struggle for racial equity. *Change: The Magazine of Higher Learning, 52*(2), 41–45. https://doi.org/10.1080/00091383.2020.1732775

Perry, P. (2001). White means never having to say you're ethnic: White youth and the construction of "cultureless" identities. *Journal of Contemporary Ethnography, 30*(1), 56–91. https://psycnet.apa.org/doi/10.1177/089124101030001002

Puwar, N. (2004). *Space invaders: Race, gender and bodies out of place.* Berg.

Reason, R. D., & Evans, N. J. (2007). The complicated realities of whiteness: From color blind to racially cognizant. In S. R. Harper & L. Patton (Eds.), *Responding to the Realities of Race on Campus* (New Directions for Student Services, no. 120, pp. 67–75). Jossey-Bass. https://doi.org/10.1002/ss.258

Reason, R. D., Millar, E. A. R., & Scales, T. C. (2005). Toward a model of racial justice ally development. *Journal of College Student Development, 46*(5), 530–546. https://doi.org/10.1353/csd.2005.0054

Robbins, C. K. (2016). White women, racial identity, and learning about racism in graduate preparation programs. *Journal of Student Affairs Research and Practice, 53*(3), 256–268. https://doi.org/10.1080/19496591.2016.1143834

Rodriguez, N. M. (1998). Emptying the content of Whiteness: Toward an understanding of the relation between Whiteness and pedagogy. In J. L. Kinchcloe, S. R. Steinberg, N. M. Rodriguez, & R. E. Chennault (Eds.), *White reign: Deploying whiteness in America* (pp. 31–62). St. Martin's.

Stewart, D-L (2019). Whiteness as collective memory in student publications at midwestern liberal arts colleges, 1945–1965. *American Educational Research Journal, 56*(1), 3–38. https://doi.org/10.3102%2F0002831218788326

Tapia-Fuselier, N. & Irwin, L. (2019). Strengths so white: Interrogating StrengthsQuest education through a critical whiteness lens. *Journal of Critical Scholarship on Higher Education and Student Affairs, 5*(1), 30–44.

Tevis, T. (2020). Exploring whether white male postsecondary presidents respond to racism. *Whiteness and Education, 5*(1), 91–111. https://doi.org/10.1080/23793406.2019.1711150

Thompson, B., & Watson, V. T. (2016). Theorizing white racial trauma and its remedies. In S. Middleton, D. R. Roediger, & D. M. Shaffer (Eds.), *The construction of whiteness: An interdisciplinary analysis of race formation and the meaning of a white identity* (pp. 234–255). University Press of Mississippi.

Turner, C. S. V. (1994). Guests in someone else's house: Students of color. *The Review of Higher Education, 17*(4), 355–370.

Warikoo, N. K., & De Novais, J. (2015). Colour-blindness and diversity: Race frames and their consequences for white undergraduates at elite US universities. *Ethnic and Racial Studies, 38*(6), 860–876. https://doi.org/10.1080/01419870.2014.964281

Watt, S. K. (2007). Difficult dialogues, privilege and social justice: Uses of the privileged identity exploration (PIE) model in student affairs practice. *College Student Affairs Journal, 26*(2), 114–126.

Weaver, K. E., Lange, A. C., & Linley, J. L. (2021, April 1). White student leaders' deflections of diversity conversations. *International Journal of Qualitative Stud-*

ies in Education. Advance online publication. https://doi.org/10.1080/09518398.2021.1900619

Whitehead, M. A. (2021). Whiteness, anti-blackness, and trauma: A grounded theory of white racial meaning making. *Journal of College Student Development, 62*(3), 310–326. http://doi.org/10.1353/csd.2021.0027

Wootson, C. R. (2018). A Black Yale student fell asleep in her dorm's common room. A white student called police. *The Washington Post.* https://www.washingtonpost.com/news/grade-point/wp/2018/05/10/a-black-yale-student-fell-asleep-in-her-dorms-common-room-a-white-student-called-police/

Yancy, G. (2018). *Backlash: What happens when we talk honestly about racism in America.* Rowman & Littlefield.

PART ONE

THEORETICAL FOUNDATIONS

2

TOWARD DEFINITIONS OF WHITENESS AND CRITICAL WHITENESS STUDIES

Disruption and Response-ability

Moira L. Ozias and Penny A. Pasque

As we walk across most colleges campuses, look at retention rates across race and ethnicity, and listen to students, staff, and faculty of color share about their experiences on campus, it is clear that race shapes people's access, experiences in, and success in college. Race not only affects People of Color, however; it also shapes the lives of white people, the structures of our programs and institutions, and our ideologies, psychologies, material resources, space, and emotions. Too often conversations about college and higher education focus on students of color as the unit of analysis for understanding racism, when racism—and whiteness as a normative way of structuring and understanding society—shapes much more than People of Color's experiences. To fully understand and begin to resist racism, we must understand whiteness and white supremacy as the often unnamed power "behind the curtain" of racism for People of Color *and* for white people.

U.S. institutions of higher education, particularly historically white institutions, were built by the forced labor of Black people on stolen Indigenous land (Wilder, 2014). The wealth that sustains the institutions in which we work is wealth accumulated by the enslavement of Black people (Brown University, 2006) and the theft of mineral and land wealth of Indigenous people (Lee & Ahtone, 2020). Further, the knowledge that has been overvalued by our institutions—even knowledge about students and their development and learning—has not only centered the experiences of white people (primarily white, nontrans, straight Christian men), but has also silenced and denied the white violence and racism that is the foundation of higher education in the United States. Higher education faculty and administrators have to contend with these histories and the ways they shape practices, policies, programs, institutions, and communities to this day. If professionals are not actively engaging issues of power, systemic oppression, and whiteness in our daily practice, we are not only supporting but building on this foundation of white domination and violence. And we—white people—end up doing harm. Silence perpetuates violence.

As two white women working as faculty in higher education, with experience as academic and student affairs administrators, we have found it essential to critically reflect on our own whiteness and the ways it shapes how we see and interact in the world, and our relationship to white supremacy. Theories and scholarship from critical whiteness studies help us see ourselves, our campuses, and the world in clearer ways to understand how we contribute to racism and how we can shift to resist it so that our students and colleagues of color may live freer, safer lives, and their contributions and talents are able to take center stage on our campuses when they have for so long been pushed away and punished. Critical whiteness studies "brings whiteness (as a concept) into the center of analysis in order to locate it, demystify it, and, if possible, discontinue its hold on education" (Leonardo, 2013, p. 91). Everyone benefits when faculty, administrators, and institutions address—and act on—critical understandings of whiteness and white supremacy; yes, this means white people benefit, too.

White supremacy not only harms and dehumanizes Black, Indigenous, and People of Color, but it also harms white people in a different way; it normalizes white violence against People of Color and infects the souls of white folks (Du Bois, 1920). As Garvey and Ignatiev (1996) wrote, "Treason to whiteness is loyalty to humanity" (p. 105), and therefore "loyalty to whiteness pulls one's soul *away* from humanity" (Matias & Mackey, 2016, p. 34). When white people support the normalization of white domination, we participate in the dehumanization of People of Color. And similarly, when white people resist whiteness, we work in concert with People of Color–led liberation efforts. In other words, when white people move in sync with racist systems and institutions, our souls suffer as we participate in systemic violences that harm People of Color; when we resist systemic and institutionalized white supremacy, we work toward the good of People of Color and improve our own human condition in the process. For white faculty and higher education professionals, the study of critical whiteness can provide "a process of learning (our) own whiteness and how the exertions of whiteness create a violent condition within which People of Color must racially survive" (Matias & Mackey, 2016, p. 35). If white people choose to ignore this knowledge, we are left with a partial understanding of race and racism, at best, and one that "cannot fully allow for commitment to racial justice" (p. 35).

Higher education faculty, as well as academic and student affairs administrators, must work against white supremacy in order to fully support Black, Indigenous, Latinx, and Asian people and communities on campus. When faculty and administrators understand, unlearn, and resist white-dominant ways of being and systemic white supremacy, we work to create more equitable, life-affirming, and justice-oriented learning spaces where all students can work without oppressive barriers to become their full selves in community with others.

This chapter introduces critical whiteness studies and how they may help both white people and People of Color to better understand and resist white supremacy. First we offer important definitions to ground the conversation, and then we describe the history and inherent challenge of critical whiteness studies. Next we describe our own positionality and processes in writing this chapter as two white women contributing to a book on whiteness, with chapters authored and edited by people from many racial identities. We then outline theories that help us understand whiteness, describing how they might look in practice. And we close with questions for white people and People of Color that may help in reflecting on and practicing response-ability (Battiste, 2013) and—for our white colleagues—accountability for our complicity in white supremacy.

Important Definitions

To understand how whiteness and white supremacy work, we must first understand what they are. After all, there are many definitions and misunderstandings about racism floating about our world. First, *white supremacy* is a system of white racial domination that normalizes violence, discrimination, and unequal power relations that privilege white people and harm People of Color (Leonardo, 2009). Under this system, white people desire and protect power, access, resources, and rights, working to exclude People of Color from the same. Whites become numb to violence and discrimination against People of Color, both witnessing it and participating in it. White supremacy is rooted in anti-Blackness and anti-Indigeneity (Dunbar-Ortiz, 2014; Sharpe, 2016). This violence and exclusion is so normalized that white people claim not to see it, even believing our own denials (Matias, 2016; Mills, 2007). In this way, white supremacy becomes like air for white people—unrecognizably lived and breathed as though it is not there, when it is all around, and within, us. People of Color have to know white supremacy intimately in order to survive its violence, but white people learn to ignore it in order to preserve our sense of ourselves as "good people" (Applebaum, 2010; Thompson, 2003), even as we watch our neighbors die because of it. For example, a Black applicant for an academic advisor position may understand that she needs to wear a weave instead of her natural puff and communicate with White Mainstream English in an interview, whereas her white interviewers would deny they hold racial bias, even as they make assessments about interviewees' "professionalism" and "fit" based on white European beauty standards and white language politics (Baker-Bell et al., 2020; Reece et al., 2019).

Whiteness, then, is "the ideology that works to normalize and promote white supremacy" (Nishi et al., 2016, p. 2). It is "the attitude and philosophy that positions the white race as superior, whether through intelligence, beauty, or culture/traditions" (Nishi et al., 2015, p. 2). It is also the discourse, or ways of talking and making meaning of the world, that grows out of this attitude and philosophy (Leonardo, 2009). Although sometimes this still happens explicitly in the United States—think of the white people at the "Unite the Right" rally in Charlottesville, Virginia, in 2017—this promotion of white supremacy is more often normalized and considered the "way things are done." For example, 74% of vice presidents of student affairs are white (National Association of Student Personnel Administrators [NASPA], 2014), standards of professionalism privilege white ways of being and dressing (Reece et al., 2019), and foundational research that higher education faculty and administrators use to understand student experiences and student development centers white, male students (Jones & Stewart, 2016), despite contemporary scholars working to center student of color perspectives (Patton et al., 2016). When whiteness operates unchecked in graduate admissions, white, economically privileged applicants are admitted over applicants of color (Posselt, 2016). Whiteness also shapes faculty hiring processes, blocking the hiring of faculty of color and maintaining white majority faculty in most academic departments in the United States (Sensoy & DiAngleo, 2017).

Both white people and People of Color can support whiteness and white supremacy as a system and ideology, but when white people do, they (we) benefit, whereas when People of Color support white supremacy, they end up harming themselves (e.g., internalized oppression; Huber et al., 2006). For example, when a Person of Color practices respectability politics that privileges white definitions of professionalism within the workplace, they ultimately harm communities of color, and themselves, in the process; not only do People of Color not get hired and promoted but also knowledges held within communities of color get suppressed and silenced. When a white person demands the same respectability politics, she benefits by hoarding more power and resources for herself and her white community by excluding People of Color and their knowledges and expertise. White people, by virtue of showing up in the world as white, are always and already complicit in white supremacy (Applebaum, 2010). We have to take concerted action in order to interrupt the centering of whiteness. White people immediately benefit from whiteness, even if we struggle because of our class, dis/ability, gender, or other social positions. Because of this, white people, ourselves included, have a particular moral responsibility to resist white supremacy in ourselves and the world at every turn.

Further, Cabrera (2017) called for a shift in language from white privilege to the more accurate "white immunity," where white immunity "means that People of Color have not historically, and are not contemporarily, guaranteed their rights, justice, and equitable social treatment; however, White people are because they have protection from this disparate treatment" (p. 82). White privilege pedagogy teaches that white people individually benefit from whiteness, downplaying the way that white supremacy depends on the subjugation and exclusion of People of Color both systemically and relationally (Applebaum, 2010). Often, concepts of white privilege are based on Peggy McIntosh's (1988) knapsack metaphor, and the solution to racism becomes "taking off the knapsack," when being white in a white supremacist society is not something any white person can "take off," "unpack," or change. White privilege is often framed as benefits white people "just get," as if we are walking down the street and someone just happens to drop money into our pockets without our knowledge (Leonardo, 2009, citing Scheurich). Instead we must understand that white people, whether intentionally or not, take an active role in practicing and maintaining white domination. These everyday actions that maintain white dominance are driven by whiteness as an ideology and discourse. Leonardo (2009) described that there is a cost of "downplaying the active role of whites who take resources from People of Color all over the world, appropriate their labor, and construct policies that deny minorities' full participation in society" (p. 76). The term *white privilege* "conjures up images of domination happening behind the backs of whites, rather than on the backs of People of Color" (p. 76). Instead, to return to the pants pocket metaphor:

> The experience of People of Color is akin to walking down the street having your money taken from your pocket. Historically, if "money" represents material, and even cultural, possessions of People of Color then the agent of such taking is the white race, real and imagined. The discourse on privilege comes with the unfortunate consequence of masking history, obfuscating agents of domination, and removing the actions that make it clear who is doing what to whom. (p. 76)

Therefore, when we shift from talking about "white privilege" to talking about "white immunity" or "white domination," we locate the action of racial injustice with white people and white people's historically and contemporarily instituted laws, policies, and practices. When we get specific about the what and who, we can more effectively understand our roles moment by moment and day by day to resist white supremacy and its longstanding harms.

Although we are careful about defining *white supremacy* as systemic, and *whiteness* as the ideology and discourse that maintains white supremacy, we often use these terms interchangeably, as do others. This is in part because systemic power is re/produced day by day and moment by moment in interactions and relationships. Individuals in relationship constitute the system. Institutions, including higher education, that have historically denied power to and harmed People of Color continue to operate inequitably because policies, processes, and practices are maintained by individuals in relationship to each other. Every individual has agency and makes choices to resist or comply. And white people in particular have responsibility to use our power and position to question, resist, and block the workings of systemic white supremacy and whiteness.

History and the Challenge of Critical Whiteness Studies

People of Color have been writing about whiteness for centuries and yet white people continue to turn away, not doing enough to heed the calls from Black, Brown, and Indigenous people for racial justice (Leonardo, 2013). (Reflect: If you're white, did you read this sentence, and think, "That is not me; that is other white people"? If so, consider what this means in your own life, and if you have—or have yet to—go "far enough" with heeding the calls.) These descriptions of white supremacy and calls for racial justice have taken various forms. For example, Black scholars and activists write about whiteness as a force of terror and anti-Black racism in the context of chattel slavery and its aftermath in the United States (Baldwin, 1965; Du Bois, 1920; Fanon, 1952/2008; Hartman, 2008; Sharpe, 2016; Wells-Barnett, 1894). Women of color, especially Black and queer Black women, write about white cisheteropatriarchy[1] and the particular ways it violates and shapes the lives of Black women, as well as the ways that Black women resist (Collins, 2000; Crenshaw, 1990; Gossett, 2017; hooks, 1986; Lorde, 1984/2020). Women of color from across the world offer transnational and decolonial feminist perspectives of whiteness as a western, patriarchal power structure that shapes globalization and women of color's lives across the "global assembly line" and delineates definitions of citizenship and rights (Bhattacharya, 2009; Jayawardena,

2014; Mohanty, 2003; Pala, 1977). Latinx scholars have described how colonial and governmental categories of whiteness, and European colonization, shape *Latinidad* (Lopez, 1997; Rodriguez, 2000; Valdez, 1996). Asian American scholars have described how whiteness has created nativist ideologies as well as legal and citizenship barriers for Asian Americans, and how the model minority myth supports whiteness and harms Asian American, Black, and Indigenous communities in the United States (Chang, 2000; Poon et al., 2016; Suzuki, 2002; Tuan, 1998). And Indigenous scholars have written about how white supremacy and settler colonization work in tandem via whiteness and settler ways of being to rob Indigenous people of land, minerals, and water, as well as Indigenous ways of being, living, and learning (Battiste, 2013; Moreton-Robinson, 2004; Reardon & TallBear, 2012; Shotton et al., 2013; Smith, 2012; Tuck & Yang, 2012).

Despite this long history of People of Color witnessing and writing about the violence of whiteness, white people have done two things: (a) We have not listened to these calls, in fact deliberately ignoring them (Mills, 2007), and (b) when we do acknowledge them, white people pretend that we discovered them, appropriating this intellectual work by People of Color and profiting from it (Painter, 1994; Thompson, 2003). As Leonardo (2013) described: "Whiteness Studies arrives on the scene precisely at the moment when minorities have gained a legitimate foothold in curricular, instructional, and cultural reform of education" (p. 89). This fact alone is an example of what legal scholar and critical race theorist Bell (1980) called "interest convergence," or the pattern of white people in power only supporting legal, political, or educational racial justice change when it is in their collective best interest, and blocking any change that serves the interests of People of Color and disadvantages white people.

Leonardo (2013) outlined the following key questions with which critical whiteness studies grapples:

> How does a privileged group work through the reasons to dissolve its own advantages? What could possibly motivate Whites to undo their domination after they have enjoyed it for so long? How could Whites be trusted to lead a movement against their own interests, indeed against themselves? (p. 86)

We, as white people, need to be willing to cede resources and power by taking risks in support of People of Color–led liberation efforts. In turn we will gain back pieces of our humanity stolen by the violence of white supremacy into which we've been socialized. In fact, we as two white women coauthoring this piece, and working through our own whiteness, are subject to and tarrying with (Yancy, 2012, 2015) these same questions on a lifelong basis. For us, and for Yancy (2015), to tarry is to "dwell with the emotional and cognitive dissonance" that we experience every time we feel the crush of the ways in which "we are entangled in the social and psychic web of white racism" (p. 26). The "trick is not to flee," but to stay with the discomfort through courageous listening, humility, and the capacity to be touched and shaken by witness that People of Color give to the white racism (p. 26).

Tarrying With Whiteness

As we began writing this chapter, we started with critical reflection and dialogue. We cocreated a list of reflective questions that we used as prompts in conversation (see Appendix 2.A at the end of the chapter). We knew that one of the traps of whiteness is intellectualizing discussion about racism and white supremacy in order to distance ourselves from it emotionally and physically, so we challenged each other to be vulnerable and honest. Our long-standing relationship and previous collaborations helped us, but we still found it challenging to move out of our academic selves—where we are drawn to perform "already knowing" and being the "good white person"—and into a more vulnerable and challenging discussion that is less about performance and more about our lived experiences. We are both faculty now, who have, taken together, decades of experience as faculty and higher education administrators. And in this process of coauthoring we were reminded again and again about how being a scholar-practitioner often means feeling compelled to act like we know, when what would really benefit us is building community around not knowing, vulnerability, and learning, starting from a place of naming and working through our own complicity with white supremacy (which we will talk about in more detail later).

For now, suffice it to say that there is a whole industry of white antiracism that rewards white people for repeating and appropriating messages about whiteness that People of Color (a) know firsthand through experience and (b) have been talking and writing about for centuries. We, in fact, are participating in this dynamic even as we write this chapter. Who are we as two white women to collect and write about the work that People of Color have been doing for so long? And yet what responsibility do we have to do the work of undoing and resisting whiteness among white people—and in ourselves—that People of Color have called us to do for so long? We cannot escape this conundrum of both participating in white supremacy at the same time that we are trying to resist it. (This is why white people have to be always open to critique and accountability, including in the critique of this piece, too.)

Ways of Understanding Whiteness and White Supremacy

Many people think about whiteness as an identity. Whiteness is something white people are or have. Although this may be true in a limited sense, whiteness is much more than an identity that individuals hold. Systemic white supremacy and whiteness (the ideology and racial discourse that maintain systemic white supremacy) influence everything from our most widespread global social and economic structures to our institutions, interpretations of history, our families, our relationships, even our feelings and the ways we relate to ourselves and others in our bodies.

White supremacy also works in tandem with other systems of oppression like patriarchy, classism, ableism, ageism, religious hegemony, trans* oppression, heterogenderism, and settler colonialism (J. C. Harris & Patton, 2019; Stewart & Nicolazzo, 2018). Different understandings of whiteness help us see how it works in our lives and in the world in different ways. Each of these understandings of whiteness provides a different lens through which higher education faculty and administrators can see our practice, our lives, and the lives of our students. When we use them all, we have a fuller, clearer picture of how white supremacy shapes our world and lives, as well as how we can resist it in big and small ways on campus, at home, and in our communities.

Whiteness approached as an identity is a way of understanding individuals as part of a socially constructed group—white people. White racial identity development models like Helms's (1995) and white racial consciousness models like Rowe et al.'s (1994) describe different ways in which white people understand what it means to be a white individual living in a racist society. These models can be valuable for helping us understand how white people make meaning of their own whiteness (as an identity) in relation to People of Color, but they can also leave understandings of whiteness at the level of the individual. What good is describing white people's racialized identities and racial consciousness if larger institutions, social systems, and norms continue to exclude and harm People of Color while benefiting whites? Not much.

So if whiteness is not only identity, what is it? Here are some ways of understanding whiteness that can help us see how it works in the world. Seeing how whiteness works, after all, is itself a resistance to the power of whiteness to remain invisible (especially for white people). Seeing how whiteness works is not enough, however; white people especially must work to resist the ways that whiteness works in and around us in order to reduce the harm that People of Color experience under white supremacy. When People of Color resist whiteness in their lives, they are able to work toward communal and individual healing and freedom (Menakem, 2017; Singh, 2019). We offer six ways of understanding whiteness.

1. Whiteness as Ideology

One way of understanding whiteness is as ideology. Ideology is essentially a web of interconnected ideas that give shape to and help us understand the world. Schwandt (2015) defined *ideologies* as "a set of social, political, and moral values; attitudes; outlooks and beliefs that shape a social group's interpretation of its behavior and its world" (pp. 150–151). Ideologies shape the meanings we make, our relationships, and the ways we move and act in the world. This means that ideologies influence our institutions and systems, affecting how they distribute resources like money, time, water, land, and influence, as well as access to health care and education.

The ideology of white supremacy influences what Feagin (2020) called the *white racial frame* or "the dominant racial frame that has long legitimated, rationalized, motivated, and shaped racial oppression and inequality" (p. 4) in the United States. Whiteness as an overarching ideology, then, shapes racial stereotypes and prejudices, interlinked interpretations and narratives, visual images, racialized emotions, racialized language politics, and discriminatory actions (Feagin, 2020). It becomes a way of interpreting our senses and perceptions, putting them into larger context, and even distorting them so that one feeling or understanding can get mistaken or understood as another (Matias & Zembylas, 2014). Whiteness ideology can be taken up by people of any race, although only white people as a group benefit. As an example, when a white teacher assumes that a Latina student is speaking Spanish because she is lazy or less proficient with English, the teacher is working from whiteness ideology that shapes her assumptions and feelings, impacting her actions and relationship with the Latina student.

2. Whiteness as Discourse

Whiteness also operates as a way of communicating about and acting in the world. As Johnstone (2018) pointed out, discourse is both the source of this knowledge and the result of it; in other words, we create reality as we speak it. When we understand whiteness as a racial discourse, we understand that whiteness involves patterns of communication and that these ways of communicating shape our practices, relationships, and institutions (Foste & Irwin, 2020; Frankenberg, 1993; Leonardo, 2009). According to Cabrera et al. (2017, drawing on Leonardo, 2009, and Frankenberg, 1993) this discourse of whiteness includes three central components: "(a) an unwillingness to name the contours of systemic racism, (b) an avoidance of identifying with a racial experience or minority group, and (c) the minimization of the US history of racism" (p. 18). When white people claim that "slavery is over," argue that race does not matter, make racial jokes (Cabrera, 2014), or avoid talking about race altogether (Hill, 2008), they are practicing whiteness as a discourse, as a way of communicating that denies the realities of People of Color who know and experience white supremacy. When we understand whiteness as a discourse, we can also see how People of Color can practice these same ways of talking and understanding (e.g., internalized oppression; Huber et al., 2006; Tatum, 1997), although People of Color do not benefit from these practices in the same ways that white people do.

Whiteness as a discourse is so important because "discourse is both the source of [this] knowledge (people's generalizations about language are made on the basis of the discourse they participate in) and the result of it (people apply what they already know in creating and interpreting new discourse)" (Johnstone, 2018, p. 2). As such, people create reality into existence by speaking it. Interrogation of our discourse, interruption of existing patterns, interventions into the silence that perpetuates white supremacy (what is said and what is not said), and intentional language that names racism and white supremacy can be a form of anti-oppressive action.

3. Whiteness as a Racial Contract

One of the particular ways that whiteness shapes relationships and the ways we come to relate to each other is through what Charles Mills (1997) called *the racial contract.* Mills described that global political and economic structures have been built by colonization, and that these systems privilege white people while exploiting the bodies, land, and resources of People of Color. The benefits of the system also require white misunderstanding, misrepresentation, evasion, and self-deception, so that white people can believe in our inherent goodness while still participating in "conquest, colonization, and enslavement" (p. 19). This deliberate, social misunderstanding—that is accepted as true by a majority and those in power—is called *white ignorance* (Mills, 1997, 2007). It creates a structured evasion, veiling, and hiding of racism in order to maintain white racial superiority and dominance.

For example, when history classes do not teach about Indigenous genocide or the enslavement of Africans, schools created—then continued to perpetuate—white ignorance about the history of racism. Or, for Moira, when she was in fifth grade and her class re-enacted "Thanksgiving" in a class play, her education normalized white violence and genocide, telling false stories about white colonization and Indigenous life. Similarly, when a child asks about why her friend's skin is darker and why that friend's family cannot join the country club, and her parent tells her to be quiet because those questions are not polite, this parent is reinforcing white ignorance. And when a sexual assault advocacy program focuses on histories of abuse and assault in white communities but neglects to address the history of rape as a tool of white colonization and racism in Indigenous and Black communities, it contributes to white ignorance and its attendant harms against women of color.

By way of another example, when Penny was a hall director and director of special programs at a small liberal arts college, there was an annual euchre tournament with cash prizes. The white students played euchre in their rooms. The Black students played spades every night in the lounge and were never included in the annual euchre tournament, despite the fact that both are quick-play card games and the tournament was publicly advertised. This practice of formally supporting white students' cultural practices white excluding Black students' similar cultural practices reinforced white ignorance and dominance. Even more, cash prizes were given in the formal euchre tournaments, distributing university funds to white students via white cultural practices, which amassed resources among white students and not Black students. White students participated in the racial contract by excluding, intentionally or not, spades players in their tournament series, until someone pointed out the inequity and the tournament was expanded to include spades and euchre.

The understanding of whiteness as a racial contract (Mills, 1997) involves the reality that although not all white people may sign on to the contract, or agree to the terms of it, all white people benefit from this social arrangement. As Mills put it, "All whites are beneficiaries of the Contract, though some whites are not signatories to it" (p. 11). To use a higher education example, we as white faculty do not agree that we should have immunity from the harms that faculty of color face; however, every day we benefit from white immunity in the academy. We are not considered a "threat" or "difficult" like many of our colleagues of color; we are more readily identified as experts (though less than white men in our departments), and we face fewer risks to our safety at the hands of police. Further, the racial contract is a contract among white people that defines and excludes People of Color. Because of this, to build resistance, People of Color must imagine and build alternative structures of power, of mutual aid, and of knowing (outside of white ignorance). Robin D. G. Kelley's (2002) *Freedom Dreams*, Gerald Vizenor's (1999) *survivance*, and the activist visions and work of people like Grace Lee Boggs, Rosa Clemente, Patrisse Cullors, Alicia Garza, Che Gosset, Dolores Huerta, CeCe McDonald, and Opal Tometi suggest ways to do this in resistance to the racial contract.

White people, however, if we are to work toward racial justice, must start from the reality that we always already benefit from the racial contract—from histories of wealth built on the violence of colonization, genocide, land theft, and slavery—even if we also attempt to resist and undermine it. White people may not all benefit in the same ways, depending on our gender, class, religion, or ability, but we all benefit in some way. This starting place is white complicity. Regardless of intention, white people inevitably benefit from showing up as white in a white supremacist society. We have all the immunity of whiteness, even if we do not want it. And so we must start from the place of understanding that we are reproducing white supremacy just by showing up as white. White people need to practice vigilance, or constant recognition of our complicity with white supremacy, and constant work to resist (Applebaum, 2010). If white people start by acknowledging these benefits and our own complicity in systems of race domination, regardless of intention, then we can with sharper senses see, hear, and understand our position in these global and local systems of race domination and work to resist.

4. *Whiteness as Property*

Whiteness as property is the legal legacy of the colonization and seizure of land from Indigenous people of the Americas and the white ownership of Black bodies through enslavement in the Americas (C. I. Harris, 1993). It has shifted through time, denying Black and Indigenous people reparations for their labor, land, and resources, and imbues white people with particular rights that People of Color in the United States do not in practice have. Harris (1993) stated that "the law has established and protected an actual property interest in whiteness itself, which shares the critical characteristics of property and accords with the many and varied theoretical descriptions of property" (p. 1724). Here, whiteness is not just an identity; it becomes a systemic method for convincing white people that it is their intrinsic and extrinsic right to own something or someone, and to exclude others, particularly People of Color. These rights are supported through custom and sovereign power and, in turn, become the "common sense" of colonizers.

Whiteness as property continues through intergenerational oppression and intergenerational privilege (Pasque & Rex, 2010), which means oppression and/or privileges are passed down from generation to generation. For example, white people believe and act on whiteness as a property right when we exclude People of Color from our neighborhoods through redlining (and modern equivalents), from our schools through white flight, or from spaces on campus due to fear that "that office is becoming too Black/Brown/radical and white students won't be comfortable here." It continues generationally in predatory lending practices, voter suppression, college athletics that depend on the labor of Black and Brown athletes while white students buy elite access to college through athletics (Haslerig, 2017; Hextrum, 2021), real estate practices (Gotham, 2002), legacy admittance to college (Hurwitz, 2011), and beyond.

5. Whiteness as Feeling and Affect

Whiteness not only shapes our cognitive structures, ways of understanding and perceiving the world, knowledge building (or evading), and the distribution of resources, labor, and safety, but it also shapes how emotions and feelings wrap around and through these same structures. In fact, emotions—acknowledged and unacknowledged—drive our practices (Ahmed, 2014). And white supremacy shapes the ways we feel toward, practice in, and relate to the world.

For administrators and scholars this becomes important because in educational spaces, and the world at large, white feelings end up taking precedence over the safety and life chances of Black, Brown, and Indigenous people. Leonardo and Zembylas (2013) described this by exploring how white people strive to create distinctions between "good whites" and "bad whites," always creating ways to see ourselves as one of the "good ones." We do this because we continue to be emotionally invested in our own goodness, which is a product of whiteness itself (that frames white people as good and human, and nonwhite people as bad and less than human). To do this we create *white intellectual alibis*, or ways to feel safe and maintain our "good white" status in race dialogues, shielding ourselves from the feelings of discomfort when confronted with the realities of our own complicity in the violence of white supremacy against People of Color. These emotional shields, or white intellectual alibis, can look like claims to be a "good white," intellectualization of racism and race talk, confessions to racism that only center white feelings and white tears (Accapadi, 2007), or altogether avoidance and disengagement. White intellectual alibis and feelings also happen anytime a Person of Color names a white person as "one of the good ones," as though this validation absolves any individual white person of the past horrors of white supremacy.

For faculty and administrators in higher education these examples pop up everywhere: conceivably in staff meetings; in conduct processes; in decisions about how to allocate resources; in performance reviews, tenure, and promotion processes; in program planning; and in conference presentations.

Although any educational or helping work may be framed as a caring or "touchy feely," white faculty and administrators must engage the underbelly of feeling and affect—feelings of hatred, apathy, fear, greed, disgust, guilt, pain—in order to squarely confront histories of white supremacy that shape not only our institutions but also our feelings and ways of relating as they shape daily practice.

For example, I, Moira, vividly remember being in an antiracism workshop and being asked the question, "What keeps you from stepping in when you witness racism?" Several white folks, including myself, mentioned fearing loss of status, loss of jobs, loss of relationships with other white people. When it was finally the turn of a participant of color—a Black woman with whom I worked—she paused and finally said, "It feels like we heard different questions. When I consider interrupting racism I worry that people I love—my brother, my sister, myself—will end up arrested, or dead." I felt a heaviness—guilt, sadness, disgust with myself—when I realized I had contributed to Black death and violence by letting my loyalty to whiteness and white "likeability" stop me from stepping in and standing by friends and colleagues of color in so many moments. The risks I felt—and continue to feel—were fabricated by white supremacy to buy my loyalty at the cost of Black lives.

Cheryl Matias (2016) further described whiteness as a sadomasochistic social pathology, and posited critical love as the antidote to the desires of whiteness for Black and Indigenous dehumanization:

> If treason to whiteness really is loyalty to humanity, then the greatest act of love Whites can show humanity is to end whiteness itself, to love so much as to send whiteness to its grave. Given that whiteness is mainly a sadomasochistic construction, Whites need to not only undo racist ideologies and organize acts of racial disobedience, but also bear the emotional pain necessary to lovingly end the White race as a sociopolitical form of human organization. (p. 62, internal citation omitted)

Higher education and student affairs educators must grapple with our connections and loyalties to whiteness not only cognitively but also emotionally at the level of feelings and affect.

6. *Whiteness as Interactional and Interlocking*

Finally, whiteness can and should also be understood as one part of a matrix of domination (Collins, 2000) that involves interlocking systems of oppression and their intersecting and compounding effects on social structures and human beings. Focusing on whiteness and white supremacy in an interactional theory "does not end the analysis, but arguably begins it" (Leonardo, 2013, p. 93). An interactional theory of whiteness asks how cisheteropatriarchy reinforces whiteness and how whiteness reinforces cisheteropatriarchy.

Stewart and Nicolazzo (2018) referred to these interlocking and interacting oppressions by describing "whiteness as a container," as an "ideological and epistemological perspective that consolidates and promotes hegemony and normalization across various interlocking systems of domination and oppression to further white supremacy. As such, it is a way of knowing and set of knowledges that drives white supremacy" (pp. 134–135). We concur and see whiteness as a circular construction of epistemology (knowing), ontology (being), and axiology (ethics), one that becomes the living and being of a person; it is the essence of what one lives and breathes (Pasque et al., 2012). And, as such, we can make intentional change to the iterative nature of whiteness. Here we want to emphasize that to work against white supremacy, practitioners and scholars must always hold whiteness as a part of our analysis, while also understanding that whiteness is a starting place, but never the end of fully articulating the ways that interlocking systems of oppression crosscut the world, our campuses, and our lives. To take white supremacy as a starting point for understanding interlocking systems of oppression moves us at least part way toward fulfilling J. C. Harris and Patton's (2019) call to use intersectionality in a "manner that advances a transformative social justice agenda" (p. 347).

Theories in Practice: Politics of Disruption for White People

To follow the calls of critical scholars like J. C. Harris and Patton (2019), Collins (2000), and Crenshaw (1990), critical whiteness studies must ultimately lead to critical praxis. Critical whiteness scholars such as Leonardo (2013) have also emphasized that the end goal should be praxis guided by a politics of disruption. He and others have argued that white people should "look, but not act White" (p. 110). What he means is that white people should work so hard to disrupt the dominating practices of whiteness that we make it at least inconvenient, if not impossible, for other white people to enforce white domination. Although we are always read as white and benefit from whiteness, we must act in every way we can to resist the mechanisms of white supremacy and expose whiteness as violence. After all, how often do People of Color have to name and interrupt racism, even while they are targeted by that same racism and are punished for any resistance, while white colleagues watch silently? Leonardo explained a politics of disruption for whites:

> Discombobulating Whiteness includes thwarting the police, who are inclined to enact less harsh tactics toward Whites; calling into question racial favors from everyday interactions, like car sales people who charge less to White buyers; and the subtle yet felt dynamic of presumed agreement, such as participating in racial jokes about People of Color. (p. 109)

On our campuses this might look any number of ways, always guided by critical theory and knowledge of local contexts, histories, and power dynamics. In administrative settings a politics of disruption might look like white staff sharing salary offers and ranges with colleagues of color and pointing out to Human Resources or the broader public the racial discrepancies in pay, flex time, or vacation. It might look like white staff taking extra hours to support Black student activists at a sit-in at the president's office or white staff questioning rationales like "fit" for hiring white staff over staff of color (Reece et al., 2019). It might also look like white staff stepping back from opportunities assigned to them because of their whiteness in order to make space for their colleagues of color to hold meaningful leadership positions, receive grants, or be assigned leave time. Simultaneously, disruption also requires being careful not to use this as an excuse to give People of Color more work when many racially minoritized people are already expected to do more work than white peers in myriad ways. For example, "the Black tax" is commonly known to faculty who acknowledge their additional investment in Black students toward the collective good, similar to a tax paid to the government to support the community (Griffin et al., 2011).

In classrooms a politics of disruption could take the form of a white instructor strategizing with Black students so that time spent at a Black Lives Matter rally counts as class participation, white students stepping in to ask why scholars of color are only included on the syllabus during the week on "diversity," or a white teacher refusing to let white tears (Accapadi, 2007) derail a class discussion on racism. It may also look like white students refusing to participate in racist jokes about professors of color, or interrupting other student complaints like "All she wants to do is talk about race" with a professor of color. Among researchers, this might look like white faculty challenging colleagues who complain that students of color want to do "navel gazing" research while white students do similar research but are not critiqued. Or it may look like challenging assumptions that graduate students should be trained and socialized to be just like faculty in the department, instead of being encouraged to grow in their own racial identities and community connections.

When doing assessment this looks like centering assessments on the experiences of multiple marginalized students and working from frameworks like trickle-up high-impact practices (Stewart & Nicolazzo, 2018) or using assessment to question *what*, not just *if*, students are learning in cocurricular environments (McCloud, 2019; Mitchell et al., 2012; Yosso, 2002).

Disrupting Whiteness: Questions for Response-ability and Answerability

We write this section as white people to other white people and to People of Color as we understand that the audience for this book is not limited to white readers. We recognize that People of Color resist white supremacy every day simply by surviving—and thriving—in a white supremacist world. The responsibility and accountability People of Color may need is not to us as white women! Instead it is to each other, to building freedom-seeking and healing relationships and community that may not include (and certainly do not center) white people.

Here, instead, we write to and for higher education professionals and scholars who are serious about resisting whiteness in ourselves and in the institutions, neighborhoods, and worlds around us. Marie Battiste (2013) suggested that as higher education scholars and practitioners we should seek relationships of answerability with communities of color. Battiste called educators to center Indigenous communities and develop the ability to respond to histories and present practices of settler colonialism and white supremacy. She called this ability to be responsive and responsible *response-ability*. We are all offered "an opportunity to rededicate [ourselves] to protecting humanity, redressing the damage and losses of Indigenous peoples, and enabling Indigenous communities to sustain their knowledge for their future and the future of humanity" (p. 189). Patel (2016) extended this notion, emphasizing that educators and researchers need to move from thinking about knowledge, learning, and place from a framework of ownership to a framework of answerability:

> Because coloniality has been so pervasive, we can think about how our actions, our research agendas, the knowledge we contribute, can undo coloniality and create spaces for ways of being in relation that are not about individualism, ranking, and status. Answerability includes aspects of being responsible, accountable, and being part of an exchange. It is a concept that can help to maintain the coming-into-being with, being in conversation with. (p. 73)

When we—as practitioners, leaders, educators, and a field—center the need, knowledges, and worldmaking (Blockett, 2018) of Black and Indigenous people, white people will need to stand back. White people must become comfortable with *not* being centered, and in fact being questioned, critiqued, and "not getting it." It is okay, in fact, for white people not to be included, not to get the joke, not to be centered. And, taken further, we, as white people, must work toward centering conversations and interests of People of Color, and standing back, letting folks of color *stay* centered, leading and building without our interference. White people's work, then, lies in working on ourselves, listening to communities of color, taking their lead, and building our own capacity to resist white supremacy in and around us, what Battiste (2013) called *response-ability* and Patel (2016) named *answerability*.

For White Readers (and Ourselves)

We offer the following questions as starting places for putting the theories and concepts introduced in this chapter into action. We invite white folks to engage these questions both individually and collectively with other people. Consider what questions you can add to this list based on other chapters in this book, as well.

- What was I taught about race and racism growing up? How does that influence how I think about myself as a white person now? How does it influence how I think about racism and racial justice now?
- How do I feel when the topic of race, racism, and whiteness comes up? When I think about being racist (as all white people are when socialized in a white supremacist world), how do I feel? "Tarry" with this feeling, as Yancy (2015) recommended. Consider journaling about this feeling.
- How do I seek to be a "good white" as a way to ease my discomfort with racism? How can I resist the desire and accolades as a "good white person"?
- How am I complicit in systemic racism? In what ways do I benefit from being white at work? At home? In the community?
- How can I learn more about racism and whiteness without burdening People of Color to teach me?
- How do I actively listen to people and communities of color and their calls to white people? How do I seek out and stay open to perspectives that challenge my whiteness, and act on them?

- Do I have white people in my life who can be honest with me, and with whom I can be honest, about my own participation in racism and whiteness?
- What stops me from disrupting and intervening in racism when I see it? What do I need to do to build more courage to speak and act to resist whiteness and white supremacy at work? At home? In the community?

For Our Colleagues of Color

For our colleagues of color—many of whom are contributors of book chapters interrogating important conceptualizations of whiteness for the survival of People of Color—we offer these questions.

- What was I taught about race and racism growing up? How does that influence how I think about myself as a Person of Color in the academy now? How does it influence how I think about racism and racial justice now?
- How do I feel when the topic of the "Black tax" for faculty—or for administrators—comes up? Am I able to see where I or other minoritized faculty and administrators are suffering from this taxation? How might I interrupt this and still be supportive of Black students and minoritized students from my own racial identity?
- How do I perpetuate the notion of a "good white" person as a way to ease the discomfort of racism for white colleagues? How can I resist giving accolades to "good white" colleagues? How can I refocus on freedom dreaming with other people of color?
- How can I join or build communities of healing and resistance with other people of color? How does whiteness interfere with this community and relationship building? What do I need to continue resistance and healing in the face of ongoing racial violence under white supremacy?

This list of questions may mean different things to you/us at different times in our careers. We encourage you—and promise to ourselves—to come back to this list on a regular basis to interrogate its meaning, our actions, and what we need to do to further resistance of racism and white supremacy. This requires white people to be actively engaged in centering the issues, programs, policies, and interests of People of Color. It also requires People of Color to be reflective about the ways whiteness and white supremacy pervasively operate in the academy. Whiteness, after all, pervades our living and being whether or not we are aware.

We need collectives—including you (and us)—to do this ongoing work. It is a lifelong process. May we all find ways to sustain the resistance, find joy in the struggle, and continue the processes of healing and freedom dreaming that activists, scholars, and change-makers before us have pointed us toward.

Notes

1. Although we focus on whiteness and white supremacy in this chapter, we stand with women of color and trans People of Color who understand white supremacy, cisheteropatriarchy, and globalized capitalism as intertwined systems of oppression that work not only across nation-states and institutions, but also within interpersonal relationships. Stewart and Nicolazzo (2018) called this "whiteness as a container": "Whiteness [is] an ideology of interlocking tacit assumptions that shape and support racism, patriarchy, classism, ableism, ageism, religious hegemony, trans* oppression, heterogenderism, and settler colonialism" (p. 134).

References

Accapadi, M. M. (2007). When white women cry: How white women's tears oppress Women of Color. *College Student Affairs Journal, 26*(2), 208–215.

Ahmed, S. (2014). *Cultural politics of emotion*. Edinburgh University Press.

Applebaum, B. (2010). *Being white, being good: White complicity, white moral responsibility, and social justice pedagogy*. Lexington Books.

Applebaum, B. (2017). Comforting discomfort as complicity: White fragility and the pursuit of invulnerability. *Hypatia, 32*(4), 862–875. https://doi.org/10.1111/hypa.12352

Baker-Bell, A., Williams-Farrier, B. J., Jackson, D., Johnson, L., Kynard, C., & McMurtry, T. (2020). *This ain't another statement: This is a DEMAND for Black linguistic justice*. Conference on College Composition & Communication. https://cccc.ncte.org/cccc/demand-for-black-linguistic-justice

Baldwin, J. (1965). White man's guilt. *Ebony Magazine, 20*, 47–48.

Battiste, M. (2013). *Decolonizing education: Nourishing the learning spirit*. UBC Press.

Bell, D. A. (1980). *Brown v. Board of Education* and the interest-convergence dilemma. *Harvard Law Review, 93*(3), 518–533. https://doi.org/1340546

Bhattacharya, K. (2009). Negotiating shuttling between transnational experiences: A de/colonizing approach to performance ethnography. *Qualitative Inquiry, 15*(6), 1061–1083. https://doi.org/10.1177/1077800409332746

Blockett, R. A. (2018). Thinking with Queer of Color critique: A multidimensional approach to analyzing and interpreting data. In R. Winkle-Wagner,

J. Lee-Johnson, & A. N. Gaskew (Eds.), *Critical theory and qualitative data analysis in education* (pp. 109–122). Routledge.

Brown University Steering Committee on Slavery and Justice. (2006). *Slavery & justice: A report of the Brown University Steering Committee on Slavery and Justice.* http://brown.edu/Research/Slavery_Justice/report/

Cabrera, N. (2017). White immunity: Working through some of the pedagogical pitfalls of "privilege." *Journal Committed to Social Change on Race and Ethnicity, 3*(1), 77–90. https://doi.org/10.15763/issn.2642-2387.2017.3.1.77-90

Cabrera, N. L. (2014). But we're not laughing: White male college students' racial joking and what this says about "post-racial" discourse. *Journal of College Student Development, 55*(1), 1–15. http://doi.org/10.1353/csd.2014.0007

Cabrera, N. L., Franklin, J. D., & Watson, J. S. (2017). Whiteness in higher education: The invisible missing link in diversity and racial analyses [Special issue]. *ASHE Higher Education Report, 42*(6). Wiley.

Chang, R. (2000). *Disoriented: Asian Americans, law, and the nation-state.* NYU Press.

Collins, P. H. (2000). *Black feminist thought: Knowledge, consciousness, and the politics of empowerment.* Routledge.

Crenshaw, K. (1990). Mapping the margins: Intersectionality, identity politics, and violence against women of color. *Stanford Law Review, 43*(6), 1241–1299.

Du Bois, W. E. B. (1920). *Darkwater: Voices from within the veil.* Harcourt Brace. https://www.gutenberg.org/files/15210/15210-h/15210-h.htm

Dunbar-Ortiz, R. (2014). *An indigenous peoples' history of the United States* (Vol. 3). Beacon Press.

Fanon, F. (2008). *Black skin, white masks.* Grove Press. (Original work published 1952)

Feagin, J. R. (2020). *The white racial frame: Centuries of racial framing and counter-framing.* Routledge.

Foste, Z., & Irwin, L. (2020). Applying critical whiteness studies in college student development theory and research. *Journal of College Student Development, 61*(4), 439–455. https://doi.org/10.1353/csd.2020.0050.

Frankenburg, R. (1993). *White women, race matters: The social construction of whiteness.* Routledge.

Garvey, J., & Ignatiev, N. (1996). The new abolitionism. *Minnesota Review, 47*(1), 105–108.

Gossett, C. (2017). Blackness and the trouble of trans visibility. In C. Gosset, E. A. Stanley, & J. Burton (Eds.), *Trap door: Trans cultural production and the politics of visibility* (pp. 183–190). The MIT Press.

Gotham, K. F. (2002). *Race, real estate, and uneven development: The Kansas City experience, 1900–2000.* SUNY Press.

Griffin, K. A., Bennett, J. C., & Harris, J. (2011). Analyzing gender differences in Black faculty marginalization through a sequential mixed-methods design. In K. A. Griffin & S. D. Museus (Eds.), *Using Mixed-Methods Approaches to Study Intersectionality in Higher Education* (New Directions for Institutional Research, no. 151, pp. 45–61). Jossey-Bass. https://doi.org/10.1002/ir.398

Harris, C. I. (1993). Whiteness as property. *Harvard Law Review, 106*(8), 1708–1791. https://doi.org/1341787

Harris, J. C., & Patton, L. D. (2018). Un/doing intersectionality through higher education research. *The Journal of Higher Education, 90*(3), 347–372. https://doi.org/10.1080/00221546.2018.1536936

Hartman, S. (2008). *Lose your mother: A journey along the Atlantic slave route*. Macmillan.

Haslerig, S. J. (2017). Graduate(d) student athletes in Division I football: Redefining archetypes and disrupting stereotypes or invisible? *Sociology of Sport Journal, 34*(4), 329–343. https://doi.org/10.1123/ssj.2017-0003

Helms, J. E. (1995). An update of Helm's white and People of Color racial identity models. In J. G. Ponterotto, J. M. Casas, L. A. Suzuki, & C. M. Alexander (Eds.), *Handbook of multicultural counseling* (pp. 181–198). SAGE.

Hextrum, K. (2021, May 18). White property interests in college athletic admissions. *Journal of Sport and Social Issues*. Advance online publication. https://doi.org/10.1177/01937235211015352

Hill, J. H. (2008). *The everyday language of white racism*. Wiley.

hooks, b. (1986). Sisterhood: Political solidarity between women. *Feminist Review, 23*(1), 125–138. https://doi.org/10.1057/fr.1986.25

Huber, L. P., Johnson, R. N., & Kohli, R. (2006). Naming racism: A conceptual look at internalized racism in US schools. *Chicano-Latino Law Review, 26*(1), 183–206.

Hurwitz, M. (2011). The impact of legacy status on undergraduate admissions at elite colleges and universities. *Economics of Education Review, 30*(3), 480–492. https://doi.org/10.1016/j.econedurev.2010.12.002

Jayawardena, K. (2014). *The white woman's other burden: Western women and South Asia during British rule*. Routledge.

Johnstone, B., (2018). *Discourse analysis*. Wiley.

Jones, S. R., & Stewart, D-L (2016). Evolution of student development theory. In E. S. Abes (Ed.), *Critical Perspectives on Student Development Theory* (New Directions for Student Services, no. 154, pp. 17–28). Jossey-Bass.

Lee, R., & Ahtone, K. (2020, March 30). Land grab universities. *High Country News*. https://www.hcn.org/issues/52.4/indigenous-affairs-education-land-grab-universities

Kelley, R. D. (2002). *Freedom dreams: The black radical imagination*. Beacon Press.

Leonardo, Z. (2009). *Race, whiteness, and education*. Routledge.

Leonardo, Z. (2013). *Race frameworks: A multidimensional theory of racism and education*. Teachers College Press.

Leonardo, Z., & Zembylas, M. (2013). Whiteness as technology of affect: Implications for educational praxis. *Equity & Excellence in Education, 46*(1), 150–165. https://doi.org/10.1080/10665684.2013.750539

Lopez, I. H. (1997). *White by law: The legal construction of race*. NYU Press.

Lorde, A. (2020). *Sister outsider: Essays and speeches*. Penguin Classics. (Original work published 1984)

Matias, C. E. (2016). *Feeling white: Whiteness, emotionality, and education*. Brill/Sense.

Matias, C. E., & Mackey, J. (2016). Breakin' down whiteness in antiracist teaching: Introducing critical whiteness pedagogy. *The Urban Review, 48*(1), 32–50. https://doi.org/10.1007/s11256-015-0344-7

Matias, C. E., & Zembylas, M. (2014). "When saying you care is not really caring": Emotions of disgust, whiteness ideology, and teacher education. *Critical Studies in Education, 55*(3), 319–337. https://doi.org/10.1080/17508487.2014.922489

McCloud, L. I. (2019). *Engaging with the other: Black college students' perceptions of perspective taking at historically White colleges and universities* (Doctoral dissertation, University of Iowa). Iowa Research Online. https://ir.uiowa.edu/etd/6992/

McIntosh, P. (1988). *White privilege and male privilege: A personal account of coming to see correspondences through work in women's studies.* https://www.wcwonline.org/images/pdf/White_Privilege_and_Male_Privilege_Personal_Account-Peggy_McIntosh.pdf

Menakem, R. (2017). *My grandmother's hands: Racialized trauma and the pathway to healing our hearts and bodies.* Central Recovery Press.

Mills, C. (2007). White ignorance. In S. Sullivan & N. Tuana (Eds.), *Race and epistemologies of ignorance* (pp. 26–31). SUNY Press.

Mills, C. W. (1997). *The racial contract.* Cornell University Press.

Mitchell, T. D., Donahue, D. M., & Young-Law, C. (2012). Service learning as a pedagogy of whiteness. *Equity & Excellence in Education, 45*(4), 612–629. https://doi.org/10.1080/10665684.2012.715534

Mohanty, C. T. (2003). *Feminism without borders: Decolonizing theory, practicing solidarity.* Duke University Press.

Moreton-Robinson, A. (Ed.). (2004). *Whitening race: Essays in social and cultural criticism* (No. 1). Aboriginal Studies Press.

National Association of Student Personnel Administrators. (2014). *Who are VPSA's?* http://census.naspa.org/who-are-vpsa

Nishi, N. W., Matias, C. E., & Montoya, R. (2015). Exposing the white avatar: Projections, justifications, and the ever-evolving American racism. *Social Identities, 21*(5), 459–473. https://doi.org/10.1080/13504630.2015.1093470

Nishi, N. W., Matias, C. E., Montoya, R., & Sarcedo, G. L. (2016). Whiteness FAQ: Responses and tools for confronting college classroom questions. *Journal of Critical Thought and Praxis, 5*(1), 1–34. https://doi.org/10.31274/jctp-180810-55

Painter, N. I. (1994). Representing Truth: Sojourner Truth's knowing and becoming known. *The Journal of American History, 81*(2), 461–492. https://doi.org/2081168

Pala, A. O. (1977). Definitions of women and development: An African perspective. *Signs: Journal of Women in Culture and Society, 3*(1), 9–13. https://doi.org/10.1086/493434

Pasque, P., Carducci, R., Kuntz, A. K., & Gildersleeve, R. E. (2012). Qualitative inquiry for equity in higher education: Methodological innovations, implications, and interventions. *ASHE Higher Education Report, 37*(6), 1–121. Wiley. https://onlinelibrary.wiley.com/toc/15546306/2012/37/6

Pasque, P. A., & Rex, L. A. (2010). Complicating "just do it": Leader's frameworks for analyzing higher education for the public good. *Higher Education in Review, 7*, 47–79.

Patel, L. (2016). *Decolonizing educational research: From ownership to answerability*. Routledge.

Patton, L. D., Renn, K. A., Guido, F. M., & Quaye, S. J. (2016). *Student development in college: Theory, research, and practice*. Wiley.

Poon, O., Squire, D., Kodama, C., Byrd, A., Chan, J., Manzano, L., Furr, S., Bishundat, D. (2016). A critical review of the model minority myth in selected literature on Asian Americans and Pacific Islanders in higher education. *Review of Educational Research, 86*(2), 469–502. https://doi.org/10.3102/0034654315612205

Posselt, J. R. (2016). *Inside graduate admissions: Merit, diversity, and faculty gatekeeping*. Harvard University Press.

Reardon, J., & TallBear, K. (2012). "Your DNA is our history": Genomics, anthropology, and the construction of whiteness as property. *Current Anthropology, 53*(5), 233–245. https://doi.org/10.1086/662629

Reece, B. J., Tran, V. T., De Vore, E. N., & Porcarro, G. (Eds.). (2019). *Debunking the myth of job fit in higher education and student affairs*. Stylus.

Rodriguez, C. E. (2000). *Changing race: Latinos, the census, and the history of ethnicity in the United States*. NYU Press.

Rowe, W., Bennett, S. K., & Atkinson, D. R. (1994). White racial identity models: A critique and alternative proposal. *The Counseling Psychologist, 22*(1), 129–146. https://doi.org/10.1177/0011000094221009

Schwandt, T. A. (2015). *The SAGE dictionary of qualitative inquiry* (4th ed.). SAGE.

Sensoy, Ö., & DiAngelo, R. (2017). "We are all for diversity, but . . .": How faculty hiring committees reproduce whiteness and practical suggestions for how they can change. *Harvard Educational Review, 87*(4), 557–580. https://doi.org/10.17763/1943-5045-87.4.557

Sharpe, C. (2016). *In the wake: On blackness and being*. Duke University Press.

Shotton, H. J., Lowe, S. C., & Waterman, S. J. (Eds.). (2013). *Beyond the asterisk: Understanding Native students in higher education*. Stylus.

Singh, A. A. (2019). *The racial healing handbook: Practical activities to help you challenge privilege, confront systemic racism, and engage in collective healing*. New Harbinger.

Smith, L. T. (2012). *Decolonizing methodologies: Research and Indigenous peoples*. Zed Books.

Stewart, D-L & Nicolazzo, Z. (2018). High impact of [whiteness] on trans* students in postsecondary education. *Equity & Excellence in Education, 51*(2), 132–145. https://doi.org/10.1080/10665684.2018.1496046

Suzuki, B. H. (2002). Revisiting the model minority stereotype: Implications for student affairs practice and higher education. In M. K. McEwen, C. M. Kodama, A. N. Alvarez, S. Lee, & C. T. H. Liang (Eds.), *Working With Asian American College Students* (New Directions for Student Services, no. 97, pp. 21–32). Jossey-Bass.

Tatum, B. (1997). *"Why are all the Black kids sitting together in the cafeteria?"* Basic Books.

Thompson, A. (2003). Tiffany, friend of People of Color: White investments in antiracism. *International Journal of Qualitative Studies in Education, 16*(1), 7–29. https://doi.org/10.1080/0951839032000033509

Tuan, M. (1998). *Forever foreigners or honorary whites? The Asian ethnic experience today*. Rutgers University Press.

Tuck, E., & Yang, K. W. (2012). Decolonization is not a metaphor. *Decolonization: Indigeneity, Education & Society, 1*(1), 1–40.

Valdez, F. (1996). Latina/o ethnicities, critical race theory, and post-identity politics in postmodern legal culture: From practices to possibilities. *La Raza Law Journal, 9*, 1.

Vizenor, G. R. (1999). *Manifest manners: Narratives on postindian survivance.* University of Nebraska Press.

Wells-Barnett, I. B. (1894). *Southern horrors: Lynch law in all its phases.* New York Age. https://www.publicdoman.com/SouthernHorrors2.pdf

Wilder, C. S. (2014). *Ebony and ivy: Race, slavery, and the troubled history of America's universities.* Bloomsbury.

Yancy, G. (2012). *Look, a white! Philosophical essays on whiteness.* Temple University Press.

Yancy, G. (2015). Tarrying together. *Educational Philosophy and Theory, 47*(1), 26–35. https://doi.org/10.1080/00131857.2013.861197

Yosso, T. J. (2002). Toward a critical race curriculum. *Equity & Excellence in Education, 35*(2), 93–107. https://doi.org/10.1080/713845283

APPENDIX 2.A

Reflexivity Questions as Coauthors

Questions for Both of Us (Use "I Statements")

- How are you feeling?
- What does it look like to center Black, Indigenous, and People of Color people in this work?
- What is hard about race for you?
- How does white supremacy operate in society? Higher education? Programs and departments? Professional organizations? Neighborhoods? Families?
- What are the PREs (perfectly reasonable explanations) we see on a daily basis that allow us to claim "plausible deniability" rather than own our complicity in white supremacy?
- What can we do as individuals to take this up? As a program? College? Institution? Community member? Neighbor?
- What is our responsibility as white people who know about this to bring it up? What can each of us do to take this up *without* being a "know it all"? What struggles do I have around this with white people? With People of Color?
- What does accountability mean to you?
- What is one thing you will commit to doing?
- What does white supremacy look like in research and research designs?
- What is important to include in this chapter?
- What does it mean to be for us as white people to be vulnerable (Applebaum, 2017)? What does vulnerability look like? What does vulnerability mean to you? What is scary about talking about race, oppression, violence, and white supremacy?

Other Questions That Come Up in Our Conversations

- Can you write about theory vulnerably? What does theoretical vulnerability look like?
- How does "white immunity" show up in your life? How do you hold yourself accountable in these times?

3

WHITE NORMATIVITY

Tracing Historical and Contemporary (Re)Productions of Whiteness in Higher Education

Lauren N. Irwin

In 1890, W.E.B. Du Bois graduated cum laude with a bachelor's degree in philosophy from Harvard. That year, as one of five student commencement speakers, Du Bois delivered a sensational speech about Jefferson Davis and slavery. In his address, Du Bois (1960/2013) reflected on Davis by considering "the type of civilization which his life represented" (p. 374). Du Bois argued Davis's brutality and heroism, as a soldier, represented the contradictions of a civilization based on white supremacy. In highlighting such contradictions, Du Bois asserted that a civilization predicated on violence against People of Color is hardly a civilization. In response to this address, a Harvard professor applauded Du Bois's intellectual and oratory skills, stating that Du Bois "doubtless has some white blood in his veins" (p. 375). This celebration is notable for two reasons. First, Du Bois directly critiqued racism and white supremacy but was commended, not for the message of his address, but for his style, intelligence, and objective consideration of Davis. Apparently, the Harvard professor was unwilling to recognize how he was implicated in Du Bois's speech. Second, his praise for Du Bois effectively attributed Du Bois's intellect to whiteness, diminishing his contributions and experiences as a Black man.

In this chapter I endeavor to detail how whiteness functions as the norm against which students, faculty, staff, and all members of the higher education ecosystem are evaluated and assigned worth. Simply put, this chapter defines white normativity and traces how whiteness's normative nature manifests on college campuses in the United States. I focus on whiteness in the context of dominant or white-serving[1] colleges and universities. In particular,

I describe how whiteness operates across multiple levels—structural (e.g., racial categories), ideological (e.g., beliefs), and discursive (e.g., patterns of communication)—and argue that white normativity persists because of whiteness's dominance across the social structure (Bonilla-Silva, 1997).

I do not use this chapter to argue that higher education is the sole context in which white normativity manifests. Rather I use higher education as one example of white normativity's functioning across the U.S. social structure. Some assert that whiteness operates as an invisible or taken-for-granted standard (Frankenberg, 1993). However, such assertions center whiteness by failing to recognize that whiteness is often only invisible or taken for granted for those who benefit from whiteness (Frankenberg, 2001; Owen, 2007; Yancy, 2012, 2018). People and Scholars of Color have long named, interrogated, and rejected whiteness (e.g., Anzaldúa, Baldwin, Du Bois, Fanon, Morrison). Whiteness's normative nature is not a given; rather, it is constructed as normal by those in power. In short, whiteness became meaningful as European colonizers, and their descendants, used skin color to justify their own violent and imperial pursuits and enact a social hierarchy in which white people presumed themselves to be superior to Black and Indigenous peoples. In the United States, white people—especially elites—have sought to create institutions and practices that reinforce this violent legacy.

As a white woman, I write this chapter with the uneasy recognition that for me, whiteness was invisible, unmarked, and taken for granted for much of my life. My experience is not unique among white people in the United States, as white people and dominant institutions (e.g., schools, courts) are invested in masking whiteness's dominance and normative nature (Mueller, 2020). Accordingly, white privilege is continually reproduced, across contexts, when white people and white cultural values and ways of knowing are constructed as the norm (Mueller, 2020; Ray, 2019). The claims detailed in this chapter are likely too familiar for People of Color in the United States, as the ostensibly normative nature of whiteness enacts violence and domination across higher education contexts (e.g., cocurricular spaces, classrooms, hiring; Cabrera et al., 2017). I hope this chapter can bear witness to such violence.

Most higher education institutions in the United States were established on stolen land, propagating colonization and genocide while profiting off the labor of enslaved Black peoples (Nash, 2019; Wilder, 2014). Although the form and function of U.S. higher education has evolved over the last 400 years, the reality is that higher education institutions legitimated whiteness and racism and continue to do so. Academia implicitly and explicitly affirms certain ways of knowing, being, and doing (Ladson-Billings, 2000; Minthorn

& Nelson, 2018; Stewart, 2019; Watt, 2020). These messages often position white people and whiteness as proper, best, or legitimate (Patton, 2016). Higher education institutions, as sites of knowledge production and learning, further racialized notions of belonging, expertise, knowledge, and merit (Patton, 2016; Posselt et al., 2020; Warikoo, 2016). In sum, what has been constructed as valuable or normal in higher education is not race-neutral. Notions of belonging and success across higher education contexts are imbued with racial meaning in which white people and whiteness are rewarded and normalized. This is white normativity.

In what follows, I illustrate how whiteness is continuously constructed as legitimate and used as the standard for access, belonging, and success in higher education. Legitimacy, or the perception of belonging or appropriateness in context (Tyler, 2006), is a vital currency in higher education (Gonzales, 2013; Gonzales & Terosky, 2016; O'Meara et al., 2018). Insidiously, white normativity functions to reproduce whiteness as legitimate in higher education—mirroring racism's functioning across the U.S. social structure (Bonilla-Silva, 2001; Jung, 2015). In what follows, I first define *whiteness* and *white normativity* in greater detail. Then, I summarize white normativity's functioning in and structuring of higher education by highlighting manifestations of anti-Blackness and settler colonialism, detailing how whiteness is protected in higher education, and tracing whiteness in the production of academic knowledge. In short, the ongoing construction of whiteness as normal results in systems that operate to marginalize and exclude People of Color and their contributions across higher education.

Unpacking Whiteness and White Normativity

Whiteness and race are interrelated and socially, historically, and relationally constructed. Race, as a socially constructed category, results in embodied and material realities and structures. To say that race and whiteness are socially constructed is not to deny their real effects, but to recognize their historical and relational nature. Race, as a tool of hierarchy and categorization (Jung, 2015; Lowe, 2015), is continuously constructed through racialization, or the production of racial meaning (Omi & Winant, 2015). In short, racialization assigns historically and contextually specific racial meanings to people, actions, and knowledge in support of racism (Hall, 2017). Racialization, in creating racial categories in relation to whiteness, functions to confer or deny humanity, positioning certain peoples—namely People of Color—as inhuman and unfit for civilization (Gilroy, 2000; Jung, 2015). Thus, race is "integral to the emergence, development, and transformations of the modern nation-state" (Goldberg, 2002, p. 4). State institutions, like colleges and universities, play a powerful role in reproducing race and racism through their widespread grounding in whiteness (Bonilla-Silva, 1997; Jung, 2015; Omi & Winant, 2015).

Additionally, whiteness is historically and relationally constructed. Together, settler colonialism and anti-Blackness provide a foundation through which whiteness is constructed as normal and human—whiteness is only made real and visible through its relational opposition to People of Color. White normativity persists because what is constructed as normal is racialized as white—positioning whiteness as legitimate, human, moral, and normal (Jung, 2015; Owen, 2007). Morris (2016) detailed the pervasive nature of white normativity in describing how medical knowledge and practice is often based on studies of mostly white men, resulting in racial and gender bias in diagnosing patients and prescription drug efficacy, alongside stereotypes that paint Black and Latinx patients as having higher pain tolerance. Put simply, white normativity is a matter of life and death.

The construction of whiteness as human and normal relies on the creation of racial categories that position People of Color as separate from and inferior to whiteness. Namely, U.S. settler colonialism and anti-Blackness are central to whiteness's construction and evolution (Dumas, 2016; Tuck & Yang, 2012). Settler colonialism is characterized by colonizers' efforts to possess land and resources by making use of Indigenous labor before eliminating Indigenous peoples (Cavanagh & Veracini, 2013). Wolfe (2006) argued that settler colonialism "destroys to replace" (p. 388). The destruction perpetuated by whiteness is also evident in anti-Blackness, or a "paradigm that works against the survival and life chances of Black people, ideas, and ways of being in the world through structures of white supremacist domination" (Stewart, 2019, p. 18). Afro-pessimist scholars recognize that mainstream frameworks of humanity rely on white supremacist definitions of *humanity*, which largely exclude Black people (Stewart, 2019; Wilderson et al., 2017).

Historically, powerful elites produced and normalized racial categories that constructed white people and whiteness as human and moral while simultaneously constructing Indigenous peoples and enslaved Black peoples as uncivilized, impulsive, and deviant—and thus, not worthy of citizenship, property ownership, or subsequent human rights or autonomy (Bonilla-Silva, 1997; C. I. Harris, 1993; McClintock, 1995). Herein lies whiteness's violence: By constructing and categorizing People of Color as less than human, violence is legitimated and endorsed in the name of whiteness (Jung, 2015). This sinister legacy is foundational to understanding race and whiteness in the contemporary United States.

Defining Whiteness as Structure, Ideology, and Discourse

Whiteness refers to more than white people or a racial identity. Rather, understanding whiteness as a structure, ideology, and discourse is central to detailing white normativity. Despite the overrepresentation of white people across higher education (Davis & Fry, 2019), focusing solely on demographics neglects white normativity's systemic nature (Cabrera et al., 2017). Thus, it is important to consider how whiteness functions as a structure, ideology, and discourse. Positioning whiteness as a structure illuminates how whiteness "infects all aspects of the life-world" (Owen, 2007, p. 214). As a structure, whiteness creates a hierarchical order—this ordering informs individuals' thoughts and social practices (Owen, 2007). Within this structure, white ideologies, or systems of ideas, are characterized by valorization of individualism, color-evasiveness, and merit (Annamma et al., 2017; Bonilla-Silva, 2017; Lewis, 2004). When deployed, such beliefs minimize the realities of racism.

Ideologies of whiteness shape whiteness as discourse, or patterns of communication that reproduce white domination (Leonardo, 2002). Three features characterize whiteness as discourse: minimization of racism in the United States, ignorance and avoidance of the racialized experiences of People of Color, and a refusal to acknowledge systemic racism (Leonardo, 2009). These discourses often obfuscate the realities of racial domination, not because white people and institutions do not know about racism, but because they benefit from actively ignoring racism (Bonilla-Silva, 2017; Mills, 2007; Mueller, 2017, 2020). In the post–civil rights era, color-evasiveness has proliferated as the dominant ideology in the United States, facilitating a set of cognitive and linguistic resources that allow white people to talk about race without naming race, racism, or white people's complicity (Bonilla-Silva, 2017). Such color-evasive practices contribute to the normalization of whiteness by attributing the material and social benefits afforded to white people as the result of merit and hard work, rather than unequal access to resources and opportunities. Racial ignorance and color-evasiveness, at the ideological and discursive level, reinforce structural whiteness, by rewarding practices that preserve white dominance (Cabrera et al., 2017; Owen, 2007; Ray & Purifoy, 2019). Owen (2007) argued that the normalization of whiteness preserves white supremacy. Thus, we turn our attention to white normativity, as a core function of whiteness and contributor to the fallacy of white supremacy.

White Normativity

As detailed previously, whiteness is relationally, socially, and historically constructed, reproducing white normativity across multiple levels of the social structure. Simply put, whiteness's normative nature functions so that "[w]hat is associated with whiteness becomes defined as natural, normal, or mainstream" (Owen, 2007, p. 216). Further, white normativity constructs white people's emotions, knowledge, and behaviors as representative of humanity, normality, and rationality (Owen, 2007; Smith, 2013; Yancy, 2018). Thus, whiteness serves as the standard by which people's humanity, knowledge, and ways of being are judged—and deemed worthy, human, and legitimate, or not (Dumas, 2016; Jung, 2015; Yancy, 2018). Yet this reality is largely invisible to many white people—white people's active ignorance of whiteness and racism both results from and ensures whiteness persists as a dominant force (Mueller, 2020; Owen, 2007; Yancy, 2018). Jung (2015) argued that the pervasive nature of white normativity, and its legitimation across dominant institutions, like colleges and universities, has produced physical, intellectual, and structural violence against People of Color. In short, white normativity seeks to ensure a small portion of humanity can access the privileges of being human—and this reality powerfully structures higher education.

White Normativity in Higher Education

White normativity manifests in multiple ways in higher education. At white-serving institutions, those racialized as white are likely to encounter other white people in positions of power (e.g., faculty, administrators; Davis & Fry, 2019), to find their history and knowledge in the curriculum (Patton, 2016; Smith, 2013), and to locate clubs, activities, and resources that reflect their priorities, interests, and values (Gusa, 2010). Gusa's (2010) notion of white institutional presence explains how white normativity operates in higher education. White institutional presence manifests "in the practices, traditions, and perceptions of knowledge that are taken for granted as the norm at institutions of higher education" (p. 464). Effectively, Gusa argued that white institutional presence pervades higher education, resulting in racism, exclusion, and marginalization for People of Color across higher education (see, e.g., Cabrera et al., 2017; Caplan & Ford, 2014; Gildersleeve et al., 2011; Harper & Hurtado, 2007; Patton, 2016). In short, the normative nature of whiteness undergirds higher education in several ways: U.S. higher education is rooted in racism and white supremacy (Patton, 2016), resulting from imperialism and capitalism (Nash, 2019; Wilder, 2014), and serving as a venue through which formal knowledge production rooted in whiteness is generated (Patton, 2016; Smith, 2013). In what follows, I offer examples in three categories: manifestations of anti-Blackness and settler colonialism, protecting whiteness, and knowledge production. Collectively, these examples highlight how the normative nature of whiteness pervades higher education, ensuring whiteness is legitimated and normalized.

Manifestations of Anti-Blackness and Settler Colonialism

In detailing the construction of race, racism, and whiteness in the United States, I situated the history of higher education and white racial identity in relation to anti-Blackness and settler colonialism. If white normativity constructs white people as the standard for humanity, then we must consider how higher education institutions continue to ensure that white students are made to belong on campus. Although belonging can refer to a psychosocial state of perceived fit or connectedness on campus (Maslow, 1962; Rosenberg & McCullough, 1981; Strayhorn, 2012), I use belonging here in a structural sense—to refer to whose bodies, histories, and practices are assumed (and made) to seem natural or at home on college campuses (Stewart, 2019). In examining which students are considered traditional or at home on college campuses, white normativity—and its preservation through anti-Blackness and settler colonialism—becomes even more evident.

Policing White Space

Three national news stories from 2018 exemplify how white normativity is protected via surveillance and policing of People of Color on college campuses. At Colorado State University, a white mother on a college tour called the police on two Indigenous teenagers whom she claimed looked like "they don't belong" (Levin, 2018, para. 1). Subsequently, these two teenagers were interrogated and missed their campus tour. A few weeks later, a white student at Yale University, Sara Braasch, called the police on a Black student, Lolade Siyonbola, who was napping in the student lounge (Wootson, 2018). That same month, a white Smith College employee called the police on a Black graduate student, Omou Kanoute, who was presumed to be "out of place" for daring to eat lunch (Whitford, 2018, para. 1). These teenagers and students were presumed not to belong, simply because they occupied space on campus. In short, these campuses exist as white spaces, or spaces dominated by white people that subsequently mark People of Color as out of place (E. Anderson, 2015; Puwar, 2004). In all three instances, white people acted to protect their unfettered access to campus by calling the police. However, these incidents are neither isolated nor rare. Jenkins et al. (2021) offered a critical race theory analysis, as Black male collegians and scholars, of their own encounters with campus police as a result of racial profiling at three different white-serving institutions. They demonstrated how Black students' access to campus is surveilled and viewed with suspicion because of their embodied transgressions from whiteness (Jenkins et al., 2021).

These examples highlight how, through the normative nature of whiteness, Black and Indigenous people are presumed and made to not belong, especially at white-serving institutions. Stewart (2019) explained how ideologies of anti-Blackness and unbelonging shape the experiences of Black students and Black student affairs practitioners across higher education. Particularly, Stewart (2019) argued belongingness is a "condition produced by institutional systems and structures," where being made to belong is a "privilege bestowed upon those who have assimilated to ways of being and doing that have been normalized . . . based on whiteness" (p. 22). Some are made to belong whereas others are excluded. Across higher education, where whiteness is normalized, Black students and student affairs professionals are made not to belong for any number of reasons, including for wearing natural hairstyles, being perceived as unapproachable, for communicating directly, and for expressing stress and exhaustion for managing ongoing racism (Stewart, 2019). The institutional production of unbelonging for Black students and student affairs professionals cannot be separated from whiteness's origins—where white elites asserted their entitlement to land, resources, labor, and power by denigrating the worth and humanity of Black and Indigenous peoples. These examples represent how higher education institutions preserve white normativity by reproducing anti-Blackness.

Settler Colonialism

White normativity is further perpetuated through ongoing settler colonialism in higher education. Minthorn and Nelson (2018) traced how campus tours embrace settler colonial, racist, and genocidal histories and values. Campus tours often highlight the founding of the college's "first" building—such histories generally erase any presence of Indigenous peoples on the land that institutions now occupy (Minthorn & Nelson, 2018). Further, campuses often name buildings and important landmarks after figures of prolific colonizers—by doing so, the prototypical campus tour becomes a narrative of white-serving institution building that perpetuates white normativity. Thus, while white people actively exclude Indigenous peoples from college campuses (Levin, 2018), institutions also position their histories of colonization, racism, and genocide as points of institutional pride. Such warped histories erase the legacies and contributions of Indigenous peoples, ensuring Indigenous histories, traditions, and values do not belong on college campuses (Minthorn & Nelson, 2018). In addition to the multiple ways that campus structures and narratives further racism and settler colonialism, scholars document Indigenous students' experiences with racism, stereotypes, distance from family, and cultural isolation as a result of conflict between the normative, Eurocentric culture of white-serving institutions and their Indigenous heritage (Brayboy, 2015; Caplan & Ford, 2014; Jackson et al., 2003; Tachine et al., 2017). White institutional presence reinforces the normative nature of whiteness across college campuses, perpetuating racism and unbelonging through settler colonialism and anti-Blackness. Next, I offer several examples of how white people actively protect whiteness in higher education.

Protecting Whiteness in Higher Education

As detailed previously, ideologies of anti-Blackness and settler colonialism affect belonging on campus—structurally, physically, and psychologically. Often, higher education institutions are places where white students are made to belong and are disproportionately entitled to resources (Cabrera et al., 2016). Thus, white normativity is evident when institutions center white students' needs, histories, experiences, and privileges within and beyond the classroom.

Higher Education and Student Affairs Programs and Students

Recently, scholars have interrogated how whiteness is reproduced in higher education and student affairs (HESA; see, e.g., Bondi, 2012; Poon, 2018; Robbins, 2016). Notably, Bondi (2012) critically examined white students in HESA graduate programs and detailed how racism resulted in material inequities between white students and Student of Color. For many white students, their HESA graduate experience required them to consider racism and whiteness more critically than they had before. In response, white students focused on their good intentions and learning needs, without concern for the needs of or harm enacted on Students of Color in the class (Bondi, 2012). Further, white HESA students excluded Students of Color from social gatherings and expected Students of Color to value, validate, and center their contributions in the classroom—with no regard for how such expectations perpetuated racism and exclusion (Bondi, 2012). J. C. Harris and Linder (2018) also echoed these realities, in detailing how HESA programs and faculty largely cater to the needs of white students, resulting in isolating and invalidating experiences for Students of Color, as they were expected to educate their white peers and serve as representatives of diversity within HESA programs. Here, white normativity is exemplified in HESA programs' centering of white students' needs and learning.

White Students' Resistance

These findings also align with research that broadly documents white students' resistance to learning about racism and privilege (Cabrera, 2017, 2019; Watt, 2007). Specifically, white women often respond with emotional outbursts (e.g., crying) when confronted with the realities of racism or their own racist actions. Such emotional responses protect whiteness by expecting People of Color and other people in the space to attend to white feelings, rather than considering the continued marginalization such actions enact against People of Color (Accapadi, 2007; Matias, 2016; Robbins, 2016). In short, white students often enter college classrooms with an assumption of racial comfort (Cabrera et al., 2016; Leonardo & Porter, 2010) or the expectation that they can exist in a state of social comfort by avoiding direct engagement with racism and feelings of dissonance, even in dialogue about racism. White students' assumed racial comfort can also lead to resistance to curricula that center racism and the experiences of People of Color (Stanley, 2006). White students' preservation of racial comfort stems from whiteness's normative nature, as white students can actively center their own needs and evade the realities of racism because they are often rewarded—with comfort, relationships, access to education, and promotion in organizations—for doing so (Mueller, 2020; Ray, 2019).

Legacies of Whiteness Across Higher Education

It is important to put such actions of white resistance in context, as higher education institutions often validate white students' responses and reinforce white normativity. For much of higher education's history, institutions were racially segregated and exclusionary, as race determined access to higher education (Harper et al., 2009; Karabel, 2005; Wilder, 2014). In the 1940s, most white-serving universities refused to hire exceptionally qualified Black scholars, despite claims that race was not a central qualification for faculty hiring (J. D. Anderson, 1993). These same patterns persist today, as faculty hiring committees often use the language of "fit" to evade discussing race and to disqualify People of Color (Liera, 2020; White-Lewis, 2020) and graduate admissions committees perpetuate racism by relying on biased metrics like GRE scores (Alon & Tienda, 2007; Posselt, 2016). However, access alone is not the only problem. Institutions also perpetuate racism, exclusion, and marginalization through microaggressions and racist climates (Harper & Hurtado, 2007; Harper & Quaye, 2009; Solórzano et al., 2000); lowered expectations for Students of Color (Gildersleeve, 2010; Ladson-Billings & Tate, 1995); biased tenure, promotion, and evaluation processes (Bernal & Villalpando, 2002; Croom, 2017; Urrieta et al., 2015); and curricula that largely center white histories, peoples, and knowledge or position the contributions of People of Color as additive to the white core curriculum (Linley, 2017; Milem et al., 2005; Patton et al., 2007). Further, widely used practices and tools, like service-learning and StrengthsQuest, often normalize whiteness by centering white students' needs, experiences, and learning (Irwin & Foste, 2021; Mitchell et al., 2012; Tapia-Fuselier & Irwin, 2019). Thus, it is important to consider how whiteness is normalized and protected in academic knowledge production.

Production of Legitimate Knowledge

Having detailed how white normativity is (re)produced through anti-Blackness and settler colonialism on campus, and the protection of whiteness by white people and institutions, I turn to a final example of white normativity in higher education—the dominance of whiteness in what is deemed legitimate knowledge. White normativity in the production and legitimation of knowledge directly contributes to ideologies of whiteness, anti-Blackness, and settler colonialism, and leads to curricula that continue to center whiteness and white people. In short, academic knowledge production is implicated in the creation of a racial hierarchy that protects whiteness and continues to reproduce white normativity.

Traditional Academic Methods and Knowledge

First, academic knowledge production is implicated in the creation and preservation of racial hierarchy—resulting in real, material, and violent effects. The creation of a racial hierarchy ensured that race became a marker of more than just difference, but a mode to differentiate among humanity, thereby positioning white people as human, superior, and civilized, and People of Color as inhuman and uncivilized (McClintock, 1995; Steinberg, 1998). Scientists played an integral role in creating and furthering race science—creating racial hierarchies and classifications to justify enslavement and colonization (Gilroy, 2000; Smith, 2013; Zuberi & Bonilla-Silva, 2008). White people largely controlled these efforts and created scientific methods, procedures, and claims that ensured white people's dominance. Modern tools of statistical analysis were developed in support of eugenics (Zuberi, 2001) and are often still taken up by scholars in ways that reify racial categories (James, 2008). For example, contemporary social science scholarship furthers racism by locating the effects of racism as the result of cultural differences—such practices essentially preserve racism and white normativity by positioning racial inequality as the result of People of Color's failings, rather than the terrors of racism and white supremacy (Steinberg, 1998). In higher education research, Harper (2012) illustrated how scholars preserve the status quo by attributing inequities to race, not racism. Ascribing inequities to race avoids naming the realities of systemic white supremacy in higher education and society broadly. Thus, it is not just the content of what the academy has legitimated that has furthered white normativity, but also how such knowledge is created.

Numerous scholars have demonstrated how dominant ways of knowing—ontologies and epistemologies—that are valued and legitimated across disciplines are rooted in racism, white supremacy, and colonialism (see, e.g., Almeida, 2015; Collins, 1989; Ladson-Billings, 2000; Scheurich & Young, 1997; Smith, 2013; Zuberi & Bonilla-Silva, 2008). Smith (2013) explained that positivism, as the dominant epistemology of western science, reduces the world to what can be measured. Further, James (2008) traced how social scientists use census data for various analyses and, in doing so, treat race as a fixed variable. By treating race as a fixed variable, researchers often attribute racial inequities, resulting from racialization and racism, to differences in racial groups or fail to adequately consider the complexity and fluidity of racism in the United States (James, 2008). Positivist approaches to knowledge facilitate four practices: (a) the classifying of "others" into categories, (b) condensing the complexity of societies and their imaginations, (c) the creation of standard models, and (d) providing criteria by which other societies can be ranked (Smith, 2013). Zuberi and Bonilla-Silva (2008) referred to this practice as "white logic" (p. 17). Effectively, positivistic approaches to knowledge helped construct a racial hierarchy by positioning white people and Eurocentric culture as the foundation by which to evaluate and categorize everything and everybody. Thus, the unquestioned acceptance and protection of such knowledge as legitimate and universal reinforces white normativity.

Devaluation of Knowledge

Second, I trace the ongoing violence, erasure, and marginalization enacted through dominant norms of academic knowledge production. In response to the dominant nature of white, western knowledge, minoritized scholars have brought additional perspectives and ways of knowing and doing research to the academy (e.g., critical race theory, intersectionality, Black feminist thought). Although many of these theories and methodologies have traveled across the academy, their proliferation has largely resulted from the increased presence of minoritized scholars across the academy and their efforts to challenge legitimated norms of knowledge production (Collins, 2012, 2015). However, institutions still reward scholarship that privileges whiteness (Bernal & Villalpando, 2002). Effectively, Scholars of Color must be bicultural to navigate the academy—preserving their own values and ways of knowing while navigating the academy's white norms (Ladson-Billings, 2000; Scheurich & Young, 1997). In short, the process of evaluating and producing legitimate knowledge is highly political, and the contributions of Scholars of Color can be devalued, because of their deviations from whiteness (Bernal & Villalpando, 2002). The academy's and white scholars' continued blithe acceptance and endorsement of this reality exemplifies and perpetuates white normativity.

Scholars of Color and other minoritized scholars sometimes receive pushback for doing work that is community oriented (Smith, 2013), are critiqued as biased or lacking objectivity for centering racism and People of Color in their scholarship (Bernal & Villalpando, 2002; Gonzales et al., 2013; Solórzano & Yosso, 2002; Stanley, 2007), have their contributions devalued for publishing in languages other than English or in open-access journals (Bernal, 2002; Bernal & Villalpando, 2002; Gonzales & Núñez, 2014), and are penalized for deviating from the "canon" or dominant topics or theories in their field (Brunsma & Wyse, 2019). This epistemological racism often ensures that race-based epistemologies are excluded from top journals and competitive grant funding, and subsequently the core knowledge of many academic disciplines (Apple & Christian-Smith, 1991; Scheurich & Young, 1997; Stanfield, 2016). In short, the norms of academic knowledge production ensure that the existing forms of legitimated knowledge, which largely privilege white knowers, dominant ways of knowing, and the existing racial hierarchy, are protected. Accordingly, white normativity is continually reproduced across higher education.

Conclusion

In this chapter, I described how white normativity manifests on college campuses—their physical environments, the knowledges they legitimate, and the students, staff, and scholars involved. I offered three examples of white normativity in higher education: anti-Blackness and settler colonialism as preserving white normativity, white students and institutions protecting whiteness, and the production of legitimate knowledge and white normativity as mutually reinforcing. Across all three instances, I described how whiteness's normative nature enacts violence and marginalization—ensuring that higher education is anything but inclusive, just, and equitable. To this end, Patton (2016) asserted that

> the reproduction of racism [in higher education] occurs without much disruption because those with the power to change institutions were also educated by these institutions, meaning they graduate from their institutions and often perform their lives devoid of racial consciousness. (p. 324)

In short, white normativity persists across higher education. This reality was established with higher education's roots in enslavement, genocide, and land theft, and persists by continuously legitimating and protecting knowers and knowledge that reinforce whiteness. The embedded, dynamic, and evolving nature of white normativity is precisely what makes it so hard to disrupt.

I am not denying the progress that has occurred across higher education—increased access to higher education for People of Color and other historically excluded and minoritized groups (Thelin, 2011), the creation of ethnic studies and inclusion of minoritized scholars and epistemologies in the curriculum (Gutierrez, 1994), more visible racial diversity among staff and faculty (Davis & Fry, 2019), and the creation and implementation of various curricular and cocurricular efforts to validate and support Students of Color (Quaye et al., 2020). However, institutions largely remain preoccupied with diversity, rather than transformation. Although Ahmed's (2012) work comes from a British context, her arguments about the shortcomings of diversity efforts as transformative tools speak to white normativity in U.S. higher education and are echoed by U.S. scholars like Stewart (2017). Ahmed (2012) claimed that diversity efforts are often "about changing perceptions of whiteness rather than changing the whiteness of organizations" (p. 34). White normativity, and its continued manifestation across higher education, persists as a central problem. This chapter characterized white normativity as a socially constructed source of violence and marginalization. Although uncovering and detailing whiteness's normative nature will not ensure transformation on its own, I hope this chapter has helped readers deepen their conceptual understanding of white normativity in pursuit of transforming and disrupting whiteness within and beyond higher education.

Notes

1. I use the language of *white-serving institutions* (Rodriguez, 2019), rather than historically or predominantly white, because the language of "white-serving" recognizes who disproportionately attends these institutions and to whom these institutions cater.

References

Accapadi, M. M. (2007). When white women cry: How white women's tears oppress women of color. *College Student Affairs Journal, 26*(2), 208–215. https://files.eric.ed.gov/fulltext/EJ899418.pdf

Ahmed, S. (2012). *On being included: Racism and diversity in institutional life.* Duke University Press.

Almeida, S. (2015). Race-based epistemologies: The role of race and dominance in knowledge production. *Wagadu: A Journal of Transnational Women's & Gender Studies, 13*, 79–105. http://sites.cortland.edu/wagadu/wp-content/uploads/sites/3/2015/07/4-FOUR-Almeida.pdf

Alon, S., & Tienda, M. (2007). Diversity, opportunity, and the shifting meritocracy in higher education. *American Sociological Review, 72*(4), 487–511. https://doi.org/10.1177/000312240707200401

Anderson, E. (2015). The white space. *Sociology of Race and Ethnicity, 1*(1), 10–21. https://doi.org/10.1177/2332649214561306

Anderson, J. D. (1993). Race, meritocracy, and the American academy during the immediate post-World War II era. *History of Education Quarterly, 33*(2), 151–175. https://doi.org/10.2307/368340

Annamma, S. A., Jackson, D. D., & Morrison, D. (2017). Conceptualizing color-evasiveness: Using dis/ability critical race theory to expand a color-blind racial ideology in education and society. *Race Ethnicity and Education, 20*(2), 147–162. https://doi.org/10.1080/13613324.2016.1248837

Apple, M. W., & Christian-Smith, L. K. (1991). The politics of the textbook. In M. W. Apple & L. K. Christian-Smith (Eds.), *The politics of the textbook* (pp. 1–21). Routledge.

Bernal, D. D. (2002). Critical race theory, Latino critical theory, and critical raced-gendered epistemologies: Recognizing students of color as holders and creators of knowledge. *Qualitative Inquiry, 8*(1), 105–126. https://doi.org/10.1177/107780040200800107

Bernal, D. D., & Villalpando, O. (2002). An apartheid of knowledge in academia: The struggle over the "legitimate" knowledge of faculty of color. *Equity & Excellence in Education, 35*(2), 169–180. https://doi.org/10.1080/713845282

Bondi, S. (2012). Students and institutions protecting Whiteness as property: A critical race theory analysis of student affairs preparation. *Journal of Student Affairs Research and Practice, 49*(4), 397–414. https://doi.org/10.1515/jsarp-2012-6381

Bonilla-Silva, E. (1997). Rethinking racism: Toward a structural interpretation. *American Sociological Review, 62*(3), 465–480. https://doi.org/10.2307/2657316

Bonilla-Silva, E. (2001). *White supremacy and racism in the post-civil rights era.* Lynne Rienner.

Bonilla-Silva, E. (2017). *Racism without racists: Color-blind racism and the persistence of racial inequality in the United States* (5th ed.). Rowman & Littlefield.

Brayboy, B. (2015). Indigenous peoples in the racial battle land. In K. Fasching-Varner, K. A. Albert, R. W. Mitchell, & C. M. Allen (Eds.), *Racial battle fatigue in higher education* (pp. 45–58). Rowman & Littlefield.

Brunsma, D. L., & Wyse, J. P. (2019). The possessive investment in white sociology. *Sociology of Race and Ethnicity, 5*(1), 1–10. https://doi.org/10.1177/2332649218809968

Cabrera, N. L. (2017). White immunity: Working through some of the pedagogical pitfalls of "privilege." *Journal Committed to Social Change on Race and Ethnicity,*

3(1), 78–90. https://www.ncore.ou.edu/media/filer_public/43/cd/43cd1bc4-e1db-41a8-a787-23d1527174b2/cabrera___white_immunity_.pdf

Cabrera, N. L. (2019). *White guys on campus: Racism, white immunity, and the myth of "post-racial" higher education*. Rutgers University Press.

Cabrera, N. L., Franklin, J. D., & Watson, J. S. (2017). Whiteness in higher education: The invisible missing link in diversity and racial analyses. *ASHE Higher Education Report, 42*(6), 7–125. https://doi.org/10.1002/aehe.20116

Cabrera, N. L., Watson, J. S., & Franklin, J. D. (2016). Racial arrested development: A critical whiteness analysis of the campus ecology. *Journal of College Student Development, 57*(2), 119–134. https://doi.org/10.1353/csd.2016.0014

Caplan, P., & Ford, J. (2014). The voices of diversity: What students of diverse races/ethnicities and both sexes tell us about their college experiences and their perceptions about their institutions' progress toward diversity. *Aporia, 6*(3), 30–69. https://doi.org/10.18192/aporia.v6i4.2828

Cavanagh, E., & Veracini, L. (2013). Editor's statement. *Settler Colonial Studies, 3*(1), 1. https://doi.org/10.1080/18380743.2013.768169

Collins, P. H. (1989). The social construction of Black feminist thought. *Signs, 14*(4), 745–773. https://www.journals.uchicago.edu/doi/abs/10.1086/494543?journalCode=signs

Collins, P. H. (2012). Social inequality, power, and politics: Intersectionality and American pragmatism in dialogue. *The Journal of Speculative Philosophy, 26*(2), 442–457. https://doi.org/10.5325/jspecphil.26.2.0442

Collins, P. H. (2015). Intersectionality's definitional dilemmas. *Annual Review of Sociology, 41*(1), 1–20. https://doi.org/10.1146/annurev-soc-073014-112142

Croom, N. N. (2017). Promotion beyond tenure: Unpacking racism and sexism in the experiences of Black womyn professors. *The Review of Higher Education, 40*(4), 557–583. https://doi.org/10.1353/rhe.2017.0022

Davis, L., & Fry, R. (2019). *College faculty have become more racially and ethnically diverse, but remain far less so than students*. Pew Research Center. https://www.pewresearch.org/fact-tank/2019/07/31/us-college-faculty-student-diversity/

Du Bois., W. E. B. (2013). A negro student at Harvard at the end of the 19th century. *The Massachusetts Review, 54*(3), 364–380. http://www.jstor.com/stable/24494510 (Original work published 1960)

Dumas, M. J. (2016). Against the dark: Antiblackness in education policy and discourse. *Theory Into Practice, 55*(1), 11–19. https://doi.org/10.1080/00405841.2016.1116852

Frankenberg, R. (1993). *White women, race matters: The social construction of whiteness*. University of Minnesota Press.

Frankenberg, R. (2001). The mirage of an unmarked whiteness. In B. B. Rasmussen, E. Klinenberg, I. J. Nexica, & M. Wray (Eds.), *The making and unmaking of whiteness* (pp. 72–96). Duke University Press.

Gildersleeve, R. E. (2010). *Fracturing opportunity: Mexican migrant students and college-going literacy.* Peter Lang.

Gildersleeve, R. E, Croom, N. N., & Vasquez, P. L. (2011). "Am I going crazy?!": A critical race analysis of doctoral education. *Equity & Excellence in Education, 44*(1), 93–114. https://doi.org/10.1080/10665684.2011.539472

Gilroy, P. (2000). *Against race: Imagining political culture beyond the color line.* Harvard University Press.

Goldberg, D. T. (2002). *The racial state.* Blackwell.

Gonzales, L. D. (2013). Faculty sensemaking and mission creep: Interrogating institutionalized ways of knowing and doing legitimacy. *The Review of Higher Education, 36*(2), 179–209. https://doi.org/10.1353/rhe.2013.0000

Gonzales, L. D., Murakami, E., & Núñez, A. M. (2013). Latina faculty in the labyrinth: Constructing and contesting legitimacy in Hispanic serving institutions. *Educational Foundations, 27*(1–2), 65–89. https://eric.ed.gov/?id=EJ1013719

Gonzales, L. D., & Núñez, A. M. (2014). The ranking regime and the production of knowledge: Implications for academia. *Education Policy Analysis Archives, 22*(31), 1–24. http://dx.doi.org/10.14507/epaa.v22n31.2014

Gonzales, L. D., & Terosky, A. L. (2016). From the faculty perspective: Defining, earning, and maintaining legitimacy across academia. *Teachers College Record, 118*(7), 1–44. https://www.tcrecord.org/Content.asp?ContentId=20805

Gusa, D. L. (2010). White institutional presence: The impact of whiteness on campus climate. *Harvard Educational Review, 80*(4), 464–490. https://doi.org/10.17763/haer.80.4.p5j483825u110002

Gutierrez, R. A. (1994). Ethnic studies: Its evolution in American colleges and universities. In D. T. Goldberg (Ed.), *Multiculturalism: A critical reader* (pp. 157–167). Blackwell.

Hall, S. (2017). *The fateful triangle.* Harvard University Press.

Harper, S. R. (2012). Race without racism: How higher education researchers minimize racist institutional norms. *The Review of Higher Education, 36*(1), 9–29. https://doi.org/10.1353/rhe.2012.0047

Harper, S. R., & Hurtado, S. (2007). Nine themes in campus racial climates and implications for institutional transformation. In S. Harper & L. Patton (Eds.), *Responding to the Realities of Race on Campus* (New Directions for Student Services, no. 120, pp. 7–24). Jossey-Bass.

Harper, S. R., Patton, L. D., & Wooden, O. S. (2009). Access and equity for African American students in higher education: A critical race historical analysis of policy efforts. *The Journal of Higher Education, 80*(4), 389–414. https://doi.org/10.1080/00221546.2009.11779022

Harper, S. R., & Quaye, S. J. (2009). Beyond sameness for engagement and outcomes for all. In S. R. Harper & S. J. Quaye (Eds.), *Student engagement in higher education: Theoretical perspectives and practical approaches for diverse populations* (pp. 1–15). Routledge.

Harris, C. I. (1993). Whiteness as property. *Harvard Law Review, 106*(8), 1707–1791. https://www.jstor.org/stable/1341787?seq=1

Harris, J. C., & Linder, C. (2018). The racialized experiences of students of color in higher education and student affairs graduate preparation programs. *Journal of College Student Development, 59*(2), 141–158. https://doi.org/10.1353/csd.2018.0014

Irwin, L. N., & Foste, Z. (2021). Service-learning and racial capitalism: On the commodification of People of Color for white advancement. *The Review of Higher Education, 44*(4), 419–446. https://muse.jhu.edu/article/796155

Jackson, A. P., Smith, S. A., & Hill, C. L. (2003). Academic persistence among Native American college students. *Journal of College Student Development, 44*(4), 548–565. https://doi.org/10.1353/csd.2003.0039

James, A. (2008). Making sense of race and racial classification. In T. Zuberi & E. Bonilla-Silva (Eds.), *White logic, white methods: Racism and methodology* (pp. 31–45). Rowman & Littlefield.

Jenkins, D. A., Tichavakunda, A. A., & Coles, J. A. (2021). The second ID: Critical race counterstories of campus police interactions with Black men at historically white institutions. *Race Ethnicity and Education, 24*(2), 149–166. https://doi.org/10.1080/13613324.2020.1753672

Jung, M. K. (2015). *Beneath the surface of white supremacy: Denaturalizing US racisms past and present.* Stanford University Press.

Karabel, J. (2005). *The chosen: The hidden history of admission and exclusion at Harvard, Yale, and Princeton.* Houghton Mifflin.

Ladson-Billings, G. (2000). Racialized discourse and ethnic epistemologies. In N. D. Denzin & Y. S. Lincoln (Eds.), *Handbook of qualitative tesearch* (2nd ed., pp. 257–277). SAGE.

Ladson-Billings, G., & Tate, W. (1995). Toward a critical race theory of education. *Teachers College Record, 97*(1), 47–68. https://eric.ed.gov/?id=EJ519126

Leonardo, Z. (2002). The souls of white folk: Critical pedagogy, whiteness studies, and globalization discourse. *Race Ethnicity and Education, 5*(1), 29–50. https://doi.org/10.1080/13613320120117180

Leonardo, Z. (2009). *Race, whiteness, and education.* Routledge.

Leonardo, Z., & Porter, R. K. (2010). Pedagogy of fear: Toward a Fanonian theory of "safety" in race dialogues. *Race Ethnicity and Education, 13*(2), 139–157. https://doi.org/10.1080/13613324.2010.482898

Levin, S. (2018). "They don't belong": Police called on Native American teens on college tour. *The Guardian.* https://www.theguardian.com/us-news/2018/may/04/native-american-students-colorado-state-college-tour-police

Lewis, A. E. (2004). "What group?": Studying whites and whiteness in the era of "colorblindness." *Sociological Theory, 22*(4), 623–646. https://doi.org/10.1111/j.0735-2751.2004.00237.x

Liera, R. (2020). Moving beyond a culture of niceness in faculty hiring to advance racial equity. *American Educational Research Journal, 57*(5), 1954–1994. https://doi.org/10.3102/0002831219888624

Linley, J. L. (2017). Teaching to deconstruct whiteness in higher education. *Whiteness & Education, 2*(1), 48–59. https://doi.org/10.1080/23793406.2017.1362943

Lowe, L. (2015). *The intimacies of four continents.* Duke University Press.

Maslow, A. H. (1962). *Toward a psychology of being.* Van Nostrand Reinhold.

Matias, C. E. (2016). *Feeling white: Whiteness, emotionality, and education.* Sense.

McClintock, A. (1995). *Imperial leather: Race, gender and sexuality in the colonial contest.* Routledge.

Milem, J. F., Chang, M. J., & Antonio, A. L. (2005). *Making diversity work on campus: A research-based perspective.* Association of American Colleges and Universities.

Mills, C. (2007). White ignorance. In S. Sullivan & N. Tuana (Eds.), *Race and epistemologies of ignorance* (pp. 11–38). SUNY Press.

Minthorn, R. S., & Nelson, C. A. (2018). Colonized and racist Indigenous campus tour. *Journal of Critical Scholarship on Higher Education and Student Affairs, 4*(1), 73–88. https://ecommons.luc.edu/jcshesa/vol4/iss1/4/

Mitchell, T. D., Donahue, D. M., & Young-Law, C. (2012). Service learning as a pedagogy of whiteness. *Equity & Excellence in Education, 45*(4), 612–629. https://doi.org/10.1080/10665684.2012.715534

Morris, M. (2016). Standard white: Dismantling white normativity. *California Law Review, 104*(4), 949–978. https://www.jstor.org/stable/24758741

Mueller, J. C. (2017). Producing colorblindness: Everyday mechanisms of white ignorance. *Social Problems, 64*(2), 219–238. https://doi.org/10.1093/socpro/spw061

Mueller, J. C. (2020). Racial ideology or racial ignorance? An alternative theory of racial cognition. *Sociological Theory, 38*(3), 142–169. https://doi.org/10.1177/0735275120926197

Nash, M. A. (2019). Entangled pasts: Land-grant colleges and American Indian dispossession. *History of Education Quarterly, 59*(4), 437–467. https://doi.org/10.1017/heq.2019.31

O'Meara, K., Templeton, L., & Nyunt, G. (2018). Earning professional legitimacy: Challenges faced by women, under-represented minority and non-tenure track faculty. *Teachers College Record, 120*(12), 1–38. https://doi.org/10.1177/016146811812001203

Omi, M., & Winant, H. (2015). *Racial formation in the United States.* Routledge.

Owen, D. S. (2007). Towards a critical theory of whiteness. *Philosophy and Social Criticism, 33*(3), 203–222. https://doi.org/10.1177/0191453707074139

Patton, L. D. (2016). Disrupting postsecondary prose: Toward a critical race theory of higher education. *Urban Education, 51*(3), 315–342. https://doi.org/10.1177/0042085915602542

Patton, L. D., McEwen, M., Rendón, L., & Howard-Hamilton, M. F. (2007). Critical race perspectives on theory in student affairs. In S. Harper & L. Patton (Eds.), *Responding to the Realities of Race on Campus* (New Directions for Student Services, no. 120, pp. 29–53). Jossey-Bass.

Poon, O. (2018). Ending white innocence in student affairs and higher education. *Journal of Student Affairs, 27,* 13–24. https://sahe.colostate.edu/journal/journal-board-archives/

Posselt, J. R. (2016). *Inside graduate admissions.* Harvard University Press.

Posselt, J. R., Hernandez, T., Villareal, C., Rodgers, A. J., & Irwin, L. N. (2020). Evaluation and decision making in higher education: Creating equitable repertoires of practice. In L. Perna (Ed.), *Higher education: Handbook of theory and research* (Vol. 35, pp. 1–63). Springer.

Puwar, N. (2004). *Space invaders: Race, gender, and bodies out of place.* Berg.

Quaye, S. J., Harper, S. R., & Pendakur, S. L. (2020). *Student engagement in higher education: Theoretical perspectives and practical approaches for diverse populations* (3rd ed.). Routledge.

Ray, V. (2019). A theory of racialized organizations. *American Sociological Review, 84*(1), 26–53. https://doi.org/10.1177/0003122418822335

Ray, V., & Purifoy, D. (2019). The colorblind organization. In M. E. Wooten (Ed.), *Race, organizations, and the organizing process* (pp. 131–150). Emerald.

Robbins, C. K. (2016). White women, racial identity, and learning about racism in graduate preparation programs. *Journal of Student Affairs Research and Practice, 53*(3), 256–268. https://doi.org/10.1080/19496591.2016.1143834

Rodriguez, P. D. M. (2019). *Past talks.* https://www.priscadorcas.com/pasttalks/

Rosenberg, M., & McCullough, B. C. (1981). Mattering: Inferred significance and mental health among adolescents. *Research in Community and Mental Health, 2,* 163–182. https://psycnet.apa.org/record/1983-07744-001

Scheurich, J. J., & Young, M. D. (1997). Coloring epistemologies: Are our research epistemologies racially biased? *Educational Researcher, 26*(4), 4–16. https://doi.org/10.3102/0013189X026004004

Smith. L. T. (2013). *Decolonizing methodologies: Research and Indigenous peoples.* Zed Books.

Solórzano, D., Ceja, M., & Yosso, T. (2000). Critical race theory, racial microaggressions, and campus racial climate: The experiences of African American college students. *The Journal of Negro Education, 69*(1/2), 60–73.

Solórzano, D. G., & Yosso, T. J. (2002). Critical race methodology: Counter-storytelling as an analytical framework for education research. *Qualitative Inquiry, 8*(1), 23–44. https://doi.org/10.1177/107780040200800103

Stanfield, J. H. (2016). The ethnocentric basis of social science knowledge production. *Review of Research in Education, 12*(1), 387–415. https://doi.org/10.3102/0091732x012001387

Stanley, C. A. (2006). Coloring the academic landscape: Faculty of color breaking the silence in predominantly white colleges and universities. *American Educational Research Journal, 43*(4), 701–736. https://doi.org/10.3102/00028312043004701

Stanley, C. A. (2007). When counter narratives meet master narratives in the journal editorial-review process. *Educational Researcher, 36*(1), 14–24. https://doi.org/10.3102/0013189X06298008

Steinberg, S. (1998). The role of social science in the legitimation of racial hierarchy. *Race and Society, 1*(1), 5–14. https://doi.org/10.1016/S1090-9524(99)80183-1

Stewart, D-L (2017). Language of appeasement. *Inside Higher Ed.* https://www.insidehighered.com/views/2017/03/30/colleges-need-language-shift-not-one-you-think-essay

Stewart, D-L (2019). Ideologies of absence: Anti-Blackness and inclusion rhetoric in student affairs practice. *Journal of Student Affairs, 28,* 15–30. https://sahe.colostate.edu/wp-content/uploads/sites/10/2019/10/csu308099-SAHE-journal-2019-guts-web.pdf#page=15

Strayhorn, T. L. (2012). *College students' sense of belonging: A key to educational success for all students.* Routledge.

Tachine, A. R., Cabrera, N. L., & Yellow Bird, E. (2017). Home away from home: Native American students' sense of belonging during their first year in college. *The Journal of Higher Education, 88*(5), 785–807. https://doi.org/10.1080/00221546.2016.1257322

Tapia-Fuselier, N., & Irwin, L. N. (2019). Strengths so white: Interrogating StrengthsQuest through a critical whiteness lens. *Journal of Critical Scholarship on Higher Education and Student Affairs, 5*(1), 30–44. https://ecommons.luc.edu/jcshesa/vol5/iss1/4/

Thelin, R. (2011). *A history of American higher education.* Johns Hopkins University Press.

Tuck, E., & Yang, K. W. (2012). Decolonization is not a metaphor. *Decolonization: Indigeneity, Education, & Society, 1*(1), 1–40. https://jps.library.utoronto.ca/index.php/des/article/view/18630

Tyler, T. R. (2006). Psychological perspectives on legitimacy and legitimation. *Annual Review of Psychology, 57*(1), 375–400. https://doi.org/10.1146/annurev.psych.57.102904.190038

Urrieta, L., Jr., Méndez, L., & Rodríguez, E. (2015). "A moving target": A critical race analysis of Latina/o faculty experiences, perspectives, and reflections on the tenure and promotion process. *International Journal of Qualitative Studies in Education, 28*(10), 1149–1168. https://doi.org/10.1080/09518398.2014.974715

Warikoo, N. K. (2016). *The diversity bargain: And other dilemmas of race, admissions, and meritocracy at elite universities.* University of Chicago Press.

Watt, S. K. (2007). Difficult dialogues, privilege and social justice: Uses of the privileged identity exploration (PIE) model in student affairs practice. *The College Student Affairs Journal, 26*(2), 114–126. https://files.eric.ed.gov/fulltext/EJ899385.pdf

Watt, S. K. (2020). *When addressing anti-racism—not just what, but how: Introducing the theory of being.* ACPA. https://www.myacpa.org/blogs/black-lives-matter-blog/not-just-what-how-theory-being-process-oriented-principles-anti-racism

White-Lewis, D. K. (2020). The facade of fit in faculty search processes. *The Journal of Higher Education, 91*(6), 833–857. https://doi.org/10.1080/00221546.2020.1775058

Whitford, E. (2018). Police called on Black student eating lunch. *Inside Higher Ed.* https://www.insidehighered.com/quicktakes/2018/08/03/police-called-black-student-eating-lunch

Wilder, C. S. (2014). *Ebony and ivy: Race, slavery, and the troubled history of America's universities.* Bloomsbury.

Wilderson, F. B., III, Hartman, S., Martinot, S., Sexton, J., & Spillers, H. J. (2017). *Afro-pessimism: An introduction.* Racked & Dispatched.

Wolfe, P. (2006). Settler colonialism and the elimination of the native. *Journal of Genocide Research, 8*(4), 387–409. https://www.tandfonline.com/doi/full/10.1080/14623520601056240

Wootson, C., Jr. (2018). A Black Yale student fell asleep in her dorm's common room. A white student called police. *The Washington Post.* https://www.washington-post.com/news/ grade-point/wp/2018/05/10/a-black-yale-student-fell-asleep-in-her-dorms-common-room -a-white-student-called-police/?noredirect=on&utm_term=.697305387b4a

Yancy, G. (2012). *Look, a white!: Philosophical essays on whiteness.* Temple University Press.

Yancy, G. (2018). *Backlash: What happens when we talk honestly about racism in America.* Rowman & Littlefield.

Zuberi, T. (2001). *Thicker than blood: How racial statistics lie.* University of Minnesota Press.

Zuberi, T., & Bonilla-Silva, E. (2008). Introduction. In T. Zuberi & E. Bonilla-Silva (Eds.), *White logic, white methods: Racism and methodology* (pp. 3–27). Rowman & Littlefield.

4

WHITE RACIAL IGNORANCE

White Lies and Inverted Epistemologies

Chris Corces-Zimmerman and Tonia Guida

It is certain, in any case, that ignorance, allied with power, is the most ferocious enemy justice can have.

—James Baldwin, *The Price of the Ticket*

"I don't see race!" "There is no racism in this country; we've had a Black president!" "Affirmative action is a form of reverse racism!" How many times have these exclamations and proclamations been uttered by white[1] people as a means of both protecting our[2] racial innocence and denying our complicity in and white supremacist systems? And for those of us white people reading this, how many times have we ourselves said or thought these retorts over the years? On a surface level, statements like these can be interpreted as somewhere between naïve denial and outright ignorance. However, to understand them as isolated comments made by individual white people is to miss the deeper power that such rhetorical and epistemological strategies have on the maintenance and advancement of white supremacy in the United States. Just as James Baldwin stated in the epigraph, it is the combination of individual ignorance with structural power that leads to a society where racism and white supremacy become accepted as inherent and normalized.

As many scholars of race and whiteness have explained (Ahmed, 2012; Omi & Winant, 2014), the insidiousness of whiteness in higher education and society more broadly stems equally, if not more, from its connection to systems and structures than its ties to the thoughts and actions of individuals. The threads that hold these systems and structures together are a combination of ideology (ways of thinking), epistemology (ways of knowing), and ontology (ways of being) that unite all people who are identified as white together in a mutually reinforcing allegiance to and complicity with whiteness and white supremacy. Central to this bond is an epistemology of white racial ignorance that Mills (1997) described as being structured by the "Racial Contract," which he explains as

> [a] set of formal or informal agreements or meta-agreements between members of one subset of humans, henceforth designated as "white," and coextensive with the class of full persons, to categorize the remaining subset of humans as "non-white" and of a different and inferior moral status. (p. 11)

Put simply, the racial contract is an agreement, formal and otherwise, among people identified as "white," to create a society in which we are the superior class and all others, designated as "nonwhite," are inferior. The racial contract is crucial to the maintenance of whiteness and white supremacy as it creates an unspoken and largely unacknowledged accord between white people to preserve the racial status quo through the way we come to know the society and world in which we live.

The epistemological component of the racial contract structures how we as white people come to know about the world around us and is grounded in what Mills (1997) described as an epistemology of ignorance. By this he refers to a way of knowing, and not knowing, about the world that is the product of a collective compact between white people to misinterpret and obfuscate the realities of racism and whiteness in our lives and society more broadly. For Mills, this way of knowing is fundamental to the ability of white people to maintain our racial dominance while justifying our moral superiority and racial innocence. In essence, an epistemology of ignorance is both the logic and language of the racial contract, and represents a way of knowing about race and whiteness to which all white people are socialized.

A common manifestation of an epistemology of ignorance is the ideology of "color-blindness" or what Annamma et al. (2017) referred to as *color-evasiveness*. In articulating a color-evasive ideology when confronted with accusations of racist thoughts or actions, white people who think or say phrases like "I don't see race" or "I don't care if you are white, Black, green, or purple," in effect accomplish two goals crucial to the maintenance of the racial contract. First, the statements seek to negate the accusation of racism by establishing the white person as "good" and unbiased. More importantly however, they also contest the significance of race more broadly, implying that race is not a factor that impacts the lived experiences of all people, and particularly People of Color. This invisibility of race and whiteness in the minds of white people is central to the racial contract as Mills (1997) described, wherein "the only people who can find it psychologically possible to deny the centrality of race are those who are racially privileged, for whom race is invisible precisely because the world is structured around them" (p. 76). This example of an "inverted epistemology" is illustrative of the concept of white racial ignorance because it demonstrates how a way of knowing about racism and whiteness can not only shield white people from having to reckon with our own individual racism but also serves to obfuscate a much larger system of white supremacy that maintains a deeply inequitable racial status quo.

Throughout this chapter we will thoroughly explore the intricacies of Mills's theorization of the racial contract and his conceptualization of epistemologies of ignorance in order to better understand the concept of white racial ignorance and how it can be applied to research and practice in higher education and student affairs. As white scholar-practitioners of higher education and student affairs, we believe that this understanding is essential, not just because it allows us to better challenge manifestations of white racial ignorance in the students and institutions that we work with(in) but, perhaps more importantly, because it forces us to challenge the epistemologies of white racial ignorance that we ourselves rely upon in our daily understandings of racism and whiteness. In the following pages we (a) present an overview of the concept of white racial ignorance as explained by Mills (1997, 2007, 2017), (b) then provide an overview of higher education and student affairs scholarship that applies and explores the dynamics of white racial ignorance, and lastly (c) discuss practical manifestations of white racial ignorance and how practitioners may work to challenge it at both individual and structural levels. Our hope is that by the end of this chapter readers will have a deeper understanding of the overall concept of white racial ignorance, an appreciation for the nuances that make it different from an everyday form of lacking information, and a piqued interest in further exploring how they might apply this concept to their work and personal lives.

As scholars who ourselves have struggled to understand and make meaning of the work of Mills (1997) and others, prior to moving into the overview of the concept of white racial ignorance we offer a brief note on the meaning of epistemology that we would have liked to have had when we first encountered these concepts. The term *epistemology* is both an incredibly opaque concept and a fundamental component to understanding Mills's theorization of white racial ignorance and the racial contract. As defined by Rallis and Rossman (2012), *epistemology* describes "the assumptions about what knowledge really is, what is accepted as knowledge claims, and what is taken as evidence" (p. 28). Although much of what is considered under the umbrella of epistemology may seem inherent or taken for granted, the reality is that these assumptions about what knowledge is and why it is taken to be true are almost entirely socially constructed and are central to how we as people make sense of the world.

Overview of White Racial Ignorance

In understanding the concept of white racial ignorance, the most important idea to grasp is that white racial ignorance is not simply a lack of information about racism or whiteness, but it is also a willful ignorance through which white people agree to wrongly understand the world through what Mills (2007) referred to as a socially induced ignorance. As is the case with many concepts related to racism (Ahmed, 2012), the first instinct for many white people when thinking about white racial ignorance and an epistemology of ignorance is to focus primarily on the *ignorance* (a lack of understanding) of individuals as opposed to the *epistemology* (ways of knowing) that is more structural in nature. However, we believe that a focus on the epistemological component is critical to understanding that white racial ignorance describes a way of knowing that is both intentional and structural. Although this racial amnesia may appear to be rooted in an individual's lack of knowledge and understanding about race and racism, the reality is that an ascription to an epistemology of white racial ignorance is just as much about the desire of white people to structurally maintain racial power and dominance. In this way, the idea of white racial ignorance is central to Mills's (1997) conceptualization of the racial contract as an agreement between white people to maintain a white-dominant social structure through a combination of political, social, and epistemological norms. In other words, white people enter an informal agreement, consciously or unconsciously, to maintain a white supremacist system through policies, culture, and the ways that we understand the world in which we live.

This active and passive ascription to a way of knowing about racism and whiteness through an epistemology of ignorance is most directly described by Mills (1997) when he explained,

> Thus, in effect, on matters related to race, the Racial Contract prescribes for its signatories an inverted epistemology, an epistemology of ignorance, a particular pattern of localized and global cognitive dysfunctions (which are psychologically and socially functional), producing the ironic outcome that whites will in general be unable to understand the world they themselves have made. (p. 18)

In this passage Mills (1997) cogently outlined many of the most central and important components of the concept of white racial ignorance. First is the establishment of an "inverted epistemology" by which he refers to a way of knowing about the world that deliberately distorts the historical and present-day realities of racial inequity and structural oppression faced by People of Color. In addition, he explains that this epistemology of ignorance is both psychologically and socially functional, meaning that although this way of thinking may be in opposition to reality, it is accepted and normalized at both individual and systemic levels by the dominant white society. Lastly, Mills explains that the result of this inverted way of understanding racism and whiteness results in a distinct inability on the part of white people to understand the delusional world that we have fabricated to serve our need for racial superiority and domination.

Mills (1997) poignantly described this agreement by stating,

> So here, it could be said, one has an agreement to *mis*interpret the world. One has to learn to see the world wrongly, but with assurance that this set of mistaken perceptions will be validated by white epistemic authority, whether religious or secular. (p. 18)

Although he stated that not all white people are necessarily signatories to the racial contract at all times, we are always beneficiaries of it and isolated moments of resistance are temporal and fleeting. As those who benefit from this racial accord, Mills (1997) suggested that white people have established what he called a "culture of forgetfulness" (p. 97) that allows us to maintain a sense of moral peace and superiority that is rooted in an evasion of our social and moral misgivings and a self-deception that we ever engaged in them in the first place. He also described this state as a "consensual hallucination" (p. 18) and an "inverted delusional world" (p. 18) as a way of communicating the complex mental work in which white people must engage to maintain our allegiance to a collective white racial ignorance. In many ways this accord is also a central reason why presenting white people with arguments rooted in logic and facts about racism and whiteness does not work to penetrate the force field of white racial ignorance. For example, as Foste and Irwin (2020) explained in speaking about the identity development of white students,

> If white students' behaviors towards, attitudes about, and knowledge of race and racism were merely the result of limited exposure, then content knowledge about institutional racism, white privilege, and histories of racial exclusion would logically lead to a more enlightened and racially progressive racial consciousness by fostering dissonance. (p. 447)

Rather, because this consensual hallucination stems from a socialized racial ignorance, barriers to the racial identity development of white students are much more likely the result of an inability or unwillingness to accept that racism and whiteness exist as to do so would upend their entire epistemological framework of the world in which they live. This also returns to the prominence of *epistemology* over that of *ignorance* in how we understand the concept of an epistemology of ignorance.

This dynamic is also what leads to the frequent surprise or outright denial expressed by white people when we are confronted with the realities of systemic racism in the United States. For example, in discussing the tendency of white people to claim that antiracist policies like affirmative action or educational reparations are actually examples of anti*white* racism, Eddie Glaude (2020) cited James Baldwin in saying,

> What is most terrible is that American white men are not prepared to believe my version of the story, to believe that it happened. . . . In order to avoid believing that, they have set up in themselves a fantastic system of evasions, denials, and justifications, [a system that] is about to destroy their grasp of reality, which is another way of saying their moral sense. (p. 47)

Baldwin's quote also brings to focus the deeply intersectional nature of white racial ignorance and its important connections to systems of patriarchy and white male dominance to create in effect a white male racial ignorance.

White Racial Ignorance Is Socially Sanctioned and Agentic

It is equally important to note that ascription, by white people, to the racial contract is not just a matter of one's thoughts and ideas, but it also impacts how society is structured to maintain white racial dominance. As Applebaum (2010) explained, white racial ignorance also has a powerful impact on the material and social realities of white people in that "such ignoring is not a lack of knowledge but a particular kind of knowledge that does things" (p. 37). In highlighting the productive nature of white racial ignorance, Applebaum (2010) made clear that there is a purpose and a consequence for the maintenance of this inverted epistemology as it serves to preserve and amplify white supremacy and white privilege as opposed to being simply a neutral stasis of obliviousness. Specifically, an epistemology of white racial ignorance is agentic in that it creates a racialized society in which,

> because of the reciprocally dependent definitions of superior whiteness and inferior nonwhiteness, whites may consciously or unconsciously assess how they're doing by a scale that depends in part on how nonwhites are doing, since the essence of whiteness is entitlement to differential privilege vis-à-vis the exploitation of nonwhites as a whole. (Mills, 1997, p. 95)

This maintenance of the racial status quo at a structural level has both material benefits (e.g., the disproportionate accumulation of wealth by white people) as well as psychosocial benefits (e.g., a freedom from the everyday stressors of racial oppression).

Given the ways that whiteness and white epistemologies are normalized in U.S. society, white racial ignorance can often fade into the background (Ahmed, 2012) and is frequently unintelligible to most white people, and that is perhaps the most fundamental characteristic of white racial ignorance. It is what Applebaum (2010) explained as both "not knowing, but also not knowing what one does not know and believing that one knows" (p. 39), which she described as a "safeguard to privilege" (p. 38) and a "form of ignorance that arrogantly parades as knowledge" (p. 39). Moreover, the relationship between white racial ignorance and systemic racism and white supremacy is symbiotic in that racist structures are necessary to maintain a society rooted in an epistemology of ignorance, and this inverted epistemology simultaneously allows for the maintenance of racist structures. For example, when white people advance a revisionist history of the Civil War or deny the incorporation of an ethnic studies curriculum because it teaches children to hate white people, we are in effect denying the historical truths of white supremacy and negating the need for structural changes to correct for structural racism in the present day. Walker and Newlove (2020) exemplified this dynamic in saying "ignorance in this sense is not a passive event, but is rather inherent to the processes for the production and maintenance of particular kinds of knowledge that benefit the dominant group" (p. 62). Given both the past and present centrality of racism and white supremacy in U.S. society, white people must consent to both not knowing, and not acknowledging what we don't know, about racism and whiteness.

Reflecting on Mills's (1997) foundational concepts of the racial contract and epistemologies of ignorance, coupled with the extension provided by Applebaum (2010) and others, we offer three central characteristics that define and enable white racial ignorance. First, it is both a not knowing as well as an unwillingness or inability to acknowledge what one does not know, all the while believing that we are fully informed. Second, although white people may have moments of awareness in which we are able to resist or think outside of this inverted epistemology, the reality that we live in a white supremacist society means that our default will always be a state of white racial ignorance. And third, white racial ignorance is not merely an individual trait or phenomenon but rather a systemically reinforced way of thinking that serves the purpose of maintaining a collective investment in white supremacy and white racial dominance. With this overview of the concept of white racial ignorance in mind, the following section serves to further illuminate the nuances of the concept by discussing both theoretical and practical applications to scholarship within the fields of higher education and student affairs. What is important to keep in mind throughout the following sections is that, although extreme or aberrant examples of white racial ignorance may be the easiest to identify and address, they are not nearly as important to challenge as the everyday, often invisible manifestations of white racial ignorance that are truly foundational to the structure and maintenance of white supremacy.

Empirical Manifestations of White Racial Ignorance in Higher Education

Applied to the study of higher education and student affairs, the concept of white racial ignorance has served as an important tool to help us understand how white supremacy is maintained. This work has primarily focused on white undergraduate students and how they use epistemologies of ignorance to uphold white supremacy. In this section, we highlight three key manifestations of white racial ignorance as seen in the higher education empirical scholarship and literature. First, white racial ignorance allows white students to claim reverse racism and negate white privilege (Cabrera & Corces-Zimmerman, 2017; Cabrera et al., 2016, 2017; Mueller, 2017). Second, white racial ignorance allows white students to maintain innocent perceptions of the campus racial climate (Foste, 2019). Third, white racial ignorance is the mechanism that allows white people to profess a historical amnesia (Foste & Irwin, 2020; Mueller, 2020).

White racial ignorance, when applied to the study of higher education, helps to explain how white students use the myth of reverse racism to negate white privilege. These claims of reverse racism are often unsubstantiated by concrete evidence, which in turn prevents and distracts us as white people from taking up and confronting racism on campus (Cabrera et al., 2017). The work of Cabrera and Corces-Zimmerman (2017) serves to illustrate how white participants downplayed the contemporary significance of white privilege by conveying the belief that their white identity was meaningless, denying the impact that white privilege had in their lives (even when challenged to engage in these conversations), and expressing the view that conversations about identity have minimal impact on changing their views about race and racism. As discussed earlier, white racial ignorance is not just a passive, naïve state where white people lack information about racism but rather a strategically crafted culture of ignorance that intentionally maintains obliviousness. One example of how this manifested in Cabrera and Corces-Zimmerman's (2017) study involved a participant discussing how he was taught by his family to acknowledge anti-Semitism, while simultaneously arguing that People of Color see racism in places where it does not exist. In this scenario, the interviewer then challenged the participant regarding this discrepancy by asking how they juxtapose their belief and understanding of anti-Semistism being everywhere with their view that "Black people are reading too much into racism?" (p. 308). The participant replied by stating,

> It's different when you say reading too much or into it. . . . I see what you did there. I see it there. But I can't juxtapose it, all right? Because there is . . . there's no measure . . . . I didn't measure anything. I didn't measure, you know, how prevalent it really is to how prevalent they perceive it to be. (p. 308)

This example illustrates how white racial ignorance often manifests as both a distorted reality for white undergraduate men and a means of evading responsibility for their complicity in racism and white supremacy.

White students also engage in this form of white racial ignorance when assessing their own learning and competency around topics of race and racism (Mueller, 2017). For instance, Mueller (2020) argued that ignorance is produced via specific social processes that include "nondiscursive and tacit maneuvers" where "white people evade and distort the perspectives of people of color and empirical facts of racism" (p. 155). An example of this in practice can be seen in her students' final papers when taking a course on Social Problems or Racial and Ethnic Relations. Applying white racial ignorance to students' family wealth assessment assignments, Mueller (2017) found students used "creative racial logics" to bypass racial awareness (p. 225). Throughout Mueller's course, students were presented with material that explored and documented the social reproduction of racial inequality and the racial wealth gap. One of the epistemic maneuvers students engaged in included highlighting how their families benefited from things like the GI Bill, family wealth related to slavery, and financial support that kick-started home down payments, but then retreated to reject racialized arguments related to these family wealth advantages. For example, one student stated,

> The transfer of wealth is more than just giving your kids money and assets. I believe it's living in decent neighborhoods with good schools and having the opportunity to attend college. I don't feel that the color of my skin or of my ancestors necessarily made it easier on them than other immigrant families. My grandfather came to the U.S. not knowing a word of English and owning only the clothes on his back. Primarily through hard work and our own merit my family has been able to accumulate a little wealth and . . . pass some of that on to the next generation. (p. 227)

Here, the student relies on the socially constructed notion of merit in order to rationalize the ways in which whiteness has allowed his family to amass generational wealth while simultaneously denying those opportunities to People of Color. The ascription to an ideology of meritocracy is central to how we as white people obfuscate systemic privilege under the guise of hard work and deservedness.

Not only does white racial ignorance minimize white individuals' understandings of white privilege, but it also allows white students to maintain inaccurate perceptions of the campus racial climate (Foste, 2019). For instance, white collegians use narratives of campus racial harmony and solidarity to underwrite racist campus climates (Foste, 2019). These two narratives uphold the racial status quo by maintaining perceptions of the racial innocence and morality of white students and the institutions more broadly. Students advanced a narrative of campus racial harmony in saying things like, in college, there are "better race relations than there are in society." For instance, one participant stated, "Our education does have an emphasis on inclusion and diversity and understanding other people . . . . State [university pseudonym], I think, creates good human beings. And part of being a good human being is not being a racist. And like, they've done that" (p. 246). This serves as another example of how white students employ an inverted epistemology, in this case in understanding diversity as equity and justice, to essentially acquit the institution of all responsibility for racist experiences on campus. Moreover, this mindset likely reinforced to the student that because they had attended this nonracist institution, they too were unable to hold or be accused of holding racist views.

Lastly, white racial ignorance functions as the mechanism that allows white students to participate in a historical amnesia (Mills, 1997), which becomes particularly important as practitioners attempt to apply student development research and theory to their work with students. For example, Foste and Irwin (2020) explained that the third wave of research on student development pays particular attention to power and oppression. Thus, using concepts like epistemologies of ignorance has significant implications for how we understand the moral and cognitive development of both white students and Students of Color, most notably in how white students come to think about the complex legacy of racism and white supremacy in society. Foste and Irwin (2020) provided the example of a collective forgetting of the contributions of Communities of Color and a simultaneous erasure of white terror and violence inflicted by white people to uphold white supremacy to describe this "selective remembering" (p. 446) as a means of advancing a moral interpretation of a good white racial self. As such, the presence of cognitive dissonance, which was central to second-wave identity development models, doesn't necessarily lead to white identity development because of the ways that white students default to an epistemology of white racial ignorance (Foste & Irwin, 2020). As a result, Foste and Irwin (2020) highlighted that practitioners must consider the concept of epistemologies of ignorance when trying to make sense of "college students' engagement with race and the racial self" (p. 447). Given that barriers to the racial identity development of white students are much more likely the result of an inability or unwillingness to accept that racism and whiteness exist, practitioners must do the work of breaking down their socialized epistemologies of ignorance rather than simply providing them with facts and information about the existence of racism and whiteness. This again returns to the prominence of *epistemology* over that of *ignorance* in how practitioners challenge the ways of knowing of white students.

Practical Manifestations of White Racial Ignorance

In addition to examples of white racial ignorance that can be understood through existing empirical studies on whiteness in higher education, practical examples of how an epistemology of white racial ignorance manifests in practitioner and administrative spaces can also be helpful in illuminating the nuances of this inverted epistemology. Throughout this chapter we have stressed the significance of focusing on the epistemological component (over that of ignorance) when working to challenge an epistemology of white racial ignorance. Although that may have appeared to be a matter of semantics, it is in the applications and impacts on higher education and student affairs practice that the importance of this distinction becomes more apparent. As higher education and student affairs practitioners, and particularly those of us who identify as white, reflect on and implement practices that will serve to challenge white racial ignorance, we must first understand what we are working with, against, and toward.

The distinction between epistemology and ignorance in this case challenges us to acknowledge that what we are trying to do is as much, if not more, about changing *how* white students and colleagues know than it is about changing *what* they know. For example, many white people tend to engage in some sort of formal or informal book club or reading group in an attempt to better understand the nuances of whiteness and anti-Black racism in higher education and society more broadly (in fact, you may be reading this book right now in that exact scenario). Although such acts are important, they are largely focused on gaining information as a way of changing *what* the reader knows. We believe that this is only a small part of the process of challenging white racial ignorance, as the much more difficult change comes in *how* we know about race, racism, and whiteness. This is a process of changing behaviors, patterns of thought, and ways of knowing that goes beyond the basic acquisition of facts and histories. Moreover, because the work is grounded in changing behaviors, white practitioners must be mindful that efforts to challenge white racial ignorance must be recurring, span a duration of time, and involve a range of modalities in order to fully uncover the nuanced and often-invisible nature of a white epistemology of ignorance. We must also remain mindful that this work is as much self-work as it is challenging white racial ignorance in the students and colleagues with whom we work. In the following section we provide concrete, practical examples for how practitioners can engage in this process of transformative, epistemological change at both the individual and institutional level.

Racism and Whiteness as Systemic

Perhaps one of the most insidious examples of how white people utilize an epistemology of white racial ignorance to maintain the racial status quo manifests in the way we learn to think about racism and whiteness as individual-level characteristics as opposed to systemic-level racial projects. This individualization of racism and white supremacy as individual character flaws used to distinguish "good" white people from the anomalous, bigoted, or racist white person ultimately serves to obfuscate the larger, more problematic ways that racism and whiteness are embedded in the policies, structures, and norms of our society and institutions. Sara Ahmed (2012) poignantly addressed this distinction and its role in maintaining white supremacy by explaining,

> In other words, racism should not be seen as about individuals with bad attitudes (the "bad apple model"), not because such individuals do not exist (they do) but because such a way of thinking underestimates the scope and scale of racism, thus leaving us without an account of how racism gets reproduced. The argument can be made in even stronger terms: the very identification of racism with individuals becomes a technology for the reproduction of racism of institutions. (p. 44)

By coming to know about racism and whiteness through this individualized lens, we as white people engage in a collective not knowing about structural oppression that both permits us to feign ignorance of our collective and individual complicity in the oppression of People of Color and largely prevents us from understanding oppression as something that occurs regardless of individual animus or intent. As white educators we believe that it is our role not just to inform white students and colleagues about the nature of racism and whiteness as systemic, but it is also our responsibility to challenge others to change *how* they think toward a systemic way of knowing about oppression.

In practice, we have observed that white educators frequently engage with racism and whiteness at an individual level both in how they respond to incidents of racism on campus and how those responses serve to socialize students to think at an individual level. What follows is an example of how one might consider challenging this juxtaposition between individual and systemic understandings of racism and whiteness more concretely, specifically through the lens of interactions that might take place over the course of resident assistant training within an office of residential education. For instance, a common scenario discussed in many training modules considers how a student staff member might respond if a racist incident were to occur between two residents within the residence hall. Frequently, the response taken by white practitioners and administrators, and the advice given to student staff, is to understand the conflict as solely a matter of a racist act perpetrated by one racist student against another. This individualization is embodied in the tendency to isolate the act to the individual student, declare them as aberrant, and address their ignorance or animus through some form of training, counseling, or other remediation measure. By responding in this way, administrators are not only treating the act as that of one bad apple when it is more likely a symptom of a larger system of white supremacy, but they are also communicating that the appropriate "solution" is to change what the perpetrating student thinks and not how they think. Although requiring white students who engage in acts of racism against Students of Color to attend a short-term training or dialogue group may provide them with some additional knowledge about racism in society, it is unlikely to fundamentally change how they think about racism as the acts of individuals.

In contrast, a systemic approach to the scenario might involve an examination, with student staff and residents, of the norms and culture prominent in the dorm and on campus more broadly. Importantly, this signals to students that the issue is not with the individual perpetrating student, but rather with the institution that has permitted a culture of racism and white supremacy to thrive on campus. Similarly, it engages students in a way that asks them to (re)consider how the norms, policies, and agreements within a community function to challenge or maintain inequities and racial hierarchies. Going beyond general signaling from the institution, white practitioners could also work explicitly with student staff (or all residents) over the course of multiple engagements to consider how the culture in the residence hall, on campus, and in society more broadly created the environment in which the incident could occur. Lastly, students could be asked to work collectively to develop responses, both proactive and reactive, that would then be implemented by the dorm or institution more broadly to challenge racism and whiteness at both an individual and systemic level. This type of response differs from the previous individualized example in that it both addresses the problem at a structural level within the dorm and institution, and it socializes students to change *how* they think and know about racism in a way that resists the epistemological norms of white racial ignorance. Importantly, this shift in challenging how students know about racism and whiteness must go beyond efforts to address single acts of racism to the point where it is woven and embedded throughout as many curricular and cocurricular programs within the institution as possible.

Whiteness as Normal

Equally pervasive, although often much harder for white people to identify, is the way that we as white people come to know whiteness as normal and all other ways of being, thinking, and knowing as aberrant. As Mills (1997) argued, race and whiteness have always been at the center of the U.S. colonial project and continue to influence each and every aspect of life from larger institutions of wealth and education to fundamental needs like the air we breathe and the water we drink. Yet, despite its pervasiveness, white people are socialized to not notice race precisely because it blends into the background; it is the white noise that passes by unnoticed. This way of thinking about whiteness as normal permits white people to make claims of reverse racism, advance color-evasive ideologies, or fail to identify ways that we are privileged regardless of socioeconomic status, gender, or other identities.

To further illuminate the way that an epistemology of whiteness as normal may manifest within student affairs practice, we draw on the frequent challenge offered by white students and others to the existence of racial, cultural, or resource communities on campuses. On an almost annual basis, a story emerges of a group of white students who have decided that, as white people, they too are oppressed and that they should be able to have a "white cultural center" on campus in the same way that race-specific or general multicultural centers exist at many institutions (e.g., Towson University's white Student Union). They frequently make claims that there are no spaces "for white people" on campus and that this is in and of itself an example of reverse racism against white people. It should be noted that although these groups are often vocal and aggressive in their calls, the same sentiment is frequently thought or expressed by almost every white person in one way or another (e.g., thinking that there are no scholarships for white people, claiming that a Person of Color was only hired because of their minoritized racial identity, etc.). At the core of such efforts is an epistemology of white racial ignorance through which white people have agreed to (mis)understand the ways that whiteness as the norm impacts the racialization of space on college campuses. As many scholars have suggested, the reason that there is no need for expressly white spaces is because every space on campus is rooted in an "enwhitened" norm that centers white culture and ways of being (Harris, 2019; Keels, 2020). When confronted with such a demand from white students for a white cultural center, white student affairs professionals and administrators have the choice to address the proposal by challenging either *what* the students think (that there is a need for a white-specific space on campus) or *how* they think (the inability to understand whiteness as normalized on campus).

In many instances, the default response from administrators and educators is to treat these demands as individual manifestations of white ignorance, and thus to challenge *what* the white students know about the dynamics of race and racism on campus. Responding from this lens, practitioners often consider the students to be a few vocal outliers and will resolve to address the matter by having them meet with an administrator to explain why such a center is not necessary. At most, there may be some sort of campus town hall meeting to address the concerns of the students and to provide information about racial demographics at the university or the nature of systemic racism in society.

However, for those white practitioners who want to challenge the epistemological components of white racial ignorance by pushing the students to change *how* they are thinking about the normalized relationship between whiteness and space, they will need to engage them in a more sustained and nuanced dialogue. One example response might be to ask the students to develop a full proposal for why they believe that a space specifically for white people is necessary. In this proposal they should be required to include significant research on the history, importance, and impact that cultural centers have on the educational experiences of minoritized student groups (e.g., Bradley, 2018; Cole, 2020; Wilder, 2014). They should also include a list of spaces on campus (e.g., dorms, Greek life housing, libraries, the student union, etc.) and a reflection on what cultures and ways of being are normed in each. Lastly, they should be required to attend several programs sponsored by various cultural centers or other broader campus programs focused on race and racism, and to explain the role they believe such programs play for students and the campus more broadly. In short, they should be asked to engage in a sustained period of reflection and information gathering that challenges them to think about the relationships between race and space on campus and in society more broadly, with the ultimate goal of not only understanding why their demands are misplaced but also how whiteness functions more broadly on campus.

An Institutional Focus on Diversity Over Justice

Whereas the two previous examples have demonstrated how white racial ignorance manifests and may be addressed at a student level, it is important to remember that organizations like colleges and universities also operate under and maintain an epistemology of white racial ignorance. As Ray (2019) explained, not only do institutions of higher education serve as mechanisms for socializing white students into an epistemology of ignorance but their actions and policies are also deeply rooted in the same delusional ways of thinking about racism and whiteness. As such, just as you might encounter white people who understand racism as an individual-level phenomenon, white-serving colleges and universities may express a similar individualized understanding of racism through their communications, policies, and actions. For example, when confronted with calls to address structural racism within their institutions, most colleges and universities focus on individual-level questions of diversity and inclusion as opposed to structural-level questions of equity and justice.

To understand the notion of institutional white racial ignorance, we draw here on the work of Sara Ahmed (2012), who discussed how white-serving institutions of higher education utilize the rhetoric and promise of diversity as a way of maintaining a white-dominant status quo. In exploring how a focus on diversity can serve as a tool of white supremacy, Ahmed explained, "Diversity appeals are often made because diversity seems appealing: it is more consistent with a collaborative style. If the word 'diversity' is understood as less confronting, then using the language of diversity can be a way of avoiding confrontation" (p. 65). She went on to describe the institutional performativity of diversity as a way of appearing to address issues of systemic racial inequity by changing numbers as opposed to organizational values and policies. Similarly, Ahmed (2012) confronted the destructive nature of diversity as a mechanism of white racial ignorance by saying that "diversity pride becomes a technology for reproducing whiteness: adding color to the white face of the organization confirms the whiteness of that face" (p. 151).

Just as efforts to challenge manifestations of white racial ignorance at the individual level can focus on either *what* or *how* one understands racism and whiteness, similar interventions play out in initiatives to resist white racial ignorance at the institutional level. In the previous example, *what* institutions think is that issues of structural racism can be addressed simply by increasing the number of Students, Staff, and Faculty of Color. Ahmed (2012) poignantly described this dynamic of addressing structural racism through changes to demographic representation when saying,

> Diversity still tends to be associated with those who "look different." Perhaps the promise of diversity is that it can be both attached to those bodies who "look different" and detached from those bodies as a sign of inclusion. The promise of diversity could then be described as a problem: the sign of inclusion makes the signs of exclusion disappear. (p. 65)

Through this institutional epistemology of ignorance, white-serving institutions might advance the idea that change can happen by ensuring that institutions uphold their promises to hire more Faculty of Color or to increase the percentage of Black, Indigenous, and Latinx students admitted to the university each year.

In contrast, efforts to challenge *how* white-serving institutions understand and act against racism and whiteness must center on a reimagining of institutional logics as expressed through policies, values, and culture. Although this work is far more difficult, and can feel quite nebulous at times, that is largely because the racial contract ensures that white institutions, just like white people, can rely on white racial ignorance to obfuscate their investment in whiteness and white supremacy. Challenging institutional ways of knowing and being requires white leaders to identify points of inequity within the institution (e.g., admissions practices, hiring processes, resource allocation, etc.) and reflect on what logics or beliefs facilitate the existence and maintenance of such barriers. In the current example, the logic that demographic diversity equates to equity and justice must be identified through university actions and communications, and then challenged via collective action and advocacy for policies that actively push the institution toward a radical understanding of equity and justice. This might look like a shift in tenure and promotion practices that reward faculty whose research and activism center racial and social justice. Similarly, an institution may require academic departments to offer multiple mandatory courses that explore the impacts of racism and racial justice within their discipline (e.g., biology, public health, creative writing). Lastly, institutions could allocate budgets in a way that structurally prioritizes those units and services that specifically work to advance opportunities for Students of Color, resulting in an increased support for those programs whose work advances racial justice.

Concluding Thoughts

Reflecting on the insights and examples presented throughout this chapter, there are three central components to white racial ignorance that we hope that readers will take away and apply to both their personal and professional lives. The first is that white racial ignorance does not merely describe white people who are unaware of or uninformed about aspects of racism and whiteness, but rather it speaks to a much larger and insidious form of willful ignorance that is deployed by white people to maintain racial dominance through a culture of intentional oblivion. Additionally, white racial ignorance is not exclusively an individual-level phenomenon or state of being but rather is deeply structural both in how it is organized (through the racial contract) and how it is deployed (through norms, policies, and institutions). Lastly, efforts to challenge or address an epistemology of white racial ignorance at both individual and systemic levels must focus equally, if not more, on changing the epistemological ways that white people and white institutions come to know about race and racism than on simply providing facts and information to white people as though the root of white racial ignorance is *what* we think and not *how* we think.

As we opened this chapter with the words of James Baldwin, it only seems fitting to conclude with one of the more powerful observations that he made on the role that we as white people have in the fight for racial and social justice. In his final novel, *Just Above My Head*, Baldwin proclaimed, "Not everything is lost. Responsibility cannot be lost, it can only be abdicated. If one refuses abdication, one begins again" (Glaude, 2020, p. 193). We find this quote powerful not because it provides a sense of inspiration and possibility but rather because it focuses our attention as white people on our individual and collective responsibility in challenging racism and whiteness. This is a choice that we make each day, each moment; whether that is an active commitment to resist or a passive decision to remain neutral in maintaining the dominant status quo, both must be understood as choices. We must accept that the active or passive abdication of our responsibility as white people (and subsequent denial or deflection of this abdication) is in itself a central component of the racial contract and the perpetuation of white racial dominance. In this sense, the process of beginning again, although appealing, requires constant vigilance, commitment, and humility on the part of us as white people. As Mills (1997) explained, although "all whites are beneficiaries of the Contract" (p. 11), it is our responsibility to withhold our signatures by actively challenging and resisting white racial ignorance in ourselves and society more broadly.

Notes

1. In this chapter, we follow the lead of scholars like Matias (2016) and Pérez Huber (2010) in refraining from capitalizing the word *white* and all of its derivatives in order to challenge hegemonic grammatical norms and "reject the grammatical representation of power capitalization brings to the term 'white'" (Pérez Huber, 2010, p. 93).

2. Throughout this chapter we have opted to use first-person plural nouns *we/us* as a way of, as authors, acknowledging our complicity and including ourselves in the racist and white supremacist epistemologies and ideologies about which we write.

References

Ahmed, S. (2012). *On being included: Racism and diversity in institutional life*. Duke University Press.

Annamma, S. A., Jackson, D. D., & Morrison, D. (2017). Conceptualizing color-evasiveness: Using dis/ability critical race theory to expand a color-blind racial ideology in education and society. *Race Ethnicity and Education, 20*(2), 147–162. https://doi.org/10.1080/13613324.2016.1248837

Applebaum, B. (2010). *Being white, being good: White complicity, white moral responsibility, and social justice pedagogy*. Lexington Books.

Baldwin, J. (1985). *The price of the ticket: Collected nonfiction, 1948–1985*. Macmillan.

Bradley, S. M. (2018). *Upending the ivory tower: Civil rights, Black power, and the Ivy League*. NYU Press.

Cabrera, N. L., & Corces-Zimmerman, C. (2017). An unexamined life: White male racial ignorance and the agony of education for students of color. *Equity & Excellence in Education, 50*(3), 300–315. https://doi.org/10.1080/10665684.2017.1336500

Cabrera, N. L., Franklin, J. D., & Watson, J. S. (2017). Whiteness in higher education: The invisible missing link in diversity and racial analyses. *ASHE Higher Education Report, 42*(6), 7–125.

Cabrera, N. L., Watson, J. S., & Franklin, J. D. (2016). Racial arrested development: A critical whiteness analysis of the campus ecology. *Journal of College Student Development, 57*(2), 119–134. https://doi.org/10.1353/csd.2016.0014

Cole, E. R. (2020). *The campus color line: College presidents and the struggle for Black freedom*. Princeton University Press.

Foste, Z. (2019). Reproducing Whiteness: How White students justify the campus racial status quo. *Journal of Student Affairs Research and Practice, 56*, 241–253. https://doi.org/10.1080/19496591.2019.1576530

Foste, Z., & Irwin, L. (2020). Applying critical whiteness studies in college student development theory and research. *Journal of College Student Development, 61*(4), 439–455. https://doi.org/10.1353/csd.2020.0050

Glaude, E. S. (2020). *Begin again: James Baldwin's America and its urgent lessons for our own*. Crown.

Harris, J. C. (2019). Whiteness as structuring property: Multiracial women students' social interactions at a historically white institution. *The Review of Higher Education*, *42*(3), 1023–1050. https://doi.org/10.1353/rhe.2019.0028

Keels, M. (2020). *Campus counterspaces: Black and Latinx students' search for community at historically white universities*. Cornell University Press.

Matias, C. E. (2016). *Feeling white: Whiteness, emotionality, and education*. Brill.

Mills, C. W. (1997). *The racial contract*. Cornell University Press.

Mills, C. W. (2007). White ignorance. In S. Sullivan & N. Tuana (Eds.), *Race and epistemologies of ignorance* (pp. 26–31). SUNY Press.

Mills, C. W. (2017). *Black rights/white wrongs: The critique of racial liberalism*. Oxford University Press.

Mueller, J. C. (2017). Producing colorblindness: Everyday mechanisms of white ignorance. *Social Problems*, *64*(2), 219–238. https://doi.org/10.1093/socpro/spw061

Mueller, J. C. (2019). Racial ideology or racial ignorance? An alternative theory of racial cognition. *Sociological Theory*, *38*(2), 142–169. https://doi.org/10.1177/0735275120926197

Mueller, J. C. (2020). Racial ideology or racial ignorance? An alternative theory of racial cognition. *Sociological Theory*, *38*(2), 142–169. https://doi.org/10.1177%2F0735275120926197

Omi, M., & Winant, H. (2014). *Racial formation in the United States*. Routledge.

Pérez Huber, L. (2010). Using Latina/o critical race theory (LatCrit) and racist nativism to explore intersectionality in the educational experiences of undocumented Chicana college students. *Educational Foundations*, *24*, 77–96.

Rallis, S. F., & Rossman, G. B. (2012). *The research journey: Introduction to inquiry*. Guilford Press.

Ray, V. (2019). A theory of racialized organizations. *American Sociological Review*, *84*(1), 26–53. https://doi.org/10.1177%2F0003122418822335

Walker, D. S., & Newlove, P. M. (2020). But I just never knew!: Theorizing and challenging the ideologies of whiteness in social studies. In A. M. Hawkman & S. B. Shear (Eds.), *Marking the invisible: Articulating whiteness in social studies education* (pp. 55–71). Information Age.

Wilder, C. S. (2014). *Ebony and ivy: Race, slavery, and the troubled history of America's universities*. Bloomsbury.

5

RELINQUISHING WHITE INNOCENCE

Slaying a Defender of White Supremacy

Douglas H. Lee, Ellie Ash-Balá, Anton Ward-Zanotto, James Black, and OiYan A. Poon

In 2015, members of the Sigma Alpha Epsilon (SAE) fraternity at the University of Oklahoma (OU) were caught in a viral video singing a racist song proclaiming "there will never be a [n-word] in SAE" (Desmond-Harris, 2015, para. 2). Through the disturbing song performance, fraternity members invoked lynching and racial segregation, key elements of anti-Black racism representing historical and contemporary racial violence. On the Monday morning after the video went viral, OU president David Boren condemned the fraternity members' behaviors, stating, "You should not have the privilege of calling yourselves 'Sooners.' Real Sooners believe in equal opportunity. Real Sooners treat all people with respect. Real Sooners love each other and take care of each other like family members" (News 9, 2015, para. 6). Boren suspended the fraternity, closed the SAE chapter house at OU, and called for a redoubling of "efforts to create the strongest sense of family and community" (para. 8).

These redoubled efforts included meetings between the campus's Black Student Association president, several student athletes, and members of historically Black fraternities with President Boren and several members of the SAE fraternity. In these meetings, SAE members offered their apologies. Boren also requested that the national fraternity investigate the song and its origins. The investigation revealed that the fraternity's national administration taught the song to members during a national leadership cruise 4 years before the OU incident in 2015 (New, 2015). The fraternity responded with mandatory diversity training for its members nationwide and set up a confidential hotline for people to report inappropriate behaviors. At OU, the administration disbanded the fraternity and expelled two SAE student leaders from the university. Boren stated that he would be glad if the students in the video left campus because "we don't provide student services for bigots" (Richinick, 2015, para. 3). OU also created a new senior-level position focused on diversity and provided additional training for staff and faculty.

How many of our institutions have experienced similar events, where we respond with initiatives, positions, money, and statements of support? How many campus leaders espouse the concepts of diversity, equity, and inclusion (DEI) in their annual addresses, convocations, and fireside chats? We use institutional processes to remove offending individuals or organizations, while highlighting initiatives and chartering workgroups to draft reports and strategic plans. Our institutions publicly take our penance, accept (or demand) our absolution, and move on with a sense of innocence intact.

Some might praise OU's leadership response to the fraternity members' boldfaced performances of anti-Black racism. President Boren received praise from leaders across the nation. Even President Obama commended his swift action. However, the Boren administration's actions represent an effective, rapid public relations strategy to assuage public outrage and ridicule. The university proclaimed a "zero-tolerance policy," quickly labeling the offending students as deviants. It expelled the students and suspended the SAE chapter. The university leadership also announced diversity trainings on campus as part of their response to the SAE incident. Notably, plans for new mandatory diversity training programs preceded the SAE incident, due to an earlier racist campus event (Bennett, 2015). These leadership responses at OU framed racism as a problem situated within the hearts and minds of individuals that could be primarily remedied through training and the expulsions of students seen as outliers. The publicly announced strategies in light of the SAE incident tended to frame the problem of racism as an individual problem, and not a problem of systems. Beyond mandatory trainings, it remains questionable whether the university engaged in deeper organizational and systemic changes (e.g., daily norms and practices in recruitment, hiring, promotions, admissions, scholarship distributions, curriculum, classroom teaching, etc.) that uphold white dominance under the surface of spectacles like the SAE incident and many other public relations challenges.

A closer analysis of the Boren administration's response in the SAE scandal through a theoretical lens of white innocence reveals no acknowledgment of OU's role as a racialized organization (Ray, 2019) in reproducing campus climate and systems that are racially hostile, particularly for Black, Indigenous, and other People of Color (BIPOC) students, staff, and faculty.

The theoretical concept of white innocence allows a naming of how organizations and individuals absolve themselves of their complicity in the maintenance of white dominance (Gutierrez, 2006; Poon, 2018). White innocence is a social phenomenon that maintains a cycle of (performative) shock and response to momentary spectacles of racist incidents, which then prevent collective interrogation of systems that reproduce white supremacy (Gotanda, 2004; Gutierrez, 2006; Leonardo, 2009; Poon, 2018). It is the resistance and refusal of responsibility to dismantle systems and practices that maintain white dominance.

White innocence is a profound denial of responsibility and complicity in the systemic reproduction of white supremacy and structural inequities. It serves to absolve people and institutions, particularly white people and institutions, of blame for the persistence of white supremacy (Gotanda, 2004; Poon, 2018). Through performances of moral innocence, there is a conscious or unconscious choice to ignore one's complicity in systemic realities and unjust structures harming BIPOC (Leonardo, 2009). Many have shown the pervasiveness of white innocence and how it helps maintain white supremacy through inaction and denial of responsibility (Gotanda, 2004; Gutierrez, 2006; Poon, 2018). Through white innocence, people inaccurately define and frame racism as individual acts of bad faith, perpetuating a false belief that repudiating a handful of individuals as proverbial bad apples (e.g., SAE members, individual police officers who carry out extrajudicial state killings of Black people, etc.) can solve the problem of systemic racism. White innocence allows people to overlook their own complicity in racist structures and uphold their self-image of a "good" person. As some have pointed out, BIPOC can also contribute toward reinvestments in white innocence (Ahmed, 2007; Gutierrez, 2006).

In this chapter, we explore the theoretical concept of white innocence and trouble its pervasiveness in higher education. First, we engage past research to define the theory of white innocence in relation to white supremacy. We then explore specificities of how white innocence shows up in higher education. We end the chapter with a call on higher education to relinquish white innocence, which serves to defend systemic white dominance.

In higher education, white innocence allows people and institutions to perform an "aha!" moment of realization while feigning innocence and avoiding liability for racist systems and actions. The desire for innocence pushes individuals to cleanse themselves of the sin of culpability. This impulse, common among those who often proclaim not to have a "racist bone in their body," is a strategy to reconcile their actions (or inactions) with their claims of innocence. Institutions and their members can issue support statements, share social justice and antiracist resources, and perform campus climate studies while avoiding deep systemic change (Gonzales et al., 2018). By unmasking white innocence, we challenge individuals and organizational collectives to accept responsibility and recognize their agency in maintaining or dismantling unjust systems of white supremacy. We are all faced with choices to maintain the status quo or interrogate and change systems and organizational practices.

White Innocence: An Analytic Lens

We situate our definition of *white innocence* in critical whiteness studies (CwS). Seemingly contrary to its name, CwS seeks not to center whiteness, but to critique whiteness and the myriad material harms it creates for BIPOC individuals and communities (Cabrera, 2019). CwS "attempts to unmask the seemingly invisible privileges of whites and demonstrates that the privileges are real" (Cabrera et al., 2016, p. 120). Simultaneously, CwS critiques and reveals new methods for understanding and reconstructing the world toward an antiracist vision (Leonardo, 2009). CwS analysis turns a critical eye on the ways our institutions through systems—that is, policies and practices—work to reinforce ideologies of whiteness and white supremacy. For example, institutions of higher education are built on the land, labor, and lives of BIPOC (Red Shirt-Shaw, 2020; Voss, 2018; Wilder, 2013). By focusing on the centrality of ideologies of whiteness and white supremacy in the reproduction of systemic racism, CwS complements critical race theory (CRT), which interrogates systemic racism. Through a CwS framework, we can interrogate structures and practices through which institutions perpetuate systemic white supremacy (e.g., racially segregated Greek organizations, adherence to narrow notions of meritocracy, exclusivity and elitism, the maintenance of barriers to enrolling and supporting BIPOC students, faculty, and leaders) and dismantle them in forging more just realities. This analytic tool allows us to problematize whiteness, and thus critique and transform systems. We center the concept of whiteness, not white people, in order to enter the discussion with this problematizing lens.

Within the CwS paradigm, the concept of white innocence serves as a foundational component of whiteness and serves to uphold white supremacy. In critical race legal studies, Gotanda (2004) defined *white innocence* within the context of the landmark 1954 Supreme Court ruling in *Brown v. Board of Education* as an "Aha! moment" (p. 670) for the Court (and by extension, predominantly white society) that racially segregated schools are harmful to Black children. The Supreme Court justified its unanimous ruling against the "separate but equal" doctrine from *Plessy v. Ferguson* (1896) by arguing that they had a "new understanding to explain the past failure to act and why action is now appropriate" (Gotanda, 2004, p. 670).

However, as Bell (2004) documented, this realization of the right thing to do considering supposedly new evidence was performative at best. Driven by Cold War–era logics, the Truman administration advocated for the end of school segregation to counter Communist powers (e.g., USSR, Cuba, People's Republic of China, etc.) pointing out racism in the United States to undermine the American agenda for global influence (Bell, 2004). As U.S. Attorney General McGranery stated in the *amicus* brief on behalf of the U.S. government (*Brown v. Board of Education*, 1952) to the Supreme Court,

> The United States is trying to prove to the people of the world of every nationality, race and color, that a free democracy is the most civilized and most secure form of government yet devised by man. . . . The existence of discrimination against minority groups in the United States has an adverse effect upon our relations with other countries. Racial discrimination furnishes grist for the Communist propaganda mills. (p. 7)

In other words, blatant displays of racism at home were not helping the advancement of U.S. neocolonial empire building efforts around the globe. Thus the U.S. government's interest in the legal overturn of the "separate but equal" doctrine had less to do with advancing racial justice, for which the *Brown* decision is celebrated, than promoting the country's global influence. Perhaps these central U.S. global empire interests in the *Brown* case help explain why racially segregated and unequal schooling remain problems in the 21st century (Bell, 2004). There was never a true systemic interest in school integration beyond ending *de jure* (i.e., legal) segregation. Moreover, with school segregation policies outlawed, *de facto* (i.e., in fact) school segregation became a debatable problem. Although racial segregation in schools remained a persistent and growing problem in the United States, there were no laws that forced segregation (Orfield et al., 2019). Yet there have also been few policy solutions and little political will to combat the persistent anti-Black segregation and unequal schooling (Dumas, 2011; Snyder, 2020).

The maintenance of racial segregation and racism more generally in education rely on white innocence, which is reproduced through master narratives, such as those celebrated in the *Brown* case. Calling for education researchers to rethink theoretical perspectives, methods, and practices within systems of power, Gutierrez (2006) challenged scholars, and by extension educators, to disrupt white innocence endemic to dominant epistemologies that feed into the rationalization of racist ideologies and practice. White innocence allows individuals and organizational actors to deny complicity in the systemic reproductions of racial inequalities and injustice. It prevents an acknowledgment of, and action to, "challenge the underlying logic of the inhumanity and inequity that fuels racism" (p. 226). As an analytic frame, white innocence opens interrogations of "how the educational researcher [and educator] maintains *innocence* through the Aha! Moment . . . [and is able to] detach herself from historical, social, economic, and political ties" (p. 226). Notably, Gutierrez (2006) reminded readers that "*white innocence* does not refer to the racial category of whiteness but rather to the dominant subject-position that preserves racial subordination and the differential benefits for the *innocent* who retains her own dominant position vis-à-vis the 'objects' of study" or education (p. 226). As such, white innocence as a theoretical tool offers a lens to focus attention on interrogating cultural hegemony, relational power, and systems of dominance central to sustaining systemic white supremacy.

A white innocence framework problematizes how people and organizations detach themselves from systems of dominance and power by refusing to accept how they are embedded in systems of oppression. The white innocence lens compels us to name and reveal how complicity in systemic white supremacy helps support the reproduction of oppression in education. The maintenance of white innocence delivers absolution of one's sins through a catechism of innocence that allows individuals and organizational actors, who are complicit in subordination, to continue benefiting from whiteness and white supremacy with impunity. Therefore, white innocence is a key protector of white supremacy and a barrier to institutional and systemic antiracist change. If one is innocent and detached from systems of oppression, then there is no need to acknowledge and "examine our own responsibility and accountability for maintaining *innocence*" and, consequently, our complicity in racial dominance and inequities (Gutierrez, 2006, p. 228). To be clear, although white people and institutions can engage in counter-hegemonic acts to counteract whiteness and systemic white dominance, it is not possible for them to completely detach or remove themselves from systems of white supremacy (Leonardo, 2009). Accordingly, in the next sections we contextualize white innocence in relationship to systemic white supremacy and other CwS concepts. We also offer examples of white innocence preventing change in higher education.

White Innocence in Relationship to Other CwS Concepts

White innocence is one of many guardians for white supremacy that create a barrier to antiracist change. White immunity (Cabrera, 2018b) and white fragility (DiAngelo, 2011) represent two other protectors of systemic white dominance. Like the multiple heads of the monstrous Hydra of Lerna in Greek mythology, these variations on white innocence form a fierce, manipulative team, working together to fend off attempts to slay the beast-as-gestalt. Even if a social justice warrior manages to lop off one of the Hydra's heads, it regenerates and goes back to work. To defeat the Hydra, Hercules worked in collaboration with others to systematically prevent the beast's regeneration and buried the source of its power—its one immortal head. If the Hydra is white racial dominance, we must first understand how the beast regenerates to figure out how to put a stop to it.

White innocence and the related constructs discussed here work together to replicate and maintain white supremacy by coming to its defense, like the Hydra's multiple heads protecting the body of the beast. Constructs such as (white) normality, invisibility, immunity, and privilege maintain the status quo, reinforcing the underpinnings of white supremacy by normalizing racism (Ahmed, 2007; Cabrera, 2018b; DiAngelo, 2011; Gillborn, 2006; Jayakumar & Adamian, 2017; Leonardo, 2009; Winans, 2005). These constructs are not passive, as they work together to strategically obfuscate and preserve white supremacy. White normality establishes whiteness as the social and cultural default because the "interests and perceptions of white subjects are continually placed centre stage" (Gillborn, 2006, p. 319). This placement is neither arbitrary nor neutral, and to reign supreme as what is normal, whiteness as ideology undermines the legitimacy of communities that are not white (Jayakumar & Adamian, 2017). With normality comes white invisibility for bodies and spaces perceived as white (Ahmed, 2007). "Whiteness," explained Ahmed (2007), "is only invisible for those who inhabit it, or those who get so used to its inhabitance that they learn not to see it, even when they are not it" (p. 157). In this assertion, Ahmed (2007) was making an important point to indicate how BIPOC can also align with white normality. As Gutierrez (2006) asserted, "We are all implicated in some way in maintaining white innocence" (p. 226). Such invisibility allows whites and whiteness to move through the world uninterrupted due to unearned advantages, which McIntosh (1989) described as white privilege, to which white people can be oblivious. Cabrera (2018b) deepened the discussion of whiteness and systemic white supremacy by pointing out that the concept of white immunity can more accurately point out how white people are not only privileged but also generally protected from—or immune to—directly experiencing how systemic racism targets BIPOC. Alongside these various constructs of whiteness, white innocence prevents clear and collective interrogations of systems of oppression to develop and implement strategies to dismantle white supremacy.

Additionally, white ignorance and emotionality are key constructs contextualizing white innocence. Although white ignorance suggests a lack of understanding about race and racism, ignorance is a decidedly willful and privileged choice to opt out of struggles against oppression (Wildman & Davis, 2002). The performance of white ignorance works until it fails, as was evident in the Supreme Court's assertion of ignorance that racial segregation was violent in its 1954 *Brown* decision. "While they may claim that they know very little about race," Leonardo (2009) explained that "whites suddenly speak volumes about it when their racial ideology is challenged" (p. 114). They might act out and reject interrogations of whiteness and white supremacy (DiAngelo, 2011), fueled by unbridled emotion (Matias, 2016). According to Matias (2016), the white innocent's allegedly sudden awareness about racism inspires an emotional response that can involve guilt, helplessness, self-victimization, disrespect, or any combination of those responses. Within this context of emotional denial of complicity in systemic white dominance, when white ignorance is called out, a wellspring of emotionality can come to the fore, resulting in calls for absolution through claims of white innocence. White innocence, thus, can be a reactionary response to the emotionality of confronting the ugly realities of systemic racism, serving to shut down dialogue necessary to critically analyze and change oppressive conditions (Matias, 2016).

We assert that the revelation of the existence of racism is not what surprises as much as the fear of being implicated in its reproduction and maintenance. For example, Winans (2005) found that white undergraduate students "seek to remain safe from the threat of being perceived as racist" (p. 257). In other words, white students felt endangered by the possibility of having their image of innocence threatened. Such expressions of white innocence are the most recent echoes in the long history of attempts to justify white supremacy in colonized North America.

In sum, white innocence serves a pivotal role in relationship with various constructs of whiteness to maintain and defend white supremacy. It serves to refute individual complicity in the reproduction of racism and white racial dominance (Gotanda, 2004; Leonardo, 2009; Poon, 2018; Ross, 1990; Wildman & Davis, 2002; Winans, 2005), although both whites and BIPOC contribute in small and significant ways to their perpetuation (Ahmed, 2007; Gutierrez, 2006). White innocence insists on the normalization of whiteness, relying on widespread ignorance about race and racism. White innocence maintains that white people and organizational actors are not responsible for systemic white dominance and therefore they are not obligated to act differently or make meaningful and sustained change (Baldwin, 1964; Gutierrez, 2006; Leonardo, 2009; Ross, 1990).

White Innocence in Higher Education

In this section, we turn our attention to organizational change and leadership in postsecondary education, and we apply the white innocence analytic lens to unveil and critically examine barriers to antiracist change in higher education. White innocence works to prevent deep institutional change in higher education, which includes a range of institutions—four-year private and public colleges and universities, community colleges, and so on—that almost all universally claim commitments to and values of DEI (Stewart, 2018). By focusing on Princeton University (2015–2020), we also identify how the state can reinforce white innocence, preventing pathways to racial reconciliation.

Following the murder of George Floyd in May 2020 and subsequent protests reinvigorated in summer 2020 in response to the continuing pandemic of anti-Black racist violence and police killings of Black people (#Sayeveryname, n.d.), numerous universities and colleges released public statements to convey a range of messages of acknowledgment and care. Notably, most of these statements rarely mentioned key factually descriptive terms connected to Floyd's murder, such as "murder/killing" (Charaniya, 2020). Some universities, such as Auburn University and Baylor University, did not even mention George Floyd's name, whereas others, like Bucknell and Grinnell College, never released a statement (Charaniya, 2020). Charaniya's rapid response analysis and past research of institutional statements reveal a persistent pattern in U.S. higher education of releasing a statement of varying quality, few details for tangible antiracist organizational action or systemic change leadership, and little follow-up (Cole & Harper, 2017).

Students, alumni, faculty, and staff have called on higher education leaders to respond to violent events, such as the extrajudicial murders of George Floyd, Nina Popp, Breonna Taylor, and so many other Black people, with more than statements. One might argue that these killings and other current events have no ties to campuses. However, these events are symbolic of the social currents and realities of systemic racism that infuse and manifest themselves in colleges and universities, particularly through campus policing (Cole, 2021; Morgan & Davis, 2019). As such, students and other stakeholders in higher education logically call on institutional leaders to engage in actionable and meaningful measures to enact antiracist systemic change, going beyond superficial public relations efforts—deeper than the brand management efforts that President Boren announced immediately following the SAE incident at OU, which we discussed previously. Although launching diversity training series, announcing task forces, and hiring professionals to lead university organizational change efforts toward DEI goals represent important institutional investments, there remain questions about the effectiveness of such pronouncements to fundamentally change higher education (Cole & Harper, 2017). As Kelley (2016) asserted:

> The fully racialized social and epistemological architecture upon which the modern university is built cannot be radically transformed by "simply" adding darker faces, safer spaces, better training, and a curriculum that acknowledges historical and contemporary oppressions. This is a bit like asking for more black police officers as a strategy to curb state violence. We need more faculty of color, but integration alone is not enough. (para. 11)

Without fundamentally questioning and transforming the conditions and organizational structures in higher education, such programmatic pronouncements are often set up for failure if the goal is to reconstitute the institution to live out DEI and antiracist values (Ahmed, 2012).

In this radical spirit of reimagining higher education, some have called on universities to cut ties with municipal police departments and divest from policing more generally (Davis & Dizon, 2020). Policing plays a key role in reinforcing anti-Blackness and anti-Black racism in higher education (Cole, 2021; Dancy et al., 2018; Squire et al., 2018). By divesting from policing, colleges and universities can make substantial and necessary investments in campus infrastructures to create equitable educational supports and environments by centering BIPOC students and communities in higher education (Dizon et al., 2020).

Student activists have also called for more modest changes to make the university a more inclusive place for Black students. As Taylor (2016) explained, modest demands for reform "have the potential to crack open debates about racial inequality on campus, thereby creating a larger platform to address the history and contemporary practices of racism in these institutions. Small victories can empower one to fight larger battles" (para. 7) that can result in more radical change. For example, some student activists have called for the removal of monuments and the renaming of buildings honoring racist segregationists, Confederate Civil War leaders, and other white supremacists (Taylor, 2016). Princeton University's reckoning with the contemporary legacies of its white supremacist founding and history, and the Trump administration's actions in 2020, offers a case study of white innocence in higher education as interconnected with the state.

Since at least 1995, student activists and other community members at Princeton have presented several demands to administration, calling on the university to confront its history and engage meaningful actions for racial reconciliation and antiracist change (Kerr, 2015). Principal among the 2015 Black Justice League (BJL) and student coalition demands was a call, and subsequent administrative leadership agreement, to examine Woodrow Wilson's legacy at the university and the white supremacist ideologies he advanced (Black Justice League [BJL] at Princeton University, 2015; Princeton University, 2015). It was a notable call and agreement between student activists and university leaders to reckon with its history of white supremacy, as embodied and symbolized by monuments celebrating Woodrow Wilson. In demanding the removal of Wilson's name from buildings and the School of Public Policy, BJL (2015) stated students "understand that a name change does not dismantle racism, but also know that the way we lionize legacies set precedents" (para. 2). Their calls identified a lack of congruence between institutional value claims, actions, and cultural symbols.

In response to the 2015 agreement, Princeton's Board of Trustees convened a committee to consider the demands and make recommendations. In 2016, this special committee recommitted "to making Princeton a more diverse, inclusive, and welcoming community," and encouraged "members of the University community to think creatively and expansively" to make progress (Trustees of Princeton, 2016, p. 8). The university adopted the committee's recommendations, such as creating pipeline programs for students from underrepresented groups to pursue doctoral degrees, modifying Princeton's informal motto popularized by Wilson, and adopting several educational and transparency initiatives (Trustees of Princeton, 2016). However, the trustee committee did not recommend removal of Wilson iconography, including the School of Public Policy's name, claiming that the "use of his name implies no endorsement of views and actions" (p. 12).

On June 22, 2020, hundreds of student signatories from the Princeton class of 2020, 2021, and 2022 renewed and detailed six demands for racial justice from the university, following the growing public antiracist movement that summer (Change WWS Now, 2020). Their demands included changes to the School of Public and International Affairs (SPIA) core curriculum, diversification of faculty and transparent antidiscrimination procedures, scholarly recognition of antiracist undergraduate work, a faculty–student research task force to explore implementation of reparations, the removal of Wilson's name from the school, and divestment from the prison-industrial complex and fossil fuels (Change WWS Now, 2020). Almost immediately, university president Christopher Eisgruber (2020a) announced in a national *Washington Post* essay that the Board of Trustees had voted to remove Wilson's name from the school, crediting his sudden realization that his 2015 refusal to acknowledge Wilson's avowed racist ideals was wrong. He did not acknowledge the Black Justice League and other student coalitions and campaigns, nor did he discuss actions to address the other five student demands for justice. *The Daily Princetonian* Editorial Board (2020) called out President Eisgruber's essay as a performance for good publicity and demanded the university to take action after 5 years of activism. *The Daily Princetonian* Editorial Board (2020) explained:

> Since re-naming the SPIA, the University has not taken any material actions to combat systemic racism—beyond creating committees. Time and again, the administration has used its own bureaucratic hurdles to silence student activists' demands, exclude them from decision making processes, and out-wait them by remaining complacent and slow-moving. (para. 9)

Perhaps the Eisgruber administration and university trustees believed that changing building names would offer a powerful enough symbolic action to absolve the university from answering the other listed demands. However, the student newspaper editorial board collectively called for action beyond "performative gestures" (para. 10).

Interestingly, Eisgruber (2020b) issued a public statement almost 3 months later at the start of the fall 2020 term, stating,

> Racism and the damage it does to people of color nevertheless persist at Princeton as in our society, sometimes by conscious intention but more often through unexamined assumptions and stereotypes, ignorance or insensitivity, and the systemic legacy of past decisions and policies. (para. 6)

Without corresponding national publicity efforts, the president's September 2020 statement presented a set of institutional steps for material intersectional, antiracist change. The admission of intentional and unintentional racism was a significant and notable step for a university, and necessary for reconciliation.

Perhaps the notability of Princeton's confession of its role in contributing to white supremacy garnered negative attention from the Trump Department of Education, which sent a letter requesting an account of Princeton's actions deemed racist (Stratford, 2020). Days after announcing the federal investigation at Princeton, the Trump White House also issued Executive Order

13950 (2020), which threatened to withhold federal dollars from organizations if they support programs that problematize racism and patriarchy. Between the investigation of Princeton and the executive order, the federal government reinforced institutional demands on leaders to refuse organizational responsibility for systemic racism. While Princeton seeks to do better, white supremacy punishes the university as a white "race traitor" that refused white innocence (Leonardo, 2015). Still, this case demonstrates that sustained antiracist student leadership plays a key dialectical role in demanding that institutional leadership relinquish white innocence. Without an acceptance of culpability, there can be no progress in racial reconciliation and effective dismantling of systemic white supremacy. In the face of political threat, will other higher education leaders let go of white innocence? Most postsecondary institutions lack the deep resources that Princeton possesses to withstand such government attacks. Ironically, its resources were obtained through chattel slavery, labor exploitation, and continued investments in private prisons (Princeton University, 2018).

Relinquishing White Innocence: A Call to Divest From White Supremacy in Higher Education

The impacts, both visible and invisible, of white innocence can impede progress we want to make toward creating antiracist and equitable campus communities. One of the most prevalent themes in critical whiteness research in education is the call to make visible obscured systems of whiteness (Cabrera, 2018a; Gusa, 2010; Gutierrez, 2006; Leonardo, 2009; Orozco, 2019). Until we actively name, define, and disrupt white innocence, our institutions will continue to (un)intentionally uphold white supremacy and marginalize BIPOC students, faculty, staff, and other stakeholders.

Many DEI efforts in higher education rightly focus on the experiences of BIPOC students and others, and how to support them on their educational and career journeys. Fewer conversations involve naming and interrogating the systems and practices that reproduce inequitable educational conditions that hinder BIPOC trajectories in the first place. Systems of whiteness, which serve to maintain white power through white norms and racial domination, serve to uphold white supremacy. This system of power and domination manifests as racism in both word and deed. Ignoring tangible and material realities of systemic racism, held up by systems of whiteness, in our institutions reinforces white innocence and preserves the status quo of white dominance. Allowing whiteness to persist uninterrogated and unchallenged does a disservice to BIPOC, who are forced to navigate hostile spaces, and to possibilities of racial reconciliation, which requires community stakeholders to own up to their complicity and responsibilities to contribute toward change.

Higher education and its organizational leaders that claim to value and seek to advance DEI must relinquish white innocence. We call on higher education researchers and leaders to stop shirking complicity and responsibility for structural inequities that reproduce whiteness and white dominance. Without accepting responsibility, DEI efforts will be in vain. This is our call to action—relinquish the mask of white innocence. Accept liability with courage.

We know there will be resistance to relinquishing innocence. As we conclude this chapter with a discussion of strategies for dismantling white innocence in higher education contexts, we are mindful of the long-standing barriers to confronting the truth of systemic white supremacy. We are inspired by James Baldwin's observation about "the tensions of American life, as well as the possibilities," and his call on American society to relinquish the lie that this nation is purely a force of good (as cited in Patell, 2011, p. 356). As Glaude (2020) explained, Baldwin called on the United States to

> grapple with the contradiction at the heart of its self-understanding: the fact that in this so-called democracy, people believed that the color of one's skin determined the relative value of an individual's life and justified the way American society was organized. That belief and justification had dehumanized entire groups of color. White Americans were not excluded from its effects. "In this debasement and definition of black people," Baldwin argued, white people "debased and defined themselves." (pp. 6–7)

Accordingly, the call to let go of white innocence may provoke raw feelings of defensiveness, shame, guilt, fear, and denial. But the call to action remains. We must confront, expose, and relinquish white innocence in our institutions as necessary steps toward justice, reconciliation, and healing. This stance and long-standing resistance to it raise new questions. How can we expose these systems and practices of white innocence? As Glaude (2020) asked through his analysis of Baldwin, how can we root out the deep denial and lies that white innocence rests on?

First, we must expose white innocence for what it is: a tool that protects white supremacy. Only then can we take steps to pull it apart systemically. White innocence operates in a context where whiteness remains uninterrogated, and it prevents critical interrogation of systemic white supremacy—an admittedly cyclical condition. We can begin by asking:

Where is racism and whiteness at play but not identified in our policies, practices, institutional cultures, and work norms? How might it be explicitly named? What if we specifically named the disruption of white innocence as part of our institutional diversity plan? We can start with the past by publicly naming racist ideas, practices, and historical roots in our institutions to break open white denial (Gutierrez, 2006; Orozco, 2019). Instead of hiding behind well-worded "diversity statements," we can publicly own and apologize for the problematic parts of institutional history and make meaningful change and/or restitution, if possible.

In everyday practices, organizations should also routinize equity checks by analyzing relevant data and evidence. As Posselt, Hernandez, Villareal, et al. (2020) explained, "Evaluative criteria, deliberative processes, and decision outcomes constitute three key equity checkpoints at which decision stakeholders can bring equity-mindedness to check their evaluation and decision-making practice" (p. 22). Indeed, there are large and small, notable and routinized, daily decisions and work practices that contribute toward systemic distributions of material opportunities and advancements (e.g., admissions, employment, promotion, purchasing, contracting, evaluation rubrics, etc.) and equity implications. Reviewing relevant data on outcomes of varied processes and systems can allow an analytic and thoughtful identification of areas for change in work practices, routines, and systems. Posselt, Hernandez, and Villareal (2020) offered a robust framework to guide everyday decision-making in higher education to be more equitable.

Second, we must address the present legacies of that past and acknowledge the tangible realities of racism as a current organizational dynamic (Ray, 2019). We have discussed the damaging impact of normative cultures of whiteness on college campuses (Gusa, 2010). We must name this environment and work to disentangle it from our structures and practices, through data- and evidence-informed approaches (Posselt, Hernandez, & Villareal, 2020). We must resist the pull toward the familiar (i.e., normative) because it is what we know, and be willing to explore other ways of knowing and being. We can publicly acknowledge contemporary issues of intersectional racism and commit to doing better. We can invite, appoint, and hire leaders and teams—administrative, faculty, and students—that are empowered to actualize these commitments with necessary resources such as financial support and political capital.

As other scholars have highlighted, we can ask key questions to examine the implications of how we view and frame DEI and theories of change in higher education organizations (Orozco, 2019; Poon, 2018). Diversity statements and initiatives can be an important force for change, or they can be merely a "warm-fuzzy discourse" (Berrey, 2018, p. 546) that reinforces white innocence and prevents systemic justice. Without dismantling the underlying infrastructure, white supremacy will continue to adapt to maintain its power.

Additionally, DEI programs are often defended by the rationale that they are good for white people, too (Berrey, 2011). Thus, they are treated as an add-on option that helps everyone instead of naming them as critical efforts to address ongoing inequity. In what ways are DEI values and efforts centered as critical or merely an "add-on" in our work? Are we embracing the notion of "diversity" as a mere numbers game to produce a benign and superficial multiculturalism that can still uphold white innocence to defend systemic white dominance? How might we reject these "narrow frameworks of multiculturalism, void of power analysis" and embrace a practice that more directly challenges the stronghold of systemic oppression that is white innocence (Poon, 2018, p. 17)? Advancing a superficial notion of "diversity" can simply be about maintaining palatable appearances for white institutions to benevolently invite "others" to participate in opportunities while not changing structures and norms of practices (Ahmed, 2012). Although the inclusion of BIPOC in participating in dominant and predominantly white—in demographics and/or power structures—institutions is important and central to many frameworks of DEI, does your organization's DEI framework go beyond diversifying the face of stakeholder demographics? Does it compel transformations in systems and practices for equity (Stewart, 2018)?

By asking these questions and examining and discussing relevant data and evidence with organizational stakeholders, leaders can engage in organizational learning and sensemaking agendas to make tangible, small, and large systemic changes toward equity (Kezar, 2014; Posselt, Hernandez, Villareal, et al., 2020). In the process, and from our own organizational experiences, we know there may be resistance to questioning past and current practices as contributing to the reproduction of inequities and ultimately systemic white dominance. Mindful and context-specific organizational learning projects are necessary. Learning activities and programs can include opportunities for students, administrators and staff, and faculty to recognize often unconscious frameworks and discursive strategies that reinforce white innocence that prevents accountability and deep change. Orozco (2019) identified these strategies as misrecognition, deniability, excuses, justifications, generalizations/scripts, and distillations. Although learning programs can be offered to support the development of organizational stakeholders, we also recognize that for some no amount of organizational learning and sensemaking will lead to renouncement of white innocence and recognizing one's responsibilities. In these circumstances, there are also difficult decisions to be made, which should also be guided by organizational mission and value claims. After all, it is not uncommon for leaders to decide to remove stakeholders from an organization when they consistently create barriers to achieving organizational imperatives.

Additionally, how might we deliberately interrogate our rhetoric and identify ways it might be framing white subjectivity as innocent and BIPOC as problematic (Orozco, 2019)? How do we talk about BIPOC students? Is it from a deficit frame that labels them "at risk," "disadvantaged," or in need of intervention and fixing? How does this approach and lens prevent a critical analysis of normative systems and practices that produce inequalities in advantage and risk? Such frames uphold whiteness as the innocent norm to which people must conform, the standard by which they are measured. Instead, we can use language like "dominant" and "nondominant" to name power dynamics and structures of dominance and oppression involved, as Gutierrez (2006) suggested.

Finally, we must ask ourselves, how might we work to disentangle our own defensiveness and desire to be blameless in systems and organizations that reproduce inequalities? In what ways are we downplaying or denying the real consequences of racism on our campuses out of fear of criticism, which might include federal investigations and litigation? Scholars and activists are calling on higher education and leaders to fully own our past misdeeds and present norms that are rooted in racism and settler colonialism (Cabrera, 2018a; Gutierrez, 2006; Leonardo, 2009; Wilder, 2013). We must not seek to avoid responsibility and accountability for our active or passive complicity in perpetuating systemic white dominance through white innocence. We must stop denying our participation and get to work effecting change. If we are more invested in protecting our own sense of moral goodness, we will never make progress toward real equity.

Conclusion

> *I'm not interested in anybody's guilt. Guilt is a luxury that we can no longer afford. I know you didn't do it, and I didn't do it either, but I am responsible for it because I am a man and a citizen of this country and you are responsible for it, too, for the very same reason. . . . Anyone who is trying to be conscious must begin to dismiss the vocabulary which we've used so long to cover it up, to lie about the way things are.*
>
> —James Baldwin, remarks at Hampshire College

The murder of George Floyd by members of the Minneapolis police department and the continued extrajudicial violence and killings of Black people amid the COVID-19 pandemic in 2020 catalyzed a renewed national reckoning with systemic racism. The question posed by many throughout this period was, How is it that so many are only now "waking up to the everyday racism and trauma that Black Americans have lived intimately every day for hundreds of years" (Martin, 2020, para. 8)? A partial answer to that question is found in understanding the insidious nature of white innocence and its role in defending systems of white dominance.

We can get to work creating more equitable systems in higher education and elsewhere by exposing white innocence as a tool that shields individuals and organizations from rejecting the myths that maintain white hegemonic society, organizations, norms, and practices. White innocence ultimately preserves both the unearned privileges of whiteness and the oppressive nature of whiteness. White innocence is deeply embedded in our institutions, and it will take collective work and creative effort to eliminate it. But once we shine a light on it, it can no longer hide behind our well-meaning diversity statements. If we believe education can be a powerful force for equity, we must commit to educating everyone on systems of white supremacy and the practices like white innocence that uphold them.

Although calls to make changes in society writ large can be overwhelming and result in inaction, defining the scope for discrete changes can be an effective strategy to build momentum and movements for revolutionary change (brown, 2017; Weick, 1984). In higher education—a complex and large-scale system containing multitudes of organizational structures—organizational stakeholders and members can act strategically as individuals and collectives to advance significant systemic changes that bring forth new futures (la paperson, 2017). The first step is to take responsibility. As civil rights leader Grace Lee Boggs stated, "You cannot change any society unless you take responsibility for it, unless you see yourself as belonging to it and responsible for changing it" (as quoted in Yellow Horse et al., 2021, p. 168). White innocence is the antithesis of this truth.

Author Note

Correspondence concerning this book chapter should be addressed to OiYan Poon. Email: opoon@spencer.org.

Note

1. Throughout this chapter, we make an intentional choice to write *whiteness* with a lowercase *w*. This is an intentional inversion of common linguistic and rhetorical practices that capitalize *whiteness*, thereby putting it in a place of prominence. It is also a choice to reflect that whiteness in our discussion represents systemic power and cultural status.

References

#SayTheirNames. (n.d.). *Home page.* https://sayevery.name

Ahmed, S. (2007). A phenomenology of whiteness. *Feminist Theory, 8*(2), 149–168. https://doi.org/10.1177/1464700107078139

Ahmed, S. (2012). *On being included: Racism and diversity in institutional life.* Duke University Press.

Baldwin, J. (1964). The white problem. In R. Goldwin (Ed.), *100 years of emancipation* (pp. 80–88). Rand McNally.

Bell, D. (2004). *Silent covenants:* Brown v. Board of Education *and the unfulfilled hopes for racial reform.* Oxford University Press.

Bennett, B. (2015, January 28). Alleged "cowboys and Indians" party prompts mandatory diversity trainings. *OU Daily.* http://www.oudaily.com/news/alleged-cowboys-and-indians-party-prompts-mandatory-diversity-trainings/article_655bcaa4-a675-11e4-bd03-9f6f0a45438d.html

Berrey, E. C. (2011). Why diversity became orthodox in higher education, and how it changed the meaning of race on campus. *Critical Sociology, 37*(5), 573–596. https://doi.org/10.1177/0896920510380069

Berrey, E. C. (2018). Ivory tower fantasies about affirmative action [Review of the book *Ivory tower fantasies about affirmative action*, by N. K. Warikoo]. *Contemporary Sociology, 47*(5), 544–549. http://dx.doi.org/10.1177/0094306118792218b

Black Justice League at Princeton University. (2015). *#OccupyNassau meet Black student's demands.* change.org. http://chng.it/vRg2sDRfTG

Brief for the United States Government as *Amicus Curiae* Supporting Plaintiffs, Brown v. Board of Education, 347 U.S. 483 (1952).

brown, a. m. (2017). *Emergent strategy: Shaping change, changing worlds.* AK Press.

Cabrera, N.L. (2018a). Where is the racial theory in critical race theory? A constructive criticism of the crits. *The Review of Higher Education, 42*(1), 209–233. https://doi.org/10.1353/rhe.2018.0038

Cabrera, N. L. (2018b). White immunity: Working through some of the pedagogical pitfalls of "privilege." *JCSCORE, 3*(1), 77–90. https://doi.org/10.15763/issn.2642-2387.2017.3.1.77-90

Cabrera, N. L. (2019). *White guys on campus: Racism, white immunity, and the myth of "post-racial" higher education.* Rutgers University Press.

Cabrera, N. L., Watson, J. S., & Franklin, J. D. (2016). Racial arrested development: A critical whiteness analysis of the campus ecology. *Journal of College Student Development, 57*(2), 119–134. https://doi.org/10.1353/csd.2016.0014

Change WWS Now. (2020, June 22). *Demands of the undergraduate students of Princeton University's School of Public and International Affairs.* https://drive.google.com/file/d/1lpxEuLY_5rV4VTwC1Ly8sa2r77XuMVEE/view

Charaniya, A. [@amaan_c]. (2020, June 4). *I went through and pulled 189 statement's from different schools and checked them for to address 6 things* [Tweet]. Twitter. https://twitter.com/amaan_c/status/1268556137877643269?s=20

Cole, E. R. (2021, June 2). The racist roots of campus policing. *The Washington Post.* https://www.washingtonpost.com/outlook/2021/06/02/racist-roots-campus-policing/

Cole, E. R., & Harper, S. R. (2017). Race and rhetoric: An analysis of college presidents' statements on campus racial incidents. *Journal of Diversity in Higher Education, 10*(4), 318–333. http://dx.doi.org/10.1037/dhe0000044

Daily Princetonian Editorial Board. (2020, July 2). After five years of student activism, it's time for the U. to stop dragging its feet. *The Daily Princetonian.* https://www.dailyprincetonian.com/article/2020/07/princeton-woodrow-wilson-renaming-bjl-student-activism

Dancy, T. E., II, Edwards, K. T., & Davis, J. E. (2018). Historically white universities and plantation politics: Anti-Blackness and higher education in the Black Lives Matter era. *Urban Education, 53*(2) 176–195. http://dx.doi.org/10.1177/0042085918754328

Davis, C. H. F., III., & Dizon, J. P. M. (2020, June 2). More colleges should divest from the institution of policing. *Inside Higher Ed.* https://www.insidehighered.com/views/2020/06/02/heels-george-floyd-killing-colleges-have-moral-imperative-not-work-local-police

Desmond-Harris, J. (2015, March 12). Reaction to the Oklahoma frat scandal shows just how poorly Americans understand racism. *Vox.* https://www.vox.com/2015/3/12/8199343/oklahoma-sae-racist-song

DiAngelo, R. (2011). White fragility. *International Journal of Critical Pedagogy, 3*(3), 54–70.

Dizon, J. P. M., Salazar, M. E., Yucel, E., & Lopez, E. F. (2020). *Campus policing: A guide for higher education leaders.* USC Rossier School of Education.

Dumas, M. J. (2011). A cultural political economy of school desegregation in Seattle. *Teachers College Record, 113*(4), 703–734. http://dx.doi.org/10.1177/016146811111300402

Eisgruber, C. L. (2020a, June 27). I opposed taking Woodrow Wilson's name off our school Here's why I changed my mind. *The Washington Post.* https://www.washingtonpost.com/opinions/2020/06/27/i-opposed-taking-woodrow-wilsons-name-off-our-school-heres-why-i-changed-my-mind/

Eisgruber, C. L. (2020b, September 2). *Letter from President Eisgruber on the University's efforts to combat systemic racism.* Princeton University. https://www.princeton.edu/news/2020/09/02/letter-president-eisgruber-universitys-efforts-combat-systemic-racism

Exec. Order No. 13,950, 3 C.F.R, 60683–60689 (2020). https://www.federalregister.gov/documents/2020/09/28/2020-21534/combating-race-and-sex-stereotyping

Gillborn, D. (2006). Rethinking white supremacy: Who counts in "WhiteWorld." *Ethnicities, 6*(3), 318–340. https://doi.org/10.1177/1468796806068323

Glaude, E. S., Jr. (2020). *Begin again: James Baldwin's America and its urgent lessons for our own.* Crown.

Gonzales, L., Kanhai, D., & Hall, K. (2018). Reimagining organizational theory for the critical study of higher education. In M. B. Paulsen (Ed.), *Higher education: Handbook of theory and research* (Vol. 33, pp. 505–559). Springer. https://doi.org/10.1007/978-3-319-72490-4_11

Gotanda, N. (2004). Reflections on Korematsu, Brown and white innocence. *Temple Political and Civil Rights Law Review, 13,* 663–674.

Gusa, D. L. (2010) White institutional presence: The impacts of Whiteness on campus climate. *Harvard Educational Review, 80*, 464–490. http://dx.doi.org/10.17763/haer.80.4.p5j483825u110002

Gutierrez, K. (2006). White innocence: A framework and methodology for rethinking educational discourse and inquiry. *International Journal of Learning, 12*(10), 223–229. https://doi.org/10.18848/1447-9494/CGP/v12i10/48224

Jayakumar, U. M., & Adamian, A. S. (2017). The fifth frame of colorblind ideology: Maintaining the comforts of colorblindness in the context of white fragility. *Sociological Perspectives, 60*(5), 912–936. https://doi.org/10.1177/0731121417721910

Kelley, R. D. G. (2016). *Forum: Black study, Black struggle*. Boston Review. http://bostonreview.net/forum/robin-d-g-kelley-black-study-black-struggle

Kerr, O. (2015, November 20). Princeton University student protests, 1995 vs. 2015. *The Washington Post*. https://www.washingtonpost.com/news/volokh-conspiracy/wp/2015/11/20/princeton-university-student-protests-1995-vs-2015/

Kezar, A. (2014). *How colleges change: Understanding, leading, and enacting change*. Routledge.

Leonardo, Z. (2009). *Race, whiteness, and education*. Routledge.

Leonardo, Z. (2015). Contracting race: Writing, racism, and education. *Critical Studies in Education, 56*(1), 86–98. https://doi.org/10.1080/17508487.2015.981197

Martin, R. (2020, June 26). *Journalist Kevin Powell on his new book and his hopes and fears for his future child* [Interview]. NPR Morning Edition. https://www.npr.org/2020/06/26/883823660/journalist-kevin-powell-on-his-new-book-and-his-hopes-and-fears-for-his-future-c

Matias, C. E. (2016). *Feeling white: Whiteness, emotionality, and education*. Sense.

McIntosh, P. (1989, July/August). White privilege: Unpacking the invisible knapsack. *Peace and Freedom Magazine, 59*, 10–12.

Morgan, D. L., & Davis, C. H. F., III. (Eds.). (2019). *Student activism, politics, and campus climate in higher education*. Routledge.

New, J. (2015, March 15). SAE at sea. *Inside Higher Ed*. https://www.insidehighered.com/news/2015/03/30/u-oklahoma-chapter-learned-racist-song-sae-leadership-cruise

News 9. (2015, March 9). *President Boren: OU has zero tolerance for racism*. https://www.news9.com/story/5e34c821e0c96e774b34cc3b/president-boren:-ou-has-zero-tolerance-for-racism

Orfield, G., Frankenberg, E., Ee, J., & Ayscue, J. B. (2019). *Harming our common future: America's segregated schools 65 years after Brown*. The Civil Rights Project/Proyecto Derechos Civiles. https://www.civilrightsproject.ucla.edu/research/k-12-education/integration-and-diversity/harming-our-common-future-americas-segregated-schools-65-years-after-brown

Orozco, Richard A. (2019). White innocence as an investigative frame in a schooling context. *Critical Studies in Education, 60*(4), 426–442. https://doi.org/10.1080/17508487.2017.1285335

Patell, S. R. K. (2011). "We the people," who? James Baldwin and the traumatic constitution of these United States. *Comparative Literature Studies, 48*(3), 356–387. http://dx.doi.org/10.5325/complitstudies.48.3.0356

Plessy v. Fergusson, 163 U. S. 537 (1896)

Poon, O. (2018). Ending white innocence in student affairs and higher education. *Journal of Student Affairs*, *27*, 13–23.

Posselt, J., Hernandez, T., & Villarreal, C. D. (2020). Choose wisely: Making decisions with and for equity in higher education. In A. Kezar & J. Posselt (Eds.), *Higher education administration for social justice and equity: Critical perspectives for leadership* (pp. 43–66). Routledge.

Posselt, J., Hernandez, T. E., Villarreal, C. D., Rodgers, A. J., & Irwin, L. N. (2020). Evaluation and decision making in higher education. In L. W. Perna (Ed.), *Higher education: Handbook of theory and research* (Vol. 35, pp. 1–63). Springer.

Princeton University. (2015, November 19). *University, students reach agreement on campus climate concerns* [Press release]. https://www.princeton.edu/news/2015/11/19/university-students-reach-agreement-campus-climate-concerns

Princeton University. (2018, April 20). *Resources Committee issues report on private prison divestment* [Press release]. https://www.princeton.edu/news/2018/04/20/resources-committee-issues-report-private-prison-divestment

Ray, V. (2019, November 19). Why so many organizations stay white: Understanding how race is historically and structurally built into the workplace. *Harvard Business Review.* Advance online publication. https://hbr.org/2019/11/why-so-many-organizations-stay-white

Red Shirt-Shaw, M. (2020). *Beyond the land acknowledgement: College "LAND BACK" or free tuition for Native students.* https://hackthegates.org/wp-content/uploads/2020/08/Redshirt-Shaw_Landback_HTGreport.pdf

Richinick, M. (2015, March 9). *University president: "We don't provide student services for bigots."* MSNBC. https://www.msnbc.com/msnbc/fraternity-under-fire-after-video-showing-racist-chant-surfaces-msna546256

Ross, T. (1990). The rhetorical tapestry of race: White innocence and Black abstraction. *William and Mary Law Review*, *32*, 41.

Snyder, J. (Producer). (2020, July 23). Nice white parents [Audio podcast]. *The New York Times.* https://www.nytimes.com/2020/07/23/podcasts/nice-white-parents-serial.html

Squire, D., Williams, B. C., & Tuitt, F. (2018). Plantation politics and neoliberal racism in higher education: A framework for reconstructing anti-racist institutions. *Teachers College Record, 120*, 1–20. http://dx.doi.org/10.1177/016146811812001412

Stewart, D-L (2018). Minding the gap between diversity and institutional transformation: Eight proposals for enacting institutional change. *Teachers College Record, 120*(14), 1–16. http://dx.doi.org/10.1177/016146811812001411

Stratford, M. (2020, September 17). Education department investigates Princeton for admitting "systemic racism" on campus. *Politico.* https://www.politico.com/news/2020/09/17/education-department-investigates-princeton-for-systemic-racism-417454.

Taylor, K.-Y. (2016). *Forum response: Black study, Black struggle.* Boston Review. http://bostonreview.net/forum/black-study-black-struggle/keeanga-yamahtta-taylor-keeanga-yamahtta-taylor-response-robin

Trustees of Princeton University. (2016, April 2). *Report of the Trustee committee on Woodrow Wilson's legacy at Princeton.* https://www.princeton.edu/sites/default/files/documents/2017/08/Wilson-Committee-Report-Final.pdf

Voss, B. L. (2018). The archaeology of precarious lives: Chinese railroad workers in nineteenth-century North America. *Current Anthropology, 59*(3), 287–313. http://dx.doi.org/10.1086/697945

Weick, K. E. (1984). Small wins: Redefining the scale of social problems. *American Psychologist, 39*(1), 40–49. http://dx.doi.org/10.1037/0003-066X.39.1.40

Wilder, C. (2013). *Ebony and ivy: Race, slavery, and the troubled history of America's universities.* Bloomsbury.

Wildman, S. M., & Davis, A. D. (2002). Making systems of privilege visible. In P. S. Rothenberg (Ed.), *White privilege: Essential readings on the other side of racism* (pp. 89–95). Worth.

Winans, A. E. (2005). Local pedagogies and race: Interrogating white safety in the rural college classroom. *College English, 67*(3), 253–273. https://doi.org/10.2307/30044636

Yellow Horse, A. J., Kuo, K., Seaton, E. K., & Vargas, E. D. (2021). Asian Americans' indifference to Black Lives Matter: The role of nativity, belonging and acknowledgment of anti-Black racism. *Social Sciences, 10(5),* 168. https://doi.org/10.3390/socsci10050168

PART TWO

PRACTICAL CONSIDERATIONS

6

EPISTEMIC ASPHYXIATION

Whiteness, Academic Publishing, and the Suffocation of Black Knowledge Production

Wilson Kwamogi Okello

I can't read this . . . he [Author] will have to do it again.

—Grammar school teacher

The way you move through the world is beautiful and creative, but others will not always be able to see it.

—Author's mother

Breathing is a fugitive act. For Black people, attempts at the vivifying circulation of air, the enunciation of life, inhalation, and exhalation has been met with angst and anxiety historically and in this temporal moment. Eric Garner. George Floyd. I can't breathe. And the scene repeats. This project, the eclipsing of air such that it stills or brings under control unruly objects, tongues, and bodies, is not new. Indeed, as the weight of history and signification converge, and revolve on white[1] epistemologies (Wynter, 2003), the violent theft of breath has taken the form of state-sanctioned authority (e.g., law enforcement chokeholds), fulfilling the script of American grammar (Spillers, 1987). In its fulfillment, Dumas (2014) called *the Black*, sutured to bestiality and nonhumanness, anxiety-producing in the white imagination, doubling as the rival to western, U.S. epistemological constructions of identity.

This conceptualization of the Black (Wilderson, 2010) adds credence to Audre Lorde's (1978) warning that as Black (and so, too, Indigenous, People of Color), "we were never meant to survive" (p. 31). Instantiations to seize Black breath issue the urgent question: What is it about endarkened

(Dillard, 2000) breathing that is so threatening that it deserves enclosure? Wynter (1994), offering insight into this question, pointed to the governing nature of the sociogenic principle, which bounds the modern construction of knowledge to European representations of humanity, that, too, decisively makes claims about what can be included within its bounds and those/that which can never be human. For Wynter (1994), lack of regard is rooted in conquest, settler colonialism, and enslavement. She concluded,

> All our present struggles with respect to race, class, gender, sexual orientation, ethnicity, struggles over the environment, global warming, severe climate change, the sharply unequal distribution of the earth resources . . . these are all differing facets of the central ethnoclass Man vs. Human struggle. (Wynter, 2003, pp. 260–261)

Furthermore, destruction of the Other is located in "what Michel Foucault identifies as the 'invention of Man'—that is, by the Renaissance humanists' epochal redescription of the human outside the terms of the then theocentric, 'sinful by nature' conception/'descriptive statement' of the human" (Wynter, 2003, p. 263). Following Baszile (2019), this sociogenic algorithm morphs and "manifests in our present Humanities and Social Sciences [and Education] and their production of 'inner eyes' that cannot conceive of humanity outside of race, class and gender hierarchies among others" (p. 9). Building on the work of Black feminist philosopher Kristie Dotson (2011) and her attention to testimonial quieting and smothering, alongside Paul Butler's (2017) conceptualization of the chokehold, this conceptual chapter explores what I will term here *epistemic asphyxiation.*

Here, western constructions of epistemology function to control and surveil the production of knowledge, research, and value in academic spaces and beyond. Moreover, returning to the notion of breathing, Masaoka et al. (2001) contended that "emotional experiences are not only productions within the brain accompanied by physiological activity such as sweating, increased heart rate, and respiration; these activities result from an unconscious process" (p. 55). Thus, if Blackness in the white imagination (hooks, 1992) yields anxiety-producing responses, then epistemic asphyxiation is the rationalized attempt(s) to restore a normative pattern of breathing—that is, coherence to a white western epistemological ideal.

To expound on this theorization, I examine two recent epistemic asphyxiation scenes in the tenure denials of Ashley Woodson at the University of Missouri and Paul Harris at the University of Virginia. Woodson, a Black woman scholar, and Harris, a Black man scholar, were denied tenure at their respective institutions. Across their careers, each scholar garnered praise and collegial respect for outstanding contributions to their universities, their discipline, and fields through advising, service, and publishing. For the length of their academic appointments, both received supportive reviews from reappointment, promotion, and tenure committees, and yet, as discussed in the following, they were denied tenure. The reasoning offered for the denial differs, but this chapter will expose the ways academic publishing processes are manifestations of the white gaze, designed to protect white spaces (Anderson, 2015). I place these scenes in conversation with the first authored Black woman (poet) in the western Americas, Phillis Wheatley, to demonstrate the ways whiteness has exercised this project over time. Conducting a critical discourse analysis (Van Dijk, 2003) of media, social media, and official documents, I ask, How does whiteness epistemically function to terrorize Black onto-epistemologies in and beyond educational contexts? By examining what Wolfe (2006) called the "logic of elimination" (p. 402), this chapter attempts to contribute to the discourse on anti-Black technologies in and beyond higher education, with specific attention to the academic publishing process. Further, it endeavors to draw out otherwise possibilities for existence in the wake of anti-Blackness (Sharpe, 2016).

Scripting Blackness in the White Imaginary

Black people, and People of Color more broadly, grapple indefinitely with histories that deem them intellectually inferior. In *Notes on the State of Virginia*, Thomas Jefferson would go to great lengths to suggest that "in reason [Black people] were much inferior" (Kendi, 2016, p. 109). He continued, stating that "it would be unfair to follow them to Africa for this investigation. We will consider them here, on the same stage with the whites, and where the facts are not apocryphal on which judgment is to be formed" (p. 109). Here, "he could never find that a Black had uttered a thought above the level of plain narration" (p. 109). His ideas were consistent with the intellectual movement that would ultimately establish the epistemological canon at the root of academic knowledge production and publishing, Enlightenment.

Birthed in the 1600s and the scientific revolution, Enlightenment brought together "all philosophical experiments that let light into the nature of things" (Kendi, 2016, p. 80). The metaphor of light referenced Europe's rediscovery of knowledge after years of darkness, and more drastically, embodied the distinction between whiteness and its metaphysical other, Black(ness). Put simply, Enlightenment ideas granted legitimacy to anti-Black ideas and policies.

Black Bodies and Minds

Whiteness as an impediment to Black breath and breathing, as noted previously, has been etched into the western, U.S. fabric. This impediment served and, indeed, works to define the boundaries of western knowing and knowledge production. Moreover, Black people's history and Black bodies are linked indelibly to histories of whiteness that have sought to frame them as inferior and an object to be controlled. According to Yancy (2008), the Black body is a thing to be feared, represented by sadism, terror, and the very idea of criminality itself. Constructed in the white imaginary as madness and the absence of rightness, vis-à-vis, whiteness, Blackness is the embodiment of anguish and despair.

Solidifying patterns of encounter, "The Black body is constructed as antithetical within a binary logic that points to the white body's own 'signifying [and material] forces to call attention to itself' as normative" (Yancy, 2008, p. 13). Simultaneously strange and an object of ascension, Blackness is fixed in the white imaginary as an object to be resolved (Yancy, 2008). In this way, whiteness functions as the norm, or standard by which people are measured, and too, deploys disciplinary control in policies, practices, and the idea of personhood in the United States. Furthermore, White identity was constructed along these disciplinary lines, ensuring and expanding the racial hierarchy that established chattel slavery.

Whiteness as Property

Blackness symbolized racial otherness and subordination, a system bound to descent and national origin, that ultimately became a justification for slavery (C. Harris, 1993). Here, conceptualizations of property formed and took on new meaning that would disregard Black intellect and knowledge as illegible in the white imagination. Higher education, as an institution, is rooted in whiteness (Wilder, 2013), and thus, it is a holder of property rights unavailable to Black people. Property as determined by classical theorists included external objects as determined by one's ownership capacities (read: proximity to whiteness). Property also concerned the rights, immunities, and privileges afforded to, and for, a human's well-being in a social setting. As such, humans should be afforded freedoms of expression, opportunity, and the ability to live free from the harm of others (C. Harris, 1993). Whiteness as property, the normative set of conditions that outlines who and what counts, confers tangible, protected social and economic benefits, a guarded possession reserved for those who meet white identity qualifications.

hooks (1992) discussed power as that which is habitually passed on as white normativity. Jordan (1988) concluded that white normativity persists uncritiqued and underquestioned despite the shifting culture and language demographics in the United States. White normativity, instead, defines the boundaries of what is considered correct and deviant with respect to language and being. Said differently, property establishes and regulates expectations, and who can draw advantages from those expectations, what counts as knowledge, and who will be read as legible in the production of knowledge. Academia, and academic publishing more specifically, mirrors this sentiment by regulating what is produced.

Emblematic of the white supremacist intent to place a stranglehold on knowledge and, in turn, the suffocation of all other ways of knowing and being, settler colonialism functioned as an extension of property seizure and ownership. Tuck and Gaztambide-Fernández (2013) noted that settler colonialism is a method by which colonizers stake their claim to a place and exercise sovereignty. Colonizers—whiteness—in this way define citizenship and knowing in a particular context. Wolfe (2006) called this process the *logic of elimination*. Here, the destruction of place is thrust into settler-colonial social and political structure and norms, such that colonialism survives as more than the event; rather, it becomes the normative structure. Furthermore, settler colonialism demands that nonwhite people be read, engaged, and interpreted as outside of the norm and incapable of meeting the qualifications for full citizenship. This organizing practice ensures that whiteness remains normal (Tuck & Gaztambide-Fernández, 2013).

The creation of property, norms, and expectations as the enforcement of power is neither ambiguous nor inevitable; instead, it is a specific and intentional move to structure society (C. Harris, 1993). Norms, as the creation of laws and practices, set whiteness as the essence of property and personhood. Further to the point, whiteness as an objective fact ensures that social and political relations take on its essence, acquiring objectivity, rationality, and insolubility that make it difficult to trace (C. Harris, 1993). One of the main methods by which higher education has wielded whiteness as a controlling metric is the academic publishing process.

Remarking on the politics of academic writing, Cooper (2017) contended that the template, or the normative frame, for producing knowledge should be understood in reference to its guiding epistemology. It is the episteme that outlines what knowledge can be accepted and that which falls outside of the knowledge canon. Academic writing, epistemically, is rooted in the scientific method's linearity as the benchmark for legitimate academic production.

Baszile (2019) added, the "template" is "reproduced by scholars in westernized peer networks, and its episteme allows certain knowledge and refuses other kinds of knowledge which are inexpressible and/or incomprehensible within the given template" (p. 14). Moreover, the framing stresses technicality, calling for a wider division between plain, ordinary expression and academic standards of writing and citing that maintain the episteme. This template congeals as the dominant method for legitimate knowledge and, ultimately, what counts as legible. Sharpe (2016) anchored this point, stating, "to produce legible work in the academy often means adhering to research methods that are drafted into the service of a larger destructive force thereby doing violence to our own capacities to read, think, and imagine otherwise" (p. 13). Moreover, as a disciplining function, Black, Indigenous, and other non-White scholars are trained to produce knowledge through a scientific method that reinforces their already Other status in academe. It should be noted that even if minoritized scholars gain the language of acculturation and can produce in a way that is consistent with academic legibility, their very presence, in-text and material body, is yet in lack of what it means to be legitimate (Sharpe, 2016).

Theoretical Framework

Whiteness, as the arm of academic publishing, is a form of epistemic violence. Dotson (2011) discussed epistemic violence as a refusal, intentional or unintentional, of an audience to reciprocate a linguistic exchange owing to pernicious ignorance communicatively. The injurious nature of epistemic violence is sustained, and therefore reliable in a particular context. In the world of academic publishing, epistemic violence monitors the production of knowledge, in its selection of what gets accepted and disseminated, and as noted previously, asks that scholars adopt a narratively condemned status (Sharpe, 2016) that would have them satisfy the appetite of whiteness (Morrison, 1992). Dotson (2011) continued by calling reliable that "ignorance that is consistent or follows from a predictable epistemic gap in cognitive resources" (p. 238). Black onto-epistemologies exist outside of white, enlightenment sensibilities, thereby failing to meet the linguistic exchange's dependencies. Hornsby (1995) explicated the condition and relationship between speaker/writer and listener/reader, writing,

> I give the name "reciprocity" to the condition that provides for the particular way in which successful illocutionary acts can be performed. When there is reciprocity among people, they recognize one another's speech as it is meant to be taken: An audience who participates reciprocally does not merely (1) understand the speaker's words but also, in (2) taking the words as they are meant to be taken, satisfies a condition for the speaker's having done the communicative thing she intended. (p. 134)

Plainly, Hornsby's offering emphasized reciprocity in linguistic exchange; thus, "the success of a speaker's attempt to communicate ultimately depends upon audiences" (Dotson, 2011, p. 238). As an audience misinterprets and fails to meet the terms of exchange, thereby participating in epistemic violence, two particular forms of silence emerge—testimonial quieting and testimonial smothering. First, testimonial quieting occurs as processes fail to identify the writers/speakers as qualified knowers. Illustrating this point, Dotson (2011), for example, lifted Collins (1990), who maintained that she was already underrecognized as a knower by virtue of her Black womanhood. Moreover, Black women are less likely to be perceived as competent knowers beyond the historically anchored presuppositions that persist. Tuana (2006) expounded on this notion, writing, "In instances such as these [where epistemically disadvantaged identities produce ignorance] it is not merely facts, events, practices, or technologies that are rendered not known, but individuals and groups who are rendered not knowers" (p. 13). The inability to (un)recognize knowers outside of the normative, white racial frames (Feagin, 2010) can harm.

Feagin (2010) discussed the prevalence of white racial frames as ways of seeing that are "combined racial stereotypes, metaphors, and interpretive concepts, images, emotions, and inclinations birthed out of the materiality of racial oppression. This dominant framing has functioned to preserve whiteness and benefit White people" (p. 423). Importantly, white racial frames are rooted in colonization and enslavement, and have functioned, since the period of conquest, as the parameters for goodness and citizenship. White racial frames are an assault on one's intellectual courage, epistemic agency, and, more broadly, the intellectual traditions of a people (Collins, 1990; Dotson, 2011). The resultant attitude for writers and speakers, made to be unknown, manifest in what Dotson (2011) called testimonial smothering. In this instance, as unknowns anticipate the ways whiteness curtails one's voice, individuals truncate their testimony to ensure that the linguistic act is intelligible for the audience. In other words, "testimony that meets the dictates of accurate intelligibility for an audience is testimony that is clearly comprehensible and defensibly intelligible to that audience" (p. 245). Thus, whiteness maintains its overarching standard as *deviant* voices are brought into the order of things.

Epistemic violence manifests as testimonial quieting and smothering, exemplifying whiteness as a form of constraint. Theorizing whiteness as a form of epistemic asphyxiation can also locate its practice in surveillance literature, particularly Butler's (2017) notion of the chokehold. Conceptually, the chokehold is an alarmingly accurate maneuver to describe the principled consistency of whiteness. For Butler (2017), the chokehold "is a process of coercing submission that is self-reinforcing. A chokehold justifies additional pressure on the body because it does not come into compliance, but the body cannot come into compliance because of the vice-grip" (p. 4). Accordingly, the chokehold does not allow for reasoned responses by individuals, such that those held are in violation with every movement. The only option available to those held is one of submission. Where whiteness is concerned, its grip compels compliance, as it simultaneously provokes resistance. Therefore, the chokehold's sinister nature is magnified because the resistance it causes redistributes one's resistance upon the self, tightening. One way of reading this redistribution is in the popularized adage "working within the system to change it." This custom would have authors believe that paying one's dues, so to speak, will grant them legitimacy, and once they demonstrate legitimacy, they can do differently. Whiteness, however, seemingly predicts this logic and ensures that standards outside of itself do not accumulate in excess to pose a threat.

Siting and Citing Epistemic Asphyxiation

This chapter draws out the tenets of epistemic asphyxiation by putting epistemic violence in conversation with Butler's (2017) framing of the chokehold to explicate several anti-Black violence scenes related to knowledge production processes. I conducted a critical discourse analysis (van Dijk, 2003) of media, social media, and official documents, involving two academicians and one of the premiere writers in U.S. memory. Guiding this analysis, I asked, How does whiteness inform knowledge production, research, and what is valued in academic spaces? Critical discourse analysis (CDA), according to van Dijk (2003), is an analytical type of research that examines the way power and dominance are embedded in and reproduced by various texts in sociopolitical contexts. Moreover, because power is discursive, CDA surfaces the multiple and varied expressions of power by keying into historical patterns and the present-day manifestations of those patterns. Additionally, CDA accounts for epistemology as socialized and fungible, intent on disrupting how whiteness has normalized what counts as valid knowledge. Van Dijk (2003) illuminated two particular CDA sites, the micro and macro. Micro-level analysis interrogates text and verbal communications, whereas a macro-level review grapples with power relations, laws, and the silent norms that govern society.

To expose the ways whiteness gets expressed in knowledge production, I analyze voices that it attempted to suffocate. I do this to locate how whiteness is actively contending for their language and being by claiming an objective stance. Additionally, I attempt to allow them to talk back (hooks, 1989) to whiteness by focusing on the language of their appeal and those advocating for the three Black writers as they encounter these scenes.

Black (In)capacity for Whiteness in Three Scenes

I begin theses analyses with the case of Ashley Woodson. In the petition that follows, Cheryl Matias (2020) wrote in support of Woodson's record and case for tenure:

> We write to express our concern and dismay regarding the failure to grant tenure to Dr. Ashley Woodson, Assistant Professor and the William A. and Jean S. Stauffer Faculty Fellow in Education. In supporting her, we note that she has published over 17 peer reviewed and other research papers, presented at dozens of professional conferences and frequently invited to guest lecture. In the past couple of years she has received external funding in excess of 40k, and has received the AERA Social Studies Early Career Award (2020) from her own Division. In 2018, Dr. Woodson received the following recognitions regarding her teaching and mentorship: the College of Education Faculty Commitment to Diversity Award, Dean's Faculty Leadership Fellow award, and the student award for mentorship. Similar awards are present for previous years. With regards to service, she sits on several editorial boards of major academic journals [which] include Urban Education, Theory and Research in Social Education, etc. In terms of University Service, she sits on no less than 10 University committees of which she has served in leadership in 3. This is the record of a star, devoted to her profession and dedicated to rendering the best she can. (para. 1)

I highlight Woodson's case as an example of how whiteness adamantly resents and ignores scholarship on and about Black people. Even when published research is available and should inform policies and practices, the objectivity of whiteness and cultures of white supremacy maintain a set of values that refuses to acknowledge anti-Black racism.

CDA Analysis of Woodson

Woodson's case surrounds teaching evaluations and, in particular, scores and comments made by students of her teaching. Teaching, as evaluated by the University of Missouri's *Collected Rules and Regulations* pamphlet, in section 320.035, "Policy and Procedures for Promotion and Tenure," reads (in part),

> Questionnaires developed at the college or school level in cooperation with the faculty committees on promotion and tenure may be used for this purpose, or a similar procedure can be followed which is designed to reflect comprehensive student judgment concerning teaching qualities. Data from questionnaires should be buttressed by interpretation and comparative data. Simple numerical summaries of evaluations are not sufficient to judge teaching ability. Faculty members whose records consistently reflect poor teaching will normally not be recommended for promotion. Other indicators may be used to point out good teaching. Good teachers receive public recognition in a variety of ways. Students, both individually and through organizations, seek them out more often. Such teachers make more innovative contributions in courses, sometimes whole curricula. Their students demonstrate achievement in learning. They often serve on more student activity committees and carry heavier advising loads. . . . Extension and continuing education activities represent an extension of the teaching and research functions of the institution. Faculty engaged in this mission will be evaluated by the same criteria applied to other faculty. Outstanding performance in extension leads to special recognition of faculty by groups, individuals, and organizations. (University of Missouri System, n.d., part B.2.c, para. 3)

As expressed in the advocacy letter noted previously, Woodson is a critical social studies scholar. In this way, her presence and scholarship are already out of place in the university structure that stresses white normativity and a university context with a storied history of exclusion. In 2015, the University of Missouri faced criticism because of its willful (Sullivan & Tuana, 2007) unresponsiveness to Black students' experiences of racial violence on campus. Ironically, Woodson's research and teaching squarely take up the tension of that moment. It should come as no surprise then that a university invested in epistemologies of ignorance (Sullivan & Tuana, 2007), resistant to the cause of Black pain and suffering, and epistemically a maker of it, would show itself incapable of attending to the racialized and gendered nature of Woodson's case.

In my initial read of the policies, students' voice as knowers and participants in their learning is a significant portion of a candidate's record. As a site of mutuality and learning, the classroom is fulfilled when all voices have a say in how space is realized. However, the objectivity of this expectation is interrupted due to the ongoing and ever-present specter of race and racism. For faculty of Color, and Black faculty in particular, race is always present and, thus, anti-Black racism is forcefully at play in implicit and explicit decisions, during and beyond the classroom space, inclusive of but not limited to student evaluations. Current practice among colleges and universities in the United States permits promotion and tenure committees to use student evaluations as instruments of teaching effectiveness. Research notes the ways racial bias influences teaching evaluations (see Reinsch et al., 2020). The previously quoted policy seemingly ignored these findings, which would otherwise advocate for faculty of Color, in favor of generic language and uncritical interpretation.

Notably, the lines that read, "Questionnaires developed at the college or school level in cooperation with the faculty committees on promotion and tenure may be used for this purpose. . . . Data from questionnaires should be buttressed by interpretation and comparative data," demonstrate a pernicious form of ignorance as they flagrantly dismiss the possibility that anti-Black racism could be present in the thinking and evaluative measures of promotion and tenure committees and students' judgments. The policy relies on students to acknowledge and respond to their potentially racist behaviors and situates the interpretation of mostly White faculty at the university as an unarguable standard. What's more, "the validity of anonymous students' evaluations rests on the assumption that, by attending lectures, students observe the ability of the instructors, and that they report it truthfully" (Reinsch et al., 2020, p. 115). Moreover, as the promotion and tenure committee has oversight of the evaluative measures, they, too, become the instrument's interpreters with the power to make decisions about what and who counts. The promotion and tenure committee, with research available to them that stated "even those who are explicitly supportive of equity and sure they are unbiased can demonstrate implicit bias" (p. 121) and "the method most universities now use allows for, and even encourages, immutable characteristics such as gender, race, national origin, and age to color the results" (p. 122), seemingly ignored this research in their evaluation of Woodson.

As whiteness frames evaluative measures, Black faculty are placed in suffocating situations, such that even when they meet and exceed standards set by the university and the records of their peers, their efforts fail as insufficient. An example of this can be seen in how Woodson exceeded other teaching measures recognized by the university and larger discipline. According to her April 2020 curriculum vitae, Woodson wrote five peer-reviewed articles with undergraduate students, an extraordinary research effort, and one that requires teaching and mentoring prowess. Again, this willful oversight by the committee lends itself to an arbitrary deployment of rules and an unwillingness to see Woodson beyond some students' evaluations of her teaching. Moreover, the anonymity of evaluative processes engineers a panoptic watchfulness that ensures Woodson is monitored by visible and invisible structures, and that she does not disturb the tranquil experience of whiteness. When Woodson, and others like her, do disturb these sensibilities, the white gaze, as a site of power and control, responds violently, and with dehumanizing processes, to put Blackness in its place.

Furthermore, "if implicit bias involves any of the protected categories under the law and evaluations are used to make employment decisions, then those employment decisions are based on some factors that are discriminatory and therefore illegal" (Reinsch et al., 2020, p. 116). Thus, even though the University of Missouri can write, as previously noted, that applicants "will be evaluated by the same criteria applied to other faculty," ultimately, whiteness is impacting employment decisions ensuring that Woodson will lose the protections of tenure and, in essence, some ability to contribute to the university's production of knowledge. This policy, a standard clause for many institutions, fails at its mission as it doesn't account for systems of power and privilege as they act upon the multiple identities named. Woodson's knowledge production is not only called into question; it is perceived as less valuable and ultimately squeezed out.

Scene II

The following is a portion of Paul Harris's appeal letter, written on March 9, 2020. I quote the letter at length to capture the fullness of Harris's critique:

> It is clear from the information provided by Dean Pianta in his letters of February 3 and 11, 2020 (Appendix A), that a negative assessment of my scholarship led to the negative tenure recommendation. The letters show that the recommendation, unfortunately, rests on untruths and egregiously misleading information that expose and reinforce long-standing structural preferences that privilege the work of some scholars and marginalize the work of others, despite their work being recognized as significant in their discipline. Patently false claims about the number of articles I have published in peer reviewed journals, incongruent metrics applied to the number of citations, and inappropriate value ascribed to impact factors related to my work presented an inaccurate view of my scholarship in my evaluation. This narrative tainted my entire evaluation process as it informed the Curry faculty vote on my dossier and the promotion and tenure committee's recommendation to the Dean about my case. These structural preferences (which also give disproportionate weight to quantitative research; more than half of my work is qualitative research) help explain why my dossier was required by University policy, in the context of my field of academic inquiry. (P. Harris, 2020, paras. 2–3)

Compounding this statement and the white gaze that accompanied historically White institutions, according to Harris, there were no persons of Color on his promotion and tenure committee. This structural ordering reinforces the notion that academe, and authorities on the production of knowledge, are patrolled by whiteness.

CDA Analysis of Harris

Whiteness as property (C. Harris, 1993) was at the center of Harris's racial violence scene. As noted in his appeal letter, "patently false claims" related to his publication record led to an unfavorable promotion and tenure decision. Specifically, the promotion and tenure committee appeared to take issue with one of his publications. In a blog written by Harris's wife, Taylor Harris, she noted, in the committee's words, that at least one of his peer-reviewed journal articles "*appeared to be self-published.* It was the *Journal of African American Males in Education.* The acceptance rate for articles? About 20 percent. Some of the biggest names in his field publish in that journal" (T. Harris, 2020, para. 19). In this instance, whiteness is deployed with the power to name that which is and is not proper knowledge. This statement about an academic journal having the appearance of "self-publishing" is an indictment on what can and should be considered scholarly.

Furthermore, the statement echoes the ways Black bodies and minds are constructed in and through white racial frames. These frames, seeded in colonization and enslavement, are imbued with timeless tropes about Black people and Black intelligibility that understand them as inferior, purely affective, and less inclined to rigorous study. The claim presumes that a title that advances a specific regard for Black humanity in education could not meet others' standards (read: White-led, neutral) outlets, who seemingly hold authority over what counts. The language of self-publishing also suggests that Black people authoring themselves has limited value in academic spaces and, broadly, the white imagination.

According to Harris, every year that he was on the tenure track, his departmental evaluations suggested that he met or exceeded expectations related to his scholarship. Yearly evaluations are central to the promotion and tenure process as they are in place to provide scholars with feedback. Over 5 years, Harris received no feedback from review committees that his scholarship was in question. Thus, as the chokehold would have it, Harris was invited to continue his effort to meet terms of compliance that were ever-shifting. Related to meeting standards that, as evidenced, were unclear, the review of Harris's record demonstrated the ways, again, that whiteness is rooted in epistemologies of ignorance (see Sullivan & Tuana, 2007), which demands willful ignorance, shifting scales of acceptability, and attempts to map egalitarian appearances onto racist, anti-Black structures. As noted previously, for a speaker/writer to be understood, the audience/reader must be competently able to read and receive what is spoken/written. In Harris's case, this fact of communication was not met, and placed an impossible burden on Harris to convey his value.

As a Black scholar, the white imaginary already positioned him as a nonknower, such that what he did produce was considered lower quality, extending these presuppositions, the promotion and tenure committee quantitatively ignored Harris's contributions by failing to document the impact that his scholarship made in the field. Harris's citation count was understated by more than five times its stated count. Therefore, even though scholars in the field are attempting to legitimate Harris's work, the promotion and tenure committee refused to regard him. Lastly, as research illustrates that scholars of Color are judged by a higher standard, the promotion and tenure committee took no steps to guard themselves from the inherent bias seeded in the process.

Scene III

In October of 1772, Phillis Wheatley, then 18 years old, had been in the Americas for 11 years. Wheatley was purchased by Susanna and John Wheatley, who named her after the slave ship that brought her to the Americas. According to Kendi (2016), Phillis quickly learned Latin, Greek, the classics, and English literature and wrote her first poem at age 11. Demonstrating her proficiency, skill, and talent, Wheatley published her first poem, "On Messrs. Hussey and Coffin," in 1767. Several years later, Wheatley compiled a collection of her works to publish in a press. Sensing that Phillis Wheatley's gifts, of themselves, would not sufficiently convince publishers to contract with her, John Wheatley assembled Boston's elites (read: educated White men) to engage in what might be understood as a "peer review." The following is the preface to Phillis Wheatley's collection, *Poems on Various Subjects*, a letter from her White male purchaser, John Wheatley, and the review from 18 white men. I quote the passages at length:

> PHILLIS was brought from Africa to America, in the Year 1761, between Seven and Eight Years of Age. Without any Assistance from School Education, and by only what she was taught in the Family, she, in sixteen Months' Time from her Arrival, attained the English Language, to which she was an utter Stranger before, to such a Degree, as to read any, the most difficult Parts of the Sacred Writings, to the great Astonishment of all who heard her. As to her WRITING, her own Curiosity led her to it; and this she learnt in so short a Time, that in the Year 1765, she wrote a Letter to

> the Rev. Mr. OCCOM, the Indian Minister, while in England. She has a great Inclination to learn the Latin Tongue, and has made some Progress in it. This Relation is given by her Master who bought her, and with whom she now lives. (Bartleby, 2020, paras. 5–7)

The white men regarded as "the Public" attested:

> AS it has been repeatedly suggested to the Publisher, by Persons, who have seen the Manuscript, that Numbers would be ready to suspect they were not really the Writings of PHILLIS, he has procured the following Attestation, from the most respectable Characters in Boston, that none might have the least Ground for disputing their Original. WE whose Names are underwritten, do assure the world, that the POEMS specified in the following Page, 1 were (as we verily believe) written by PHILLIS, a young Negro Girl, who was but a few Years since, brought an uncultivated Barbarian from Africa, and has ever since been, and now is, under the Disadvantage of serving as a Slave in a Family in this Town. She has been examined by some of the best Judges, and is thought qualified to write them. (Bartleby, 2020, paras. 8–9)

CDA Analysis of Wheatley

Readings of Wheatley can interpret her achievements as Black exceptionalism, lifting her not as a brilliant Black woman in her own right but as an exception to the masses of Black people, and evidence of the ways Black people could adjust to whiteness. In this assessment, whiteness maintains the defining standard by which all else was given value. The Wheatleys recognized Phillis's prodigious capacity and took delight in extending to her an education that was typically only available to White men. After a year of being purchased on the auction block, Phillis was fluent in scriptures and her slaveholding language (Jordan, 2002). As noted by Jordan (2002), Phillis Wheatley longed to show appreciation to the Wheatley's for their kindness. Jordan (2002) wrote, "She says that her poetry results from 'an intrinsic ardor,' not to dismiss the extraordinary kindness of the Wheatley's, and not to diminish the wealth of White men's literature with which she found herself quite saturated" (para. 13). Although this can true, it is worth noting that Phillis was creating something that was never expected in the Americas, a Black poet. A careful reading of Phillis Wheatley's early works shows the ways whiteness had infiltrated her episteme and spilled out over her words. Jordan (2002) identified these suffocating gestures:

> It's simple enough to track the nonsense about herself "benighted": *benighted* means surrounded and preyed upon by darkness. That clearly reverses what

> had happened to that African child, surrounded by and captured by the greed of white men. Nor should we find puzzling her depiction of Africa as "Pagan" versus somewhere "refined." (para. 14)

Whiteness as a controlling mechanism was actively scripting Black bodies and minds into the broader literature canon; it should be assumed that as an enslaved Black girl, regardless of John and Suzanna's well-meaning attributes, Phillis Wheatley would not be educated by or in the service of her cultural origins. Instead, the Wheatleys wanted to show their divine stewardship and benevolence as generous slaveholding people. Thus, readers see in Phillis's words the language of forced assimilation to whiteness, which is revealed most in the denigration of Black.

Phillis's early works recite the attitudes of slaveholding culture as onto-epistemological rescue from the void of darkness that was Africa. Importantly, enslavement does not allow for free choice—Wheatley did not have a choice in what she was introduced to or taught, as survival required compliance, and more so, the suffocation of a native, deviant tongue. Whiteness, too, is on display in the exotification of Phillis Wheatley. First, John Wheatley had to be a man of status to access the elites in the region. His ability to beacon their gathering to provide a review of Phillis Wheatley, a Black girl no less, is an example of the power of privilege to give an audience to work he believes is worthy of publication. In John Wheatley's justification, he highlighted Phillis's ability to learn the "Sacred Writings," the "English Language," and the "Latin Tongue." The subtext here is that Phillis could learn, read, and write like men. As her "Master," he was advocating for her goodness and acceptability. This situation, consistent with the scenes noted previously, exemplifies the function of whiteness as a structure of control and evaluation, and too, points to ways the project of whiteness has long been operationalized as a tool to keep Black, and nonwhite people and ideas, at bay.

A review of Phillis's work by Boston's elite would be an early indication as to how Black literacies would be assessed and interpreted in America. The process taught Phillis that she would need the white gaze's approval if she were to attain relevance. Holding power to accept and reject, the 18 elite White men owned the power to "assure the World" that Phillis's writings were, indeed, written by her. Importantly, there is no affirmation of the Black girl Phillis; instead, the emphasis is on the writings Phillis produced. This calculative decision wrests any dignifying assessment of Phillis away from the situation, as she was and would continue to be a slave girl, and as such, not quite, never human. On this premise, Blackness could never come into being, and whiteness could validate its civilizing essence by extending those nonhuman the opportunity to take on shards of whiteness. That is, Black people could continue to produce to the disposition and enjoyment of whiteness (C. Harris, 1993), but never attain full humanity, and therefore their work would always be met with suspicion.

Epistemic Asphyxiation and Breathing Elsewhere

Whiteness intends to preserve the norm, and as shown in the preceding analysis, accomplishes this through policy, standard practices, and maintaining the white gaze—that is, ensuring that white normativity surveilles nonnormative bodies, minds, and epistemologies. If the presence of nonnormative epistemologies is still and always threatened by asphyxiation, how does one draw breath, or otherwise possibilities in the wake of anti-Blackness (Sharpe, 2016)? As shown previously, for every case that manages to escape the grasp of whiteness (Harris and Wheatley), another (Woodson) is strangled by its clutch. Instances of breath and vitality call forth forms of existence that are ever mindful of context. However, tracing the histories of Black literacies and knowledge production testifies that challenging white normativity is to demand breath elsewhere. To pursue an elsewhere is to flee the concealments of whiteness, and more specifically, the comportments and routines that entrap various ways of knowing and being.

Recognizing research and scholarship as inherently fugitive opens up life-giving possibilities for those producing and those struggling for breath. Elsewhere breathing generates four questions for researchers engaging academic processes: Whom am I citing, and how am I citing them?; Where is the site of the research?; and What am I giving sight to in my work? With attention to the first question, citations are political projects that move knowledge across space and time. Citing Black epistemologies is contested work, but as mentioned previously, to be Black has often meant the absence of contribution. Citations, thus, make claims about who is capable of being a knower and the extent to which they should be known. Building on citations, the site of one's research as fugitive work, asks whose lives, whose bodies, whose voices are showing up in my work? More than noting experience, fugitive writing and research are concerned with where knowledge production is taking place and its ultimate value to the lives of real people, contexts, and situations. This component is concerned with the materiality of existence and the ethics of honoring those involved in the inquiry. Finally, fugitive writing and research should give sight to new ways of knowing and being. This recommendation recognizes Black feminist theorizations of the body as a un/doing project that stretches beyond academe.

Conclusion

My mother's offering at the top of this chapter sits with me years later for two reasons. One, she affirmed what Paul Harris, Phillis Wheatley, Ashley Woodson, and generations of scholars, creatives, and writers know about the suffocating nature of whiteness to [our] language and being. The deeply embedded, indeed, permanent nature of whiteness as an anti-Black building block of society and academe is a fixture of the current moment and future. My mother refused to gloss over this fact, and yet, while doing so, issued the reminder that I was not the problem. More than that, she told me that I was legible and that the heart of my work mattered. As whiteness problematizes Blackness and other deviant identities, fugitive claims and reminders can make room for the vivifying process that is inhaling and exhaling—breathing.

Notes

1. I follow Matias (2016) in my capitalization of *Black* and *White*, and lowercase for *whiteness*. *Black* and *White* represent racialized groups, whereas "whiteness is a state of being that goes beyond [an] individual's identity" (p. xvii). Where *white* is lowercase, it is intended to reflect the larger system of whiteness.

References

Anderson, E. (2015). The white space. *Sociology of Race and Ethnicity, 1*(1), 10–21. https://doi.org/10.1177/2332649214561306

Bartleby. (2020). Preface to *Poems on various subjects*. Bartleby. https://www.bartleby.com/150/100.html

Baszile, D. T. (2019). Rewriting/recurricularlizing as a matter of life and death: The coloniality of academic writing and the challenge of Black mattering therein. *Curriculum Inquiry, 49*(1), 7–24. https://doi.org/10.1080/03626784.2018.1546100

Butler, P. (2017). *Chokehold: Policing black men*. The New Press.

Collins, P. H. (1990). *Black feminist thought: Knowledge, consciousness, and the politics of empowerment*. Unwin Hyman.

Cooper, B. (2017). The politics of the genre of academic writing or, Professor Curtin, Professor Clegg, and the African studies network war. *Journal of Commonwealth Literature, 52*(1), 99–115. https://doi.org/10.1177/0021989415592943

Dillard, C. D. (2000). The substance of things hoped for, the evidence of things not seen. *International Journal of Qualitative Studies in Education, 13*(6), 661–681. https://doi.org/10.1080/09518390050211565

Dotson, K. (2011). Tracking epistemic violence, tracking practices of silencing. *Hypatia, 26*(2), 236–257. https://doi.org/10.1111/j.1527-2001.2011.01177.x

Dumas, M. J. (2014). "Losing an arm": Schooling as a site of Black suffering. *Race Ethnicity and Education, 17*(1), 1–29. https://doi.org/10.1080/13613324.2013.850412

Feagin, J. R. (2010). *Racist America: Roots, current realities, and future reparations.* Routledge.

Harris, C. (1993). Whiteness as property. *Harvard Law Review, 106*(8), 1709–1791.

Harris, P. (2020). *#TENUREFORPAUL.* https://sites.google.com/view/tenureforpaulharris/home

Harris, T. (2020, June 10). *Whiteness can't save us: Taylor Harris.* https://catapult.co/stories/taylor-harris-on-police-violence-racism-church-parenting-black-kids

hooks, b. (1989). *Thinking feminist, thinking Black.* South End Press.

hooks, b. (1992). *Black looks: Race and representation.* South End Press.

Hornsby, J. (1995). Disempowered speech. *Philosophical Topics, 23*(2), 127–147.

Jordan, J. (1988). Nobody mean more to me than you and the future life of Willie Jordan. *Harvard Educational Review, 58*(3), 363–375.

Jordan, J. (2002). *The difficult miracle of Black poetry in America. Something like a sonnet for Phillis Wheatley.* https://www.poetryfoundation.org/articles/68628/the-difficult-miracle-of-black-poetry-in-america

Kendi, I. X. (2016). *Stamped from the beginning: The definitive history of racist ideas in America.* Nation Books.

Lorde, A. (1978). Scratching the surface: Some notes on barriers to women and loving. *The Black Scholar, 9*(7), 31–35.

Masaoka Y., Kanamaru A., & Homma I. (2001) Anxiety and respiration. In Y. Haruki, I. Homma, A. Umezawa, & Y Masaoka (Eds.), *Respiration and emotion* (pp. 55–64). Springer.

Matias, C. (2020). *Tenure for Ashley Woodson.* https://www.gofundme.com/f/tenure-for-dr-ashley-woodson

Morrison, T. (1992). *Playing in the dark: Whiteness and the literary imagination.* Harvard University Press.

Reinsch, R. W., Goltz, S. M., & Hietapelto, A. B. (2020). Student evaluations and the problem of implicit bias. *Journal of College and University Law, 45*(1), 114–140.

Sharpe, C. (2016). *In the wake: On Blackness and being.* Duke University Press.

Spillers, H. J. (1987). Mama's baby, papa's maybe: An American grammar book. *Diacritics, 17*(2), 65–81.

Sullivan, S., & Tuana, N. (Eds.). (2007). *Race and epistemologies of ignorance.* SUNY Press.

Tuana, N. (2006). The speculum of ignorance: The women's health movement and epistemologies of ignorance. *Hypatia, 21*(3), 1–19.

Tuck, E., & Gaztambide-Fernández, R. A. (2013). Curriculum, replacement, and settler futurity. *Journal of Curriculum Theorizing, 29*(1), 72–89.

University of Missouri System. (n.d.). *Policy and procedures for promotion and tenure.* https://www.umsystem.edu/ums/rules/collected_rules/personnel/ch320/320.035_policy_and_procedures_for_promotion_and_tenure

Van Dijk, T. A. (2003). Critical discourse analysis. In D. Schiffrin, D. Tannen, & H. E. Hamilton (Eds.), *The handbook of discourse analysis* (pp. 352–371). Wiley.

Wilder, C. S. (2013). *Ebony and ivy: Race, slavery, and the troubled history of America's universities*. Bloomsbury.

Wilderson, F. B., III. (2010). *Red, white, and Black: Cinema and the structure of US antagonisms.* Duke University Press.

Wolfe, P. (2006). Settler colonialism and the elimination of the native. *Journal of Genocide Research, 8*(4), 387–409.

Wynter, S. (1994). No humans involved: An open letter to my colleagues. *Forum N.H.I.: Knowledge for the 21st Century: Knowledge on Trial, 1*(1), 42–72.

Wynter, S. (2003). Unsettling the coloniality of being/power/truth/freedom: Towards the human, after man, its overrepresentation: An argument. *The New Centennial Review, 3*(3), 257–337.

Yancy, G. (2008). *Black bodies, white gazes: The continuing significance of race.* Rowman & Littlefield.

7

DEAR WHITE PEOPLE

Black Women Students' Perspective

Kenyona N. Walker and Lori D. Patton

The summer of 2020 ushered in a racial awakening, and the United States witnessed a seismic jolt in perceptions and attitudes regarding race. The recent murders of unarmed Black people appeared to have interrupted the psyche of many. Viewers observed the video of George Floyd's death at the hands of a white officer as fellow officers failed to intervene alongside the shooting of Ahmaud Arbery by two white men. These racist events caught society's attention. Sandwiched between the loss of Floyd and Arbery was the shooting death of Breonna Taylor. Sleeping peacefully in her own home, Taylor succumbed to a barrage of bullets from police officers who later blamed her for her own death. Taylor did not garner the same attention as Arbery and Floyd, likely because mass audiences did not witness her death. Further, the politics of race and gender made Taylor's life particularly disposable.

The outcry over Taylor's death at the hands of police has since garnered national attention as top law enforcement officials involved in the case held no one accountable for her murder, but charged one officer for endangering tenants in an adjacent apartment. That Taylor was treated as an afterthought is a logical outcome of an intersectional failure rooted in white supremacy, where Black women are often forgotten (Cooper, 2020; Crenshaw et al., 2015). The idea of Black women being invisible and unremarkable is not new, but instead normal. As authors of this chapter and as Black women who are highly experienced with navigating academic terrains, we challenge the notion of Black women as afterthoughts and claim this chapter as one space for making Black women's experiences known and firmly centered.

This chapter is inspired by Patton and Haynes (2020), two Black women scholars who wrote "Dear White People: Reimagining Whiteness in the Struggle for Racial Equity." In their article, Patton and Haynes used the work of critical race legal scholar Derrick Bell as a springboard to speak directly and poignantly about the role white people should play in educating themselves about and actually working to dismantle white supremacy. Most important, they offer ways to understand the operation of whiteness. Their key premise is that whiteness resists its own undoing, is *not* invisible, is imperfection, and that despite these things, white people have "everything to gain by reimagining their whiteness" (p. 43).

In the context of this chapter, the phrase "Dear White People" is apropos because it references the title of the 2014 film (later a Netflix series) by Justin Simien. In the film, Samantha, a biracial, Black woman college student at a predominantly white institution (PWI) hosts a radio show in which she names and addresses the problematic behaviors of white people that she and other Black students regularly experience at their university. Elected as the head of a traditionally Black residence hall, Samantha uses her platform to disrupt the racial status quo. Similar to the main character Samantha in the film, this chapter is presented from the perspectives of Black women college students committed to disrupting the status quo. Inspired by Patton and Haynes (2020) their letters name and challenge the intersectional failures that Black women students endure in predominantly white academic spaces. Furthermore, the letters explore the many ways in which the identified issues can be addressed.

This chapter does three things. First, it writes Black women into existence despite overarching discourses and systems that promulgate and ultimately rely on their invisibility to maintain the status quo. Second, the chapter allows white people, particularly those who want and need, to think more deeply about their role in addressing the concerns Black women face on college campuses. Third, this chapter presents an opportunity for white people to reflect on Patton and Haynes's (2020) article and consider what it would mean to reimagine whiteness in a way that is committed to unlearning stereotypes and tropes and seeing Black women (and all marginalized communities) through a lens that honors their humanity. Such a task requires knowing and understanding how Black women traverse spaces that were never intended for them. This chapter is presented by Black women in higher education who mentor Black women students, but written in the form of several letters from a group of Black women students. We will explore how Black women navigate and operate in classroom spaces and college places that, through whiteness, challenge their mere presence.

Black Women Students Speak

Dear White People

We are a group of Black women students attending your PWI. We gather together regularly to provide each other with support. We are each other's sounding board. We listen to one another. When one of us experiences pain and hurt, we all empathize and grapple with these emotions. We have been meeting for quite some time. We do not broadcast it because we purposefully wanted and needed a space carved out and occupied by us, where we could be our whole selves. We represent a wide range of academic interests, have diverse majors, and come from different social and economic classes. Despite the diversity within our experiences, backgrounds, and academic pursuits, our conversations reveal time and again the white supremacy we regularly endure.

Recently our conversations have focused on the persistent racial crisis in our country. We have talked about the murders of Ahmaud Arbery, George Floyd, Breonna Taylor, and, more recently, Ma'Khia Bryant. The lives of countless other Black people who continue to lose their lives over the most mundane circumstances break our hearts every single time. The pain never subsides, instead prompting anguish as we anticipate the next instance in which a white person and/or a system claims another Black person's life. These wounds are even more palpable as we consider our own mortality. We are educated women. We are mothers, sisters, daughters, aunts, cousins. We are researchers, scholars, teachers, and so much more. Yet we sit daily with the weight of knowing that no matter our accomplishments and contributions, we are not immune from the fate experienced by Sandra Bland, Korryn Gaines, Atatiana Jefferson, and Breonna Taylor. More disheartening is the absence of immunity that would be extended to us in any attempt to defend ourselves. This reality is hard. State-sanctioned violence is hard.

When our community of Black women gather and unpack what is occurring in the world around us, we also discuss institution-sanctioned violence (Patton & Njoku, 2019). We discuss how being at this institution has resulted in us being targeted and subjected to a more subtle kind of violence. As Black women we are accustomed to having our voices silenced and experiences ignored. Although none of us have experienced physical violence on our campus or in the classrooms, we have experienced racial and gender epistemic violence, suppression, censoring, and silencing (Dominigue, 2015; Jones & Shorter-Gooden, 2003; Lewis et al., 2013; Walker, 2020). In fact, although the COVID-19 virus has presented additional barriers to our education, it has been somewhat of a relief for us. When the campus closed down for in-person activities, we no longer had to be subjected to an environment that was not designed for our existence.

We read the university's antiracist statements regarding a renewed focus and commitment to use teaching, research, and reflection to enact equity, social justice, and inclusion. Statements such as these are often all talk with no action. Will you follow through with all of the recommendations made by the new task force? How will you know if Black women students' experiences are adequately addressed? To ensure this occurs, we want to explain how official and unofficial university policies have negatively affected us. Not only are we centering our experiences, but we are also outlining our expectations with regard to espoused antiracist statements. These expectations and the suggestions we provide apply broadly to the university's leadership, faculty, and staff with whom we interact. These suggestions will guide you toward creating a more welcoming environment for us, other marginalized groups, and all of the rest of the students in our campus community.

Black women have disparate collegiate experiences when compared to our white peers (Borum & Walker; 2012; Callan, 2018; Shabazz, 2015). The majority of our administration, faculty, and peers are white (National Center for Education Statistics [NCES], 2020). We know whiteness confers privilege to some and disadvantages to others. In fact, whiteness creates the rules, patterns, and ideas of what is normal, whereas white supremacy ensures the benefits of whiteness are accrued and maintained. Is the university willing to address structural barriers rooted in whiteness to benefit us and future students? We are skeptical because white supremacy has existed for centuries. Yet white administration, faculty, staff, and peers are just waking up (or so they claim) to the long-standing reality that Black people consistently face racism, which for us is further compounded by sexism. They are also beginning to learn how complicit they have been and continue to be, even as they claim to be our allies and coconspirators. They are beginning to learn about white institutional presence, which is the undetectable ways in which their whiteness has operated in educational places and spaces (Gusa, 2010).

The university statement suggests that through teaching, research, and reflection many of our concerns will be addressed. Educators in our nation are grappling with the notion that American history has been whitewashed. Policymakers are creating policies to stop the accurate retelling of history, thus invalidating some of our historical experiences. How will you address these attempts to erase our histories? How will you hold resistant faculty accountable for teaching the truth, rather than allowing them to uphold institutional and historical structures that place their comfort above our realities?

The following collection of letters are written to our white administrators, faculty, and student peers, whose actions and inactions have impacted our college experiences. The letters also serve as an opportunity for you to learn about how some of us have experienced the environments created and maintained. We are pushing the boundaries of what you envision your work to be given the recent antiracist statement. We are unpacking our experiences and providing recommendations to promote your accountability for revising, creating, and enacting change on this campus via policies and practices.

Dear White Administrators

As Black women students on this campus, we first met at the Black culture center (BCC) during orientation week. This place is near and dear to us and one of the few places where we see people like us. There are events and programs that specifically cater to our interests and needs as Black women students. In this space, we have established a sister circle and have frequent interactions with Black faculty and staff (Croom et al., 2017; Steele, 2017). As such, our Black culture center provides us with a sense of belonging. In fact, Michelle Obama (2018) fondly reflected on the benefits she derived from her center when she was a student at Princeton and her ability to make connections. Likewise, the center on this campus is extremely valuable to us. We want to ensure the increased emphasis on "diversity" and sensitivity to systematic racism are framed in a way that is supportive for us as Black women. We do not want to be subjected to erasure, nor should our experiences fall through the cracks. Across the country there have been many BCCs established to address diversity and inclusion across minoritized groups (Harris & Patton, 2017; Hefner, 2002). In some instances, BCCs undergo name changes to demonstrate an institution's focus on the needs of all minoritized students, where the label that captures our identity is subtly removed.

Our BCC matters to us. It is a place where we are free to be ourselves and our burdens can be shared (Hord, 2005; Patton, 2006; Walker, 2020). These are not self-imposed burdens, but rather those placed on us as a result of our learning environment. In the broader campus spaces, we are often silenced or censored or expected to speak on behalf of all Black people. We are consistently navigating hypervisibility and invisibility, and frankly, we are tired. We do not experience that in our BCC (Dominigue, 2015; Jones & Shorter-Gooden, 2003; Lewis et al., 2013; Walker, 2020). The BCC plays a significant role in our positive educational experiences (Patton, 2006). In our center, we reflect on and share our experiences, we learn about our culture, and our collective identities are embraced.

Because we are not welcomed in the larger university spaces, our center is not only a place where we belong, but also where we have leadership opportunities. As you attempt to take up diversity, equity, and inclusion

(DEI) efforts, remember the BCC helps us form a sense of community as Black women at this university. We recognize that the center is open to all students, as it should be. However, in the future if this is one of the places where you envision blending and addressing the issues of all minoritized students, please know that this will be disruptive to our well-being. Our center should not lose its identity, but instead be afforded the resources to continue its work in providing space, support, advocacy, and representation for Black students, while partnering with other entities and offices across campus.

Outside of the BCC

There are few spaces where we are fully safe to let down our guard. We have to be prepared for racist acts even in the spaces where we should find respite. We cannot even eat in our residence halls without looking out of place (Whitford, 2018). As Black women students, our very presence can antagonize and threaten white peers and staff. We are falsely accused of attacking our white women peers, when in fact we are targets (Estrada, 2017; Miller, 2020). For example, a Black woman student, Chennel Rowe, had a typical college roommate disagreement with her white roommate, Breonna Brochu. Brochu was charged with criminal mischief after smearing her bodily fluids on multiple pieces of Rowe's belongings, including her toothbrush. This example highlights one of the many incidents that demonstrate how residence halls can be unsafe spaces for Black women. Indeed, the spaces outside of our BCC are experienced as racially radiated environments where we are constantly under surveillance while not being protected. Sometimes it feels like there is no reprieve for us as Black women students.

As undergraduate students, our randomly assigned academic advisors are the gatekeepers to our college success and potentially our future careers. Many of our graduate advising experiences are no different. Unfortunately, our interactions with our academic advisors are lackluster at best. As a distinct group, Black women students often experience poor advising, particularly in PWIs (Domingue, 2015). We can discern disbelief in our academic capabilities. When we meet, some white undergraduate advisors are disinterested and appear apathetic as they simply mark our meeting from their to-do list. Yet when we overhear our white peers discussing advising experiences, their experiences are different. And they are not scheduled for unnecessary remedial classes like we are. They find their advisors to be accessible and proactive in ensuring that they are in the right classes and complete their degrees on time.

As Black women students our negative experiences with academic advisors are more pronounced when we pursue degrees in science, technology, engineering, and mathematics (STEM), due to our race and genders (Borum & Walker, 2012). We have dealt with advisors who have attempted to counsel us out of our programs into one that they believe is easier or better suited for us (Borum & Walker, 2012; Walker, 2020). In these situations, our white advisors do not see us as academically capable of pursuing and earning a STEM-related degree. In general, white academic advisors seemingly lack cultural competence. They appear disinterested, apathetic, and/or disconnected from the needs of Black women students, creating unnecessary barriers to our persistence. In their positions of power, they do not empower us as Black women students. We find their actions to be oppressive. Their inability to appropriately advise us requires us to engage in additional efforts as we piecemeal our academic plans by seeking academic guidance from our peers or other university officials. This is unacceptable.

There are many places on our campus that we experience as unwelcoming. We see this in the large and small details in which space is used. For example, when we walk into our large lecture halls or libraries, there are pictures of past presidents, faculty, or donors prominently displayed, all of whom are white. We also see artwork that depicts wistful images, aesthetically pleasing sculptures, or nostalgia-provoking pictures of past times based on the university's history. We do not see artwork created by Black artists displayed. Even more troubling, we rarely see cultural artwork that showcases or represents Black women. These highly visible depictions of life and people, in places where we access knowledge, do not include us and it further fuels our invisibility (as cited in Reed & Lohnes, 2019). Such representation, we realize, is only symbolic in nature. However, we find no joy in learning spaces where whiteness is hyper-depicted.

Exposure to diverse experiences and perspectives is essential to fully understand the reality of the world. Conversely, exposure to positive and accurate depictions of those who look like us is crucial to the positive development of our identities in academic spaces. All students need to see artwork that honors their culture and experiences, including Black women, and not just in Black-defined spaces (e.g., culture centers).

We are bold, brave, and intelligent women. In addition to images of widely known Black women, display historical and contemporary Black women researchers, artist, physicians, and so on that represent the spectrum of our contributions. We want to see artwork created to honor the experiences and accomplishments of all Black women, with some curated by Black women artists in highly visible places. Doing so is not difficult or unreasonable. In fact, Pennsylvania State recently installed a 16-foot bust of a Black woman at the entrance of their campus. The bust, *Brick House*, was created by Simone Leigh, a Black woman artist (*U.S. News*, 2020).

How wonderful it will be when we see such artistry and representation on this campus.

Dear White Administrators, when we saw your outward responsiveness and statements regarding systematic racism, we thought, "It's about time!" But beyond talking, we expect to see action (McNair et al., 2020). You have to create, implement, and reinforce policies and practices that will fundamentally matter to us as Black women. So many of the policies and practices, written and unwritten, negatively affect us. They are rooted in Eurocentric values that have been perpetuated for centuries and infringed upon our college experiences. Disrupting a system that has largely benefited you, we acknowledge, is a challenge. We want to assure you, however, that any policy or practice you revise, disrupt, or change that benefits us will benefit all students. They will benefit this institution. If you are truly invested in all students, which includes Black women students, then we expect our recommendations and strategies to be implemented with urgency.

If you are truly committed to recruiting a diverse student population and addressing the issues we have identified, your commitment to recruiting and retaining diverse staff and faculty should be a key priority, particularly Black women. This is advice that has been shared with institutions for several decades, but is often ignored and dismissed. We believe that the same efforts you use to recruit Black athletes to increase revenue for our institution are the same efforts you should make to increase the overall Black student population at this institution. Your actions should be driven by a desire to enact equity within your faculty and student population to the point where the institution is no longer considered a PWI, and instead a model of diverse representation in higher education.

As Black women we are specifically advocating for an increased presence of Black women leaders, faculty, and staff. On average, Black women make up only 3% of full-time college faculty (NCES, 2020). We expect to see more Black women representation at all levels of the institution, especially as our faculty and institutional leaders. Their representation is crucial for us because they bolster sense of belonging and connectedness among Black women students. Sometimes you excuse this advice away by claiming that you cannot find talented Black women to work at this institution. This excuse is overwhelmingly offensive. Black women faculty are excellent mentors and often are our only true advocates (Patton & Harper, 2003). The handful of Black women faculty here have mentored us, but they also extend themselves to other students. Black women faculty not only invest their time in mentoring us, but some of them split that time between us and combating racism and discrimination while attempting to gain tenure, with very little support (Rucks-Ahidiana, 2019). They are spread thin and exhausted from providing support that their white and/or male colleagues are not expected to do.

One way for you to show your investment in us is to not only hire more Black women but invest in those currently here and those you recruit. They should be equitably paid. Unfortunately, Black women faculty compensation is significantly less than their white and Black male peers; this is especially true in PWIs (Sule, 2009). Without a doubt, our Black women faculty will be called upon to connect with, advise, mentor, serve on committees, and lead many of the new campus-wide efforts that emerge from the increased focus on DEI. Despite these meaningful contributions to this university, Black women faculty's efforts are not acknowledged in their compensation or during the tenure process (Fields, 2020). This recommendation of equitable compensation is important as we reflect on white faculty who do not face similar issues. White students see faculty like themselves each day and they have a wide selection of mentors from which to choose.

You can address this recommendation by crafting policies specifically designed to hire and increase Black women's presence on campus and ensure that practices are put in place to support them. When you begin recruitment, do not rely on graduate-level Black women to be contingent faculty (Porter et al., 2020). Instead, invest in Black women because we are deserving. We want to be student representatives on the search committee and the committee itself should be diverse. We expect you to connect with organizations, institutions, and agencies that support Black scholars and faculty. In some instances, you should anticipate doing a targeted search. An adjacent option is to start investing in our more senior Black women doctoral students and postdoctoral fellows on campus by creating a pipeline for them to become faculty and leaders at this institution.

Similar to our experiences as Black women students, Black women faculty are recruited but are difficult to retain because they face the same macroaggressions and microaggressions that we do (Kelly et al., 2017). Black women university leaders are not immune to these circumstances. In fact, Lesley Lokko, a college dean, resigned from her position after only 10 months. She cited lack of support and structural racism as the reasons behind her departure. Our university must outline, implement, and enforce clear policies that disrupt the negative climate that exists and causes barriers to Black women's retention. As you consider actualizing our antiracist statement, now would be an excellent time to do an environmental audit to understand the experiences of Black women on this campus. Ask them what they experience as barriers and what support would retain them. We urge you to seek a greater level of awareness regarding barriers that exist in the classroom and with colleagues, and to design and implement appropriate policy.

The personal experiences we have articulated as Black women students and those of others like us require that any university-created racial or diversity training be refined and customized where appropriate. We advocate for an ongoing, mandated implicit and explicit bias training for all students, faculty, and staff. This training should review our country's past as it relates to racism, bias, and privilege, and how these structures operate in education. Next, the training should explore each participant's implicit bias, while providing alternative historical facts that can be used to disrupt inaccurate, uninterrupted, and unmitigated individual conclusions, like the 1619 Project. It explores the legacy of slavery while celebrating the contributions of Black people in the United States (Hannah-Jones et al., 2019). Faculty and staff should be exposed to content that provides an explicit guide to creating antiracist classroom environments, including antiracist course material and how to address racist behavior. Lastly, similar to other mandates, the university should require faculty, students, and staff to endorse a code of conduct that would require them to engage in certain actions when racist behavior occurs. We realize this as just one of multiple efforts this institution could and should implement.

Faculty and staff should have at least one annual professional development goal that addresses racial equity, diversity, and inclusion. Likewise, faculty and staff's midyear and annual evaluations should review and address the extent to which the goals were accomplished. The university should have a zero-tolerance policy as it relates to the enactment and allowance of racist behavior. In order to understand compliance and adherence to these policies, the university should include race-specific questions on the student evaluations of faculty. These questions should provide administrators with an understanding of the climate and environment faculty create, whether or not they use racially sensitive and accurate content. Lastly, faculty should continue to be exposed to coaching and support as they engage in this work.

We have outlined various ways we experience racially charged spaces in and beyond the classroom. We know there are instances where racism occurs simply because of naïve faculty, staff, and peers. There are times when we report these issues and, in some circumstances, we have to report them to people we believe support the perpetrators. The implementation of a comprehensive racial equity, diversity, and inclusion mandate could increase the campus community's awareness, while also addressing some of the issues related to confronting racism. We as Black women students have experienced covert and overt racist behavior from faculty, staff, and our peers. We have gone through the channels that the university has outlined to address them. Unfortunately, it appears that nothing ever comes of our grievances that holds anyone accountable for offending the standards this campus espouses about racial justice.

Given the recent antiracist statement, what will be different the next time you receive a report from one of us? Will you simply use surface-level research, teaching, and reflection strategies to address faculty? Or will you follow through on your commitment to further antiracist work, even when it means concrete accountability for those who threaten this work? Addressing this concern means that when we make a complaint regarding racism or discrimination, you will follow up on it. We will no longer suffer in our silence. We have been asked to do that far too long. As Black women students, we are a protected class. We do not expect be penalized for speaking up. When an investigation has been opened, investigate! It is not our job to gather the information. And when our report is found to be true, follow through with the necessary discipline and put the antiracist statement to work. Consider these events during promotion, tenure, and when other universities are looking to hire your faculty. Don't pass along racist faculty to impact our peers in other universities.

Dear White Faculty

When you do not take a personal stance against racism, you single-handedly create racially charged classroom environments, where verbal violence is enacted upon us Black women students. Whiteness is perpetuated in the classrooms that you lead where knowledge is held and conferred by white people. Have you ever listened to our classroom discussions? Many times, you have asked for reactions or opinions about information you presented. When we add our voices to the conversation, we are typically interrogated by our white peers (Walker, 2020). Although their whiteness may be invisible to you, it is painfully visible to us as they use it to censor our voices. You do not interrupt these microaggressive behaviors, instead moving on with the discussion as if nothing occurred. When our white peers speak, you nod your head and your body language affirms their conclusions and interpretations, only. When you disregard our contributions to classroom dialogue, we feel censored and unheard. For some of our peers this behavior can have consequences for academic persistence (Walker, 2020). In addition, this behavior creates an environment that allows the behavior to continue unchecked. It also models unacceptable behavior for all of your students and continues the erroneous and damaging narrative that Black women are inferior. We encourage you to do your antiracist work. Perhaps this would yield a different experience for us.

Some of you teach our entry-level, required undergraduate courses. Did you know that the readings and materials you assign for your undergraduate classes are inaccurate and problematic? Most completely exclude Black people and more specifically Black women. It is clear that you have not done your work to be more intentional about course content. In psychology classes we hear about the "Fathers of Psychology," which routinely include white men like Erik Erikson, Sigmund Freud, and Carl Rogers, to name a few. Periodically, you may highlight Kenneth B. Clark, who conducted the infamous "Doll Study." But what about his wife, Mamie Phipps Clark, a Black woman psychologist, whose research was just as impactful? Why not highlight the contributions of contemporary Black women psychologists like Beverly Daniel Tatum, whose research is routinely leveraged and cited because she explores race and education, a topic to which all students should be exposed?

For those of you who teach our English courses, consider your selected literature. Why does literature featuring Black people or written by us only serve as a footnote or add-on? If the course is taught during the spring semester, you might highlight Black creativity during Black History Month. Otherwise, you fail students by promoting an inaccurate narrative. The narrative that runs throughout these materials is that Black people have not contributed anything to the field or that these contributions are insignificant. We think good pedagogical decisions on your part would include Black authors like James Baldwin or Langston Hughes. But there are also Black women writers and creatives like Maya Angelou, Zora Neale Hurston, Toni Morrison, and Alice Walker. The list is expansive, yet Black women writers are rarely if ever featured in your courses. The lack of inclusion on your part signals to us that these Black women writers are invisible to you, that we as Black women students are invisible to you.

Faculty, when you include film-based resources or assignments in your class, you often use racially insensitive content that promotes rather than disrupts the notion of Black inferiority. Other times, your film selection highlights the sacrifice of a white person who saves a Black person from the racial terror of other white people. Your use of these films glorifies white people, without identifying and addressing racism and white supremacy. We are tired of watching films that glorify white people, romanticize racism, and pacify white guilt. Perhaps these critiques would emerge in the class discussion if you were open to such critical dialogue. Not surprisingly, many of the films that you select are produced and directed by white men. Did you know that there are also prominent Black women filmmakers from whom you could select to expand your course content? Chinonye Chukwu, Ava DuVernay, Kasi Lemmons, and Shonda Rhimes are just a few that come to mind. Dirshe (2020) suggested, "When we remove blackness from the bottom, everybody gets to be seen," (para. 8). Exploring and using racially appropriate learning materials is a benefit to all students.

Further, White Faculty, did you know that allowing students to choose their group for classwork and assignments is one of many popular practices that ensures the exclusion of Black women or ensures we are picked last? In particular, in STEM-based classes we feel routinely excluded given the intersections of our race and gender (Dortch & Patel, 2017; Johns, 2018). You consistently allow our white peers to select each other, whereas we work alone or with fewer group members. As a result, our white peers can leverage the collective knowledge of their group members as they support one another to succeed and pass your course (Walker, 2020). This process is exclusionary and deprives our white peers of the opportunity to work with us and witness the value that Black women bring to their work.

Also, did you know that you engage in white complicity when you confer the benefits of whiteness to our white peers, while we feel the delegation of the disadvantages of our race. Embedded in your pedagogical practices is the reinforcement of the negative consequences of race. For example, we listen to your lectures in biology class when you teach about the biological nature of race, where whiteness is not explored as a race, yet it has created the concept of race and the rules that apply to the construct itself (Leonardo, 2009). Our white peers' understanding of race is aided by your teaching, where you reify the impenetrable structures of race and racism, that we have to fight against. You can address racist instruction by debunking myths of intellectual inferiority as socially constructed ideas that were fostered to protect whiteness. You do not have to be complicit. Instead, be intentional about addressing racism by using your teaching platform to dismantle lies.

Dear White Faculty, sense of belonging is critical for all college students. Without sense of belonging Black students will not thrive on campus and may be faced with early departure (Duran et al., 2020; Francique, 2018; Hurtado & Alvarado, 2015). The relationships that students have with educators is strongly connected to their academic performance. As Black women students, we are invisible in your classes, yet hypervisible when we do not attend. Honestly, we have contemplated dropping some of your courses because each session is triggering and weighs on our mental and emotional health. Did you know your courses sometimes make us sick? We mean this in a literal, not figurative, sense. One of the ways you make it difficult for us in the classroom is by confusing us for one another, simply because we are Black women. It is your responsibility to learn our names and correctly say them (Kohli & Solórzano, 2012; Michael, n.d.).

Say our names correctly. Week after week we sit in your class, only to hear you mispronounce our names or rename us by calling us another person's name. This is dehumanizing, especially as we listen to you use the correct enunciation for white students. This occurred often during slavery, when enslaved Africans were renamed like other property that was purchased by their masters (Hodge, n.d.; Roy et al., 2019). When you engage in this racist practice in the classroom, it makes us feel even more marginalized and disconnected to the spaces in which we learn. Our names are not interchangeable labels. They have meaning, and they connect us to our culture.

Can you develop a trained eye to see when a Black woman student is being marginalized? Can you be thoughtful about opportunities that benefit us? When you are contacted by a colleague regarding an employment or research opportunity, do you ever think to recommend us? When a colleague says they are looking for someone who is a "good fit," do you help them see a Black woman as a potential candidate? You never forward our names to other colleagues who have open positions. When you have a great research idea you never consider working with one of us or inviting us to join your research team. When we share a research idea that needs a little faculty guidance, you do not work with us. You do not publish with students like us. You do not advocate for Black women students. As a faculty member you have the ability to mentor and guide all students, but we do not receive much guidance and support from you. We never warrant the support and you unfortunately fail to invest in us in any meaningful way. We have become accustomed to making our own way and being successful despite the challenges. And even when you see us as capable, you view these successes as one more reason to restrict your support (Shaw, 2017).

Dear White Faculty, let us recommend a few next steps for you. Create and implement more inclusive classroom policies. For example, given what we shared about being excluded from groups, create a group-assigning policy to use when assigning project work groups. This policy is especially important in programs where students attend the same classes across several years in a cohort. Embed a randomized group selection process in your course dashboard to reduce instances where we get left out. When groups are assigned, request feedback from all group members by using group peer evaluation forms. This will allow us as well as our peers to provide specific feedback regarding the distribution of work, what we found valuable regarding group processes, and what behaviors were detrimental to the group. This would afford us the opportunity to report how we were included or excluded. And it can assist you in refining group projects to ensure equity is achieved as it relates to individual efforts, benefits, and so on.

Although we understand that all of us may struggle to appropriately articulate names at times, it is not acceptable for you to continue to misname us. This is microaggressive behavior (Torres-Mackie, 2019). At minimum, we spend a semester with you. That means you see us at least once a week for

12–16 weeks. That is more than enough time for you to learn our names and learn how to pronounce them. You may already have a picture of us; please commit our image to memory and commit to using meaningful ways to connect our faces with our names. Invest in a name pronunciation app or ask us to pronounce our names while you write them out phonetically. Once you write a name out, record yourself pronouncing it correctly until you have it. Please do this for us and our peers, especially international students. None of us should have to generate a nickname or other type of name to make it easier for you to call us by our names.

We realize faculty do not know everything about every race and culture. Nor are they experts in these areas. Yet engaging in cultural humility will allow you to acknowledge and own the fact that you do not have all the answers and that others can increase your understanding. Whiteness has always embedded the belief that white people know everything or that they are owners and producers of knowledge. In order to be the faculty we deserve, the attitude of intellectual superiority has to be rooted out. We recommend collaborating with other scholars to locate culturally sensitive and appropriate texts for our assigned readings. Use these experiences to incorporate text, films, content, and so on into course content, which would allow us to see ourselves reflected in the learning process. Furthermore, identify knowledgeable people, such as Black women, as guest speakers to present content. This practice would allow Black women students to see others like them and assist non-Black students in seeing multiple representations of Black women and diverse perspectives on course materials.

We recommend that you interrogate the impacts of race and gender in your course content and when you lecture, using widely accepted conclusions. For example, critical race theory offers a lens that inspects the often-unseen role of race, power, and the law in the experiences of Black people. Likewise, intersectionality provides a framework that explores the combined effects of overlapping minoritized identities. Applying these and similar frameworks to your work with us as Black women students will assist you in developing a keen eye to spot the ways in which oppression and privilege work and how they are denied in the content that is used to educate us.

Conclusion

White Administrators and Faculty, we would like to summarize our thoughts. As Black women students we are a unique and amazing group. However, what has recently and repeatedly occurred in our nation to Black women is reflected in our collegiate experiences. We are excited that our university has decided to offer a verbal commitment to dismantling systemic racism within its practices, policies, and faculty. Yet we do not expect to see change until changes actually occur. Renowned scholar James Baldwin (n.d.) once said, "Not everything that is faced can be changed. But nothing can be changed until it's faced" (p. 2). This letter is a memorialization of our sustained racialized experiences at this university. And it is our demand that you acknowledge and address the racist practices that have affected our educational success. Reflect on your faculty hiring decisions as you engage in realizing the university's antiracist statement. We deserve better than racially insensitive instruction or practices. We expect to see evidence of the university's follow-through on staff and faculty accountability. Furthermore, we intend to see the implementation of interventions designed to include our voices, opinions, and experience as Black women students in the spaces and places on this campus.

As Black women students, we will continue to enjoy our positive and affirming experiences at our BCC. This sacred space will continue to remain our "safe space," in the midst of the university's antiracist efforts. We will continue to welcome our non-Black peers into this space. However, our center will operate as a place where we receive support, advocacy, and representation. We will remain diligent in connecting with the Black faculty here as their guidance and mentorship has proven valuable to us, and as they continue to share academic and career opportunities with us.

You have heard our concerns regarding more visible representation of people like us on campus and we expect you to respond accordingly. We expect to celebrate new artwork that you will have displayed across campus that honors us as Black women. And we know that you will create an opportunity for us to meet the Black women artists who curated these pieces. As you have seen, these could serve as entryways into conversations about privilege, oppression, and Black contributions to the broader society. We are worth this well-deserved, yet delayed investment.

We patiently await your invitations to have us sit on faculty search and hiring committees, as a way to ensure increased representation of Black women is realized in the faculty selections at this university. Your revamped recruitment and retention policies will ensure that there is a consistent pipeline of talented Black women scholars who can mentor and guide us as we pursue our education. Based on recent university assertions we expect to see our current Black women faculty honored for their contributions and compensated in an equitable manner, because their service to us and this university is a critical component to our retention and the well-rounded experiences of peers.

In these letters, we have highlighted your anti-Black and racist behavior perpetuated against us in the classroom. Now is the time for you to reckon and reconcile your past actions. You can no longer cultivate racially charged spaces, where our white peers are comfortable excluding and demeaning us as Black women. Nor will you engage in the racist practice of interchanging our names or renaming us because it is not important enough to you to commit our names to your memory. We have put you on notice that you will be called out and reported. Additionally, as you move toward antiracist behavior that mirrors the university's statement, we look forward to reading and viewing more diverse material in your classes that pays special attention to Black women.

As we close this letter, we want you to know that we expect change. We will not settle for antiracist verbalizations of change without action. Similar to our white peers, we fully intend to benefit from new policies and practices that will be created to address these suppressive behaviors that we have outlined. We want to experience the concrete ways in which research, teaching, and reflection will produce the change. We have provided you with a view through our lens, as Black women students. Receive this as an opportunity for this university to honor our presence on this campus.

References

Baldwin, J. (1962, January 14). As much truth as one can bear. *The New York Times*, pp. 11–12.

Borum, V., & Walker, E. (2012). What makes the difference? Black women's undergraduate and graduate experiences in mathematics. *Journal of Negro Education*, *81*(4), 366–378. https://doi.org/10.7709/jnegroeducation.81.4.0366

Callan, R. D. (2018). *Black, female, first-generation college students: Perceptions of academic persistence* [Doctoral dissertation, University of Miami]. ProQuest Dissertations and Theses Global.

Cooper, B. (2020, June 4). Why are Black women and girls still an afterthought in our outrage over police violence? *Time*. https://time.com/5847970/police-brutality-black-women-girls/

Crenshaw, K., Ritchie, A. J., Anspach, R., Gilmer, R., & Harris, L. (2015). *Say her name: Resisting police brutality against black women* (Brief No. 1). African American Policy Forum. http://aapf.org/sayhernamereport

Croom, N. N., Beatty, C. C., Acker, L. D., & Butler, M. (2017). Exploring undergraduate Black womyn's motivations for engaging in "sister circle" organizations. *NASPA Journal About Women in Higher Education*, *10*(2), 216–228. https://doi.org/10.1080/19407882.2017.1328694

Dirshe, S. (2020). What does it mean to "center Black people"? *The New York Times*. https://www.nytimes.com/2020/06/19/style/self-care/centering-blackness.html

Domingue, A. D. (2015). "Our leaders are just we ourself": Black women college student leaders' experiences with oppression and sources of nourishment on a predominately white college campus. *Equity & Excellence in Education, 48*(3), 454–472. https://doi.org/10.1080/10665684.2015.1056713

Dortch, D., & Patel, C. (2017). Black undergraduate women and their sense of belonging in STEM at predominately white institutions. *NASPA Journal About Women in Higher Education, 10*(2), 202–215. https://doi.org/10.1080/19407882.2017.1331854

Duran, A., Dahl, L. S., Stipeck, C., & Mayhew, M. J. (2020). A critical quantitative analysis of students' sense of belonging: Perspectives on race, generation status, and collegiate environments. *Journal of College Student Development, 61*(2), 133–153. https://doi.org/10.1353/csd.2020.0014

Estrada, S. (2017, December 19). *Ex-student who used bodily fluids to harass Black roommate, avoids hate crime charge.* DiversityInc. https://www.diversityinc.com/ex-student-used-bodily-fluids-harass-black-roommate-avoids-hate-crime-charge/

Fields, L. N. (2020). *A case study of the experiences of Black female faculty at research-intensive schools of social work* (Publication No. 2185) [Doctoral dissertation, Washington University]. Arts & Sciences Electronic Theses and Dissertations. https://openscholarship.wustl.edu/cgi/viewcontent.cgi?article=3227&context=art_sci_etds

Francique, A. (2018). Is excellence inclusive? The benefits of fostering Black female college athlete's sense of belonging. *Journal of Higher Education Athletics & Innovation,* (3), 48–73. https://doi.org/10.15763/issn.2376-5267.2018.1.3.48-73

Gusa, D. L. (2010). White institutional presence: The impact of whiteness on campus climate. *Harvard Educational Review, 80*(4), 464–498. https://doi.org/10.17763/haer.80.4.p5j483825u110002

Hannah-Jones, N., Elliott, M., Hughes, J., Silverstein, J., & New York Times Company. (2019). *The 1619 Project: New York Times Magazine, August 18, 2019.* New York Times.

Harris, J. C., & Patton, L. D. (2017). The challenges and triumphs in addressing students' intersectional identities for Black culture centers. *Journal of Diversity in Higher Education, 10*(4), 334–349. https://doi.org/10.1037/dhe0000047

Hefner, D. (2002, February 14). *Black cultural centers: Standing on shaky ground?* Diverse Issues in Higher Education. https://diverseeducation.com/article/1952/

Hodge, A. (n.d.). *Mispronouncing your non-white students' name is a racist act: A guide for understanding a microaggression for white teachers working with students of color.* https://medium.com/@msalihodge/mispronouncing-your-non-white-students-names-is-a-racist-act-567dc33a8bdf

Hord, F. L. (Ed.). (2005). *Black culture centers: Politics of survival and identity.* Third World Press.

Hurtado, S., & Alvarado, A. R. (2015). *Discrimination and bias, underrepresentation, and sense of belonging on campus.* https://www.heri.ucla.edu/PDFs/Discriminination-and-Bias-Underrepresentation-and-Sense-of-Belonging-on-Campus.pdf

Johns, R. O. (2018). *A phenomenological investigation of the lived experiences of female African American undergraduate STEM students at an elite predominately white institution* (Publication No. 1550153720) [Doctoral dissertation, College of William and Mary]. W&M ScholarWorks. http://dx.doi.org/10.25774/w4-d0zd-zr91

Jones, C., & Shorter-Gooden, K. (2003). *Shifting: The double lives of Black women in America.* HarperCollins.

Kelly, B. T., Gayles, J. G., & Williams, C. D. (2017). Recruitment without retention: A critical case of Black faculty unrest. *Journal of Negro Education, 86*(3), 305–317. https://doi.org/10.7709/jnegroeducation.86.3.0305

Kohli, R., & Solórzano, D. G. (2012). Teachers, please learn our names!: Racial microagressions and the K–12 classroom. *Race Ethnicity and Education, 15*(4), 441–462. https://doi.org/10.1080/13613324.2012.674026

Leonardo, Z. (2009). *Race, whiteness, and education.* Routledge.

Lewis, J. A., Mendenhall, R., Harwood, S. A., & Huntt, M. B. (2013). Coping with gendered racial microaggressions among Black women college students. *Journal of African American Studies, 17*(1), 51–73. https://doi.org/10.1007/s12111-012-9219-0

McNair, T. B., Bensimon, E. M., & Malcom-Piqueux, L. (2020). *From equity talk to equity walk.* Jossey-Bass.

Michael, A. (n.d.). *Getting names right.* https://www.teachingwhilewhite.org/blog/2017/10/2/getting-names-right

Miller, J. R. (2020, December 29). Cops storm Black student's dorm after white roommates allegedly file false report. *New York Post.* https://nypost.com/2020/09/29/black-freshman-allegedly-targeted-with-false-police-report-that-led-to-raid/

National Center for Education Statistics. (2020). *The condition of education 2020* (NCES 2020-144). https://nces.ed.gov/pubs2020/2020144.pdf

Obama, M. (2018). *Becoming.* Crown.

Patton, L. D. (2006). Black culture centers: Still central to student learning. *About Campus, 11*(2), 2–8. https://doi.org/10.1002/abc.160

Patton, L. D., & Harper, S. R. (2003). Mentoring relationships among African American women in graduate and professionals schools. In M. F. Howard-Hamilton (Ed.), *Meeting the Needs of African American Women* (New Directions for Student Services, no. 104, pp. 67–78). Jossey-Bass. https://doi.org/10.1002/ss.108

Patton, L. D., & Haynes, C. (2020). Dear white people: Reimagining whiteness in the struggle for racial equity. *Change: The Magazine of Higher Learning, 52*(2), 41–45. https://www.tandfonline.com/doi/full/10.1080/00091383.2020.1732775

Patton, L. D., & Njoku, N. R. (2019). Theorizing Black women's experiences with institution-sanctioned violence: A #BlackLivesMatter imperative toward Black liberation on campus. *International Journal of Qualitative Studies in Education, 32,* 1162–1182. https://doi.org/10.1080/09518398.2019.1645908

Porter, C. J., Moore, C. M., Boss, G. J., Davis, T. J., & Louis, D. A. (2020). To be Black women and contingent faculty: Four scholarly personal narratives. *The Journal of Higher Education, 91*(5), 674–697. https://doi.org/10.1080/00221546.2019.1700478

Reed, R., & Lohnes, J. (2019). Tripping the Black fantastic at a PWI: Or how Afrofuturist exhibitions in an academic library changed everything. *Alexandria: The Journal of National and International Library and Information Issues, 29*(1/2), 116–129. https://journals.sagepub.com/doi/pdf/10.1177/0955749019876383

Roy, K., Ali, Z., & Kumar, M. (2019). *The racist practice of mispronouncing names.* NPR. https://www.kuow.org/stories/a-rose-by-any-other-name-would-not-be-me

Rucks-Ahidiana, Z. (2019, June 7). The inequities of the tenure-track system. *Inside Higher Ed.* https://www.insidehighered.com/advice/2019/06/07/nonwhite-faculty-face-significant-disadvantages-tenure-track-opinion

Shabazz, A. A. (2015). *Black women, white campus: Students living through invisibility* [Doctoral dissertation, Indiana University]. IUScholarWorks. https://hdl.handle.net/2022/19819

Shaw, M. D. (2017). Supporting students who struggle successfully: Developing and institutionalizing support for Black undergraduate women. In L. D. Patton & N. N. Croom (Eds.), *Critical perspectives on Black women and college success* (pp. 200–212). Routledge. https://doi.org/10.4324/9781315744421

Simien, J. (2014). *Dear white people: A guide to inter-racial harmony in "post-racial" America.* Atria/37Ink

Steele, T. (2017). Retaining Black female college students: The effects of meritocracy on their ideas of success. *College Student Affairs Leadership, 4*(1), Article 7. http://scholarworks.gvsu.edu/csal/vol4/iss1/7

Sule, T. (2009). Black female faculty: Role definition, critical enactments, and contributions to predominately white research institutions. *NASPA Journal About Women in Higher Education, 2*(1), 93–121. https://www.researchgate.net/publication/250147975_Black_Female_Faculty_Role_Definition_Critical_Enactments_and_Contributions_to_Predominately_White_Research_Institutions

Torres-Mackie, N. (2019, September 29). Understanding name-based microaggressions. *Psychology Today.* https://www.psychologytoday.com/us/blog/underdog-psychology/201909/understanding-name-based-microaggressions

U.S. News. (2020, November 10). Massive Simone Leigh sculpture now greets Penn students. https://www.usnews.com/news/entertainment/articles/2020-11-10/massive-simone-leigh-sculpture-now-greets-penn-students

Walker, K. (2020). *At what cost: The patterns of persistence of first-generation, urban, Black female, college students* [Unpublished doctoral dissertation]. The Ohio State University.

Whitford, E. (2018, October 30). Smith finds no bias in incident that roiled campus. *Inside Higher Ed.* https://www.insidehighered.com/news/2018/10/30/investigation-finds-no-policy- violations-when-police-were-called-black-student

8

HOW WHITENESS WERQS IN LGBTQ CENTERS

Alex C. Lange, Antonio Duran, and Romeo Jackson

Roughly 50 years ago, the first spaces dedicated to gay and lesbian students emerged on college campuses. These offices came into existence alongside movements for sexual and gender justice in the United States (Graves, 2018). In 1969, the first student space came about at the University of Minnesota, and the first staffed resource center arose at the University of Michigan (Marine, 2011). Additionally, recent decades have seen an increase in institutional efforts to teach campus communities about issues facing the LGBTQ community, often dubbed "Safe Zone" training (Woodford et al., 2014). Through these dedicated spaces and training efforts, college and university administrators have committed resources to ensure some level of inclusion for LGTBQ students in postsecondary education.

Although there has been a rise in resources like LGBTQ centers and safe zone training, potentially signaling positive changes for LGBTQ students on college campuses, scholars have also highlighted how these services benefit certain students over others (Marine & Nicolazzo, 2014). Notably, research has shown how LGBTQ+ centers revolve around white norms (Catalano & Tillapaugh, 2020). The same critiques exist for training curriculum dedicated to educating potential allies about sexual and gender diversity (Fox, 2007; Lange, 2019). In essence, whiteness circulates through these institutional commitments to LGBTQ inclusion and must be interrogated more thoroughly. Thus, it is imperative to examine how LGBTQ work within higher education institutions centers whiteness through its practices and policies. In this chapter, we use critical whiteness studies (CWS) in conjunction with queer and trans frameworks to expose how LGBTQ work on college campuses foregrounds whiteness. In addition to the CWS frameworks mentioned in Part One of the text, we briefly review theories of homonormativity and transnormativity. After discussing the relevant frameworks, we interrogate whiteness through three practices and organizational features of LGBTQ centers: training curricula, programming, and staffing/budgeting of such offices. Through our review of these features, we offer connections and disruptions to whiteness for each.

Complicating CWS With Relevant Queer and Trans Frameworks

In the first section of this book, chapter authors provided a vital introduction into concepts relative to CWS. Although this serves as a meaningful overview of the CWS scholarship, we were presented with a challenge when attempting to use a CWS lens when examining LGBTQ communities on college campuses. Namely, although scholars have mobilized critical whiteness studies to address the pervasiveness of white supremacy and whiteness in postsecondary education (e.g., Cabrera et al., 2016; Foste & Irwin, 2020), this body of literature has not largely examined how whiteness intersects with other minoritized social groups beyond cisgender, straight white men and women.

Despite some researchers having explored the gendered dynamics connected to how whiteness operates (e.g., Cabrera, 2018; Ozias, 2017), CWS lacks substantial theorizing when it comes to LGBTQ topics. To be clear, queer and trans scholars have long sought to uncover the whiteness that has manifested in queer and trans communities (e.g., Conrad, 2014; Ma'ayan, 2011; Vaid, 2012; Ward, 2008). Yet CWS higher education scholars have not explored the ways that whiteness manifests in LGBTQ communities. Therefore, to set a foundation for the investigation at the heart of this chapter, it is imperative to describe two concepts that expose how respectable, mainstream ways of being and acting queer and trans are inherently whitewashed: homonormativity and transnormativity. We will articulate how these concepts will allow us to interrogate how LGBTQ work on college campuses reproduces whiteness in queer and trans communities, later illustrating the connections to the CWS concepts introduced at the start of this text.

Homonormativity

Defined as "the myriad ways in which heterosexuality is produced as a natural, unproblematic, taken-for-granted, ordinary phenomenon" (Kitzinger, 2005, p. 478), heteronormativity is omnipresent in the United States. As LGBTQ people have been systematically excluded and othered in U.S.

society, some queer and trans people responded to this marginalization by seeking to assimilate and accommodate heteronormative cultures (Duggan, 2003). The resulting phenomenon is referred to as *homonormativity*. Articulated by Duggan (2003), homonormativity

> does not contest dominant heteronormative assumptions and institutions, but upholds and sustains them, while promising the possibility of a demobilized gay constituency and a privatized, depoliticized gay culture anchored in domesticity and consumption. (p. 50)

Homonormativity helps to explain how white, mainstream LGBTQ movements strive for inclusion in heteronormative societies by desiring rights like marriage equality, while at the same time not fundamentally questioning and disrupting the social system that privileges heterosexuality. For instance, rather than fighting for inclusion into existing arrangements of marriage rights (e.g., partner recognition, tax benefits), why not challenge the benefits that come with these arrangements for all to access them?

Significantly, and relevant to our examination, homonormativity is deeply intertwined with whiteness. Thus, it is not only that LGBTQ people attempt to be accepted in a world that systematically advantages heterosexuality. Instead, they also mimic and desire a particular kind of heterosexuality: that of a white middle class (Duggan, 2003). Homonormativity consequently obscures any movements and advocacy that "challenge the entrenchment of the transparent White subject at the heart of lesbian and gay politics" (King, 2009, p. 274), because of its very entanglements with whiteness. Those queer people who take up a homonormative ethic desire to be seen and read as respectable in their pursuit of assimilationist presentations; also seen as respectability politics, it is seemingly synonymous with whiteness (Duggan, 2003), given the desire to align with dominant white heterosexual norms. In higher education, scholars have taken up the concept of homonormativity to critique the whiteness present in LGBTQ communities, including in LGBTQ centers. For instance, the work of Jourian (2017), Pryor and Hoffman (2020), and Self and Hudson (2015) has all highlighted how homonormativity exists within LGBTQ centers, examples that we attend to in subsequent sections.

Transnormativity

In addition to homonormativity, transnormativity offers a useful framework for understanding the intersection of transgender politics and whiteness. For Glover (2016), "Transnormativity [is] a process shaped by adherence to respectability politics, heteronormative standards and class privilege" (p. 340). Transnormativity centers medical transition from one binary sex to another as *the* trans experience and forecloses the many other ways trans people come to know and express their gender. That is, white, straight, trans people who adhere to a binary gender performance are celebrated as the right kind of trans people. In turn,

> Transnormativity creates even greater difficulty for those who are gender nonconforming, genderqueer, bigender, or agender—and often subsumed under the term "transgender"—in that transnormativity does little to dismantle existing gender binaries and thus cannot sufficiently address the particular challenges that gender nonconforming, genderqueer, bigender, or agender people face on a daily basis. (Glover, 2016, p. 344)

By doing "little to dismantle existing gender binaries," transnormativity also does little to dismantle whiteness. The importing of whiteness through settler colonialism is deeply connected to ridged sex/gender binaries (Driskill, 2016). Through settler colonialism and whiteness, gender becomes an either/or between being a man/woman, female/male, or feminine/masculine (Lugones, 2008). Transnormativity helps scholars understand the ways some trans people and—by extension—some trans discourses are suitable for integration into white U.S. culture and society.

Furthermore, whiteness underlines transnormative understandings of trans people as it reproduces definitions of the right kind of trans person that are inaccessible or undesirable to many trans people. In an attempt to intervene in transnormativity discourses about her positionality, Mock (2014) wrote,

> I have been held up consistently as a token, as the "right" kind of trans woman (educated, able-bodied, attractive, articulate, heteronormative). It promotes the delusion that because I "made it," that level of success is easily accessible to all young trans women. Let's be clear: It is not. (p. xvii)

As a Black trans woman, this reflection from Mock is particularly crucial as it shows the ways that even trans people of color who adhere to respectability politics and heteronormative standards can be included in white mainstream trans discourses. Although transnormativity remains underused in higher education research, the work of Nicolazzo (2016) alongside Black trans students in higher education is helpful in understanding how these students make sense of transnormativity. Nicolazzo highlighted how Black trans students make sense of their raced and gendered identities and experiences as they navigate white LGBTQ centers. Findings revealed Black trans students felt excluded in both Black cultural centers and LGBTQ centers due to anti-trans and anti-Black discourses.

Pulling It Together

Together, homonormativity and transnormativity examine how individuals and institutions align with and adhere to standards forwarded by white, majoritized communities and ways of thinking. Related to white normativity, homonormativity and transnormativity challenge white queerness and transness as the dominant norm and representation of these communities. For instance, LGBTQ campus centers often serve many white students while framing outreach to students of color as an additional effort (Marine, 2011). In this way, white queer people's behaviors, emotions, and knowledge become the center for several campus-based centers.

Homonormative and transnormative frameworks account for the ways whiteness shows up and functions in queer and trans communities so that we as educators might challenge whiteness's grip on LGBTQ spaces. Both frameworks help scholars understand how logics of whiteness, genderism, and capitalism grow and fester in queer and trans communities, further framing white queer people and white queerness/transness as inherently innocent. Specifically, this manifestation of innocence is not the typical presumption of a lack of guilt but instead one of purity and superiority (Schick & St. Denis, 2005). White innocence—and white queer and trans innocence, in our case—acts as a cloak that protects one from being accused of perpetuating or being complicit in racism (Applebaum, 2010). For instance, white queer students can claim to understand all oppression because of their minoritized sexuality or gender identity, among potential others (Ward, 2004). This conflation of oppression however proves problematic as it builds a false sense of understanding the experiences of other forms and axes of oppression, particularly of racially minoritized communities. Said otherwise, queer and trans individuals' claims that holding a marginalized identity allows them access to understand all forms of oppression permits them to maintain their self-perception of being innocent and nonracist. Thus, through the lens of white innocence, LGBTQ center staff and the students they serve can either avoid responsibility for addressing race and racism by focusing on sexual- and gender-based oppression or gloss over the differences between those forms of marginalization and race-based oppression. Using the concepts from Part One of the book and the frameworks we presented previously, we now discuss how these frameworks help us interrogate LGBTQ campus center practices.

Critically Interrogating Whiteness in Practices Meant to Serve Queer and Trans College Students

Using concepts from CWS, homonormativity, and transnormativity, we turn our attention to standard practices and organizational structures of and within LGBTQ resource centers. Specifically, we examine gender and sexuality training, center programming, as well as budget and hiring practices. We describe each component of LGBTQ center work, name its connection to whiteness, and offer ways practitioners might interrupt these forms and patterns of dominance. First, we discuss how safe zone or safe space trainings center whiteness and white college students through homonormativity and white normativity. Second, we outline how the normative cadre of programs offered by LGBTQ center staff are rooted in white norms, making white LGBTQ students the center of concern and relegating queer and trans people of color to the margins. Finally, we offer provocations using a CWS lens related to staff hiring and retention as well as center budgeting. Though not an exhaustive list of considerations, we believe these are practices any LGBTQ staff member might take up for examination.

Safe Zone Training

Typically housed under LGBTQ centers when they are present on campus, safe zone (also referred to as *safe space* or *ally*) training and curriculum are intended to benefit LGBTQ college students by improving campus climates (Woodford et al., 2014). Namely, these trainings educate individuals about the LGBTQ community, frequently covering topics such as terminology, history, and good practices in serving LGBTQ individuals. More often than not, these trainings target students, staff, and faculty who are not part of the LGBTQ community and may have limited comprehension of LGBTQ subject matters. They vary in their timing, with some training sessions lasting an hour all the way up to daylong experiences. Finally, some campuses have multiple types of training, with LGBTQ centers developing workshops that attend to specific communities (e.g., Trans 101) or topics (e.g., Pronouns 101).

Naming Whiteness

On the surface, safe zone training is frequently regarded as a good practice in LGBTQ student affairs work (Poynter & Tubbs, 2008; Woodford et al., 2014). However, when viewed through a lens of white normativity, homonormativity, and transnormativity, several concerns arise. For instance, although these training sessions do produce beneficial outcomes by communicating knowledge of LGBTQ communities (Woodford et al., 2014), they can also perpetuate harm, especially because nonwhite, nongay, and noncisgender people are not often centered in these educational opportunities (Fox, 2007; Fox & Ore, 2010; Lange, 2019; Self & Hudson, 2015), the reason being that educators facilitate these training sessions to provide a base level of understanding regarding LGBTQ communities, which means that they regularly provide what attendees are typically looking for (i.e., lists of definitions and quick—and simple—actions they can do to support LGBTQ individuals). This simplicity means that these trainers reinforce white racial comfort, providing less nuance regarding race, class, or gender, focusing on dominant memberships in each social category.

Connected to the previous point, safe zone training sessions rarely cover the differences that LGBTQ people of color, those with disabilities, or those with other minoritized identities face in their experiences. In some cases, discussions of trans realities, much less trans people of color, are overlooked. Consequently, when taking into consideration white normativity, the baseline for LGBTQ humanity becomes white queer people, and specifically, white cisgender gay men. Additionally, LGBTQ history topics may focus on issues like the road to marriage equality, reinforcing homonormative ideas of queerness (Duggan, 2003). Thus, queerness is seen as normative, unraced, and natural—phenomena rooted in whiteness. Additionally, another way that whiteness is replicated through these trainings is represented in the product of many of these educational opportunities: stickers. Safe zone trainers regularly provide those who attend with a sticker after they complete the educational program. The intention of these stickers is to visually showcase the amount of support present for LGBTQ people on campus. And yet the appearance of safe zone stickers (as well as the content of the training sessions themselves) is frequently associated with *safety* for white gay cisgender students while leaving all those marginalized along axes of race, gender, disability, and nation status as unmarked (Fox, 2007). Safe zone stickers do little by the way of shifting climates to be more attentive to the intersecting systems of racism, trans oppression, and heterosexism—although these visual markers are often heralded as the symbol of LGBTQ inclusion on college campuses. Hence, several issues exist related to how safe zone training sessions may reinforce white normativity and homonormativity.

Interrupting Whiteness

To interrupt the whiteness inherent within safe zone curricula, practitioners must first recognize that training itself does not lead to liberation. A 1-hour or even an all-day training will not be enough to transform the nature of institutions as being rooted in white supremacy, heteronormativity, and trans oppression (Lange et al., 2021). The danger that results from these trainings is that they often default to simplifying the nature of oppression for LGBTQ individuals given these time constraints, which results in them reinforcing whiteness by centering white LGBTQ people. When designing training sessions, those facilitating should make a concerted effort to focus the workshop's content on giving people the tools necessary to disrupt institutional policies and practices that serve to disenfranchise LGBTQ individuals. Importantly, practitioners should use an intersectional lens (Crenshaw, 1989) to attend to the overlapping nature of oppressive systems. Rather than only focusing time on learning terminology or white LGBTQ history, trainers might help attendees understand how one's multiple social identities produce different experiences of marginalization within and beyond LGBTQ communities. Doing so would then challenge the normative assumptions related to whiteness that campus professionals have about LGBTQ communities.

Moreover, in one's content, professionals should always start by centering queer and trans people of color (QTPOC) in training curricula. Rather than merely mentioning the biography, lived experiences, and histories of QTPOC occasionally, curriculum designers should integrate these aspects throughout as the common thread of the educational opportunity. Doing so would interrupt the white normative standards that are largely found in gender and sexuality training sessions. For instance, one might make all examples, case studies, and images focused on QTPOC. Although these recommendations are a good place to begin, they are not exhaustive, and we encourage readers to continue to reflect on how they can address whiteness in their work from a CWS perspective, as well as one rooted in queer and trans frameworks.

Programming

Events and programs are commonplace on college campuses to support LGBTQ students. Common programming examples include National Coming Out Day (NCOD), Pride Weeks or Months, and Transgender Day of Remembrance. In this section, we illuminate the ways whiteness is centered in these programs and offer some possibilities for disrupting whiteness. We start with NCOD. Research has shown that the "coming out" experiences of QTPOC depart from coming out narratives of white gay/queer people (Duran, 2019). That is, instead of coming out through a public announcement, people of color report a coming in process that centers on self-actualizing one's identity for oneself (e.g., Tillman-Kelly, 2015). NCOD events tend to focus on proclaiming a queer and trans identity in a visible way to others. For example, while Romeo was an undergraduate student, they helped organize an NCOD event that included LGBTQ people walking through a blue door in the center of campus as a celebration. A display such as this may exclude how some QTPOC make sense of a nonstraight or cisgender identity, thus centering white understandings of coming out. We offer this example not to suggest whether it was the right or wrong approach, as that reproduces a false binary. Rather, we seek to illuminate how well intended events such as these may exclude QTPOC.

Perhaps the most constant programming centering trans people of color is Transgender Day of Remembrance (TDOR). TDOR is an annual event held on November 20th to honor trans people killed due to antitrans violence nationally and globally. Trans people of color are disproportionately most of the names listed each year since such accounts have been recorded (Gossett et al., 2017). What are the implications when one of the only canonized events for trans people of color highlights their death/dying? This pattern suggests that trans people of color are only important to center through programming in death. Lastly, college campuses may also hold week- or monthlong celebrations hosting several programs that may include 1 day centering race or may invite a speaker who is a queer and/or trans person of color. This regulation of race to a day effectively maintains whiteness while purporting to engage race in a meaningful way. However, it is problematic as these practices make white queer and trans people raceless and position QTPOC experiences as marginal.

Naming Whiteness

Taken together, one can see that various programs often associated with LGBTQ services take white normativity as the starting (and ending) point. Although one-off programs that purport to center QTPOC exist, they regulate conversations of race or racism to a day. More problematically, the programs most dedicated to addressing race are tied to the death and dying of QTPOC, especially Black trans women. In turn, this limits the possibilities for QTPOC life and places white queer realities at the center.

By relegating only certain programs as dedicated to QTPOC, LGBTQ services uphold white-dominant ways of being such and render others outside of the white frame invisible (Duran, 2021). Although it remains important to create spaces for QTPOC, what are the implications when students of color must create spaces that center race away from institutionally supported LGBTQ spaces? This move solidifies the whiteness embedded within formal LGBTQ spaces, thus pushing race/ism and people of color outside of the frame of who is queer and trans. As a reinforcement of white normativity, LGBTQ services fail to transform institutionally supported LGBTQ spaces to decenter whiteness; instead, in a move to white innocence, practitioners point to QTPOC-created spaces as a sign of racial inclusion despite their emergence from noninstitutional spaces. White innocence, homonormativity, and transnormativity help illuminate how whiteness and middle-class respectability become the center of queer life on campus colleges.

Lastly, visibility has become central to white gay/queer politics and is key to many of the events outlined in this section. However, visibility as a key tool for queer and trans social change fails to consider how hypervisibility (particularly for Black trans women/femmes) increases the likelihood of violence enacted on the body (Gossett et al., 2017). Visibility then becomes transformed into an individual choice instead of questioning systems that oppress queer and trans people.

Interrupting Whiteness

Programs that examine the intersection of race and queerness are key to unlearning and interrupting the insidious nature of whiteness in queer and trans services. Additionally, we encourage staff to not only create spaces for QTPOC but to also interrogate why institutionally backed LGBTQ spaces, clubs, and programs in centers are seen as unwelcoming for these students. Moreover, it is important to honor and remember trans people of color lost to antitrans and racist violence. Yet it is key to create programs that honor the ways that trans people of color create spaces of life and possibilities in spite of a global climate of antitransness and white supremacy. In addition, central to interrupting whiteness is making whiteness visible. One of the ways to do this is to create programs for white queer and trans students to interrogate their whiteness.

Some important questions to consider when attempting to interrupt whiteness are what might it mean to center the most marginalized of queer and trans people in LGBTQ services? What do guidelines for being in institutionally backed LGBTQ spaces look like when they center Black trans women as the predominant users of the space? For staff, how do our services center whiteness?

Staffing and Budgeting in LGBTQ Centers

In addition to programming, it is critical to also examine the operations of LGBTQ centers through their staffing and budget practices. In 2002, reportedly 70 LGBTQ resource centers existed on college campuses, staffed by either part- or full-time staff members (Sanlo et al., 2002); by 2020, over 275 such offices existed (Consortium of Higher Education LGBT Resource Professionals [Consortium], 2020). Although professional staffing and budgeting remain broader competencies for higher education and student affairs professionals (American College Personnel Association [ACPA] & National

Association of Student Personnel Adminstrators [NASPA], 2015; Wells, 2015), scholars have paid less attention to this work specifically for LGBTQ+ campus centers (Leider, 2002; Sanlo et al., 2002; Tillapaugh & Catalano, 2019). Leider (2002) described the kinds of staffing structures that should exist within a center, including full- and part-time staff members, volunteers, and supervision structures. Sanlo et al. (2002) discussed the different funding sources centers could draw from within the higher education and nonprofit ecosystem, a conversation being had across functional areas of student affairs given declines in state appropriations (Tandberg & Laderman, 2018). Graduate assistants responsible for coordinating LGBT resource centers reported a precarious financial situation for their offices, noting how they often received meager budgets for their spaces (Tillapaugh & Catalano, 2019).

Naming Whiteness

Studies of staffing in LGBTQ centers and offices suggest white people predominantly hold positions at several levels of the organization, including those roles that lead these centers' efforts (e.g., Catalano & Tillapaugh, 2020; Consortium, 2018). Although numbers do not represent destiny, white queer and trans individuals became the experts on forming and sustaining LGBTQ centers (Sanlo, 2000; Sanlo et al., 2002), inscribing white norms into the very makeup of these centers and organizations (Ward, 2008). As earlier chapters detail, whiteness functions as an ideology that upholds white dominance while oppressing racially minoritized people. This ideology leads to the inscription of white norms in LGBTQ centers, among other places on campus (Gusa, 2010). Additionally, white norms—and thus white normativity—reproduce themselves when new staff members of any race are brought on. Pressure exists to support the interests and comforts of white people in these spaces (i.e., white students and alumni; Gusa, 2010; Vaid, 2012). White queer and trans people also make moves to white innocence, sometimes noting their inability to speak to or their lack of competence surrounding issues beyond gender and sexuality (Catalano & Tillapaugh, 2020). This preservation of epistemologies of ignorance—the willful not knowing about race and racism—by white individuals in LGBTQ centers makes many feel out of place in these spaces (e.g., Duran, 2019).

Interrupting Whiteness

Interrupting whiteness in LGBTQ campus centers is not a simple matter of hiring more racially minoritized staff members. Given their sexual or gender identities, administrators often assume a staff member holding a minoritized identity provides one with enough knowledge to serve all students of a particular community on campus (Jennrich & Kowalski-Braun, 2014). However, as Tillapaugh and Catalano (2019) pointed out, "representational politics will never be successful" (p. 133). Having safe zone curricula and programming that are conscious of the realities of whiteness will require staff members with multiple racial literacies—or "the ability to examine critically and recursively the ways in which race informs discourses, culture, institutions, belief systems, interpretive frameworks, and numerous facets of daily life" (Winans, 2010, p. 476)—including those who can name and challenge whiteness. These staff members will most likely be QTPOC given the pernicious effects of whiteness on such communities (Ward, 2008); in other words, because whiteness presses on these lives most visibility, these individuals are most familiar with its shape and effects. Therefore, those with hiring authority within and over these LGBTQ centers must explore who runs these spaces and the frameworks with which they do their work. Tokenizing QTPOC should not be the strategy; intentional hiring and retention strategies must be the way forward.

For those centers with multiple staff members, how might hiring staff consider how whiteness benefits specific individuals over others? Specifically, how might certain applicants have been previously positioned—because of their privileged racial status—to acquire certain qualifications and credentials that might have been out of reach to others? For instance, if one desires national conference presentations as a marker of competence, consider how well-resourced white people may have access to greater financial capital and wealth to attend such opportunities compared to people of color. Additionally, hiring staff may consider how the concept of *fit* factors into their hiring discussion. As others point out (Ashlee, 2019; Browning & Palmer, 2019), higher education and student affairs professionals deploy the concept of fit to exclude people of color and maintain whiteness in higher education organizations. As resource center professionals assign QTPOC initiatives to a particular staff member, might these professionals also assign antiracist and white-conscious initiatives to a staff member, as well? Intentionally imbuing discussions of whiteness in the organizational chart and center staff meetings as an ongoing item may serve as initial practices for staff members to take up in their ongoing work to disrupt whiteness.

Additionally, CWS affords practitioners with frameworks that might inform the budgeting processes undertaken in these offices. If budgets reflect plans "for getting and spending money to reach specific goals" (Dropkin et al., 2007, p. 3), those with budget-setting authority within LGBTQ centers might conduct a goals audit of their programs and services. In addition to staff time dedicated to particular aims, how much does one's programming budget reflect these aims? How much money goes to programs that serve everyone compared to particular communities and efforts? For instance, does programming for events such as NCOD dwarf funding for programs for

QTPOC? How might practitioners interrupt white normative logics that promote claims that programs like NCOD are for *everyone* when they, in fact, center a particular student or community's experience of coming out? Such initiative-based budgeting and accounting may better disrupt white innocence in LGBTQ centers and forward efforts to dismantle oppression at this level.

Conclusion

LGBTQ campus centers are "situated within spaces born of protest and yet beholden to universities and administrators interested in maintaining order on campus" (Self & Hudson, 2015, p. 238). These offices—and those that work within them—may align with white norms and ideologies, at times, out of self-preservation. However, this does not preclude people and organizations from countering whiteness, particularly those that purport to be antioppressive. LGBTQ practitioners and centers must "theorize, organize, and politicize" their work beyond gender and sexual identities (p. 240). In this chapter, we took concepts from CWS paired with homonormativity and transnormativity to discuss the ways whiteness shows up in LGBTQ spaces and communities. By examining campus-based staffing, education, and programming practices, we describe current connections to whiteness and considerations for disrupting whiteness moving forward.

To achieve an intersectional vision and future, one that focuses on addressing both the simultaneity and distinctive nature of oppression, whiteness must be challenged not only among those who hold dominant identities but also those white individuals with nonracial minoritized identities. In a time where LGBTQ movements would claim victory on major aims such as same-sex marriages, hate crime legislation, and military inclusion, it remains imperative to remind ourselves as queer and trans people how whiteness shapes broader goals for queer and trans assimilation and liberation (Conrad, 2014; Duggan, 2003; Glover, 2016). As authors, we hope this chapter inspires practitioners working within LGBTQ centers and LGBTQ students to consider how whiteness may be named, confronted, and disrupted.

References

American College Personnel Association & National Association of Student Personnel Administrators. (2015). *Professional competency areas for student affairs educators*. https://www.naspa.org/images/uploads/main/ACPA_NASPA_Professional_Competencies_FINAL.pdf

Applebaum, B. (2010). *Being white, being good: White complicity, white moral responsibility, and social justice pedagogy.* Lexington Books.

Ashlee, K. C. (2019). "You'll fit right in": Fit as a euphemism for whiteness in higher education hiring practices. In B. J. Reece, V. T. Tran, E. N. DeVore, & G. Porcaro (Eds.), *Debunking the myth of job fit in higher education and student affairs* (pp. 193–216). Stylus.

Browning, H. O., & Palmer, P. M. (2019). Code word FIT: Exploring the systemic exclusion of Professionals of Color in predominantly white institutions. In B. J. Reece, V. T. Tran, E. N. DeVore, & G. Porcaro (Eds.), *Debunking the myth of job fit in higher education and student affairs* (pp. 147–165). Stylus.

Cabrera, N. L. (2018). *White guys on campus: Racism, white immunity, and the myth of "post-racial" higher education.* Rutgers University Press.

Cabrera, N. L., Franklin, J. D., & Watson, J. S. (2016). Whiteness in higher education: The invisible missing link in diversity and racial analyses. *ASHE Higher Education Report, 42,* 7–125. https://doi.org/10.1002/aehe.20116

Catalano, D. C., & Tillapaugh, D. (2020). Identity, role, and oppression: Experiences of LGBTQ resource center graduate assistants. *Journal of Student Affairs Research and Practice.* Advance online publication. https://doi.org/10.1080/19496591.2019.1699104

Conrad, R. (Ed.). (2014). *Against equality: Queer revolution, not mere inclusion.* AK Press.

Consortium of Higher Education LGBT Resource Professionals. (2018). *2018 self-study report.* https://lgbtcampus.memberclicks.net/assets/docs/Self%20Study%20Report%202018.pdf

Consortium of Higher Education LGBT Resource Professionals. (2020). *Find an LGBTQ center.* https://www.lgbtcampus.org/find-an-lgbtq-campus-center

Crenshaw, K. (1989). Demarginalizing the intersection of race and sex: A Black feminist critique of antidiscrimination doctrine, feminist theory, and antiracist politics. *University of Chicago Legal Forum, 8*(1), 139–167. https://chicagounbound.uchicago.edu/uclf/vol1989/iss1/8

Driskill, Q. (2016). *Asegi stories: Cherokee queer and two-spirit memory.* University of Arizona Press.

Dropkin, M., Halpin, J., & LaTouche, B. (2007). *The budget-building book for nonprofits: A step-by-step guide for managers and boards* (2nd ed.). Jossey-Bass.

Duggan, L. (2003). *The twilight of equality?: Neoliberalism, cultural politics, and the attack on democracy.* Beacon Press.

Duran, A. (2019). Queer *and* of color: A systematic literature review on queer students of color in higher education scholarship. *Journal of Diversity in Higher Education, 12*(4), 390–400. https://doi.org/10.1037/dhe0000084

Duran, A. (2021). *The experiences of queer students of color at historically white institutions: Navigating intersectional identities on campus.* Routledge.

Foste, Z., & Irwin, L. (2020). Applying critical whiteness studies in college student development theory and research. *Journal of College Student Development, 61*(4), 439–455. https://doi.org/10.1353/csd.2020.0050

Fox, C. O. (2007). From transaction to transformation: (En)countering white heteronormativity in "safe spaces." *College English*, *69*(5), 496–511. https://doi.org/10.2307/25472232

Fox, C. O., & Ore, T. E. (2010). (Un)covering normalized gender and race subjectivities in LGBT "safe spaces." *Feminist Studies*, *36*(3), 629–649. https://www.jstor.org/stable/27919125

Glover, J. K. (2016). Redefining realness?: On Janet Mock, Laverne Cox, TS Madison, and the representation of transgender women of color in media. *Souls*, *18*(2–4), 338–357. https://doi.org/10.1080/10999949.2016.1230824

Gossett, R., Stanley, E. A., & Burton, J. (Eds.). (2017). *Trap door: Trans cultural production and the politics of visibility*. The MIT Press.

Graves, K. (2018). The history of lesbian, gay, bisexual, transgender, queer issues in higher education. In M. B. Paulsen (Ed.), *Higher education: Handbook of theory and research* (Vol. 33, pp. 127–173). Springer.

Gusa, D. L. (2010). White institutional presence: The impact of whiteness on campus climate. *Harvard Educational Review*, *80*(4), 464–490. https://psycnet.apa.org/doi/10.17763/haer.80.4.p5j483825u110002

Jennrich, J., & Kowalski-Braun, M. (2014). "My head is spinning": Doing authentic intersectional work in identity centers. *Journal of Progressive Policy & Practice*, *2*(3), 199–212. https://caarpweb.org/?p=1438

Jourian, T. J. (2017). Trans*forming college masculinities: Carving out trans*masculine pathways through the threshold of dominance. *International Journal of Qualitative Studies in Education*, *30*(3), 245–265. https://doi.org/10.1080/09518398.2016.1257752

King, S. (2009). Homonormativity and the politics of race: Reading Sheryl Swoopes. *Journal of Lesbian Studies*, *13*(3), 272–290. https://doi.org/10.1080/10894160902876705

Kitzinger, C. (2005). Heteronormativity in action: Reproducing the heterosexual nuclear family in after-hours medical calls. *Social Problems*, *52*(1), 477–498. https://doi.org/10.1525/sp.2005.52.4.477

Lange, A. C. (2019). Envisioning new praxis for gender and sexuality resource centers: Place-consciousness in post-secondary education. *Thresholds in Education*, *42*(1), 59–73. https://academyedstudies.files.wordpress.com/2019/11/th42_1langefinal.pdf

Lange, A. C., Krestakos, B., Sylvester, A., & Bravo, N. (2021). Cultivating intersectional consciousness in undergraduate students: Considerations and suggestions. In S. Marine & C. E. Gilbert (Eds.), *Critical praxis in higher education & student affairs: Social justice in action* (pp. 107–120). Stylus.

Leider, S. J. (2002). Managing ancillary staff. In R. Sanlo, S. Rankin, & R. Schoenberg (Eds.), *Our place on campus: Lesbian, gay, bisexual, transgender services and programs in higher education* (pp. 167–170). Greenwood.

Lugones, M. (2008). *The coloniality of gender*. https://globalstudies.trinity.duke.edu/sites/globalstudies.trinity.duke.edu/files/file-attachments/v2d2_Lugones.pdf

Ma'ayan, H. D. (2011). A white queer geek at school: Intersections of whiteness and queer identity. *Journal of LGBT Youth, 8*(1), 84–98. https://doi.org/10.1080/19361653.2010.520578

Marine, S. B. (2011). Stonewall's legacy: Bisexual, gay, lesbian, and transgender students in higher education. *ASHE Higher Education Report, 37*(4), 1–145. https://doi.org/10.1002/aehe.3704

Marine, S. B., & Nicolazzo, Z. (2014). Names that matter: Exploring the tensions of campus LGBTQ centers and trans inclusion. *Journal of Diversity in Higher Education, 7*, 265–281. https://doi.org/10.1037/a0037990

Mock, J. (2014). *Redefining realness: My path to womanhood, identity, love and so much more.* Atria Books.

Nicolazzo, Z. (2016). 'It's a hard line to walk': Black non-binary trans* collegians perspectives on passing, realness, and trans*-normativity. *International Journal of Qualitative Studies in Education, 29*(9), 1173–1188. https://doi.org/10.1080/09518398.2016.1201612

Ozias, M. (2017). *White women doing racism: A critical narrative inquiry of White women's experiences of college* [Unpublished doctoral dissertation]. University of Oklahoma. https://shareok.org/handle/11244/51916

Poynter, K. J., & Tubbs, N. J. (2008). Safe zones. *Journal of LGBT Youth, 5*(1), 121–132. https://www.tandfonline.com/doi/abs/10.1300/J524v05n01_10

Pryor, J. T., & Hoffman, G. D. (2020, April 24). "It feels like diversity as usual": Navigating institutional politics as LGBTQ+ professionals. *Journal of Student Affairs Research and Practice.* Advance online publication. https://doi.org/10.1080/19496591.2020.1740717

Sanlo, R. L. (2000). The LGBT campus resource center director: The new profession in student affairs. *NASPA Journal, 37*(3), 485–495. https://doi.org/10.2202/1949-6605.1113

Sanlo, R., Rankin, S., & Schoenberg, R. (Eds.). (2002). *Our place on campus: Lesbian, gay, bisexual, transgender services and programs in higher education.* Greenwood.

Schick, C., & St. Denis, V. (2005). Troubling national discourses in anti-racist curricular planning. *Canadian Journal of Education, 28*(3), 295–317. https://doi.org/10.2307/4126472

Self, J. M., & Hudson, K. D. (2015). Dangerous waters and brave spaces: A critical feminist inquiry of campus LGBTQ centers. *Journal of Gay & Lesbian Social Services, 27*(2), 216–245. https://doi.org/10.1080/10538720.2015.1021985

Tandberg, D. A., & Laderman, S. A. (2018). *Evaluating state funding for higher education.* MHEC Policy Brief. https://www.mhec.org/sites/default/files/resources/mhec_affordability_series6.pdf

Tillapaugh, D., & Catalano, D. C. J. (2019). Structural challenges affecting the experiences of public university LGBT services graduate assistants. *Journal of Diversity in Higher Education, 12*(2), 126–135. https://doi.org/10.1037/dhe0000079

Tillman-Kelly, D. L. (2015). *Sexual identity label adoption and disclosure narratives of gay, lesbian, bisexual, and queer (GLBQ) college students of color: An intersectional grounded theory study* [Doctoral dissertation, The Ohio State University]. Electronic Theses & Dissertations Center. https://etd.ohiolink.edu/

Vaid, U. (2012). *Irresistible revolution: Confronting race, class and the assumptions of LGBT politics.* Magnus Books.

Ward, J. (2004). "Not all differences are created equal": Multiple jeopardy in a gendered organization. *Gender & Society, 18*(1), 82–102. https://doi.org/10.1177/0891243203259503

Ward, J. (2008). *Respectably queer: Diversity culture in LGBT activist organizations.* Vanderbilt University Press.

Wells, J. B. (2015). *CAS professional standards for higher education* (9th ed.). Council for the Advancement of Standards in Higher Education.

Winans, A. E. (2010). Cultivating racial literacy in white, segregated settings: Emotions as site of ethical engagement and inquiry. *Curriculum Inquiry, 40*(3), 475–491. https://doi.org/10.1111/j.1467-873X.2010.00494.x

Woodford, M. R., Kolb, C. L., Durocher-Radeka, G., & Javier, G. (2014). Lesbian, gay, bisexual, and transgender ally trainings on campus: Current variations and future directions. *Journal of College Student Development, 55*(3), 317–322. https://doi.org/10.1353/csd.2014.0022

9

INTERROGATING WHITENESS IN SORORITY AND FRATERNITY LIFE

Cameron C. Beatty and Crystal E. Garcia

Sorority and fraternity life[1] (SFL) communities are expansive networks whose membership includes collegians across the country and the world as well as grad and alumni membership in the millions. For many, these organizations, and the power they possess, are a mystery, and insight to their inner workings is only made apparent through popular media and news stories reporting incidents of binge drinking, hazing, and racism, among others. The reality is that there are many ways these organizations contribute positively to their campus communities, yet there is also truth in the media's sorority and fraternity coverage. More specifically, there are numerous examples of historically white sorority and fraternity (HWSF—those within National Panhellenic Conference [NPC] and North American Interfraternity Conference [NIC] groups) ties to racism, including how organizations were founded, the prevalence of racist incidents including themed parties, and race-based membership selection and denial (Garcia & Shirley, 2019; Gillon et al., 2019; Salinas et al., 2019). As a counter to these dominant narratives there are also myriad ways culturally based sororities and fraternities (CBSFs), such as those within a campus Multicultural Greek Council (MGC) and National Pan-Hellenic Council (NPHC) intentionally center Communities of Color (Dosono et al., 2020; Oxendine et al., 2013; Parks & Hughey, 2020).

When interrogating these examples more closely, it is clear there are overt ways racism has played out in HWSFs, including discriminatory exclusionary clauses organizations have written into early membership documents as well as myriad overt acts of racism HWSF members, chapters, and organizations wholly have engaged in (see J. C. Harris et al., 2019; James, 2000). Examples include an incident at the University of Georgia where racist messages surfaced from a group chat between members of a fraternity that targeted a Black student (Pietsch, 2020). Other overtly racist incidents include videos of fraternity members singing a racist chant (Chappell, 2015), sorority members singing a song containing racial slurs (NBC 10 News, 2020), and fraternity (Sheeler, 2018) and sorority members (Osborne, 2019) performing blackface. These explicit forms of racism are obvious ways whiteness permeates SFL communities, and because of this they often dominate conversations about racism in HWSFs. Less frequently discussed are the implicit ways race and ethnicity inform sorority and fraternity communities, including through HWSF member recruitment processes and organizational practices, among others (Salinas et al., 2019), which we will unpack further through this chapter.

Ultimately, many of the issues around race and ethnicity that have come into play in HWSFs are rooted in whiteness (Leonardo, 2002). Leonardo (2002) clarified that whiteness is a distinct concept from white people and can be described instead as "a racial discourse" and "a racial perspective or world-view" (p. 31). More specifically, "whiteness, along with race, is the structural valuation of skin color, which invests it with meaning regarding the overall organization of society" (Leonardo, 2009, p. 92). Leonardo (2013) argued that in order to critique whiteness, it must first be located. In order to further understand the relationship between HWFSs and whiteness, this chapter extends previous work by J. C. Harris et al. (2019) that examines the functionality of whiteness as property in SFL, by further connecting the practices thereof to white normativity and white racial ignorance within the context of historically white institutions (HWIs). We present the ways white normativity and white racial ignorance shape white sorority and fraternity culture as well as SFL offices by first providing examples of how these dynamics manifest within these spaces. Second, we discuss what it means to address white racial ignorance and white normativity within these communities in practice. We conclude the chapter with critical reflective questions to consider when interrogating whiteness and moving toward action for those who work with and those who are members of the SFL community.

White Normativity in SFL

In chapter 3 Irwin explained how whiteness is produced and reproduced through racialized processes of legitimation. In this section we will unpack ways these legitimation processes are embedded in HWSFs, drawing from the concept of white normativity. Gusa (2010) unpacked the ways whiteness becomes normalized within postsecondary institutions through "the practices, traditions, and perceptions of knowledge that are taken for granted as the norm at institutions of higher education" (p. 464). There are a number of ways white normativity is pervasive specifically within HWSFs. Therefore, we bring to focus how it influences who becomes a member of such organizations and how indeed whiteness is reinforced through the shared language and practices of these organizations, particularly within HWIs.

White Normativity and SFL Membership

Membership selection is a secret process, and members are exclusively privy to the conversations about who is and who is not selected to join sororities and fraternities; therefore, nonmembers cannot know the extent to which race/ethnicity informs membership selection conversations. Yet the stories of individuals who have come forth and called out racist membership intake practices, such as the example where students at the University of Alabama publicly spoke out about racism in NPC recruitment (see Ford & Crain, 2013)—a dynamic that was recently reexposed through Alabama students' posts about recruitment on TikTok (Ishmael, 2021), alongside the significant disparities in the number of Students of Color who have become members of HWSFs exemplify the ongoing centrality of whiteness in these spaces.

In the context of higher education, Cabrera et al. (2017) asserted that normalizing whiteness results in the invisibility of whiteness, and "part of this invisibility and accompanying privilege means being able to ignore issues of race" (p. 25). Indeed, this is certainly the case within sorority and fraternity communities, as has been normalized that NPC and NIC groups continue to have a majority white membership without questioning the racialized nature of membership processes, SFL office practices, and chapter/(inter) national organization operations (Salinas et al., 2019). Largely, members of these groups do not question whether these practices are intentional or problematic, and if they do, it has yet to result in organizational changes that significantly alter the demographics of NPC and NIC organizations (Gillon et al., 2019; J. C. Harris et al., 2019).

Another way white normativity informs sorority and fraternity membership is through the minimum membership requirements campuses have for student organizations to remain active. The minimum number of members required varies on each campus and is often based on "arbitrarily contrived standards" (Oxendine & Oxendine, 2021, p. 147). These requirements in and of themselves are harmful, for example, for smaller culturally based organizations that do not have the supports needed to recruit new members and sustain membership quotas. The damage of these policies is compounded by the rhetoric that MGC and NPHC groups, which are largely composed of Students of Color, want to be small at HWIs and having larger chapters would detract from the organizations' sense of community. Although MGC and NPHC members may embrace their small size within HWIs (Garcia 2019, 2020), perpetuating the notion that they must be small gives institutions the out not to provide essential resources and supports that these organizations need to thrive on campus no matter the size. Often, their low membership paired with a lack of institutional support leads to chapter sizes dwindling to the point of overtaxation on members and can easily lead to the demise of the chapter's ability to remain on campus. These outcomes then reinforce the massive presence of HWSFs on campus while almost ensuring that culturally based groups stay small enough not to garner much power or, in the worst cases, that chapters die out on campus (Garcia, 2019).

J. C. Harris et al. (2019) outlined the property functions of whiteness within sorority and fraternity culture from both a historical and present-day perspective. The framing of whiteness as property (C. I. Harris, 1993) is an analytical tool to critically deconstruct all the ways whiteness operates and is upheld in SFL. The status of whiteness may also be why some members of the SFL community continue to partake in racist behavior, such as racist theme parties and performing blackface, with minimal to no consequences (Beatty & Boettcher, 2019; Davis & Harris, 2015). Often, apology letters/statements, where institutions and organizations require white students to offer an apology to those offended by the racist incident, are the harshest forms of punishment or sanctioning that students receive for being, upholding, and perpetuating racism. This lack of accountability alone allows white normativity and white racial ignorance to fester. Furthermore, the apologies that are offered almost always "allow organizations to claim innocence rather than responsibility for the incident" (Davis & Harris, 2015, p. 72), which does little to nothing to change the status quo. A lack of accountability and the continuance of apathetic apologies may occur because white students' reputations as respectable and trustworthy people protect them from being seen as (intentionally) racist; therefore, no punishment or apology is truly necessary. Deconstructing these responses are opportunities to also interrogate whiteness.

Reinforcing White Normativity in SFL Through Institutional Language and Practices

The functional area of SFL legitimizes whiteness through NPC and NIC dominance over NPHC and MGC groups through language, practices, and resource allocation within HWIs. In terms of language, one example is the common use of the term *sorority recruitment* at the start of fall semesters to specifically promote NPC sorority recruitment. NPHC and MGC sororities typically have different recruitment processes that take place at a separate time from NPC groups; therefore labeling NPC recruitment as *sorority recruitment* reinforces white normativity and renders NPHC and MGC sororities as other. Another example is that within the field of SFL, NPC and NIC groups are commonly referred to using monikers such as "traditional" or "mainstream" sororities and fraternities. Although individuals adopt these terms because they are commonly used to distinguish these organizations from culturally based sororities and fraternities, the result is that it centers historically white organizations as the norm or the standard of SFL, and further positions race and ethnicity-based groups as other, which also reinforces white normativity.

Additional practices that normalize whiteness within SFL stem from the many ways that SFL offices expect MGC and NPHC groups to fit into initiatives and policies that were designed for NPC and NIC groups. As mentioned previously, policies on membership size, often required of all SFL chapters on campus, are notable examples (Oxendine et al., 2013; Oxendine & Oxendine, 2021). Due to the size of some small NPHC and MGC chapters, it is unreasonable to compare the GPAs of, say, six members to an organization that has over 200. To be clear, the practice of grade reporting is not necessarily a reflection of whiteness, but the enforcement of policies that were intended specifically for white groups upon organizations that were founded for Students of Color without consideration of negative ramifications those policies may have on students reinforces whiteness as center. Additionally, many SFL offices put on workshops and other events that members of sororities and fraternities are required to attend. Often, offices will enforce a chapter attendance percentage requirement. Enforcing a 75% attendance seems reasonable enough for an organization made up of 100 members, wherein 25 students could be absent without any organizational repercussions. Again, for the organization of six members, if two of those individuals are absent, their chapter would face a potential fine or other disciplinary action. Practices like these were intended for and continue to serve HWSFs, continuing their position within historically white institutional SFL spaces as the standard. When practices of advising and supporting HWFS deem culturally based organizations as the "other," whiteness is upheld and perpetuated in SFL on campus.

Another crucial way that white normativity is maintained within SFL communities is through resource allocation (i.e., financial resources, physical space, and staff support). Some research has shed light on these dynamics, wherein student members of CBSFs reflected that they sometimes do not even know who the SFL professionals are, or in other cases feel inferior to members of HWSFs when in the SFL office on campus (Garcia, 2019). Additionally, members of CBSFs often do not receive equitable attention from SFL professionals on their campus when compared to historically white organizations (Camacho, 2021; Duran et al., 2021; Garcia, 2019). These reflections of being underserved by the institution as expressed by members of CBSFs are echoed in hiring practices within SFL communities at HWIs. It is not uncommon for campuses to hire professionals who focus solely on NPC or NIC groups, whereas NPHC and MGC organizations are delegated to a graduate assistant or a professional who must split their time between councils (Duran et al., 2021). This further perpetuates inequities because historically white organizations are often in excess of support, having multiple alumni advisors, local alumni chapters, large membership bases, and dedicated professional staff on campus, whereas CBSFs often face different realities. To illuminate this point, Crystal, the second author of this chapter, served as an advisor for her NPC sorority's chapter for 5 years following her graduation. In that time, she served alongside advisors who each provided support to the undergraduate officers of the chapter; it was not unusual to have five alumni advisors present at major chapter events. This was in addition to the institution-provided professional who worked with NPC chapters on campus. Later in her career as she transitioned to serve in a faculty role, she learned that the first MGC sorority established at the institution was without an advisor for 2 and a half years following their charter date until she volunteered for the role. The institution also did not hire an SFL professional dedicated to the MGC until a year and a half after their charter. Unfortunately, situations like these are not uncommon for CBSFs. The irony is that often institutions will provide the excuse that it is because of their small size that the institution chooses not to prioritize providing resources to CBSFs, although this precise mentality ensures that they stay small and unworthy of equal support. The challenging piece, as discussed previously, is that the lack of resources and adequate support these organizations face are compounding and often result in the inability for these organizations to survive on campus, much less thrive—further normalizing the centralization and normalization of whiteness within SFL.

Disrupting White Normativity in SFL

We also wanted to draw attention to ways white normativity in SFL has been challenged. Racialized and discriminatory behaviors within HWSFs partially informed the development of CBSFs. These groups were also founded in part due to the subsequent need to form spaces for their own identity, as in response to a greater societal need to push against systemic racism and oppression (Gillon et al., 2019; Ross, 2000; Torbenson & Parks, 2009). In addition to the nine historically Black sororities and fraternities within the National Pan-Hellenic Council, there are myriad identity-based organizations that are typically categorized on local campuses within a multicultural Greek council, including historically Asian American Pacific Islander Desi American, Latinx/a/o, multicultural, and Native American organizations. Members of these CBSFs participate in acts of resistance that counter the persistent racist behaviors enacted by HWSF communities by explicitly centering Communities of Color (Dosono et al., 2020; Oxendine et al., 2013; Parks & Hughey, 2020). The very existence of CBSFs is a form of resistance to white normativity in SFL. Their presence challenges a system that was explicitly created to keep Communities of Color out, and their existence disrupts whiteness as a norm. In addition to the presence and labor of CBSFs in this effort, a new phenomenon countering white normativity in SFL recently emerged. In response to demands for racial justice and to address sexual assault on college campuses that intensified before and during the summer of 2020, the "abolish Greek life" movement surfaced at institutions across the country. Students within the movement argued that Greek life should be abolished, pointing to the problematic ways HWSFs were grounded in systems of oppression. As a result, many HWSFs have been called to reckon with the ways they have reinforced systemic racism and white normativity within their organizations. In response, many organizations have since communicated their commitment to diversity and addressing injustices within their organizational practices to varying degrees (Hauler, 2020). Time will only tell if these were merely to assuage an uprising against organizations and a show of surface-level commitments to "diversity" or if HWSFs will demonstrate genuine and sustained commitments to racial equity. We do not assert that HWSFs should be abolished; however, what is clear is that the "abolish Greek life" movement interrupted white normativity in SFL at least temporarily and to some degree.

White Racial Ignorance in SFL

In this section, we will unpack sorority and fraternity dynamics in light of the discussion on white racial ignorance, which is provided in Part One of this book. Mills's (1997, 2017) conceptualization of white racial ignorance emphasizes that individuals not only go without recognizing racial dynamics but there is also intentionality in avoiding learning about them. Such an understanding informs SFL. Patterns within SFL point to a phenomenon in which students often do not recognize the existence of or seek to understand culturally based organizations on a deeper level (i.e., beyond a fascination with cultural elements such as stepping and strolling). Frequently, members of CBSFs will share stories of encounters they had with members of HWSFs and unaffiliated students that share they did not know their organization existed or that other organizations like theirs existed on campus (Garcia, 2019). Although seemingly harmless, this pattern underscores ways white racial ignorance contributes to the erasure of organizations that were founded to center Communities of Color (Garcia & Shirley, 2019; Gillon et al., 2019). This dynamic highlights a point of privilege for members of historically white organizations, as members of culturally based organizations do not have the option of not knowing that HWSFs exist on campus because of their sheer numbers, which are frequently above CBSFs. The possession of campus space via SFL housing and HWSFs' receipt of the majority of campus and SFL professionals' attention and resources allow members of historically white organizations to believe their experience with SFL is the only experience.

Additionally, white racial ignorance is reflected in ways SFL offices offer information regarding sorority and fraternity communities. Commonly, campus orientations will feature an SFL-focused session for incoming students and parents. Within these sessions, campus professionals or designated student ambassadors present information about the organizations on campus, benefits of involvement, and how to join. Often within HWIs, these sessions focus most of the time and information on HWSFs and only offer surface-level information about culturally based sororities and fraternities or only briefly spend time mentioning them (Garcia, 2019). These sessions are a prime opportunity to educate campus communities about organizations that were founded in response to racial discrimination and how they continue to push against these systems of oppression today; as a result, practices that center HWSFs and do not share these nuances regarding CBSFs perpetuate white racial ignorance.

SFL practices that contribute to white racial ignorance are also mirrored in SFL community materials such as flyers and websites. In a recent study by Garcia et al. (2022), they focused on institutional SFL websites in the southeastern region of the United States and found that complete details were commonly offered regarding historically white organizations, whereas insufficient details of culturally based groups were provided, and in some cases, no information was provided about these sororities and fraternities at all. Furthermore, the study found that websites very rarely shared information regarding the historical emergence of CBSFs. Several sites mentioned NPHC organizations, yet they did so referring to them as "historically Black," and they did not explicitly draw lines to discriminatory SFL practices that denied membership to Black students or other Students of Color, nor did they address the foundational mission of CBSFs to serve minoritized communities in the face of societal systemic racism. These historical legacies may not be ones that communities want to discuss, and they may feel shame in discussing them; however, ignoring these realities does not mean that they are untrue, but simply reinforces white racial ignorance. We argue that SFL communities must address these truths directly, as uncomfortable as they may be; SFL communities must come to terms with the importance of their sitting in discomfort. Doing this early on models for the entire SFL community the value of CBSFs and decenters HWSFs. Coming to terms with the history also disrupts white racial ignorance through community education and acknowledgment of how whiteness has been perpetuated and maintained in SFL.

Disrupting White Racial Ignorance in SFL

Developing chapter leadership trainings and new member education curriculum rooted in acknowledging racism exists is a place to start to actively interrogate whiteness, white normativity, and white racial ignorance. Acknowledging racist histories and connecting those histories to present-day practices is a place where trainings would allow chapters to examine biases they hold and how these influence decisions on whom they recruit and invite into their organizations. Another action is to provide a curriculum on inclusive language for chapter members to help create a welcoming environment for all prospective members and current members. (Re)create a formal education for those students who assist with the recruitment and socialization processes to discuss the varied types of SFL experiences available to a student. SFL offices should center the experiences of historically Black sororities and fraternities and culturally based organizations and practice decentering whiteness. Their historical and cultural histories highlight and disrupt the master narrative of who and what is considered sorority and fraternity and what traditions and rituals are centered and valued by the larger campus community. SFL must not default all SFL members' experiences to NPC or NIC organizations. Finally, there must be conscious effort to engage members in conversations of *how* to address racism. SFL professionals can lead communities in taking an honest assessment regarding if there are actually conversations about whiteness or if they center on diversity and inclusion language—"happy talk" (Bell & Hartman, 2007, p. 895).

Implications for Practice

Whiteness is embedded throughout higher education, including in policies and procedures, campus environments, research and theory, and organizational culture (Cabrera et al., 2017; Gusa, 2010; J. C. Harris et al., 2019; Patton et al., 2015). Acknowledging the histories, traditions, and symbols rooted in whiteness is the first place to start. Deconstructing and reconstructing policies and practices to eradicate whiteness is an ongoing process. In this section we call for the SFL community, and higher education professionals specifically, to move toward action that actively engages in addressing whiteness in all its forms. We provide an exploration of how higher education professionals and SFL members can *acknowledge, deconstruct, and critically reflect to move toward action* when interrogating whiteness, white normativity, and white racial ignorance within SFL.

Acknowledge

So, what is the process for professionals and SFL members to acknowledge the normativity and ignorance of whiteness within their communities? SFL should critically identify the subtle and implicit ways whiteness is maintained through organizations' hegemonic operating processes, constructed environments, and cultures (J. C. Harris et al., 2019; Museus & Jayahumar, 2012). Gillon et al. (2019) offered some critical reflective questions as a starting point for SFL advisors, volunteers, and higher education professionals to consider when acknowledging the histories of SFL organizations:

> Going forward, we ask readers to consider, how are you engaging critically with histories of [sorority and fraternity] life? Whose histories do you know? Whose histories do you need to learn more about? Which histories are privileged in the telling of [sorority and fraternity] life, and how might you challenge this practice? (p. 15)

Acknowledging histories, traditions, and organizational cultures is a place to start. J. C. Harris et al. (2019) recommended Strange and Banning's (2015) campus ecology framework as an analysis tool to examine ritual, tradition, physical construction of spaces, and organizational symbolism and how, through SFL traditions, whiteness is maintained in the master narrative of college life. Learning of organizational histories must also acknowledge place, names, and connections to the local community. Understanding the historical legacy of inclusion and exclusion is especially important for culturally based organizations, to document the histories of their organizations in relation to the local community (J. C. Harris et al., 2019). As an

SFL community, we must be mindful to not only be critical consumers of history but also critical producers, keepers, and documenters of history (Gillon et al., 2019). Critical understandings of which places and names have colonial roots, slavery roots, and which have Indigenous roots are an important aspect of acknowledging the histories and normativity of whiteness (Sensoy & DiAngelo, 2017). Additionally, doing a critical analysis of how whiteness has been operationalized at the campus chapter level, in the community, and through the national organization is an important practical place to start when interrogating whiteness in SFL. What norms and rituals are designed to uphold the normativity of whiteness? What norms have not been interrogated and why? How do new member curricula at the chapter, campus, and national levels continue to perpetuate white racial ignorance?

White racial ignorance is reinforced by the watered-down language around diversity and inclusion and the lack of acknowledgment of the role whiteness plays in the perpetuation of inequities in SFL. Statements that have fluff and no action around racism only perpetuate whiteness and become affirming to behaviors that normalize whiteness. White normativity and white racial ignorance can have strong, negative impacts on Students of Color. During the summer of 2020, sororities and fraternities, along with other higher education entities, publicly named the histories of race and racism due to the calls for racial justice because of the killings of Ahmaud Arbery, George Floyd, and Breonna Taylor, among many others. Many of these statements sounded similar and did not clearly outline action steps to address whiteness, racism, and white supremacy that are embedded in institutions, including SFL. White ignorance is perpetuated by the watered-down language around diversity and inclusion (Sensoy & DiAngelo, 2017).

Statements acknowledging diversity alone only mask the more fundamental and important issues of inequality and lend themselves to what Bell and Hartman (2007) called the "happy talk" path. As the happy talk moves from the abstract to concrete actions, happiness disappears, and discussions of challenges and resistance emerge. This happy talk contributes to what Bell and Hartmann (2007) called this white normative center, the assumption that diversity is an add-on to an otherwise normative white experience. When diversity alone is acknowledged in the SFL community and only seen as an add-on to the historical and traditional norms, then SFL is only reproducing whiteness. Sorority and fraternity campus community members expressing frustrations and resistance to addressing diversity, equity, and inclusion efforts stem from the contradictions between talking about diversity by many white people and the very real problems they encounter in everyday life. The SFL ideal of being a diverse community is subverted by the realities that SFL professionals often produce in their actions—a color-blind, power-neutral approach to individual and collective community action (Bell & Hartmann,

2007; Burke, 2012). Acknowledging watered-down statements of valuing diversity and minoritized identities can help SFL understand the limitations of the current diversity discourse and the lengths to which we must go to start to truly interrogate whiteness.

Deconstruct

Beatty and Boettcher (2019) highlighted the role institutions play in being reactive to racist incidents in the SFL community and how these reactive actions promoted and perpetuated whiteness in SFL. Whiteness shows up in the ways higher education institutions not only respond to racism that is reactive instead of proactive (Beatty & Boettcher, 2019; J. C. Harris et al., 2019), but also in the exclusion of diversity, equity, and inclusion language in mission statements, concentration of institutional power in white (often men) administrators, minimal representation of Faculty/Staff of Color at HWIs, and a reliance upon traditional pedagogies and curricula that disregard teaching across racial difference (Cabrera, 2017; Gusa, 2010). These deconstructions and analyses can be applied to national organizations and local chapters as noted earlier. When deconstructing whiteness, one must reflect on if their SFL organization or community is being reactive or proactive when addressing racism and interrogating whiteness (Beatty & Boettcher, 2019).

When considering moving organizations toward action for the purpose of interrogating whiteness, we must first be clear that the goals should be rooted in addressing systemic racism in SFL. Before action occurs, education and acknowledgment of the ways whiteness has been perpetuated and maintained in sorority and fraternity communities at the local and national organization levels is important. To create inclusive communities of sisterhood and brotherhood for prospective and current SFL members, one must acknowledge that students are balancing their academic life, being members of a social organization, and understanding their various social identities (Salinas et al., 2019) throughout the experience. This includes an accurate and honest depiction of institutional diversity in SFL recruitment marketing material and not a false representation or performative example of compositional diversity.

Critical Reflective Questions to Consider When Moving Toward Action

We conclude the chapter by offering critical reflective questions to support those who advise SFL students and are members of the SFL chapter community and international and national leadership. The critical reflective questions that follow are a starting point for interrogating whiteness within

SFL respective campuses, chapters, and organizations. Understanding and resisting racialization and structural racism must be an explicit part of the work of SFL members, professionals, and values-oriented organizations. As this chapter calls for the ongoing work of interrogating whiteness, we hope these questions offer a guide for doing that work in values and in actions.

1. How does the office of SFL ingrain diversity, equity, and inclusion outcomes in the mission, vision, and espoused and enacted values of all programming, learning outcomes, and assessment?
2. What does critically examining the history of SFL on your campus look like through a critical whiteness lens?
3. What does antiracist training look like for recruitment and new member education programs at the chapter, campus, and national levels? In what ways do these trainings incorporate a racial justice framework to guide learning outcomes? How can these trainings interrogate whiteness?
4. How are statements drafted that respond to racist incidents so they are not reactionary, but instead offer steps toward real change rooted in interrogating whiteness and moving toward racial justice?
5. How does the SFL community celebrate and highlight initiatives that are moving to dismantle white supremacy and racism?
6. What role do campus advisors and student affairs professionals play in calling out, calling in, or calling on national organizations in revisiting their espoused values versus their enacted values around whiteness and racial justice?

Notes

1. Our intentionality in our choice to use SFL rather than FSL is to forefront sororities, which are often named secondarily to fraternities.

References

Beatty, C. C., & Boettcher, M. (2019). My culture is not a costume: Institutional practices and racism. In K. E. Gillon, C. C. Beatty, & C. S. Salinas Jr. (Eds.), *Critical Considerations of Race, Ethnicity, and Culture in Fraternity & Sorority Life* (New Directions for Student Services, no. 165, pp. 39–49). Jossey-Bass.

Beatty, C. C., McElderry, J. A., Bottoms, M., & Gray, K. (2019). Resisting and responding to racism through fraternity and sorority involvement. In K. E. Gillon, C. C. Beatty, & C. S. Salinas Jr. (Eds.), *Critical Considerations of Race, Ethnicity, and Culture in Fraternity & Sorority Life* (New Directions for Student Services, no. 165, pp. 99–108). Jossey-Bass.

Bell, J. M., & Hartmann, D. (2007). Diversity in everyday discourse: The cultural ambiguities and consequences of "happy talk." *American Sociological Review, 72*(6), 895–914. https://doi.org/10.1177/000312240707200603

Burke, M. A. (2012). Discursive fault lines: Reproducing white habitus in a racially diverse community. *Critical Sociology, 38*(5), 645–668. https://doi.org/10.1177/0896920511411207

Cabrera, N. L., Franklin, J. D., & Watson, J. S. (2017). Whiteness in higher education: The invisible missing link in diversity and racial analyses. *ASHE Higher Education Report, 42*(6), 7–125.

Camacho, T. (2021). Bridging the gap between culturally-based sororities and fraternities within larger SFL communities. In C. E. Garcia & A. Duran (Eds.), *Moving culturally-based sororities and fraternities forward: Innovations in practice* (pp. 193–220). Peter Lang.

Chappell, B. (2015, March 10). *University Of Oklahoma expels 2 students seen as leading racist chant.* NPR. https://www.npr.org/sections/thetwo-way/2015/03/10/392104932/university-of-oklahoma-expels-2-students-seen-as-leading-racist-chant

Davis, S., & Harris, J.C. (2015). But we didn't mean it like that: A critical race analysis of campus responses to racial incidents. *Journal of Critical Scholarship on Higher Education and Student Affairs, 2*(1), 62–77. https://ecommons. luc.edu/jcshesa/vol2/iss1/6/

Dosono, B., Badruddin, B., & Lam, V. W. H. (2020). History of Asian American Greek-letter organizations. In P. A. Sasso, J. P. Biddix, & M. L. Miranda (Eds.), *Foundations, research, and assessment of fraternities and sororities: Retrospective and future considerations* (pp. 25–37). Myers Education.

Duran, A., Garcia, C. E., & Reyes, H. (2021). *SFL practitioner perspectives on challenges faced by culturally-based sororities and fraternities* [Manuscript submitted for publication].

Ford, M., & Crain, A. (2013, September 11). The final barrier: 50 years later, segregation still exists. *The Crimson White.* https://cw.ua.edu/16498/news/the-final-barrier-50-years-later-segregation-still-exists/

Garcia, C. E. (2019). "They don't even know that we exist": Exploring sense of belonging within sorority and fraternity communities for Latina/o members. *Journal of College Student Development, 60*(3), 319–336.

Garcia, C. E. (2020). Belonging in a predominantly White institution: The role of membership in Latina/o sororities and fraternities. *Journal of Diversity in Higher Education, 13*(2), 181–193.

Garcia, C. E., & Shirley, Z. E. (2019). Race and privilege in fraternity and sorority life: Considerations for practice and research. In P. Sasso, P. Biddix, & M. Miranda (Eds.), *Fraternities and sororities in the contemporary era* (pp. 155–163). Stylus.

Garcia, C. E., Walker, W., Bradley, S. E., & Smith, K. (2022). Sorority and fraternity life: Examining racial discourse via institutional websites. *Journal of College Student Development, 16*(20), 37–53. https://scholarworks.wm.edu/cgi/viewcontent.cgi?article=1181&context=oracle

Gillon, K. E., Beatty, C. C., & Salinas, C., Jr. (2019). Race and racism in fraternity and sorority life: A historical overview. In K. E. Gillon, C. C. Beatty, & C. Salinas Jr. (Eds.), *Critical Considerations of Race, Ethnicity, and Culture in Fraternity & Sorority Life* (New Directions for Student Services, no. 165, pp. 9–16). Jossey-Bass.

Gusa, D. L. (2010). White institutional presence: The impact of whiteness on campus climate. *Harvard Educational Review, 80*(4), 464–489.

Harris, C. I. (1993). Whiteness as property. *Harvard Law Review, 106*(8), 1710–1791.

Harris, J. C., Barone, R. P., & Finch, H. (2019). The property functions of whiteness within fraternity and sorority culture and its impact on campus. In K. E. Gillon, C. C. Beatty, & C. S. Salinas Jr. (Eds.), *Critical Considerations of Race, Ethnicity, and Culture in Fraternity & Sorority Life.* (New Directions for Student Services, no. 165, pp. 17–27). Jossey-Bass.

Hauler, L. (2020, July 15). *Pledge against racism: Black students talk about experiencing racism in college Greek life.* Good Morning America. https://www.goodmorningamerica.com/living/story/pledge-racism-black-students-talk-experiencing-racism-college-71779145

Ishmael, A. (2021, August 18). Bama rush has swept TikTok. But what do you need to know? *Teen Vogue.* https://www.teenvogue.com/story/bama-rush-has-swept-tiktok-what-do-you-need-to-know

James, A. W. (2000). The college social fraternity antidiscrimination debate, 1945–1949. *The Historian, 62*(2), 303–324.

Leonardo, Z. (2002). The souls of white folk: Critical pedagogy, whiteness studies, and globalization discourse. *Race Ethnicity and Education, 5*(1), 29–50.

Leonardo, Z. (2009). *Race, whiteness, and education.* Routledge.

Leonardo, Z. (2013). *Race frameworks: A multidimensional theory of racism and education.* Teachers College Press.

Mills, C. W. (1997). *The racial contract.* Cornell University Press.

Mills, C. W. (2017). *Black rights/white wrongs: The critique of racial liberalism.* Oxford University Press.

Museus, S. D., & Jayakumar, U. M. (Eds.). (2012). *Creating campus cultures: Fostering success among racially diverse student populations.* Routledge.

NBC 10 News. (2020, June 18). *Members of a URI sorority suspended after racist video surfaces.* News. https://turnto10.com/news/local/members-of-a-uri-sorority-suspended-after-racist-video-surfaces

Osborne, M. (2019). *University of Oklahoma sorority kicks out member over racist Blackface video.* ABC News. https://abcnews.go.com/US/university-oklahoma-sorority-kicks-member-racist-blackface-video/story?id=60502553

Oxendine, D., Oxendine, S., & Minthorn, R. (2013). The historically Native American fraternity and sorority movement. In H. J. Shotton, S. C. Lowe, & S. J. Waterman (Eds.), *Beyond the asterisk: Understanding Native students in education* (pp. 67–80). Stylus.

Oxendine S., & Oxendine, D. (2021). Confronting colonization: Moving forward to remove barriers for historically Native American fraternities and sororities. In C. E. Garcia & A. Duran (Eds.), *Moving culturally-based sororities and fraternities forward: Innovations in practice* (pp. 139–155). Peter Lang.

Parks, G. S., & Hughey, M. W. (2020). *A pledge with purpose: Black sororities and fraternities and the fight for equality.* NYU Press.

Patton, L. D., Harper, S. J., & Harris, J. C. (2015). Using critical race theory to (re) interpret widely-studied topics related to students in U.S. higher education. In A. M. Martinez Aleman, B. Pusser, & E. M. Bensimon (Eds.), *Critical approaches to the study of higher education* (pp. 193–219). Johns Hopkins University Press.

Pietsch, B. (2020, September 22). Fraternity at University of Georgia is suspended after racist messages are exposed. *The New York Times.* https://www.nytimes.com/2020/09/22/us/fraternity-university-of-georgia-suspended-racist.html

Ross, L. C., Jr. (2000). *The divine nine: The history of African American fraternities and sororities.* Kensington.

Salinas, C., Jr., Gillon, K. E., & Camacho, T. (2019). Reproduction of oppression through fraternity and sorority recruitment and socialization. In K. E. Gillon, C. C. Beatty, & C. S. Salinas Jr. (Eds.), *Considerations of Race, Ethnicity, and Culture in Fraternity & Sorority Life* (New Directions for Student Services, no. 165, pp. 29–38). Jossey-Bass.

Sensoy, Ö., & DiAngelo, R. (2017). *Is everyone really equal? An introduction to key concepts in social justice education* (2nd ed.). Teachers College Press.

Sheeler, A. (2018, April 13). Cal Poly student apologizes for wearing blackface at frat event. *The Tribune.* https://www.sanluisobispo.com/news/local/education/article208831809.html

Strange, C., & Banning, J. (2015). Designing for learning: Creating campus environments for student success (2nd ed.). Jossey-Bass.

Torbenson, C. L., & Parks, G. S. (Eds.). (2009). *Brothers and sisters: Diversity in college fraternities and sororities.* Rosemont.

10

THE PERMEATION OF WHITENESS IN STUDENT LEADERSHIP ORGANIZATIONS

Brittany M. Williams, Bryan K. Hotchkins, and Meg E. Evans

If you ask the average *white* college student the question, "Who is the most visible student leader on your campus?," the answers will certainly vary. Yet one can infer from research and anecdotal evidence that you are likely to get the name of the campus student government association president, the strongest player on the school's best and highest rated divisional sports team, or the most visible member of a white fraternity or sorority. On a predominantly white college campus specifically, the name you are likely to hear is that of a white student—but campus leadership roles are not theirs to claim alone. Nevertheless, despite increased enrollment of students with minoritized identities on historically and predominantly white campuses (Garibay & Vincent, 2018), there remains a gap in the visibility of Black, Indigenous, and other People of Color (BIPOC) students in highly coveted campus leadership positions (Peralta, 2015). This presents a problem for students with minoritized identities as they can fail to see such leadership positions as attainable, which could lead them and their white peers to wrongly internalize a belief that white students are most qualified for campus leadership positions.

Worse yet, college student leadership organizations and cocurricular activities are touted as race-neutral campus spaces. This means many students, irrespective of race, seek out campus organizations and cocurricular activities to develop and hone their leadership skills (Arminio et al., 2000; Hotchkins, 2014; Renn, 2007), improve their job place marketability (Rahman et al., 2020), and distinguish themselves as campus visionaries amid a sea of brilliant thinkers. Such uses of these campus leadership positions, though, privilege those who are continuing generation as opposed to first generation, those who are culturally raised to prioritize individual goals over those of a collective, and those whose family connections can help to place them in front of the right people, as such students are more likely to arrive on campus preprepared (Means & Pyne, 2017). In a meritocratic realm, campus leadership opportunities would be afforded to students most qualified to hold them. However, these highly regarded positions are often held by white students who arrive on campus with a host of advantages, including their default prioritization by campus faculty and professionals.

The purpose of this chapter, then, is to explore how white normativity serves to (un)intentionally reinforce and reproduce perceptions of student leadership as spaces of whiteness and for white people. We position white identity normativity as a contributing cause for discrepancies in leadership diversity along racial identity lines. Given the growing shifts in racial demographics across the United States and within and across predominantly white institutions (PWIs), we use this chapter (a) to explore how leadership positions are synonymized with whiteness, (b) to illuminate how campus norms and policies reinforce leadership as akin to whiteness, and (c) as a space to connect contemporary examples of whiteness in student leadership to the dismissal and disenfranchisement of BIPOC students seeking leadership roles and development.

Whiteness as Normal and Central on Campus

Contemporarily, PWIs (un)intentionally default to supporting white students because historically and predominantly white campuses were initially created for white, male, wealthy, heterosexual Christians (Cabrera, 2018). This is in direct misalignment with current enrollment patterns, as poor, working-class, first-generation, and BIPOC student numbers continue to increase (Eakins & Eakins, 2017; Pérez & Sáenz, 2017; Schreiner, 2018). Despite this shift in enrollment, PWIs have historically and continue to contemporarily better support and center white students within campus leadership organizations as compared to BIPOC students, leading to white student overrepresentation. In fact, the distinct presence white students hold in these organizations can further normalize whiteness to the point of consuming the spaces and/or places within which they engage. This happens when white-normative cultural perspectives, performances, and styles of leadership are centered and replicated. We further explore the negative effects of this white reinforcement in our section on acclimation to whiteness, but we find it important to acknowledge here as we consider the history of research on student leadership.

Research Trends on Race in Student Leadership

Although we understand campus leadership organizations as places that can confirm and further or reject and disrupt the performance of normalized identities (e.g., white, male, heterosexual, and Christian) social norms, the existing research on the role of whiteness in cocurricular student leadership organizations is bifurcated. Much of the earliest research on student leaders centers white student perspectives around leadership identity development (Kodama & Dugan, 2013). As campus enrollment patterns have and continue to shift, researchers have further explored race and leadership. The findings of this research on race in historically and predominantly white campus contexts suggest BIPOC students best thrive in culturally congruent organizations where racial identity awareness is normalized and activism is actualized (Arminio et al., 2000; Harper & Quaye, 2007; B. K. Hotchkins, 2017; Museus, 2008). This means BIPOC students can and do meet and exceed performance expectations in leadership roles when those spaces are culturally and racially affirming and supportive. However, white students have no such cultural congruence to seek because the status quo is designed for their success. This suggests white students are at a sociocultural head start compared to BIPOC students if they wish to hold formal leadership roles on a PWI campus.

Proximity and Acclimation to Whiteness

Proximity and acclimation to whiteness have a range of adverse effects on BIPOC students at PWIs (Gorski, 2019; Harwood et al., 2012; Hernández & Villodas, 2019; Smith et al., 2016). However, an individual's decision to acquiesce to white cultural performance expectations, white appeasement, in white-dominant ways has short-term material benefits for Students of Color at high sociocultural and emotional costs. By this, we mean that white students' (over)presence in leadership roles can force BIPOC students who wish to disrupt white norming to engage in code-switching (Joya, 2019; Rincón & Hollis, 2018). *Code-switching* is defined as the act of shifting cultural behaviors to reflect white, middle-class standards (Hill, 2009; Rincón & Hollis, 2018; Wheeler, 2008). This manifests in a range of ways, from speaking enunciation and tonality to style(s) of dress and even racialized performance depending upon the organizational context (Boulton, 2016; Wheeler, 2008; Young et al., 2014). In addition to behavioral shifts contributing to the maintenance of a white status quo, these changes further pose a threat to the racial diversity and racial makeup of student leadership organizations, because self-preservation from anticipated racial microaggressions can become a student's priority rather than increased, authentic participation (Mills, 2020; Sarcedo et al., 2015).

Moreover, because BIPOC students are able to most authentically connect to the institution through cocurricular organizations where they feel cultural congruence (Hurtado & Carter, 1997; Jones & Reddick, 2017; Museus, 2008), their ability to persist in formal campus leadership is heavily dependent upon the actions and behaviors of their white peers. White students, particularly white male collegians, have been found to contribute to the performance of racism at PWIs, while acting in leadership roles. Whether actively telling racist jokes around Peers of Color or participating in nearly homogenous fraternities where racially degrading parties are held to mock BIPOC culture (Cabrera, 2018), we understand these types of organizations to serve as active leadership spaces where racism is reified and where culturally incongruent BIPOC student leadership is not only undermined but actively damaged.

Furthermore, at PWIs, leadership organizations operate in unchecked ways, such as having limited oversight for event planning, speakers, and so on, which can further racial privileges that only benefit white students. To this point, Jaggers (2019) found that Black women who participated in predominantly white student organizations experienced a nefarious gendered racism when interacting with white leaders, which limited their ability to practice leadership. Even when leading is not central to the discussion, additional research frames student organizations as places where interracial friendships develop while leadership occurs. Despite this, white students were more likely to participate in majority-white environments than to pursue relationships outside of their culture (Park, 2014). This type of action by white students is not framed as racial balkanization in the literature, which presents self-segregation as only occurring when BIPOC students choose to practice leadership in ethnic-based organizations where members are perceived as being self-exclusive (Gramly, 2020). These contradictions exemplify how whiteness unfurls across higher education in exhaustive yet unique ways that normalize white performance of leadership practices. Furthermore, these contradictions illustrate how cocurricular student organizations situate white racial heterogeneity as normal, a misperception in need to of greater exploration.

Ultimately, our review of current research reveals that despite attempts at holistic leadership development and campus practices to minimize white student leader racism (B. Hotchkins, 2017), the status quo continues. Formal leadership positions continue to reproduce racially homogeneous cocurricular organizations that enhance the leadership capacity and efficacy of the white student leaders who hold them (Dugan et al., 2015; Kodama & Dugan, 2013). Although we focus on race in this chapter, we acknowledge that social class and wealth homogeneity in student leadership further amplifies the racial discrepancies we are covering (Williams et al., 2021). By this we mean poor students of all races may associate social class as a reason for their inability to see themselves in "traditional" campus leadership roles. However, only white socioeconomically disadvantaged students may be able to definitively say their racial identity was not a cause for exclusion, as their subordinated class status exists alongside racial identity privileges. Nevertheless, we articulate a race-specific analysis of student leadership problems across this chapter to recenter the reality that race does, is, and continues to matter (Burt et al., 2018; Gusa, 2010; Renn & Patton, 2011).

Contemporary Examples of White Racial Norm Maintenance

Whiteness influences cocurricular organizational follower behaviors, the performance of leadership, and student leader efficacy within PWI environments. Leadership is inextricably tied to what Liu and Baker (2016) referred to as "doing whiteness" and the presumption that whiteness generally upholds white superiority and power. Liu and Baker's (2016) contention rests at the core of our understanding: The concepts and outcomes of whiteness and leadership enhance and inform one another, creating an iterative cycle that serves (many) white students while it excludes BIPOC students. We focus on the power of whiteness in leadership labels, student behaviors, and structural affirmations to emphasize the pervasive nature of whiteness in campus leadership.

Leadership Labeling

In PWI contexts, much like the larger U.S. context, white students, more specifically white men, hold most leadership roles, and thus power. This, in part, is due to white ascendancy (Gusa, 2010) or the white supremacist belief (manifested both consciously and unconsciously) that white people are better leaders. As such, many university administrators at PWIs fail to recognize how white supremacy is reified through leadership programming. Instead of leadership being tied to leaders' actions and behaviors (Komives et al., 2013), it becomes connected to the titles and positions students hold, further elevating the status of white student leaders. This labeling problem has expansive implications for students' development, safety, and sense of belonging as whiteness is reinforced and rewarded through the labeling of white students as leaders. Furthermore, this kind of labeling leads campus administrators to respond to students according to role rather than reasoning.

Take, for example, the framing of student activism in college contexts—namely, student activists who engage in identity-based work while holding racially minoritized identities. Administrators often give student leaders in more formal leadership positions and organizations, such as student government and those who serve on the student organization executive board, the benefit of the doubt when they raise questions, critique the institution, or seek to improve campus conditions. Meanwhile, student activists are often labeled as troublemakers, pushed out, and even have their funding withdrawn rather than having their leadership skills celebrated and further enhanced (Linder et al., 2020; Martin et al., 2019; Renn, 2007; Stewart & Quaye, 2019). The positioning of student activists as troublemakers and formal student representatives as leaders reinforces notions of activism as problematic and constrains our understanding of acts of leadership as bound to and by the confines of whiteness.

Existing leadership labeling and constant reinforcement of structures led students at the University of Kansas to create an entirely separate student government for BIPOC students (New, 2016). This concept of a multicultural student government is not necessarily new but was advanced out of BIPOC student activists' frustration with their largely white elected campus leaders. That very same multicultural student government was removed from the larger student senate due to low participation only 4 years later (Peterson, 2019). Although the logistics of attempting to run dual governments places additional burdens on BIPOC students, such systems are and have already operated at the University of Florida (Koman, 2016) and the University of Alabama (Bolling, 2020), where the student government systems have been maintained by shadow student governments. On both campuses, select white Greek organizations colluded to create Greek-based student government voting blocs that cemented election outcomes on campus for generations, thereby limiting the potential of BIPOC student leaders in formal leadership positions (Bolling, 2020; Koman, 2016). These power struggles further necessitate our need to nuance leadership labeling because they underscore just how much BIPOC students have to fight for inclusion in their campus's existing systems. Further, it underscores how white students who are often unaccountable for their behaviors can reproduce social inequalities.

Student Behaviors

University administrators alone do not relegate leadership to whiteness. However, campus administrators having awareness of white student behaviors, such as the existence of voting blocs and shadow governments, while doing little to hold white student leaders accountable, contributes to a *chilly campus climate* (i.e., racist) BIPOC students endure (Gusa, 2010). When students use these shadow governments as a behind-the-scenes tactic, they reinforce past racist practices by making the same practices contemporary; white students cement an inaccessible, white-centric landscape for BIPOC students daring to dream of leadership opportunities. Accordingly, students and their behaviors both within and external to their organizational involvement can (re)center whiteness in leadership. How is it possible, for instance, that we know through empirical data that white men are disproportionately responsible for conduct cases on campus (Cabrera, 2018), yet they are constantly placed in powerful campus positions (e.g., student body president, Greek council president, etc.)?

Our collective failure to acknowledge and reprimand student (mis)behavior leads to a (mis)perception of these actions as normal. Sullivan (2006) defined this way of living and engaging as *white solipsism*. Solipsism can be described as a practice that allows white student leaders to behave, create, and inform policy and practice as if only they, white people, exist and matter (Sullivan, 2006). An example of exclusive and white-centering solipsism practices created for students by students in a leadership context is the construction of the hero trope. Consider campuses like Baylor University, the University of Richmond, and the University of Tennessee, Knoxville. All three institutions exist as examples of campuses steeped in sports culture where athletes, many of them white men, are considered campus heroes. These students are often presented in the media and on campus as if they can do little wrong or harm so long as their campus wins. However, they often do. All three universities have faced public scrutiny (New, 2017) for helping student-athletes work around campus conduct and accountability processes and offices, often in cases involving harm against women (New, 2017). Though not all the student-athletes who are allowed to misbehave with little repercussions are white men, the system they uphold largely benefits powerful wealthy white men, thereby creating tiered campus experiences steeped in whiteness.

Beyond favoritism and heroics for mostly white student athletes, demeaning images in school yearbooks (Holland & Sicurella, 2019; Korn, 2019) and at campus parties (Jaschik, 2018; Tawil, 2019) are another way white student leaders enact, perform, and perpetuate whiteness. White student leaders' comfort with enacting caricatured images of BIPOC people and cultures suggests white students know they will face little, if any, consequences for their denigrating behavior. Racist images and themed parties continue to take place at campus-sanctioned and -connected events under empowered white student leaders' direction, despite media coverage of the backlash created by the overtly racist (and often sexist, homophobic, and transphobic) acts. The normalization of these behaviors and minimal accountability are exacerbated as college administrators shirk their responsibilities to harmed BIPOC students. One could argue that campus professionals cower out of fear of external organizations and critics who intentionally misinterpret free speech and the First Amendment as an all-access racism pass (Anderson, 2020).

Structural Affirmations

Students and administrators alike structurally uphold whiteness and white supremacy in student leadership. Although it is easy to say PWI campuses were not built for BIPOC students (Wilder, 2013), this point of reality is often used as an excuse to contribute to little campus change today. Campus organizations tend to use white, middle-class norms and values in campus leadership organization structures, which serve to benefit white students and whiteness more broadly. This continues, though, despite decades of advocacy for culturally relevant shifts on campus. When students invest in whiteness through personal action (e.g., white ascendency and white solipsism,) they create racist spaces to singularly occupy, often just impacting those around them. But when students bring their white dominance to their student organizations, they create campus structures that honor whiteness as the norm and believe in the singular white worldview (i.e., monoculturalism).

Functioning from a singular worldview does not just serve to keep all others out; it also deems others as inappropriate and unwanted (Gusa, 2010). An example of this gatekeeping in student organizations is the use of Robert's Rules of Order. Robert's Rules of Order stress a process that many white students see as simple and equitable, despite being deeply rooted in a monocultural (i.e., white) worldview. White students weaponize Robert's Rules of Order against BIPOC students to center civility, leaving no room to voice hurt, pain, or dissent. Worse yet, this standard is one that white students have been socialized to operationalize while BIPOC students engage in more collectivist and collegial ways.

Relatedly, whiteness is further centered and perpetuated in leadership on college campuses through dress code practices and behaviors for student leadership positions. Many university-sponsored leadership organizations abide by rules and regulations on clothing, hair, and personal grooming standards (Williams et al., 2022). For instance, campus organization policies deeming that hair must be straight, clean, and/or short leaves little room for natural hair, curly hair, and other forms of cultural hair styling (see Donahoo, 2019). Similarly, this signals to students that some students (read: biracial and lighter skinned) are more acceptable than others given the interconnections between hair and hair presentation and colorism in Communities of Color (Brown et al., 2021). For instance, Donahoo (2019) shared the trials of navigating the academy as a Black woman with natural hair and highlighted how university structural affiliations, especially as related to appearance, continue to center and function as a white-dominated and white-servicing space. Like rules and regulations around hair, college and university student leadership organizations also tend to have dress codes to keep up white, middle-class, socially acceptable appearances.

For example, at the University of Georgia, one of the most highly regarded and prestigious student leadership organizations is The Arch Society. According to their website, the members of the Arch Society—

> seek to serve the University of Georgia at all functions where it is desired to have students welcome guests and visitors to the University of Georgia. Arch Society seeks to advance the University of Georgia through service to the offices of the President, the Provost, the Vice President for Student Affairs, the Senior Vice President for External Affairs, Alumni Relations, the Athletic Association, and other University offices or officials at appropriate functions. (University of Georgia, n.d., para. 2)

As such, the organization has a strict dress code as outlined in their constitution bylaws (The Arch Society, 2018). According to their regulations, then, members must wear

> the current official uniform determined by the Vice President for Student Affairs . . . [that must] only be purchased/obtained from the designated stores. . . . The general appearance of the People of the Arch while on an official assignment shall always be polished, professional, and presentable at all times. (p. 15)

This rigid adherence to white cultural norms further feeds into Gusa's (2010) conceptualization of *white institutional presence* not only for the current students engaged in The Arch Society but also for those who may want to become involved, yet do not see the space within the static nature of the dress codes to be able to engage fully and authentically. This is a structural affirmation to BIPOC students that one's most authentic sense of self (such as wearing natural hair or cultural attire) may neither be appreciated nor welcomed in this high-profile campus leadership space.

We Owe BIPOC Students More

Although we use a few specific examples in this text, there are endless other ways that whiteness shows up, is perpetuated, and is reinforced in student leadership initiatives and organizations on PWI campuses in the United States. We offer these contemporary examples as a starting place from which we hope campus leadership professionals and student leaders can begin to recognize and interrogate the policies and expectations set for student engagement on your respective campuses. We owe it to BIPOC student leaders to do more than focus on their ability to endure and resist these campus hostilities. By naming and underscoring the ongoing and continuous patterns white students and white stakeholders use to cement whiteness in campus leadership, we can begin to focus more on proactive solutions rather than reaction-based responses.

Strategies and Opportunities for Campus Leadership Professionals

Although formal leadership spaces are an integral way for white students to uphold and recenter whiteness, there are several opportunities and implications from this chapter. Campus leadership professionals and practitioners overseeing formal student leadership spaces can implement and increase the frequency of antiracism education workshops for white student leaders. By explicitly focusing on both individual and systemic actions within a campus context, rather than race and racism broadly, these educational spaces can force students to contend with the decisions they make by, for, and in the name of their peers within their campus leadership roles. Moreover, accountability systems that center restorative justice rather than shame and punitive actions can prove useful in encouraging white student leaders to engage more ethically with their BIPOC classmates and peers. We say this not to let white students off the hook, but out of an earnest desire to ensure BIPOC students do not continue to bear the full brunt of white student misbehavior. An example of a restorative justice outcome may be students engaged in a community accountability board that cocreates outcomes to address reported incidents of bias with student organizations. Further, white student leaders should engage in bystander intervention trainings that can help them to engage in peer accountability so that the responsibility is not solely on BIPOC students who experience racial violence. Such trainings could be standardized through student group and leadership development onboarding.

Although we are mindful that organizations for BIPOC students have historically served as ethnic enclaves where culturally congruent leadership occurs that allows for the holistic development of members (Arminio et al., 2000; Harper & Quaye, 2007), students must be able to see themselves beyond these spaces. Accordingly, we believe BIPOC student leaders should be armed with racial resistance training (B. K. Hotchkins, 2017) that specifically includes strategies for ensuring campus professionals effectively acknowledge, respond to, and hold accountable white student leaders who enact racism. Further, such training should include acknowledging how internalized oppression and racial battle fatigue may impact the overall social and emotional wellness of BIPOC students who choose to seek formal leadership opportunities. Although it is unfair to place the role of resistance on the shoulders of student leaders (Linder et al., 2019), we believe it would be naïve at best and violent at worst to simply state that colleges and universities should hold white students accountable when there are few meaningful representations of such commitments.

Further, we encourage all in the field of leadership studies, campus practitioners tasked with engaging in student development work, faculty, and diversity, equity, and inclusion professionals who oversee cultural and social spaces, to rethink and reshape both what we consider and define as leadership. Our continued reliance on *formal* leadership roles as sites of prestige (including those examples in this very chapter) limits the potential for how we understand BIPOC students' leadership development (Martin et al., 2019). Namely, we believe that BIPOC students engage in leadership on and off campus, but because that work is often done in intraracial and social spaces, it is often framed as cultural and thereby minimized. Standing up to injustices on campus is leadership. Seeking accountability for discrimination is leadership. Helping fellow BIPOC students learn to resist and navigate whiteness and white supremacy in PWI contexts is leadership (Stewart & Williams, 2019). Until we collectively center (in)formal leadership and reduce the hierarchies associated with understandings of leadership, we will continue to position leadership as a duality of titled and untitled, rather than a continuum that students inhabit daily.

Concluding Thoughts

Marian Wright Edelman (2015) once said, "It's hard to be what you can't see." We believe this to be true for BIPOC students on PWI campuses who have the capacity for (in)formal leadership roles but lack the proper access and opportunity due to whiteness and racism. Across this chapter, we revealed how white student leaders and the administrators who work with them help to maintain a culture of whiteness in PWI leadership spaces. We believe a collective effort, as a field, must be made to ensure the students most rendered to the margins are able to be heard and centered in the mainstream. Accordingly, we leave campus professionals, white students, and BIPOC students with the following questions to consider:

- Campus professionals:
  - What will you and your office do to support, encourage, and prepare BIPOC students for (in)formal campus leadership roles?
  - How will you and your office contend with, and ultimately disrupt, the perpetuation of whiteness in leadership education and development?
- White student leaders:
  - How will you engage in peer accountability and bystander intervention to better support your BIPOC colleagues?
- BIPOC student leaders:
  - Who, with power on campus, will you build a relationship with to coalesce and ensure your white peers in leadership roles are held accountable?

References

Anderson, G. (2020, June 23). When free speech and racist speech collide. *Inside Higher Ed.* https://www.insidehighered.com/news/2020/06/23/first-amendment-response-first-response-racism-campus

Arminio, J. L., Carter, S., Jones, S. E., Kruger, K., Lucas, N., Washington, J., Young, N., & Scott, A. (2000). Leadership experiences of students of color. *NASPA Journal, 37*(3), 496–510. https://doi.org/10.2202/1949-6605.1112

Bolling, J. R. (2020, August 6). Tracking the machine: A timeline of UA's "underground" Greek organization. *The Crimson White.* https://cw.ua.edu/65356/news/tracking-the-machine-a-timeline-of-uas-underground-greek-organization/

Boulton, C. (2016). Black identities inside advertising: Race inequality, code switching, and stereotype threat. *Howard Journal of Communications, 27*(2), 130–144. https://doi.org/10.1080/10646175.2016.1148646.

Brown, L., Williams, B., & Williams, Q. (2021, August 19). Melanin messages: Black college women's experiences and reflections on navigating colorism. *Journal of Diversity in Higher Education.* Advance online publication. https://doi.org/10.1037/dhe0000347

Burt, B. A., Williams, K. L., & Smith, W. A. (2018). Into the storm: Ecological and sociological impediments to Black males' persistence in engineering graduate programs. *American Educational Research Journal, 55*(5), 965–1006. https://doi.org/10.3102/0002831218763587

Cabrera, N. L. (2018). *White guys on campus: Racism, White immunity, and the myth of "post-racial" higher education.* Rutgers University Press.

Donahoo, S. (2019). Owning Black hair: The pursuit of identity and authenticity in higher education. In U. Thomas (Ed.), *Navigating micro-aggressions toward women in higher education* (pp. 73–95). IGI Global.

Dugan, J. P., Turman, N. T., & Torrez, M. A. (2015). Beyond individual leader development: Cultivating collective capacities. In M. P. Evans & K. K. Abowitz (Eds.), *Engaging Youth in Leadership for Social and Political Change* (New Directions for Student Leadership, no. 148, pp. 5–15). Jossey-Bass. https://doi.org/10.1002/yd.20149

Eakins, A., & Eakins, S. L., Sr. (2017). African American students at predominantly White institutions: A collaborative style cohort recruitment and retention model. *Journal of Learning in Higher Education, 13*(2), 51–57. https://eric.ed.gov/?id=EJ1161827

Edelman, M. W. (2015, August 21). *It's hard to be what you can't see.* Children's Defense Fund. https://www.childrensdefense.org/child-watch-columns/health/2015/its-hard-to-be-what-you-cant-see/

Garibay, J. C., & Vincent, S. (2018). Racially inclusive climates within degree programs and increasing student of color enrollment: An examination of environmental/sustainability programs. *Journal of Diversity in Higher Education, 11*(2), 201–220. https://doi.org/10.1037/dhe0000030

Gorski, P. C. (2019). Racial battle fatigue and activist burnout in racial justice activists of color at predominately White colleges and universities. *Race Ethnicity and Education, 22*(1), 1–20. https://doi.org/10.1080/13613324.2018.1497966

Gramly, K. M. (2020). Misperceptions of racial and ethnic student organizations on a predominantly White campus. *Sociation Today, 19*(2), 59–69. https://sociation.ncsociologyassoc.org/wp-content/uploads/2020/10/mispreceptons_proof_10212020.pdf

Gusa, D. L. (2010). White institutional presence: The impact of whiteness on campus climate. *Harvard Educational Review, 80*(4), 464–490. https://doi.org/10.17763/haer.80.4.p5j483825u110002

Harper, S., & Quaye, J. (2007). Student organizations as venues for Black identity expression and development among African American male student leaders. *Journal of College Student Development, 48*(2), 127–144. https://doi.org/10.1353/csd.2007.0012

Harwood, S. A., Huntt, M. B., Mendenhall, R., & Lewis, J. A. (2012). Racial microaggressions in the residence halls: Experiences of Students of Color at a predominantly white university. *Journal of Diversity in Higher Education, 5*(3), 159–173. https://doi.org/10.1037/a0028956

Hernández, R. J., & Villodas, M. T. (2019). Overcoming racial battle fatigue: The associations between racial microaggressions, coping, and mental health among Chicana/o and Latina/o college students. *Cultural Diversity and Ethnic Minority Psychology, 26*(3), 399–411. https://doi.org/10.1037/cdp0000306

Hill, K. D. (2009). Code switching pedagogies and African American student voices: Acceptance and resistance. *Journal of Adolescent & Adult Literacy*, *53*(2), 120–131. https://doi.org/10.1598/JAAL.53.2.3

Holland, M., & Sicurella, S. (2019, April 4). Confronting UGA's history of blackface and racism on campus from the past 70 years. *The Red and Black*. https://www.redandblack.com/uganews/confronting-ugas-history-of-blackface-and-racism-on-campus-from-the-past-70-years/article_79d20eda-567f-11e9-bdf2-a3b6b1d7f6ba.html

Hotchkins, B. (2017). Black women students at predominantly White universities: Narratives of identity politics, well-being and leadership mobility. *NASPA Journal About Women in Higher Education*, *10*(2), 144–155. https://doi.org/10.1080/19407882.2017.1326943

Hotchkins, B. K. (2014). Guess who's coming to the meeting? African American student leadership experiences unpacked. *College Student Affairs Journal*, *32*(1), 171–188. https://www.proquest.com/openview/62433658b70f710fe28135f362ac968c/1?pq-origsite=gscholar&cbl=47847

Hotchkins, B. K. (2017). Black student leaders practicing resistance in the midst of chaos: Applying transgenerational activist knowledge to navigate a predominantly white institution. *The Journal of Negro Education*, *86*(3), 269–282. https://doi.org/10.7709/jnegroeducation.86.3.0269

Hurtado, S., & Carter, D. F. (1997). Effects of college transition and perceptions of the campus racial climate on Latino college students' sense of belonging. *Sociology of Education*, *70*(4), 324–345. https://doi.org/10.2307/2673270

Jaggers, D. L. (2019). *Navigating white spaces: A phenomenological study of Black women's involvement experiences in predominantly White student organizations* [Unpublished doctoral dissertation]. University of Tennessee.

Jaschik, S. (2018, October 29). Not just Megyn Kelly. *Inside Higher Ed*. https://www.insidehighered.com/news/2018/10/29/halloween-approaches-another-university-faces-blackface-incident

Jones, V. A., & Reddick, R. J. (2017). The heterogeneity of resistance: How Black students utilize engagement and activism to challenge PWI inequalities. *The Journal of Negro Education*, *86*(3), 204–219. https://doi.org/10.7709/jnegroeducation.86.3.0204

Joya, P. A. (2019). *"Just call me Poe": An autoethnographic look at codeswitching and passing* (Publication No. 1566) [Master's thesis, Boise State University]. Boise State University Theses and Dissertations. https://scholarworks.boisestate.edu/td/1566/

Kodama, C. M., & Dugan, J. P. (2013). Leveraging leadership efficacy for college students: Disaggregating data to examine unique predictors by race. *Equity & Excellence in Education*, *46*(2), 184–201. https://doi.org/10.1080/10665684.2013.780646

Koman, T. (2016, February 16). University of Florida senior speaks out against student government practices in troubling viral video. *Cosmopolitan*. https://

www.cosmopolitan.com/college/news/a53730/not-my-system-uf-student-government-video/

Komives, S. R., Lucas, N., & McMahon, T. R. (2013). *Exploring leadership: For college students who want to make a difference* (3rd ed.). Jossey-Bass.

Korn, M. (2019, February 14). Colleges continue to confront blackface on campus. *The Wall Street Journal.* https://www.wsj.com/articles/colleges-continue-to-confront-blackface-on-campus-11550167774

Linder, C., Quaye, S. J., Lange, A. C., Evans, M. E., & Stewart, T. J. (2020). *Identity-based student activism: Power and oppression on college campuses.* Routledge.

Linder, C., Quaye, S. J., Lange, A. C., Roberts, R. E., Lacy, M. C., & Okello, W. K. (2019). "A student should have the privilege of just being a student": Student activism as labor. *The Review of Higher Education, 42*(5), 37–62. http://doi.org/10.1353/rhe.2019.0044

Liu, H., & Baker, C. (2016). White knights: Leadership as the heroicisation of whiteness. *Leadership, 12*(4), 420–448. https://doi.org/10.1177/1742715014565127

Martin, G. L., Williams, B. M., Green, B., & Smith, M. J. (2019). Reframing activism as leadership. In G. L. Martin, C. Linder, & B. M. Williams (Eds.), *Leadership Learning Through Activism* (New Directions for Student Leadership, no. 161, pp. 9–24). Jossey-Bass. https://doi.org/10.1002/yd.20317

Means, D. R., & Pyne, K. B. (2017). Finding my way: Perceptions of institutional support and belonging in low-income, first-generation, first-year college students. *Journal of College Student Development, 58*(6), 907–924. https://doi.org/10.1353/csd.2017.0071

Mills, K. J. (2020). "It's systemic": Environmental racial microaggressions experienced by Black undergraduates at a predominantly white institution. *Journal of Diversity in Higher Education, 13*(1), 44. https://doi.org/10.1037/dhe0000121

Museus, S. D. (2008). The role of ethnic student organizations in fostering African American and Asian American students' cultural adjustment and membership at predominantly white institutions. *Journal of College Student Development, 49*(6), 568–586. https://doi.org/10.1353/csd.0.0039

New, J. (2016, May 3). One campus, two student governments. *Inside Higher Ed.* https://www.insidehighered.com/news/2016/05/03/minority-students-u-kansas-create-parallel-student-government

New, J. (2017, February 9). The "black hole" of college sports. *Inside Higher Ed.* https://www.insidehighered.com/news/2017/02/09/baylor-not-alone-shielding-athletes-accused-misconduct-punishment

Park, J. J. (2014). Clubs and the campus racial climate: Student organizations and interracial friendship in college. *Journal of College Student Development, 55*(7), 641–660. https://doi.org/10.1353/csd.2014.0076

Peralta, A. K. (2015). The underrepresentation of Women of Color in law review leadership positions. *Berkeley La Raza Law Journal, 25*, 68. https://heinonline.org/HOL/LandingPage?handle=hein.journals/berklarlj25&div=3&id=&page=

Pérez, D., & Sáenz, V. B. (2017). Thriving Latino males in selective predominantly white institutions. *Journal of Hispanic Higher Education, 16*(2), 162–186. https://doi.org/10.1177/1538192717697754

Peterson, L. (2019, September 5). "No interest": How multicultural student government came to be and how it left. *The University Daily Kansan*. https://www.kansan.com/news/no-interest-how-multicultural-student-government-came-to-be-and-how-it-left/article_d36e16c8-cf79-11e9-b6eb-6fac5c008617.html

Rahman, R. A., Zakariyab, N. H., Jannatun, S. N. H., & Ahmada, N. N. (2020, December). Enhancing students achievement through Astin theory of involvement. *Proceedings of the 4th UUM International Qualitative Research Conference (QRC 2020), 1*, 3. https://www.qualitative-research-conference.com/download/proceedings-2020/253.pdf

Renn, K. A. (2007). LGBT student leaders and queer activists: Identities of lesbian, gay, bisexual, transgender, and queer identified college student leaders and activists. *Journal of College Student Development, 48*(3), 311–330. https://doi.org/10.1353/csd.2007.0029

Renn, K. A., & Patton, L. D. (2011). Campus ecology and environments. In J. H. Schuh, S. R. Jones, S. R. Harper, & Associates (Eds.), *Student services: A handbook for the profession* (5th ed, pp. 242–256). Jossey-Bass.

Rincón, V., & Hollis, L. (2018). Cultural code-switching and Chicana/o post-secondary student persistence: A hermeneutic phenomenological analysis. *Journal of Latinos and Education, 19*(3), 232–245. https://doi.org/10.1080/15348431.2018.1499516

Sarcedo, G. L., Matias, C. E., Montoya, R., & Nishi, N. (2015). Dirty dancing with race and class: Microaggressions toward first-generation and low income college students of color. *Journal of Critical Scholarship on Higher Education and Student Affairs, 2*(1), 1. https://ecommons.luc.edu/jcshesa/vol2/iss1/1

Schreiner, L. A. (2018). Thriving in the second year of college: Pathways to success. In L. A. Schreiner (Ed.), *Sophomore Success: Making the Most of the Second Year* (New Directions for Higher Education, no. 183, pp. 9–21). Jossey-Bass. https://doi.org/10.1002/he.20289

Smith, W. A., Mustaffa, J. B., Jones, C. M., Curry, T. J., & Allen, W. R. (2016). "You make me wanna holler and throw up both my hands!": Campus culture, Black misandric microaggressions, and racial battle fatigue. *International Journal of Qualitative Studies in Education, 29*(9), 1189–1209. https://doi.org/10.1080/09518398.2016.1214296

Stewart, T. J., & Quaye, S. J. (2019). Building bridges: Rethinking student activist leadership. In G. L. Martin, C. Linder, & B. M. Williams (Eds.), *Leadership Learning Through Activism* (New Directions for Student Leadership, no. 161, pp. 51–63). https://doi.org/10.1002/yd.20320

Stewart, T. J., & Williams, B. (2019). Nuanced activism: A matrix of resistance. In A. Dache-Gerbino, S. J. Quaye, C. Linder, & K. McGuire (Eds.), *Rise up!: Activism as education* (pp. 201–223). Michigan State University Press.

Sullivan, S. (2006). *Revealing whiteness: The unconscious habits of racial privilege.* Indiana University Press.

Tawil, R. (2019, February 11). Why blackface remains popular on college campuses. *The Wall Street Journal.* https://www.wsj.com/articles/colleges-continue-to-confront-blackface-on-campus-11550167774

The Arch Society. (2018). *The Arch Society constitution.* https://uga.campuslabs.com/engage/organization/archsociety/documents/view/846376

University of Georgia. (n.d.). *Arch Society.* https://studentaffairs.uga.edu/vp/arch-society/

Wheeler, R. S. (2008). Becoming adept at code-switching. *Educational Leadership, 65*(7), 54–58. https://www.ventrislearning.com/wp-content/uploads/Wheeler_Ed_Leadership_April_08.pdf

Wilder, C. S. (2013). *Ebony and ivy: Race, slavery, and the troubled history of America's universities.* Bloomsbury.

Williams, B., Williams, Q., & Smith, C. (2021). How social class identity influences students' leadership and advocacy development. In S. Ardoin & K. L. Guthrie (Eds.), *Leadership Learning Through the Lens of Social Class* (New Directions for Student Leadership, no. 169, pp. 69–76). Jossey-Bass. https://doi.org/10.1002/yd.20422

Williams, B. M., Collier, J. N., Anderson Wadley, B., Stokes, T. N., & Coghill, K. B. (2022). Should I straighten my hair? Narratives of Black college women with natural hair. *NASPA Journal of Women and Gender.* Accepted Manuscript.

Young, V. A., Barrett, R., & Lovejoy, K. B. (2014). *Other people's English: Code-meshing, code-switching, and African American literacy.* Teachers College Press.

11

POSSIBILITIES AND FORECLOSURES

Exploring the Relationship Between Whiteness and Anti-Blackness in Higher Education

Tenisha L. Tevis and Natasha Croom

One does not need to go far to be met with practical exhibitions of whiteness. For example, in January 2021, while preparing this book chapter, whiteness was on full display in Washington DC. The storming and siege of the U.S. Capitol building demonstrated perfectly the ideological, cultural, and structural dimensions of systemic whiteness. Ideologically, whiteness undergirded the rhetoric of stolen elections (as if elections inherently belong to one person or group over the other) and the media's insistence on describing the mostly White crowd as protestors instead of rioters at the onset (a reframing that signals innocent intentions). Structurally, whiteness informed the lack of surveillance and policing of these mostly White bodies despite the premeditation afoot and the actual breaking of laws abounding (i.e., entering unauthorized spaces, stealing, vandalism, physical assault, and carrying weapons into spaces unlawfully). Lastly, within the cultural dimension, the normalcy of whiteness prevailed through the use of nooses, swastikas, and the rebel flag, most of which can be seen on a daily basis throughout the United States and serve as constant reminders of white supremacy—an overwhelming hegemonic ideology of white racial political, economic, and cultural dominance and entitlement (Ansley, 1997). Although a full analysis of the insurrection is beyond the scope of this chapter and book, it provides a pointed example of the pervasiveness of whiteness as a system of privilege—a system that extends into and has been taken up with fervor in educational contexts.

Although it is generally understood that racism is a system of oppression, there seems to be less clarity about whiteness. Additionally, although whiteness and racism have been taken up in analyses of higher education contexts, anti-Black racism/anti-Blackness,[1] explicitly, is a more recent addition to our canons and lexicons. Our overarching claims throughout this chapter are that (a) whiteness (as opposed to White *people* solely) is an overlooked progenitor to anti-Black racism, (b) whiteness is a system of privilege that is interrelated with racism as a system of oppression, and (c) we cannot end racial oppression for Black communities in higher education without interrogating and attending to systemic whiteness explicitly in conversations about anti-Black racism. Thus, we organized this chapter in the following ways. First, we define *anti-Black racism*. Second, we situate whiteness as a system intended to underscore racial privilege ideologically, culturally, and structurally. Lastly, we extract how anti-Black racism has been employed thus far in higher education scholarship and offer perspectives on what possibilities are afforded or foreclosed on when whiteness is or is not made explicit in this budding arena of research and, by extension, practice.

Anti-Black Racism in Higher Education

It is well documented that racism—a system of oppression based on the social construction of race meant to maintain white supremacy and the subordination of racially minoritized communities through resource allocation (Lopez, 2006)—is ideologically, culturally, and structurally embedded in our society and much, if not *all*, of our social institutions (Crenshaw et al., 1995; Delgado & Stefancic, 2017; Taylor et al., 2009). The ideological dimension encompasses hegemonic and normative beliefs, ideas, and concepts. The cultural dimension captures the social norms, roles, language, and everyday practices which have been normalized in social spaces. Lastly, the structural dimension embodies policies, in/formal rules, and customs enacted within and across social institutions. Where whiteness organizes racial privilege systemically, which we will unpack later in this chapter, racism organizes racial subordination systemically. Ideologically, racism encompasses hegemonic and normative beliefs and ideas held about racially minoritized communities (i.e., Black people are lazy; Mexicans are dangerous; Asians are model minorities, etc.). Culturally, racism captures the social norms and everyday practices normalized in ways that subordinate racially minoritized folks (i.e., folks surfacing how they experience racism with no recourse even after formally reporting it; revolving door of faculty of color in predominantly white institutions [PWIs]; racial microaggressions). Lastly, the structural dimension of racism embodies policies, rules, and institutional structures that maintain a one-down positionality for communities of color (i.e., separate but equal federal, state, and local laws and policies; *Brown v. Board of Education*; federal and state land-grant—or land-grab [Lee et al., n.d.]—legislation; inequitable distribution of federal, state, and local resources by institutional type [i.e., PWIs, Historically Black College and Universities, Minority-Serving Institutions, etc.]). Broadly linked to white supremacy, taken together, these interlocking dimensions create systemic racisms (Alcoff, 2013) that undergird racial subordination in society.

Anti-Black racism is a relatively new perspective being explicitly employed in higher education scholarship and practice specifically. In a later section, we surface how anti-Black racism has been taken up in the field to illuminate the ways in which whiteness has been simultaneously engaged. This approach is meant to offer some glimpse into what is afforded when whiteness is part of the framing and analysis and what is possibly foreclosed upon when it is not. For example, in recent popular writings about "how to be antiracists," authors/scholars have written about racism without addressing whiteness and/or white supremacy. These exclusions have allowed for such assertions as "people of color can be racist" rather than assertions that people of color can be prejudiced, and in some instances, engage with whiteness in ideological and cultural ways. To be sure, whiteness and anti-Black racism are related. Particularly, we understand whiteness and racism as parallel systems of privilege and oppression, respectively, which both inform the various instantiations of racisms (Alcoff, 2013) and, in this case, a more pervasive anti-Black racism. But what exactly is anti-Black racism?

For sure more scholars have employed critical framings of race and racism to examine the racist legacies that govern higher education and their subsequent impact on the status and condition of Black lives—including anti-Black racism. Drawing on an interdisciplinary body of scholarship, we offer that anti-Black racism is a specific form of racism that dictates the possibilities, or rather the impossibilities, of humanity for Black communities (Dumas, 2016). Moreover, anti-Black racism manifests in particular ideological, cultural, and structural ways, often drawing on constant psychic, physical, and material violence and surveillance to further demarcate, delineate, and fix Black people and Blackness as problematic, "other," and most importantly, nonhuman. Garner (2017) explained that "whiteness is the default setting for 'human': everything else is deviant and requires explanation" (p. 219). As Blackness has been situated on a binary continuum with whiteness, a polar opposite (Alcoff, 2003, 2013; Delgado,

1996; Perea, 1998), Blackness then becomes, in this context, nonhuman. Having humanness stripped away certainly has an adverse impact on thriving and, more immediately, surviving—and those who cannot survive are systematically pushed out (Sheth & Croom, 2021). Before delving into the ways in which anti-Black racism, and to a certain extent whiteness, has been taken up in higher education literature, we provide an unpacking of systemic whiteness.

Unpacking Systemic Whiteness

Whiteness is a system—particularly a system of privilege. As previously mentioned, social systems have ideological, cultural, and structural elements that inform how society and the social world work. Taken together, these interlocking dimensions shape a system of, in this case, whiteness that undergirds racial privilege in society. From our perspective, it is particularly important to situate whiteness as a system in order to move away from such heavy emphasis on individual White people receiving what gets taken up as individual-level privileges. Moving from an individual-level analysis to a systemic one allows scholars and practitioners, alike, to identify and thus address the ways in which whiteness permeates our ideas, everyday practices, and social rules embedded deeply across our social worlds. Moreover, "not acknowledging whiteness contributes to the permanence of race and racism" (Matias et al., 2014, p. 291). Expressly, whiteness and racism are intertwined systems based on the social construction of race—the former of privilege and the latter of oppression. More importantly, both ultimately are employed to, again, maintain white supremacy. But what exactly is *whiteness*?

Although writings on whiteness have a rich history, with works put forward by Black scholars and writers (see James Baldwin, W.E.B Du Bois, Toni Morrison), its prevalence in higher education research has acutely risen in the last decade or so in an effort to examine the unexamined. Particularly, scholars have surfaced the "White cultural ideology embedded in the language, cultural practices, traditions, and perceptions of knowledge [that] allow [postsecondary] institutions to remain racialized" (Gusa, 2010, p. 465). Through obscure diversity statements (Cole & Harper, 2017; Jones, 2019), performative responses to racism (Tevis, 2020), inequitable academic career advancement (Croom, 2017; Croom & Patton, 2011, 2015), and the ongoing treatment of Black students as "trespassers" in higher education (Haynes & Bazner, 2019), for example, institutions of higher education have and continue to be bastions of racial privilege, ultimately protecting whiteness and those who benefit from it.

More often than not, whiteness has been articulated in the following ways:

- racial privilege (Leonardo, 2009)—"the notion that white subjects accrue advantages by virtue of being constructed as white" (p. 75)
- discourse (Leonardo, 2009; McIntosh, 1989)—an articulation of said racial privilege
- social location (DiAngelo, 2011; Frankenberg, 1993, 1997; Gusa, 2010)—a positional advantage that leads to overrepresentation of White people, with embedded bias that prevents racially minoritized people from receiving its benefits
- dispositions and actions (Gillborn, 2006; Harris, 1993)—tendencies to behave in a particular way that, in this instance, afford White people the ability to maintain, pass on, or deny rights to then bolster a racial caste (Alexander, 2010; Harris, 1993) or a socioracial hierarchy
- interpretive filter (Foste & Jones, 2020)—a lens through which to understand both self and racialized others—in essence, to grant racial privilege through domination

All of these conceptualizations (a) contribute to a systemic understanding of whiteness; (b) surface whiteness as normative, universal, civilized, unmarked yet visible, and power laden; and (c) demonstrate a constant and consistent privileging of white epistemology, being, and doing (Applebaum, 2010; DiAngelo, 2011; Frankenberg, 1993, 1997; Garner, 2017; Harris, 1993; Leonardo, 2009; Mills, 2007; Perry, 2007; Sullivan, 2014; Whitehead, 2021). Due to the hegemonic normativity of whiteness, particularly in social institutions such as colleges and universities (Gusa, 2010), it becomes critically important to surface the myriad ways in which it manifests. To draw closer attention to systemic whiteness and thus its ultimate relationship to anti-Black racism, we elaborate on its manifestations ideologically, culturally, and structurally.

Whiteness Ideologically

Ideologically, whiteness shapes hegemonic, normalized ideas and beliefs about White racial epistemologies and identities—which ultimately informs behavior and practice. As Leonardo (2009) noted, "The conditions of white supremacy make White privilege possible" (p. 9); otherwise stated, the most central normalized idea about whiteness is that white ways of knowing, doing, and being are best, right, just, logical, ethical, and all around superior to any other ways of being, doing, and knowing. Whiteness embodies more than notional or abstract ideas about racial and/or ethnic groups; it embraces what are believed to be irrefutable propositions that have shaped (White) people's schema—how information is understood and interpreted. Moreover, whiteness's range, reach, power, and subjectivity demonstrate that it is far more than a trite belief in supremacism; it is epistemic—rooted in ways of knowing and *that* knowledge is validated, and dogmatic—such that beliefs are held with absolute certainty. Whiteness, informed by the ideology of white supremacy, however, does not only exist in the ideas and beliefs of White people. People of color too internalize whiteness. Its discourse spreads and is propagated, particularly in the "fears of a nonwhite nation, whites' sense of ownership and the right to exclude, and [in the] deeply racialized thinking that systematically undermines the well-being of people of color" (Pulido, 2015, p. 812; see also Rattan & Eberhardt, 2010). In its endeavor to privilege White populations, whiteness not only sustains a racial advantage but also memorializes supremacy and racial domination, thus subjugating those deemed as "other"—that is, accomplices (White allies) and activists (racially minoritized communities). This privileged epistemology, rooted in white supremacy, then imbues and pervades day-to-day activities (i.e., culture) and institutions (i.e., structures; Gillborn, 2006).

Whiteness Culturally

Desmond and Emirbayer (2009) explained that racial domination, on one hand, has the power to categorize, segregate, and deny racially minoritized communities rights and opportunities, while privileging White people. On the other hand, it is exhibited in the attitudes and behaviors of our daily lives and interactions. Hence, at the heart of cultural practices that garner (and inhibit) privilege, is the effort to preserve the narrative that White people are superior, whereas all others are inferior. Taking this into consideration, "a critical look at white privilege, or the analysis of white racial hegemony, must be complemented by an equally rigorous examination of white supremacy, or the analysis of white racial domination" (Leonardo, 2009, p. 9). Collectively, these attributes of whiteness not only contribute to the understanding of how white identity is developed specifically when compared to racially minoritized groups, but it also constructs for the imagination the cultural underpinning that constitutes whiteness (Frankenberg, 1993; Gillborn, 2015; Leonardo, 2009)—what Leonardo (2009) referred to as "the codes of white culture" (p. 9). Briefly, culture is inclusive of the shared values, convictions, behaviors, and language of a group that are learned and transmitted, whereby individuals are conditioned to develop and maintain their identity. Thus, it is clear why whiteness is expressed as a set of "assumptions, beliefs, and practices that place the interests and perspectives of White people at the center of what is considered normal and everyday" (Gillborn, 2015, p. 278). Such an understanding further brings to the forefront how whiteness has become so deeply ingrained in environments like postsecondary institutions that have a long history of exclusion, with their founding intent to reproduce structural advantage and social privilege solely for White people. Most importantly, these everyday norms, beliefs, and practices often become codified through policies, in/formal rules, and customs enacted in and through our social institutions. As Gusa (2010) explained, "[By neglecting] to find the ways in which White ideological homogenizing practices sustain the structure of domination and oppression, institutional policies and practices [come] to be seen as unproblematic or inevitable" (p. 465).

Whiteness Structurally

Since the founding of the early colonial colleges, the history of America's postsecondary system has been marred by white supremacy. Although it was the early colleges' sole intention to preserve white cultural norms, train clergy, and create and maintain the new ruling class (Arendale, 2011), this historical endeavor precipitated higher education's ongoing hostility toward racial diversity and inclusion (Tevis & Pifer, 2021). Because institutional practices remain unexamined (Gusa, 2010), whiteness remains in play, allowing the relationship between it and white supremacy to go unchecked, thus further giving way to racism and, most profoundly, the preponderance of anti-Black racism. Trite pushes for diversity, equity, and inclusion still often ignore, erase, or downplay the racist realities from which these institutions were founded.

As whiteness is viewed as normal and educational practices are characterized as neutral (Gusa, 2010), despite their inception and codifications as White-only spaces, obtuse engagement makes actors within these contexts complicit and devoid of any responsibility for naming and addressing the various ways racial privilege is amassed through institutional policies and in/formal rules and customs. As Croom and Kortegast (2018) posited, however, institutional actors "sometimes try to convince ourselves that a difference-neutral approach to our work—an approach that does not consider the effects of power and privilege associated with social differences in our beliefs, ideas, and actions—feels fair and right" (p. 27). Race-evasive and difference-neutral approaches to policy, leadership, and decision-making maintain and exacerbate, rather than eliminate, inequity—and more directly reinforce white racial privilege and a socioracial hierarchy that was always intended to oppress and subordinate racially minoritized communities (Bell, 1989, 1993).

At the beginning of this chapter, we offered that whiteness is a progenitor for anti-Black racism. It is important to be direct about our claim here. Whiteness emerged from white supremacy as a system guiding the privilege of, historically, White people and, contemporarily, those in close proximation to white skin and racial supremacist ideology. Chiefly, whiteness is embedded everywhere to the point that one does not know where it ends or where it begins; thus, defining whiteness (and white supremacy for that matter) has always come in the form of articulating what it is *not*—as it is rooted in the inferiority of others rather than an actual articulation of supremacy of a White racial collective. Here, we are asserting that whiteness is actually a system of privilege that exists parallel to racism and, in this chapter, anti-Black racism. That is to say, whiteness is a system of privilege that organizes privilege around White racial identity and hegemonic Eurocentric ideologies, cultures, and structures, whereas anti-Black racism is a system of oppression that organizes subordination around supremacist ideologies, cultures, and structures. Anti-Black racism becomes about inferiorizing and subordinating Black racial identity, epistemology, and being. Although different, white supremacy and whiteness go hand in hand—as does whiteness and anti-Black racism as two sides of the same coin of systemic dis/advantage.

Having expanded upon our understanding of whiteness and its relationship to anti-Black racism, we now turn our attention to how anti-Black racism is engaged in higher education literature. Whiteness as an analytic is a useful tool to critique, in this instance, the practices, and thus the cultures and ideologies deeply rooted and intentionally embedded in higher education. Foundational to this chapter is our belief that analyses of anti-Black racism without explicit, or minimally backgrounded, operationalization and critique/analysis of whiteness may foreclose on critical opportunities to subvert, address, and ultimately end anti-Black racism as a form of racial oppression and whiteness as a form of racial privileging.

Higher Education Anti-Blackness Literature

Stewart (2018) noted that not enough attention has been paid to anti-Blackness in higher education, and particularly student affairs, research and practice. No doubt connected to the Black Lives Matter movement and the ongoing senseless deaths and violence perpetuated against Black communities, there is a growing segment of higher education literature dedicated to surfacing, centering, and interrogating anti-Blackness/anti-Black racism explicitly toward the goals of liberating Black communities across postsecondary contexts. It is this small grouping of works we center in this chapter while recognizing that the list may not be exhaustive. For the purposes of exploring how anti-Black racism is being taken up in the higher education studies literature, we examined six articles that claimed to deal with anti-Blackness or anti-Black racism in higher education and one article that was about education policy broadly (particularly because five of the six cited the piece). In the next section we share summaries of the work and how they take up anti-Black racism and whiteness (or not).

Garriott et al. (2008) was the oldest piece found that claimed to grapple with anti-Black racism in the context of higher education. The purpose of the study was to explore the relationship between anti-Black racism and White college students' psychosocial development and self-concept. Part of their findings suggested that as more "White students express racial superiority and racial dissonance, the less socially adjusted to college they may be" (p. 54). Despite the claim to be explicitly dealing with anti-Black racism, there was no definition of *anti-Black racism*; moreover, they used *anti-Black racism* and *racism* interchangeably and did not dig into the particularities of racism as experienced specifically by Black people—other than to cite research on Black people. Further, although they did not articulate whiteness or white supremacy, they did employ the White Racial Identity Attitudes Scale and specifically included the White Superiority/Segregationist Ideology subscale. Without clear definitions of *anti-Black racism* and *whiteness* it is difficult to know what assumptions are being made theoretically and conceptually and practically (i.e., one can assume the scholars considered whiteness or white supremacy given the use of the aforementioned subscale, but it would be an assumption). Additionally, without clear articulations of either concept, it is no wonder that all of the recommendations are about heightening White students' racial awareness and ultimately intervening so that White students become more socially adjusted in college. It is not clearly articulated how these approaches eradicate anti-Black racism and, although likely inadvertent, does more to further privilege White students.

Dumas (2016) is the most cited piece among this grouping of articles. Conceptual in nature, the purpose of the article is to argue for how education policy, broadly (and primarily through the example of school desegregation), is rooted in anti-Blackness. Dumas defined *anti-Blackness* generally as the "cultural disregard for and disgust with blackness" (p. 12) and drew on the interdisciplinary work of Afro-pessimists. From the work of Afro-pessimists, Dumas further described anti-Blackness as constant forms of violence, constant surveillance, constant problematizing of Black and Blackness, and constant irreconcilability. All of this ultimately contributes to the idea that to be perceived as lacking humanness is literally akin to being "socially dead" (p. 12). With regard to education policy, Dumas wrote,

> Fundamentally, [policy as a site of anti-Blackness] is an acknowledgment of the long history of Black struggle for educational opportunity, which is to say a struggle against what has always been (and continues to be) a struggle against specific anti-Black ideologies, discourses, representations, (mal)distribution of material resources, and physical and psychic assaults on Black bodies in schools. . . . And this, then, is the essence of anti-Blackness in education policy: the Black [*sic*] is constructed as . . . inherently uneducable, or at very least, unworthy of education. (p. 16)

Although an overall compelling argument for sure, Dumas did not explicitly name whiteness in the article. Therefore, although the example of school desegregation policy is soundly analyzed through an anti-Blackness lens, it still leaves unturned and unacknowledged the ideological, cultural, and structural dimensions of whiteness manifested and maintained by such a policy. Although we do not believe this to be the intention, the lack of an explicit whiteness analysis begs the question, Is there anti-Blackness without whiteness?

Using the national political climate exacerbated by the Trump-era presidency, Haywood (2017) connected the ways anti-Black racism manifests in and across Latino communities and provided propositions for engaging Latinos in research that seeks to disrupt whiteness and anti-Black racism. Haywood drew direct connections to whiteness primarily through colorism and the privilege associated with lighter skin across Latino diasporas. She then went on to argue that such privilege opens up possibilities to internalize "racial projects" (p. 959), including hegemonic narratives about hard work that are dismissive of systemic racial privilege and oppression (e.g., meritocracy). In discussing internalized racism, that is to say the ways some Latinos may take up whiteness and White supremacy, Haywood grappled with how it is "structural, systemic, and insidious" (p. 961). Moreover, by connecting whiteness and anti-Blackness, Haywood provided compelling arguments about why White-identified Latinos might vote for Donald Trump, even if they may be voting against their overall interests.

Dancy et al. (2018) used a higher education context to connect anti-Blackness and settler colonialism. They were specifically concerned with what they called three dimensions of anti-Blackness—"(a) interpretations of Black labor through colonial arrangements; (b) relationship between labor, ownership, and education; and (c) institutionalization of Black suffering" (p. 178).

This piece is cited consistently by Haynes and Bazner (2019), Stewart (2018), and Abrica et al. (2020) and appears to be a theoretical and conceptual staple in understanding the relationship between anti-Blackness and higher education. Dancy et al. drew on scholars writing on Afro-pessimism, such as Fanon (1961) and Wilderson (2010), as well as Dumas (2016). Ultimately, they argued that within institutions of higher education Black bodies are still engaged as property employed for labor (rather than laborers laboring) and that these institutions still control and police Black bodies. To make their points, they drew on the ways in which enslaved Black people, historically, were used to build college campuses and serve as house servants and personal attendants to college presidents; the uncompensated labor of Black women academics and the disregard of intellect for nonathletic-affiliated Black men; the economic exploitation of Black men athletes; the continued connection between property ownership, education funding, and ongoing inequitable housing policy implementations; and the ongoing psychological violence enacted upon Black people in higher education and the cultural and economic devaluing of institutions created to serve them. Interestingly, there is no explicit treatment of whiteness in the article despite being wrapped up in the discussion of Mills's (1997) racial contract work as an articulation of white supremacy. In the end, the scholars invited readers to imagine "Black divestment" (p. 190) from a white racial contract. Although it is arguable if this is possible given the realities of race and racism (Bell, 1991) and the reactions of White people historically to such moves (see Messer et al., 2018), we wonder if leaving whiteness, as a system of privilege, untouched ultimately leaves anti-Black racism intact.

Stewart (2018) excavated how anti-Blackness is present in the field of student affairs through a "rhetoric of inclusion" (p. 18) that is chiefly situated in the ideologies of absence. More specifically, he extrapolated how Black graduate students and professionals are easily made objects in the inclusion rhetoric and practice, which he argued is directly connected to them not being human, rather being things to be controlled for the benefit of the institution—and ultimately whiteness. Expressly, by pointing out that Black graduate students and student affairs professionals experience the "absence as (un)belonging . . . absence as (un)safety . . . absence as (in)validation . . . absence as (un)rewarded" (pp. 22–24), he is also pointing to the privilege of White graduate students and student affairs professionals to (at least from a racial perspective and not negating intersectionality) feel belonging, safety, validation, and reward. Ultimately, Stewart proclaimed that Blackness does not have to be rooted in death and invisibility and offered Afro-futurism as a possibility for disrupting anti-Blackness in the field of student affairs by engaging a cultural collective that recognizes "Black as present and accounted for and Black as present then, now, and again" (p. 25). Stewart expressly acknowledged the role and manifestations of whiteness that allow for a deeper sensemaking of privilege and subordination.

Haynes and Bazner (2019) surfaced the demands of faculty from student activists to interrogate whiteness for the purposes of Black liberation in higher education broadly, but learning specifically. They, like most of the other pieces centered in this chapter, drew on the work of Dumas (2016) and others who theorize Afro-pessimism. Haynes and Bazner (2019) explicitly claimed that anti-Blackness cannot be addressed without attention to whiteness. They stated, "Without an interrogation of Whiteness, it might be difficult for faculty, and institutional leaders alike, to understand how anti-Blackness constitutes what it means to *Learn While Black* [*sic*] at PWIs" (p. 1149). Moreover, they posited that part of experiencing humanness is the freedom to create knowledge and learn. By connecting whiteness and anti-Blackness, Haynes and Bazner were able to extract several instantiations of privilege (as experienced by White students) and subordination (as experienced by Black students). In terms of "learning while Black" and anti-Blackness, Black students tend to not be believed about their racialized experiences; have their epistemologies and knowledges invalidated, erased, and/or added as "the other" in the curriculum; and have their racialized existence be viewed as *the* problem (rather than racism and anti-Black racism being the problem). Without an interrogation of whiteness we leave untouched the racialized existence of White people and the depth of white racial epistemic privilege embedded in the curriculum and pedagogical approaches. Additionally, untouched is the belief that because White people are seemingly without race, then (a) racism is not systemic but an abnormality experienced individually (if believed) and (b) is not the responsibility or problem of White communities (particularly those who haven't developed a critical racial consciousness) to subvert.

The last of the articles reviewed for this chapter is Abrica et al. (2020). The purpose of the research was to explore how Black men students experience anti-Blackness in a Hispanic-serving community college environment. Definitions of *anti-Blackness* were primarily drawn from Dumas (2016). Simultaneously, they drew from Harris's (1993) work, stating that whiteness is "a set of cultural, discursive, and ideological structures and practices that privileges and valorizes whites while subordinating racialized others" (p. 56). Further, with one of the more robust frameworks they also connected Hispanic-serving community college campuses to a settler colonial project, drawing significantly from Dancy et al. (2018). Similar to previous work on Black men students and Black misandry they experience on college campuses generally, they found that their participants had their intellectual capabilities challenged and erased, found themselves visible and simultaneously invisible, and were keenly aware of how Black lives movements were happening both within and outside of the institution. Abrica et al. (2020) noted that their intention was to focus on anti-Blackness explicitly in the analysis, discussion, findings, and implications, and they do just that. Namely, they argued that anti-Blackness must be attended to in minority-serving institutional contexts as to not miss the particularities of how racism (and in this case anti-Black racism) manifests in these environments. They stated, "The idea that rights granted by the state demand anti-Blackness of nonblack people of color is an interesting one with implications for how anti-Blackness within the HSI context affects Latina/o/x students" (p. 68)—which can be connected also to Haywood's (2017) work cited previously. Abrica et al. took up whiteness explicitly—again offering a more robust analysis and understanding of anti-Blackness.

Collectively, this budding body of work is engaging with anti-Black racism across a variety of contexts including Black student movements, Black graduate student and student affairs professionals' experiences, White student experiences, and Latinx communities. Despite its current limited application, the work within which it has been situated suggests that many topics are ripe for analysis using anti-Black racism as a framework. But more importantly, we were more concerned with how these scholars engaged whiteness in particular and what was afforded or foreclosed. For those articles that integrated whiteness into the work, there were more explicit interrogations of how white privilege manifested systemically, thus maintaining racism and anti-Black racism specifically. For example, Haynes and Bazner (2019) were able to surface the ideological dimension of whiteness by recognizing how white racial epistemology is privileged within postsecondary curricula, making its influence and presence deeply ingrained and seemingly innocuous to most. What Black students surfaced, however, was that their own knowledge and ways of knowing are invalidated, erased, and deemed "other." Such epistemic violence then becomes a contestation of those students' humanity and an enactment of anti-Blackness. With regard to the cultural dimensions of whiteness and anti-Blackness, Stewart's (2018) work identified how the common everyday practices of inclusion rhetoric in student affairs privileged White students and professionals by allowing them basic human needs such as safety, whereas for Black graduate students and professionals not experiencing safety is acceptable and, in some ways, necessary to maintain the inclusion rhetoric. Stewart also provided an excellent example of how the structural dimensions of privilege and subordination manifest in that White students and professionals are rewarded and compensated for their work, whereas Black students and professionals are objectified and their work is "downplayed and disregarded" (p. 24). For those pieces that did not articulate whiteness in their framings explicitly, there seemed to be missed opportunities to illuminate how privilege is maintained and accumulated for those who actually benefit from said privilege. For example, the Dumas (2016) piece surfaced for us questions such as whether it is possible to address inequity in education policy if we do not explicate how it is inequitably privileging White folks and others while simultaneously violently disenfranchising Black communities. What appears to be most foreclosed on is the opportunity to surface a fuller picture of how both subordination *and* privilege are manifested and thus upholding, in a racial context, white supremacy.

To be clear, our intention is not to inferiorize scholarship that only appears to grapple with anti-Black racism—this work is necessary and a starting point. We are, however, arguing that anti-Black racism and whiteness are two sides of the same coin and that perhaps without a clear understanding of whiteness, recommendations flowing from anti-Black racism work might foreclose on certain conclusions and possibilities for practice. For example, coming back to our commentary on the ever-popular "how to be antiracists" canon developing in higher education circles, conclusions such as "people of color can be racists" ultimately serve to keep whiteness and white supremacy alive and well, namely because the practices that flow from such a conclusion then focus on people of color as the problem, rather than whiteness and its myriad, deeply embedded manifestations. Lastly, it is important to note that surfacing whiteness in work about anti-Blackness *does not* inherently colonize the work. We invite readers to imagine other possibilities—such as the ways interrogating whiteness not only dismantles that system of racial privilege but also deepens our abilities to unearth the depths of anti-Black racism that abound.

Implications and Conclusion

In this chapter, it was our intent to ground systemic whiteness, in an effort to name its connection to not only systemic racism but more specifically the predominance of anti-Black racism. It was also our aim to take the most formidable work on anti-Black racism that has the potential to inform praxis to offer perspectives on the possibilities as well as the pitfalls when whiteness is or is not explicitly applied in this growing area of research. Our claims that undergird the development of this chapter are (a) whiteness begets anti-Black racism, (b) whiteness and racism are interrelated systems, and (c) racial oppression for Black communities in higher education will not end without explicitly examining systemic whiteness in conversations about anti-Black racism.

By understanding that whiteness and racism are parallel and simultaneously functioning systems intrinsically linked to white supremacy, it is made clear how both privileging and oppressive practices come to bear. Whiteness, both in function and in form, has ties with but does not have to be inherently dependent upon white racial dominance. However, because of socialization—the process by which we learn behavior, it has come to be indistinguishably intertwined with racial dominance out of which racism manifests. Hence, whiteness and racism are connected in that the former is a system of privilege in a matrix of domination (Collins, 1990) that marks who benefits from what, when, and how—parallel to racism, writ large, as a system of subordination that marks who is minoritized when and how. By this, their respective ties then further generate multiple forms of racism, of which we focus on the pervasiveness and ever-present anti-Black racism.

What we have found is that an anti-Black racism analysis without some form of attention to whiteness is incomplete, as whiteness is a progenitor, as is racism, to anti-Black racism and anti-Blackness. Work that draws on a more complex/robust theoretical framing (whiteness, anti-Blackness, settler colonialism, etc.) provides more robust analyses and thus opportunity for more robust subversion. It is important to note such a shift is not an "excuse" to center or recenter dominant or White voices (Gillborn, 2006), but on the contrary, such a shift is to take heed and stock of the ideological, cultural, and structural conditions in which race and racism reside. In order to do so, we make the connections between whiteness and the ideological underpinning of white supremacy and, consequently, the pervasiveness of anti-Black racism.

Note

1. These terms are often used interchangeably across literature bases; however, for the purposes of this chapter *anti-Black racism* will be used consistently. In the latter part of the essay where research in this area is discussed, the term used is the term provided by the scholars.

References

Abrica, E. J., García-Louis, C., & Gallaway, C. D. J. (2020). Antiblackness in the Hispanic-serving community college (HSCC) context: Black male collegiate experiences through the lens of settler colonial logics. *Race Ethnicity and Education, 23*(1), 55–73. https://doi.org/10.1080/13613324.2019.1631781

Alcoff, L. M. (2003). Latino/As, Asian Americans, and the Black-White binary. *The Journal of Ethics*, *7*(1), 5–27. http://www.jstor.org/stable/25115747

Alcoff, L. M. (2013). Afterword: The Black/White binary and antiblack racism. *Critical Philosophy of Race*, *1*(1), 121–124. https://doi.org/10.5325/critphilrace.1.1.0121

Alexander, M. (2010). *The new Jim Crow: Mass incarceration in the age of colorblindness*. The New Press.

Ansley, F. L. (1997). White supremacy (and what we should do about it). In R. Delgado & J. Stefancic (Eds.), *Critical White studies: Looking behind the mirror* (pp. 592–595). Temple University Press.

Applebaum, B. (2010). *Being White, being good: White complicity, White moral responsibility, and social justice pedagogy.* Lexington Books.

Arendale, D. R. (2011). Then and now: The early years of developmental education. *Research and Teaching in Developmental Education*, *27*(2), 58–76.

Bell, D. (1989). *And we are not saved: The elusive quest for racial justice*. Basic Books.

Bell, D. (1991). Racism is here to stay: Now what. *Howard LJ*, *35*, 79.

Bell, D. (1993). *Faces at the bottom of the well: The permanence of racism*. Basic Books.

Cole, E. R., & Harper, S. R. (2017). Race and rhetoric: An analysis of college presidents' statements on campus racial incidents. *Journal of Diversity in Higher Education*, *10*(4), 318. https://doi.org/10.1037/dhe0000044

Collins, P. H. (1990). *Black feminist thought: Knowledge, consciousness, and the politics of empowerment.* Routledge.

Crenshaw, K., Gotanda, N., Peller, G., & Thomas, K. (Eds.). (1995). *Critical race theory: The key writings that formed the movement.* The New Press.

Croom, N. N. (2017). Promotion beyond tenure: Unpacking racism and sexism in the experiences of Black womyn professors. *The Review of Higher Education*, *40*(4), 557–583. https://doi.org/10.1353/rhe.2017.0022

Croom, N. N., & Kortegast, C. A. (2018). When ignoring difference fails: Using critical professional praxis. *About Campus*, *23*(1), 27–31. https://doi.org/10.1177/1086482218765765

Croom, N. N., & Patton, L. D. (2011). The miner's canary: A critical race perspective on the representation of Black women full professors. *Negro Educational Review*, 62–63(1–4), 13–39.

Croom, N. N., & Patton, L. D. (2015). Using endarkened and critical race feminist perspectives to question and analyze knowledge production narratives. In F. A. Bonner (Ed.), *Black faculty in the academy: Narratives for negotiating identity and achieving career success* (pp. 67–78). Routledge.

Dancy, T. E., Edwards, K. T., & Davis, J. E. (2018). Historically White universities and plantation politics: Anti-Blackness and higher education in the Black Lives Matter era. *Urban Education*, *53*(2), 176–195. https://doi.org/10.1177/0042085918754328

Delgado, R. (1996). Rodrigo's fifteenth chronicle: Racial mixture, Latino-critical scholarship, and the Black-White binary. *Texas Law Review*, *75*(5), 1181–1202.

Delgado, R., & Stefancic, J. (2017). *Critical race theory*. New York University Press.

Desmond, M., & Emirbayer, M. (2009). What is racial domination? *Du Bois Review, 6*(2), 335. https://doi.org/10.10170S1742058X09990166

DiAngelo, R. (2011). White fragility. *International Journal of Critical Pedagogy, 3*(3), 54–70.

Dumas, M. J. (2016). Against the dark: Antiblackness in education policy and discourse. *Theory Into Practice, 55*(1), 11–19. https://doi.org/10.1080/00405841.2016.1116852

Fanon, F. (1961). *The wretched of the earth.* Grove Press.

Foste, Z., & Jones, S. R. (2020). Narrating whiteness: A qualitative exploration of how White college students construct and give meaning to their racial location. *Journal of College Student Development, 61*(2), 171–188. https://doi.org/10.1353/csd.2020.0016

Frankenberg, R. (1993). *White women, race matters: The social construction of whiteness.* University of Minnesota Press.

Frankenberg, R. (1997). Introduction: Local whitenesses, localizing whiteness. In R. Frankenberg (Ed.), *Displacing whiteness: Essays in social and cultural criticism* (pp. 1–33). Duke University Press.

Garner, S. (2017). *Racisms: An introduction.* SAGE.

Garriott, P. O., Love, K. M., & Tyler, K. M. (2008). Anti-Black racism, self-esteem, and the adjustment of White students in higher education. *Journal of Diversity in Higher Education, 1*(1), 45–58. https://doi.org/10.1037/1938-8926.1.1.45

Gillborn, D. (2006). Rethinking white supremacy: Who counts in "WhiteWorld." *Ethnicities, 6*(3), 318–340. https://doi.org/10.1177/1468796806068323

Gillborn, D. (2015). Intersectionality, critical race theory, and the primacy of racism: Race, class, gender, and disability in education. *Qualitative Inquiry, 21*(3), 277–287. https://doi.org/10.1177/1077800414557827

Gusa, D. L. (2010). White institutional presence: The impact of whiteness on campus climate. *Harvard Educational Review, 80*(4), 464–490. https://doi.org/10.17763/haer.80.4.p5j483825u110002

Harris, C. I. (1993). Whiteness as property. *Harvard Law Review, 106*(8), 1707–1791.

Haynes, C., & Bazner, K. J. (2019). A message for faculty from the present-day movement for Black lives. *International Journal of Qualitative Studies in Education, 32*(9), 1146–1161. https://doi.org/10.1080/09518398.2019.1645909

Haywood, J. M. (2017). Anti-Black Latino racism in an era of Trumpismo. *International Journal of Qualitative Studies in Education, 30*(10), 957–964. https://doi.org/10.1080/09518398.2017.1312613

Jones, V. (2019). Discourse within university presidents' responses to racism: Revealing patterns of power and privilege. *Teachers College Record, 121*(4), 1–32. https://doi.org/10.1177/016146811912100402

Lee, R., Ahtone, T., Pearce, M., Goodluck, K., McGhee, G., Leff, C., Lanpher, K., & Salinas, T. (2020, March 30). Land-grab universities. *High Country News.* https://www.hcn.org/issues/52.4/indigenous-affairs-education-land-grab-universities

Leonardo, Z. (2009). *Race, whiteness, and education.* Routledge.

Lopez, I. H. (2006). *White by law* (2nd ed.). New York: New York University NYU Press.

Matias, C. E., Viesca, K. M., Garrison-Wade, D. F., Tandon, M., & Galindo, R. (2014). "What is critical whiteness doing in OUR nice field like critical race theory?" Applying CRT and CWS to understand the White imaginations of White teacher candidates. *Equity & Excellence in Education, 47*(3), 289–304. https://doi.org/10.1080/10665684.2014.933692

McIntosh, P. (1989, July/August). White privilege: Unpacking the invisible knapsack. *Peace and Freedom Magazine, 59,* 10–12.

Messer, C. M., Shriver, T. E., & Adams, A. E. (2018). The destruction of Black Wall Street: Tulsa's 1921 riot and the eradication of accumulated wealth. *American Journal of Economics and Sociology, 77*(3–4), 789–819. https://doi.org/10.1111/ajes.12225

Mills, C. (1997). *The racial contract.* Cornell University Press.

Mills, C. W. (2007). White ignorance. In S. Sullivan & N. Tuana (Eds.), *Race and epistemologies of ignorance* (pp. 11–38). SUNY Press.

Perea, J. F. (1998). The Black/White binary paradigm of race: The normal science of American racial thought. *La Raza Law Journal, 10*(1), 127–172.

Perry, P. (2007). White universal identity as a "sense of group position." *Symbolic Interaction, 30*(3), 375–393. https://doi.org/10.1525/si.2007.30.3.375

Pulido, L. (2015). Geographies of race and ethnicity 1: White supremacy vs white privilege in environmental racism research. *Progress in Human Geography, 39*(6), 809–817.

Rattan, A., & Eberhardt, J. L. (2010). The role of social meaning in inattentional blindness: When the gorillas in our midst do not go unseen. *Journal of Experimental Social Psychology, 46*(6), 1085–1088. https://doi.org/10.1016/j.jesp.2010.06.010

Sheth, M. J., & Croom, N. N. (2021). Chronicles exploring hegemonic civility and the evisceration of academic freedom for critical Womyn of Color. In R. Dutt-Ballerstadt & K. Bhattacharya, *Civility, free speech, and academic freedom in higher education: Faculty on the margins* (pp. 145–162). Routledge.

Stewart, D-L (2018). Ideologies of absence: Anti-Blackness and inclusion rhetoric in student affairs practice. *Journal of Student Affairs, 28,* 15–30.

Sullivan, S. (2014). *Good White people: The problem with middle-class White anti-racism.* SUNY Press.

Taylor, E., Gillborn, D., & Ladson-Billings, G. (2009). *Foundations of critical race theory in education.* Routledge.

Tevis, T. (2020). Exploring whether White male postsecondary presidents respond to racism. *Whiteness and Education, 5*(1), 91–111. https://doi.org/10.1080/23793406.2019.1711150

Tevis, T., & Pifer, M. J. (2021). Privilege and oppression: Exploring the paradoxical identity of white Women administrators in higher education. *JCSCORE, 7*(2), 69–102. https://doi.org/10.15763/issn.2642-2387.2021.7.2.69-102

Whitehead, M. A. (2021). Whiteness, Anti-Blackness, and trauma: A grounded theory of white racial meaning making. *Journal of College Student Development, 62*(3), 310–326. https://doi.org/10.1353/csd.2021.0027

Wilderson, F. B. (2010). *Red, White and Black: Cinema and the structure of U.S. antagonisms.* Duke University Press.

12

THE WHITE RACIAL ENGAGEMENT MODEL

Unlearning the Oppressive Conditioning of Whiteness

Melvin A. Whitehead, Erin Weston, and Meg E. Evans

The murders of Breonna Taylor, Ahmaud Arbery, George Floyd, Tony McDade, and other Black people in the United States at the hands of white police officers and racist vigilantes in 2020 renewed a national conversation about systemic racism, anti-Blackness, and white supremacy. Their deaths have also increased student pressure on college administrators to address racism on their campuses. As U.S. colleges and universities continue to grapple with addressing the pervasive realities of racism on campus, we argue these efforts must include rethinking educators' approaches to engaging white college students constructively with the issues of race and racism. Empirical literature about white U.S. college students illustrates how they largely enter college with high levels of racial resentment, interact within predominantly white social networks, evade issues of racism, and frame race in ways that sustain whiteness and white supremacy (Bowman & Park, 2015; Byrd, 2014; Cabrera, 2011; Chesler et al., 2003). Consequently, Black students at predominantly and historically white institutions have reported experiences with racial harassment, discrimination, microaggressions, hostility, and tokenism, and hold negative perceptions of campus racial climates (George Mwangi et al., 2018; Griffith et al., 2019; Kelly et al., 2019; Morales, 2020; S. J. Robinson, 2013). Pointing to the connections between whiteness, white students' behaviors, and the marginalizing experiences of Students of Color, Cabrera (2014a) stated: "If Students of Color are experiencing hostile campus racial climates, many of their white peers are creating this marginalization" (p. 769).

Indeed, racism is a *white* problem and, as such, the work of disrupting racism requires white people to reflect critically on their connections to whiteness and act reflexively to advance racial justice. Accordingly, this chapter introduces the white racial engagement model (WREM), which conceptualizes how white people perpetuate or disrupt whiteness vis-à-vis engagement with their white racial identity. We first trace the history of early models of white racial identity development and summarize more recent literature concerning white college students and whiteness. Next, we discuss our paradigm and positionality before introducing the components of the model. We conclude with implications this model offers for practice and research.

Terminology

We define *white* as referring to those who "self-identify or are commonly identified as belonging exclusively to the white racial group regardless of the continental source . . . of that racial ancestry" (Helms & Piper, 1994, p. 126). We use this definition because it both positions race as a social construct and acknowledges that anyone who is perceived to be white—inclusive of their racial identity—can often be the recipients of white racial privilege. We define *white supremacy* as an ideological structure of white racial/racist domination (hooks, 1989; Leonardo, 2004). We define *whiteness* as both a subjective racial location of structural advantage from which white people understand themselves and People of Color (Frankenberg, 1993) and as a racial discourse that structures white supremacy (Leonardo, 2009). We use these mutually inclusive definitions of *whiteness* to highlight how it simultaneously serves as an "interpretive filter" (Foste & Jones, 2020, p. 178) and as a device for upholding systemic white racial domination.

White College Students' Racial Development

The first models of white racial identity development were proposed by Rita Hardiman and Janet Helms in the early 1980s after the height of the U.S. civil rights and Black power movements (Hardiman, 2001). In an effort to disrupt racial oppression, Hardiman's (as cited in Hardiman, 2001) white identity development model sought to explain how race and racism affected white people and explored whether or not white people could abandon their white racial socialization and become antiracist. Helms's (1995) white racial identity development model sought to understand cross-racial interactions in the counseling process. In these models, a white person moves from a state of racial unawareness toward interrogating their racial socialization and the personal meaning they ascribe to their racial identity, and ultimately adopts a nonracist white racial identity (Hardiman, 2001; Helms, 1995).

How race is largely studied and conceptualized in the literature has undergone significant changes since Hardiman (2001) and Helms (1995) initially developed their white racial identity models. Notwithstanding the historical roots of critical whiteness studies (CWS) in the work of W.E.B. Du Bois, CWS's recent evolution into a formal field of study has brought a focus on hegemonic whiteness and how it shapes white individuals' racial ideological conditioning and the maintenance of white supremacy. White racial identity development models—most notably Helms's—have been critiqued for their focus on white people's racial attitudes and consciousness concerning People of Color to the exclusion of (a) white people's meaning making of their own white racial identities within a white supremacist society, (b) a broader and collective experience of whiteness with other white people, and (c) the discursive and ideological practices that leave whiteness in place and uninterrogated (Fasching-Varner, 2012; Foste & Irwin, 2020; Hardiman & Keehn, 2012). In short, white racial identity development models largely have not drawn attention to hegemonic whiteness and white individuals' complicity in reproducing white supremacy.

Accordingly, empirical research on white college students' racial development has waned in recent years while new scholarship on white college students' racial ideologies and connections to whiteness has emerged. For example, Cabrera's (2012) research revealed some white students normalized whiteness and others worked through it. The former understood racism as a problem of individual bias (not as something systemic), framed racism as largely a relic of the past, and positioned themselves as nonracist (Cabrera, 2014a, 2014b). White participants who were working through whiteness experienced several developmental processes that included increased self-awareness of their own white racial backgrounds through cross-racial interactions, deepening their understanding of systemic oppression through the lens of minoritized identities they held, becoming aware of and identifying how they benefited from whiteness, and applying their critiques to engage in action against racism (Cabrera, 2012).

Foste and Jones's (2020) research similarly focused on how white students made sense of their racial selves in relation to People of Color and to systems of white supremacy and illuminated three constructions of whiteness. White participants in their study who were ignorant of whiteness were largely unaware of how whiteness shaped their experiences, defined *racism* as interpersonal bias, positioned themselves as victims, and evaded the salience of race in their lives and People of Color's lives (Foste & Jones, 2020). Emergent constructions of whiteness were characterized by a budding understanding of racism as both interpersonal and systemic, despite an unwillingness to identify their own complicity in perpetuating white supremacy (Foste & Jones, 2020). Finally, this same study revealed participants who held critical conscious constructions of whiteness actively explored the meaning of their white identity, held complex understandings of racism, and implicated themselves as part of the problem of racism.

Other studies have lent empirical support to the divergences of white college students' connections and disconnections with whiteness. For example, studies have found that white college students who are ignorant of whiteness (a) hold racial ideologies that position themselves as racial victims and Students of Color as sources of racial division (Bonilla-Silva, 2018; Cabrera, 2014a, 2014b, 2014c; Hikido & Murray, 2016); (b) maintain their ideologies of white racial dominance under the guise of multiculturalism discourse and the performance of pity and care (Hikido & Murray, 2016; Matias & Zembylas, 2014); and (c) minimize racism while engaging in racist jokes (Cabrera, 2014b; Picca & Feagin, 2007). These ignorant constructions of whiteness are driven by white college students' racial emotions of apathy, anger, and disgust (Cabrera, 2014a; Matias & Zembylas, 2014) and are supported through their socialization within a *white habitus* (Bonilla-Silva, 2018; Jayakumar, 2015). Research concerning white college students who work through (i.e., hold emergent or critical constructions of) whiteness illustrates the various roles of guilt, shame, fear, anger, and discomfort in their developmental pathways (Cabrera, 2012; Linder, 2015). Among the antiracist white feminist participants in Linder's (2015) study, these emotions coincided with participants' processes of initially distancing themselves from whiteness, working through their concerns of appearing racist and resistance to acknowledging themselves as beneficiaries of whiteness, and ultimately toward understanding the realities of systemic racism and engaging in antiracist action.

The body of research that has emerged over the past 10 years concerning white college students' (dis)connections with whiteness clearly illustrates divergent developmental pathways toward either sustaining whiteness or consciously critiquing and disrupting it. These studies largely do not articulate a developmental model describing how white college students engage with whiteness. Although Linder's (2015) model does so, it is based on white antiracist students and does not describe the various ways white college students engage with whiteness. In drawing needed connections between white racial identity development and whiteness, Fasching-Varner (2012) articulated the concept of a *white racial propriospect*—a person's unique characteristics that draw from broader structures of whiteness and white supremacy. Still, Fasching-Varner's (2012) model is not based in the body of empirical literature on white college students. Without robust empirical support, Fasching-Varner's (2012) model may be limited in both its application and its ability to theorize the various ways white college students engage with whiteness vis-à-vis their white racial identities.

Returning to white racial identity development models, we sought to develop a unified and conceptual articulation of the divergent developmental processes white college students undertake as they either work through or sustain whiteness, while also recognizing these processes are always and already situated within the broader system of white supremacy. With our model, we also sought to build upon the empirical research on white college students and whiteness to conceptualize white identity development through a critical whiteness lens. To date, the scholarship has largely focused on white college students who are either developing a critical consciousness of whiteness or those who sustain it. Our model seeks to move beyond this dichotomy and offer more expansive ways for considering how whiteness shapes white college students' racial identity development. For example, there is little empirical research concerning white college students who express racism openly. This omission is notwithstanding the numerous news reports of white college students who have perpetuated white supremacy in overt and explicit ways (Anderson, 2019; Money, 2020; C. Robinson, 2018; Roll, 2017; Stirgus, 2020). We argue these are also manifestations of whiteness, even if they have not been widely discussed as such in the scholarly literature, and contribute to racist campus environments for Students of Color. Our model also considers the development of white individuals who may consider themselves antiracist, yet uphold white supremacy by evading implicating themselves as a part of this system.

About the Authors

The three authors' various social identities and lived experiences also shape our individual understandings and study of whiteness, as well as our conceptualization of WREM. The first author (Melvin) is an able-bodied, middle-class Black/African American transgender man. His Black parents—both from working-class backgrounds—grew up in the U.S. South during the Jim Crow era and migrated to the U.S. North in the 1960s and 1970s. The life lessons and survival strategies Melvin's parents learned through their experiences with segregation in the Jim Crow–era South shaped his early racial socialization and understandings of whiteness. These included speaking only standardized English in and out of the home (and not African American Vernacular English), which implicitly taught Melvin that conforming to whiteness and distancing oneself from Black cultural norms were necessary for achieving success. Melvin's socialization continued to reinforce similar lessons throughout his childhood and adolescence and eventually rendered whiteness as an unquestioned, normative backdrop against which he constantly measured himself.

Melvin's later engagement with Black queer and trans communities along with conversations with Black colleagues in his doctoral program stirred his awareness of whiteness and prompted his journey toward unlearning and disrupting it. Through these conversations with friends and colleagues, Melvin began to understand the oppressive ways in which whiteness shaped his life and the extent to which he had internalized it. Melvin's experience during a study-abroad program in Ghana toward the end of his doctoral program deepened his understanding of whiteness as something profoundly pathological and dehumanizing. For Melvin, the work of facilitating white folks' constructive engagement with their racial identities is integrally connected to his own processes of unlearning and disrupting whiteness, healing, transformation, and liberation.

The second author (Erin) currently identifies as a fat-bodied, middle-class white cisgender woman. She grew up in the midwestern U.S. suburbs, in a community with a 96% white population. In 2008 she settled in a high-poverty, racially diverse rural community in the U.S. South. Over the past 10 years she has become engaged both in community-based activism and academic research on whiteness and racism. These experiences prompted her first meaningful engagement with her own white racial identity and highlighted the ways whiteness had allowed her to easily evade considering her own racial privileges. She continues to engage in the self-work necessary to understand her white racial identity and supports efforts to dismantle white supremacy in an environment designed to uphold it.

Meg (they/them) currently identifies as a queer, fat-bodied, nonbinary white person who is a parent to a brilliant and spunky multiracial/Black toddler. Meg has worked in higher education for the past 15 years, primarily in identity-based offices, and core to their student affairs praxis is the intentional centering of queer and trans Students of Color. Meg grew up in the (mostly) all-white suburbs of Chicago blissfully unaware of their white identity and the ways whiteness permeates everything. A believer in everyone's ability to learn and unlearn, Meg hopes that this model helps white people understand the ways they are invested in and colluding with white dominance and white supremacy as a means to break down systemic barriers and create more pathways to liberation. They feel a commitment to an investment in the creation and application of WREM to honor People of Color in higher education. Meg believes that all white people, themself included, have a lifetime of white nonsense to unlearn and also believes that WREM is a good place to start.

Development of WREM

Our conceptualization of WREM is informed through a transformative paradigm, which emphasizes the lives and experiences of marginalized groups, the root causes of inequities and asymmetric power relationships, and connecting research to political and social action (Mertens, 2005). A transformative paradigm acknowledges both the role of social location (e.g., race, class, gender) in constructing reality and the factors that privilege some versions of reality over others (Mertens, 2005). Although scholars have traditionally used this paradigm to explore the experiences of minoritized groups, scholars have also used this paradigm to examine the experiences of and critique the narratives perpetuated by white people (e.g., Cabrera, 2014a, 2014b; Delgado, 1989; Linder, 2015). Using a transformative paradigm allowed us to develop a model and tool through which white people can begin to trouble the dominant racial narratives they frequently have internalized that uphold white supremacy. Our use of a transformative paradigm to ultimately disrupt and eradicate white supremacy is consistent with the paradigm's goal of confronting social oppression and bringing about social transformation (Mertens, 2005).

The authors initially developed WREM in a doctoral-level student development theories course and grounded the model in tenets of critical race theory, Tatum's (1997) conceptualization of racism (described in the following), white fragility (DiAngelo, 2018), and components from critical whiteness studies in higher education (Cabrera et al., 2017). We engaged in multiple rounds of feedback on the model from peer scholars, including those who study issues related to systemic oppression through a critical lens and those with substantive knowledge of the critical whiteness literature. This process helped us identify gaps within the model and refine the applications of the model. We incorporated our peers' feedback by making more explicit how WREM relates to white people's racialized *actions*, rather than just their cognitive development. We expanded the status descriptions to include ways white people may act within each status and foregrounded the role of emotions, such as guilt and discomfort, in shaping white individuals' engagement with their racial identity. For example, individuals in the Denial status may behave with anger or guilt when engaging with race. Additional feedback from a critical whiteness scholar prompted us to engage more deeply with the empirical literature concerning whiteness, white racial identity development, and white U.S. college students. This process led us to identify additional gaps with the model and further refine the relationship between white racialized emotions and white racialized actions.

Description of WREM Statuses

Given the literature about white identity development, white racial engagement, and white racial ideologies, we proposed eight fluid statuses for WREM. There are no fixed development endpoints in WREM; individuals can easily move between statuses due to shifts in their knowledge, experiences, or environment. All statuses are positioned along a unidirectional, continuously moving pathway (see Figure 12.1), on which every white person is situated (Tatum, 1997). Tatum (1997) likened racism to a moving walkway pulling society toward white supremacy. She argued that engaging in active racist behavior is the equivalent of moving quickly on the walkway, whereas passive racist behaviors are the equivalent of being still on the walkway (albeit still moving toward white supremacy; Tatum, 1997). For white people to engage in racial justice work, they must *continuously* move in the opposite direction and move more quickly than the speed of the walkway, recognizing they can never get off (Tatum, 1997). By undergirding our model with this walkway, we acknowledge the embedded nature of systemic racism and white supremacy in U.S. society. While white individuals navigate their own racial consciousness, they continue to be both part of, and influenced by, systems of power and oppression (Foste & Irwin, 2020). We also recognize that at its core, whiteness is the actions, beliefs, and social norms that uphold white supremacy (Leonardo, 2004). White people are both influenced by Tatum's moving walkway while engaging in actions to uphold it. The arrows on each side of the model indicate the direction of the walkway toward white supremacy.

WREM is a nonlinear model with numerous pathways of engagement. Movement between the statuses is indicated by the black arrows. Movement to a new status occurs as a result of dissonance-provoking stimuli (i.e., critical encounters that prompt white people to think about and reflect on race; Chesler et al., 2003). Although dissonance occurs to move individuals to a new status, it is not needed to slip back into a previous status. Tatum's (1997) conceptualization of racism also informs movement between the statuses comprising the model. As a white individual moves toward statuses

Figure 12.1. White racial engagement model.

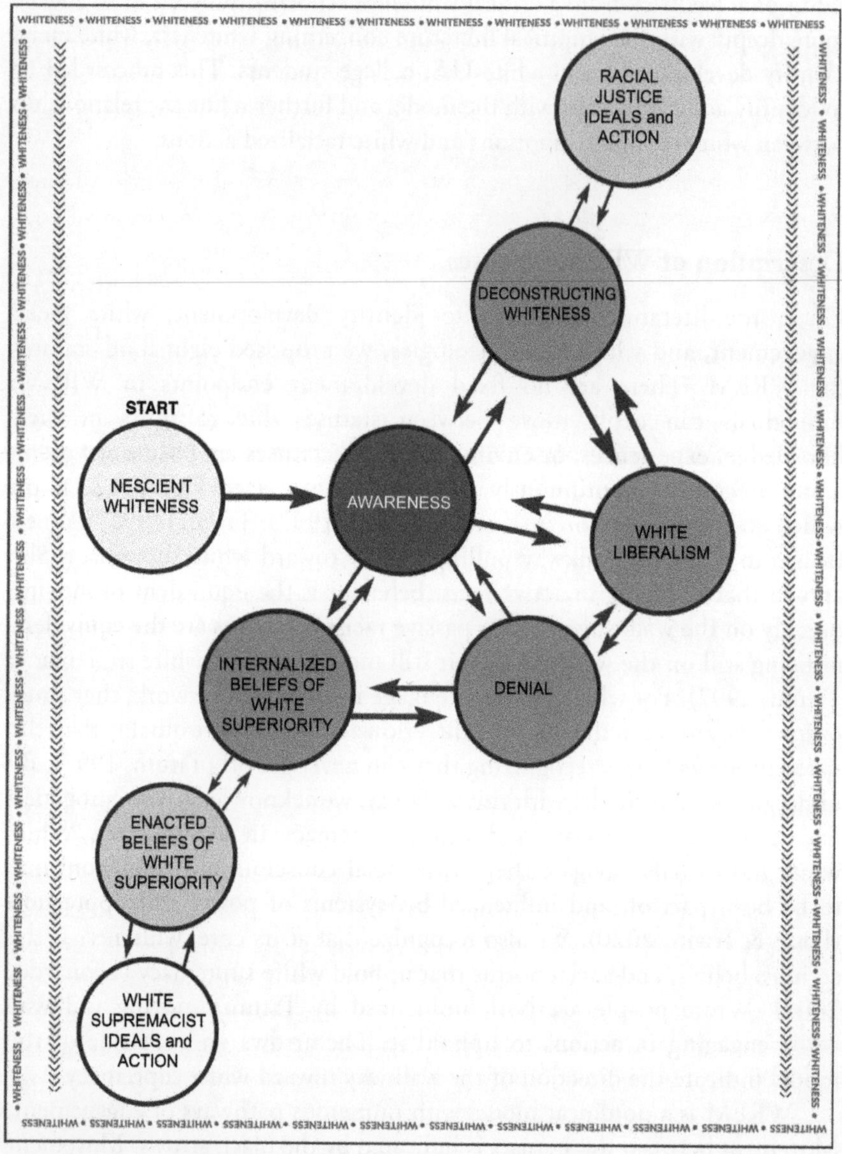

that support or facilitate white supremacy, they move along the direction of the walkway. Conversely, as an individual moves toward statuses that disrupt white supremacy, they move at an increasingly faster speed against the direction of the walkway. Moving against the pull of white supremacy requires effort, energy, and stamina reflective of the pressures of whiteness to uphold white supremacy (Leonardo, 2004; Tatum, 1997).

The model is framed by the word *whiteness*, indicating that whiteness is always present and influencing how white people are engaging with race. Such examples include white people regularly being excused for their lack of awareness of their racial identity, racialized experiences, or racial privileges, while simultaneously being given the benefit of the doubt when they make missteps related to these topics (Bebout, 2011). White people continue to hold power and access in U.S. society, while upholding a history of dominance (Bonilla-Silva, 2018; Leonardo, 2004). This reality is reflected in how structures and systems from education to criminal justice are designed to center and benefit white people (Bonilla-Silva, 2018). White people embrace the ideology of whiteness as neutral, while being exposed, almost exclusively, to white individuals in positions of power and authority (Bonilla-Silva, 2018; Foste & Jones, 2020). While an individual moves through the model they are never shielded from the constant influence of whiteness on their lived experience (Foste & Jones, 2020).

Nescient Whiteness

Nescient is defined as "uneducated in general; lacking knowledge" (Vocabulary.com, n.d.). We intentionally selected the term *nescient* to demonstrate where all white people begin their engagement with race. White people rarely reflect on their racial identity, their racialized experiences, or racial privileges (Bonilla-Silva, 2018; Hughey, 2012). White people perceive whiteness as neutral (Foste & Jones, 2020). Accordingly, this status is marked by white people's acute lack of awareness of their own racial identity and the impact of whiteness on their lives. The white habitus—a process of racialized socialization that shapes white people's racial perceptions, feelings, and views—facilitates this lack of racial awareness through white people's high levels of spatial and social segregation from People of Color (Bonilla-Silva, 2018). Depending on how insulated a white person is, they may remain in this status indefinitely. This is the only status to which an individual cannot return once they have moved to another status in the model; when the "bell has been rung" and the individual becomes aware of race, they cannot return to a state of complete nescience. However, due to the ever-present influence of whiteness, white people will continue to be ignorant of some racial issues, concepts, and constructs (Fasching-Varner, 2012). Awareness does not equate to a complete understanding of the complexities of racism. Cabrera (2014a, 2014b, 2014c) found that white students relied on individualized definitions of *racism*, equating racism with personal actions or traits as opposed to a system of oppression. The limited understanding associated with initial awareness is also reflected in Foste and Jones's (2020) description of ignorant constructions of whiteness, in which white people are unwilling to fully see how race influences both their own lives and the lives of People of Color.

Awareness

This status is similar to what Cabrera (2012) called *racial cognizance* and is characterized by white people's realization that race shapes their lived experiences. For white college students, this realization may occur through structured educational experiences (e.g., engaging in class discussions about race and reading about race), cross-racial interactions, or reflecting on experiences within other minoritized identities (Cabrera, 2011, 2012; Chesler et al., 2003). Whiteness often only becomes visible when confronted with the contrasting experiences of People of Color (Fasching-Varner, 2012). White people begin to see that their lived experiences, which they had previously viewed as race-neutral, are in fact distinct from the lived experiences of People of Color (Frankenberg, 1993). Echoing the previous status, due to the pervasiveness of whiteness, white people may develop awareness of some racial issues while continuing to be unaware of others (Fasching-Varner, 2012). However, having awareness of race and racism is distinct from having the skills and/or consciousness necessary for knowing how to cope with that awareness (Chesler et al., 2003). A white person may remain at Awareness indefinitely. This initial awareness does not encompass the deep understanding that begins at the Deconstructing Whiteness status. Individuals could enter this status through a single experience or training, or through more in-depth education (Neville et al., 2014). Awareness simply reflects the realization for white people that race shapes their lived experiences.

Denial

White people are often insulated from addressing race and racism due to their socialization within the white habitus (Bonilla-Silva, 2018). Therefore, an awareness of the saliency of race can cause race-based stress and discomfort that often lead white people to deny racism and their racially based privileges (Bonilla-Silva, 2018; Chesler et al., 2003; Frankenberg, 1993; Leonardo & Porter, 2010; Linder, 2015). This denial by white people shifts the onus of education about racism and whiteness back to People of Color

(Fasching-Varner, 2012). Denying racism and racial-based privilege after awareness is also a component of white racial ignorance (see chapter 4 for further definition and context). By ignoring the reality of racism, oppression continues to function. Common coping mechanisms and emotional responses include anger, withdrawal, emotional incapacitation, guilt, and racial color-evasiveness (Bonilla-Silva, 2018; Cabrera, 2014a; DiAngelo, 2018; Linder, 2015; Spanierman & Cabrera, 2015; Whitehead, 2021). Further exposure to racism or racially based privileges may result in an individual moving out of this status.

White Liberalism

Within this status, white individuals neglect the self-work necessary for interrogating whiteness and recognizing their role in upholding white supremacy (Fasching-Varner, 2012; Foste & Jones, 2020). Through contrasting themselves to overt racists, white individuals in this status may absolve themselves from the embedded systems of racism and white supremacy (Fasching-Varner, 2012). White folks are socialized in a racist society and must work to understand how this socialization influences their beliefs, perceptions, and lived experiences. The discomfort white people experience engaging in race-based dialogue manifests in this status as defensiveness against engaging with one's implicit biases and privileges (Leonardo & Porter, 2010; Linder, 2015). The white racial discomfort inherent to white liberalism continues to uphold racism, as white people cannot challenge their biases without first admitting they exist (Leonardo & Porter, 2010). As a result, individuals in the white liberalism status take uninformed action toward disrupting white supremacy. Their actions may cause harm to Communities of Color, ultimately upholding white supremacy. Actions in this status can manifest as performative activism or paternalistic white saviorism. Support for our conceptualization of white liberalism comes from Black feminist discourse documenting the ways in which white women's lack of self-interrogation about their whiteness have derailed or harmed intersectional feminist movements (e.g., hooks, 1981).

Deconstructing Whiteness

This status consists of significant self-interrogation concerning a white individual's complicity in white racial oppression; they begin to understand racism as systemic and structural while simultaneously developing a critique of white privilege (Cabrera, 2012). White individuals may work through feelings of guilt, fear, and shame (Linder, 2015) as they uncover and reflect on ways that whiteness has been socialized into their thinking and start to unlearn those ways of thinking. This new knowledge may spur individuals into the next status of action and commitment. However, to proceed to the next status they must reckon with the principles of a tenet of critical race theory—interest convergence (Delgado & Stefancic, 2017). Interest convergence is the idea that white people are only willing to pursue racial equality to the point that it does not jeopardize their own privilege and will benefit them. To move to the next status, white people must interrogate the ways they are benefiting from disrupting systemic racism and be willing to threaten some of their racial privilege (Bell, 1980; Delgado & Stefancic, 2017).

Racial Justice Ideals and Actions

This status occurs after a person has begun to deconstruct whiteness. It is an external commitment to a racial justice praxis and action—grounded in an understanding of Lilla Watson's concept of bound liberation (Elliott & Shatara, 2018) and the connectedness of oppression (Cabrera, 2012). In this status, individuals begin to "walk the talk" and engage in actions which may jeopardize their own privilege. Individuals recognize that disrupting racism and white supremacy cannot be achieved simply through educating oneself; action is required (Foste & Irwin, 2020). Common actions in this status include political activism, shifts in relationships, and confronting racism. Political activism in this stage is often collective and requires white individuals to listen to and follow the lead of the Communities of Color with whom they are in solidarity. Dynamic shifts are likely to occur at all levels of relationships; as white individuals are engaged in the work of disrupting whiteness, they move more quickly against the moving walkway, creating distance from friends and family. White individuals in this status regularly confront racism in their daily lives and may develop a reputation for being a person who frequently speaks up about race and racism. Confrontation again requires white individuals to listen and follow the lead of People or Communities of Color with whom they are in solidarity and may result in further straining previous relationships. Throughout this status, people continue to go through the process of unlearning whiteness. Although white individuals may benefit from these actions, white people in this status engage in the work without seeking benefit. As with all statuses in this model, this status is neither static nor permanent; to engage in racial justice ideals and actions, white people must move increasingly faster against the moving walkway, recognizing that individual actions are always occurring within the embedded systems of racism and white supremacy. There is no status within the model where the efforts of a white individual can move them outside the influence of systemic racism (Applebaum, 2016).

Unconscious Beliefs of White Superiority

Although some individuals work to move through statuses toward racial justice, others move in the direction of white supremacy. Recently, scholars have begun to name the growing resistance against efforts to call out racism, challenge white supremacy, and promote racial justice (Embrick et al., 2020). Additionally, Leonardo (2020) argued that white racial victimhood has reached normalcy and that white identity is frequently invoked as a site of injury. White victimhood discourse and racial resentment often mask an unconscious and internalized belief of white superiority (Spanierman & Cabrera, 2015). Although these beliefs may be largely internalized/subconscious, they still influence the actions of the white individuals who hold them. Individuals in this status may support policies, laws, and actions that uphold white supremacy, although they may outwardly justify this support for purportedly nonracial reasons. Scholars have argued that white racial rage and fear tied to false beliefs about People of Color, as well as perceptions of dwindling American values, threats to white survival, loss of political power, and social progress for Black people drive white supremacist discourse and ideology and radicalization (Anderson, 2016; Embrick et al., 2020; Gest, 2016). Further, these racial emotions are circulated within mainstream politics, academia, and popular culture (Ioanide, 2015). White people in this status deny or minimize the implications of systemic racism; may rely on intellectualism, exceptionalism, or meritocracy when discussing racism; often claim that white people are the real victims of modern racial oppression; and/or develop beliefs associated with symbolic racism (Bonilla-Silva, 2018; Byrd, 2014; Cabrera, 2014c; Chesler et al., 2003).

White Supremacist Ideals and Actions

This status represented an *external* commitment to a white supremacist praxis and action. In this status there is a shift from simply believing in superiority to openly promoting white supremacy. Individuals here may be members of the Klan, white nationalists, or other hate groups. Absent substantive empirical support for this status, we point to news media reports of white college students who have posted explicitly racist content on social media, used racist slurs both online and on campus, participated in white nationalist/Nazi demonstrations, promoted white supremacist ideologies through class presentations, and have otherwise perpetuated white supremacy in overt and explicit ways (Anderson, 2019; Money, 2020; C. Robinson, 2018; Roll, 2017; Stirgus, 2020). In this status a white person's individual racial identity, membership in a white racial group, superior beliefs about white people, and inferior beliefs about People of Color all coalesce to form a white supremacist identity. Although this may be the final status for some white people, it is neither static nor permanent; there is always the possibility that new knowledge, relationships, or experiences may prompt movement away from white supremacist ideas and actions. There is little research available on individuals committed to a white supremacist identity. Due to the pull toward white supremacy reflected in Tatum's moving walkway, we theorize that movement away from this status would likely be slow and incremental. We believe that moving from this white supremacist status within WREM to the other side of the model, racial justice, would require significant ongoing support and extraordinary perseverance.

WREM in Practice

Consistent with other critical whiteness scholars, we seek not to recenter whiteness—the very thing we seek to critique (Applebaum, 2016; Cabrera, 2014b); instead, we acknowledge that this work, in service to Students, Staff, and Faculty of Color, aims to assist in building a more racially just world and academy. A necessary component of justice work is bringing white people into an awareness of whiteness and into an interrogation of whiteness's continued presence and salience in shaping their experiences (see DiAngelo, 2018). To that effect, a common use for WREM includes serving as a self-reflection tool for white faculty, practitioners, and students to give language to their connections and understandings of their whiteness. For example, as part of a course, faculty could assign white students time for self-reflection using WREM, while assigning Students of Color time to reflect using other models of racial identity development or engagement (e.g., Pilipino students may be assigned Nadal's [2004] Pilipino American identity development model). Through using WREM as a tool for reflecting on their complicity with whiteness and white supremacy, white students will gain a deeper understanding of their white racial identity. As we mentioned previously, whiteness typically goes unnoticed by white people and functions as a "background experience" (Ahmed, 2007, p. 150), yet impacts many of their ideas and actions. As white students are learning concepts and practices in and outside of their classes, it is unlikely that they are learning how their whiteness impacts those concepts and/or practices. Faculty and staff, utilizing tools like WREM, must prompt students to engage critically to find the intersection between race and educational content.

Similarly, WREM serves as a guide for introducing dissonance-provoking stimuli that challenge white individuals' thinking about whiteness and race. Within the model, combined with their self-reflection praxis, white people are asked to identify what created a dissonance-provoking stimuli for them that precipitated their movement from one status to another. By gaining a clearer understanding of the "how," those engaged in a process of self-reflection utilizing WREM can look for other experiences or opportunities to engage in ways that may trigger further engagement and understanding of their white racial identity. Student-led diversity peer educator groups, often charged with facilitating discussions around diversity, could introduce WREM as a way for white students to explore their own racial identity.

In addition to providing language for self-reflection, this model provides language for future researchers to better understand how whiteness manifests in individuals and in groups. For example, researchers engaging in whiteness studies may look at how white college students come into an awareness of their white racial identity and how their understanding of their white racial identity does (or does not) impact or influence their sense of belonging on campus. WREM can provide researchers a roadmap of/for racial engagement when analyzing data, enabling a stronger understanding of white students' engagement with their racial identity.

Equally as important as guided self-reflections, faculty and practitioners should also facilitate students' understanding of their racial engagement through targeted readings about racial dynamics, issues, and engagement, power, and social identity. For example, practitioners who work with student organizations and cocurricular service-learning programs may introduce the concept of social identities and its relevance to leadership and service, respectively. Practitioners could then prompt students to identify all of their social identities and reflect on their socialization within these identities, specifically foregrounding their racial identities (see Jones & Abes, 2013, for ideas on implementing such an exercise). In these ways, practitioners can facilitate white students' processes of deconstructing whiteness in ways that are salient to them and their roles on campus. Given the discomfort many white people express during direct discussions about racial issues (Bonilla-Silva, 2018), practitioners should develop ways of cultivating spaces of mutual trust and vulnerability, foregrounding individualized (rather than group) reflection, and tending to power dynamics within interracial groups in their approaches.

Although this model is based on the empirical literature about white college students and whiteness, it is currently conceptual in nature and would benefit from empirical testing/validation. Further, WREM relies on white people's conscious awareness, and we know that whiteness often lives in the subconscious of many white people. This is why WREM must be accompanied by other readings, writings, and engagements with critical whiteness education.

WREM adds value to the critical discourse on whiteness in higher education as it poses new questions and suggests areas ripe for research. For example, what experiences and processes facilitate movement toward internalizing beliefs about white superiority, particularly among white men who—as Cabrera's (2011) findings suggest—may be the most impervious to changes in their racial ideologies during college? Why do some white people remain in a status of awareness and others do not? What developmental assumptions underlie current approaches to engaging white students in racial issues and interrogating whiteness? What new approaches could emerge?

Conclusion

This chapter introduced a new conceptualization of how white people engage with their racial identity through WREM. We traced the history of early models of white racial identity development, discussed the theoretical and conceptual underpinnings of our proposed model, outlined our proposed WREM, and provided the implications this model offers for practice and research. Developing WREM has revealed numerous avenues for future research. WREM does not address the experiences of multiracial, biracial, or white-passing individuals. WREM also does not account for the exhaustion or burnout of racial justice work, which may pull some individuals away from the status of racial justice ideals and action. WREM provides a framework for understanding and interrogating how white individuals engage with race, knowledge that could provide scaffolding for research, pedagogy, and practice. WREM can be an insightful and indispensable tool for understanding white racial identity. We encourage white scholars and practitioners to use it for doing their own work of unlearning the oppressive conditioning of whiteness and serving as needed exemplars for others.

References

Ahmed, S. (2007). A phenomenology of whiteness. *Feminist Theory*, *8*(2), 149–168. https://doi.org/10.1177/1464700107078139

Anderson, C. (2016). *White rage: The unspoken truth of our racial divide*. Bloomsbury.

Anderson, G. (2019, December 19). White supremacy in the classroom. *Inside Higher Ed*. https://www.insidehighered.com/news/2019/12/11/georgia-southern-student-promotes-white-supremacist-theory-class

Applebaum, B. (2016). Critical whiteness studies. In G. W. Noblit (Ed.), *Oxford research encyclopedia of education* (pp. 1–25). Oxford University Press. https://doi.org/10.1093/acrefore/9780190264093.013.5.

Bebout, L. (2011). Troubling white benevolence: Four takes on a scene from "Giant." *Melus, 36*(3), 13–36.

Bonilla-Silva, E. (2018). *Racism without racists: Color-blind racism and the persistence of racial inequality in America.* (5th ed.). Rowman & Littlefield.

Bowman, N., & Park, J. (2015). Interracial contact on college campuses: Comparing and contrasting predictors of cross-racial interaction and interracial friendship. *The Journal of Higher Education, 85*(5), 660–690. https://doi.org/10.1080/00221546.2014.11777344

Byrd, W. C. (2014). Cross-racial interactions during college: A longitudinal study of four forms of interracial interactions among elite white college students. *Societies, 4*(2), 265–295. https://doi.org/10.3390/soc4020265

Cabrera, N. L. (2011). Using a sequential exploratory mixed-method design to examine racial hyperprivilege in higher education. In K. A. Griffin & S. D. Museus (Eds.), *Using Mixed Methods Approaches to Study Intersectionality in Higher Education* (New Directions for Institutional Research, no. 151, pp. 77–91). Jossey-Bass.

Cabrera N. L. (2012). Working through whiteness: White, male college students challenging racism. *Review of Higher Education, 35*(3), 375–401. https://doi.org/10.1353/rhe.2012.0020

Cabrera, N. L. (2014a). "But I'm oppressed too": White male college students framing racial emotions as facts and recreating racism. *Journal of Qualitative Studies in Education, 27*(6), 768–784. https://doi.org/10.1080/09518398.2014.901574

Cabrera, N. L. (2014b). But we're not laughing: White male college students' racial joking and what this says about "post-racial" discourse. *Journal of College Student Development, 55*(1), 1–15. https://doi.org/10.1353/csd.2014.0007

Cabrera, N. L. (2014c). Exposing whiteness in higher education: White male college students minimizing racism, claiming victimization, and recreating white supremacy. *Race Ethnicity and Education, 17*(1), 30–55. https://doi.org/10.1080/13613324.2012.725040

Cabrera, N. L., Franklin, J. D., & Watson, J. S. (2017). *Whiteness in higher education: The invisible missing link in diversity and racial analyses.* Association for the Study of Higher Education monograph series. Jossey-Bass.

Chesler, M. A., Peet, M., & Sevig, T. (2003). Blinded by whiteness: The development of white college students' racial awareness. In A. Doane & E. Bonilla-Silva (Eds.), *Whiteout: The continuing significance of racism* (pp. 215–230). Routledge.

Delgado, R. (1989). Storytelling for oppositionists and others: A plea for narrative. *Michigan Law Review, 87*, 2411–2441. https://doi.org/10.2307/1289308

Delgado, R., & Stefancic, J. (2017). *Critical race theory: An introduction* (3rd ed.). NYU Press.

DiAngelo, R. (2018). *White fragility: Why it's so hard for white people to talk about racism.* Beacon Press.

Elliott, K. C., & Shatara, L. H. (2018). Your liberation is bound up in mine: Bringing our whole selves to EDU 342. *Women, Gender, and Families of Color, 6*(1), 37–42. https://doi.org/10.5406/womgenfamcol.6.1.0037

Embrick, D. G., Carter, J. S., Lippard, C., & Thakore, B. K. (2020). Capitalism, racism, and Trumpism: Whitelash and the politics of oppression. *Fast Capitalism, 17*(1), 203–224.

Fasching-Varner, K. J. (2012). *Working through whiteness: Examining white racial identity and profession with pre-service teachers*. Lexington Books.

Foste, Z., & Irwin, L. (2020). Applying critical whiteness studies in college student development theory and research. *Journal of College Student Development, 61*(4), 439–455. https://doi.org/10.1353/csd.2020.0050

Foste, Z., & Jones, S. R. (2020). Narrating whiteness: A qualitative exploration of how white college students construct and give meaning to their racial location. *Journal of College Student Development, 61*(2), 171–188. https://doi.org/10.1353/csd.2020.0050

Frankenberg, R. (1993). *The social construction of whiteness: White women, race matters*. University of Minnesota Press.

George Mwangi, C., Thelamour, B., Ezeofor, I., & Carpenter, A. (2018). "Black elephant in the room": Black students contextualizing campus racial climate within U.S. racial climate. *Journal of College Student Development, 59*(4), 456–474. https://doi.org/10.1353/csd.2018.0042

Gest, J. (2016). *The new minority: White working class politics in an era of immigration and inequality.* Oxford University Press.

Griffith, A. N., Hurd, N. M., & Hussain, S. B. (2019). "I didn't come to school for this": A qualitative examination of experiences with race-related stressors and coping responses among Black students attending a predominantly white institution. *Journal of Adolescent Research, 34*(2), 115–139. https://doi.org/10.1177/0743558417742983

Hardiman, R. (2001). Reflections on white identity development theory. In C. L. Wijeyesinghe & B. W. Jackson III (Eds.), *New perspectives on racial identity development: A theoretical and practical anthology* (pp. 108–128). NYU Press.

Hardiman, R., & Keehn, M. (2012). White racial development revisited. In C. L. Wijeyesinghe & B. W. Jackson III (Eds.), *New perspectives on racial identity development: Integrating emerging frameworks* (2nd ed., pp. 121–137). NYU Press.

Helms, J. E. (1995). An update of Helms' white and People of Color racial identity models. In J. G. Ponterotto, J. Manuel Casas, L. A. Suzuki, & C. M. Alexander (Eds.), *Handbook of multicultural counseling* (pp. 181–198). SAGE.

Helms, J. E., & Piper, R. E. (1994). Implications of racial identity theory for vocational psychology. *Journal of Vocational Behavior, 44*(2), 124–136.

Hikido, A., & Murray, S. B. (2016). Whitened rainbows: How white college students protect whiteness through diversity discourses. *Race Ethnicity and Education, 19*(2), 389–411. https://doi.org/10.1080/13613324.2015.1025736

hooks, b. (1981). *Ain't I a woman: Black women and feminism.* South End Press.

hooks, b. (1989). *Talking back: Thinking feminist, thinking Black.* South End Press.

Hughey, M. W. (2012). Stigma allure and white antiracist identity management. *Social Psychology Quarterly*, (3), 219–240. https://doi.org/10.1177/0190272512446756

Ioanide, P. (2015). *The emotional politics of racism: How feelings trump facts in an era of colorblindess*. Stanford University Press.

Jayakumar, U. M. (2015). The shaping of postcollege colorblind orientation among whites: Residential segregation and campus diversity experiences. *Harvard Educational Review, 85*(4), 609–645. http://doi.org/10.17763/0017-8055.85.4.609

Jones, S. R., & Abes, E. S. (2013). *Identity development of college students: Advancing frameworks for multiple dimensions of identity*. Jossey-Bass.

Kelly, B. T., Gardner, P. J., Stone, J., Hixson, A., & Dissassa, D.-T. (2019). Hidden in plain sight: Uncovering the emotional labor of Black women students at historically white colleges and universities. *Journal of Diversity in Higher Education, 14*(2), 203–216. http://dx.doi.org/10.1037/dhe0000161

Leonardo, Z. (2004). The color of supremacy: Beyond the discourse of "white privilege." *Educational Philosophy and Theory, 36*(2), 137–152. https://doi.org/10.1111/j.1469-5812.2004.00057.x

Leonardo, Z. (2009). *Race, whiteness, and education*. Routledge.

Leonardo, Z. (2020). The Trump presidency, post-colorblindness, and the reconstruction of public race speech. In O. K. Obasagie (Ed.), *Trumpism and its discontents* (pp. 18–55). Berkeley Public Policy Press.

Leonardo, Z., & Porter, R. K. (2010). Pedagogy of fear: Toward a Fanonian theory of "safety" in race dialogue. *Race Ethnicity and Education, 13*(2), 139–157. https://doi.org/10.1080/13613324.2010.482898

Linder, C. (2015). Navigating guilt, shame, and fear of appearing racist: A conceptual model of antiracist white feminist identity development. *Journal of College Student Development, 56*(6), 535–550.

Matias, C. E., & Zembylas, M. (2014). "When saying you care is not really caring": Emotions of disgust, whiteness ideology, and teacher education. *Critical Studies in Education, 55*(3), 319–337. https://doi.org/10.1080/17508487.2014.922489

Mertens, D. M. (2005). *Research and evaluation in education and psychology* (2nd ed.). SAGE.

Money, L. (2020, February 6). Chapman student arrested after racist, homophobic rant is caught on video. *Los Angeles Times*. https://www.latimes.com/california/story/2020-02-06/chapman-student-arrested-after-racist-homophobic-rant-is-caught-on-video

Morales, E. (2020). "Beasting" at the battleground: Black students responding to racial microaggressions in higher education. *Journal of Diversity in Higher Education, 14*(1), 72–83. http://dx.doi.org/10.1037/dhe0000168

Nadal, K. L. (2014). Pilipino American identity development model. *Journal of Multicultural Counseling & Development, 32*(1), 45–62.

Neville, H. A., Poteat, V. P., Lewis, J. A., & Spanierman, L. B. (2014). Changes in white college students' color-blind racial ideology over 4 years: Do diversity experiences make a difference? *Journal of Counseling Psychology, 61*(2), 179–190. https://doi.org/10.1037/a0035168

Picca, L. H., & Feagin, J. R. (2007). *Two-faced racism: Whites in the backstage and frontstage*. Routledge.

Robinson, C. (2018, January 16). *University of Alabama investigates sorority member's racist video.* AL.com. https://www.al.com/news/birmingham/2018/01/university_of_alabama_investig.html

Robinson, S. J. (2013). Spoketokenism: Black women talking back about graduate school experiences. *Race Ethnicity and Education, 16*(2), 155–181. http://dx.doi.org/10.1080/13613324.2011.645567

Roll, N. (2017, August 15). When your students attend white supremacist rallies. *Inside Higher Ed.* https://www.insidehighered.com/news/2017/08/15/college-students-unmasked-unite-right-protesters

Spanierman, L. B., & Cabrera, N. L. (2015). The emotions of white racism and anti-racism. In V. Watson, D. Howard-Wagner, & L. B. Spanierman (Eds.), *Unveiling whiteness in the 21st century: Global manifestations, transdisciplinary interventions* (pp. 9–28). Lexington Books.

Stirgus, E. (2020, July 28). Wesleyan College expels student for racist social media posts. *Atlanta Journal-Constitution.* https://www.ajc.com/news/local-education/wesleyan-college-expels-student-for-racist-social-media-posts/Q8mhMvlHx82h-fZTgy2lRGJ/

Tatum, B. D. (1997). *"Why are all the Black kids sitting together in the cafeteria?": And other conversations about race.* Basic Books.

Vocabulary.com. (n.d.). *Nescient* [Def. 1]. https://www.vocabulary.com/dictionary/nescient

Whitehead, M. A. (2021). Whiteness, anti-Blackness, and trauma: A grounded theory of white racial meaning-making. *Journal of College Student Development, 62*(3), 310–326. https://doi.org/10.1353/csd.2021.0027

13

WHITENESS AND THE ERASURE OF INDIGENOUS PERSPECTIVES IN HIGHER EDUCATION

Jameson D. Lopez and Felisia Tagaban Gaskin

Whiteness has systematically erased Indigenous peoples and their perspectives in higher education. White supremacy is a system of oppression normalizing discrimination, violence, and unequal distribution of power that has allowed whiteness or the normalization of white supremacy to permeate the institutions that sit on Indigenous land to infiltrate the very existence of Indigenous people. The erasure of Indigenous folks exists in almost every aspect in higher education, such as the institutional data found in higher education, underfunded institutional initiatives for Indigenous students, lack of commitment to Indigenous people from land-grant institutions, erasure of Indigenous people through admissions practices, microaggressions from university administrators, and so on. Nonetheless, the lack of data and especially quantitative data that are lacking on Indigenous experiences and perspectives in higher education is extremely troubling. One of the most common ways researchers erase Indigenous folks from higher education *is* through exclusion, blaming statistical limitations for their erasure of Indigenous people as opposed to their own flawed methods of research. Researchers may or may not know that their tradition of upholding whiteness under the guise of statistical limitations statements for statistical rigor are excluding and erasing Indigenous people in their data, when in reality these researchers and scholars should own that possibly their variables in the data are irrelevant to Indigenous people and, to put it plainly, wholly inadequate. In the following sections we will interrogate the ways in which whiteness (as well as white supremacy) has discarded Indigenous perspectives on colonized land through quantitative data.

The quantitative research that does exist on Indigenous people is usually about how quantitative research on Indigenous people doesn't exist. There are a few quantitative studies about the Indigenous experience that are outside the norm of only saying the data don't exist, but there are other difficulties that we run into, such as that Indigenous people are not monolithic given there are 574 federally recognized tribes, and that number is increased even more by the state-recognized tribes. Even as Indigenous people, it's difficult to understand all the experiences of Indigenous people. Whiteness exacerbates these issues whereas IT privileges white perspectives that can (a) cause researchers to measure Indigenous people from ideals other than our own and (b) not recognize the existence of forced assimilation, to the point of not even knowing we as Indigenous people are assimilated. Later in this chapter we discuss these two topics but first we ground this work within the broader erasure of Indigenous populations within the context of higher education.

The Erasure of Indigenous People in Higher Education

The erasure of Indigenous people in higher education is an issue previously interrogated by several Indigenous scholars (see Shotton et al., 2013). At the core of Indigenous erasure is invisibility, where Indigenous students in higher education are seen as a monolithic group or homogenous group of students (Shotton, 2020). In reality there are 574 Indigenous nations that are federally recognized and another 66 state-recognized Indigenous nations (Indian Affairs, 2021). These nations have tribal sovereignty—the right to self-govern—and unique cultural contexts that include different languages, ceremonies, and traditions. However, these Indigenous nations and subsequently Indigenous students have been forced into assimilative educational environments since the early 1800s (Windchief, 2018). Nonetheless, one of the keys to the erasure of Indigenous people has been seeing us as a monolithic group of people and then forcing non-Indigenous values into Indigenous students' education.

The values in which Indigenous people are measured against were invented by white imperialism and the whiteness that permeates higher education. Smith (2021) wrote

> Imperialism tends to be used in four different ways when describing the form of European imperialism which 'started' in [the] fifteenth century: (1) imperialism as economic expansion; (2) imperialism as the subjugation of 'others'; (3) imperialism as an idea or spirit with many forms of realization; and (4) imperialism as a discursive field of knowledge. (pp. 23–24)

The measurements against which Indigenous people have been measured in higher education have been a means of economic expansion into Indigenous lands, subjugating Indigenous people to the values of whiteness and attempting forced assimilation on Indigenous students into the discursive field of knowledge in which Indigenous values are invisible and erased.

Measuring Indigenous People From Values Other Than Our Own

In higher education quantitative research, we often measure academic achievement through grade point average, 1st- to 2nd-year persistence, and graduation rates. However, if we were to look at academic achievement from an Indigenous perspective, the outcomes may look different, especially given that these are values not rooted in the values of Indigenous people. In many ways, measuring academic achievement through how higher education scholars traditionally have measured academic achievement upholds these different forms of imperialism to keep Indigenous people in deficit views. In reality we need to stop and think about how we might measure Indigenous values that could be seen in the realities by which Indigenous people live. Whiteness has systematically erased Indigenous peoples and their perspectives in higher education by allowing only measurement based on the values of the dominant narrative. With the long history of disparities in educational achievement of Indigenous peoples, finding solutions to gaps in educational achievement is challenging (see Tachine & Lopez, 2020). Part of the struggle may be due to current datasets not accurately measuring or sampling Indigenous educational experiences. For example, scholars may only partially, or not at all, reflect Indigenous reality or experience. For that reason, there were many studies that collected, analyzed, and documented the factors influencing educational achievement for Indigenous students. However, the majority of these studies were qualitative or contained significant limitations (Carmen, 2006; Huffman, 2008; Pavel & Padilla, 1993; Shotton et al., 2007; Waterman, 2007). The following two studies demonstrate some of the limitations and the need for more accurate measuring and sampling of Indigenous educational experiences.

The first report is the Meriam Report (1928), and the second is the National Indian Education Study (National Center for Education Statistics [NCES], 2012). Although the Meriam Report is not exclusively on Indigenous education, it was one of the first reports that had data on Indigenous education with major implications and substantial limitations. Also included in the conversation is the National Indian Education Study because it contains data from national datasets addressing Indigenous education using a larger sample of Indigenous students, but also has substantial limitations. Although this paper relates mostly to Indigenous postsecondary data regarding access and persistence, collectively these two studies illustrate the minimal change in evidence found in quantitative data examining Indigenous students over the past 9 decades. Furthermore, they will illuminate some of the factors influencing Indigenous postsecondary persistence. In the following section, there is a discussion of these two reports based on their purpose, methods, results, and limitations using internal, external, statistical conclusion, and measurement validity/reliability issues.

The Meriam Report

The Meriam Report's purpose was to survey the economic and social conditions of Indigenous people during the 1920s. The full report contains information on Indigenous policy, health, education, economic conditions, family and community life, Indigenous relocation, legislation affecting Indigenous people, and missionary work among Indigenous communities. However, given the focus of this chapter, the present discussion focuses on the education portion. This study was one of the first documenting the insufficient educational opportunities provided by the U.S. government to Indigenous students (Meriam, 1928).

The researchers behind the Meriam Report knew it was impractical to gather information for their survey from each tribe in the allotted year, so they visited larger and more influential Indigenous areas. They collected data from 95 jurisdictions, including reservations, Indigenous agencies, hospitals, schools, and highly populated Indigenous communities. The education data collection focused on nonreservation boarding schools, reservation boarding schools, and Indigenous children in public schools. Data collection came primarily from interviews and surveys with superintendents, principals, teachers, day school inspectors, and students. Also, the research team visited Indigenous homes and attended the Indigenous councils to understand school problems from the Indigenous perspective. Indian advisers interpreted the survey to Indigenous participants when the researchers collected information from second-language speakers.

The Meriam Report found Indigenous education was largely inadequate. The finding was especially true in boarding schools where poor diet, overcrowding, and a lack of teacher quality existed. The report suggested there was a need for educational methods based on individual tribes, as each tribe is unique. This suggestion was contrary to the notion that Native children must leave their home to receive an education (Meriam, 1928). Furthermore, the report found a need for reservation teachers to develop higher standards of instruction. The report also recommended that reservation teachers instruct without standardized test books or curriculum and have the ability to formulate material from the life of Natives. Finally, the report suggested more time to educate advanced Indigenous students in school and providing these advanced students with scholarships for postsecondary education. The findings resulted in the expansion of Indigenous educational policies, and most notably through legislation passed in 1934, attempting to decrease federal control and increase self-governing of Indigenous tribes (Indian Reorganization Act of 1934). Although researchers collected data in an efficient manner, given the time and geographic constraints, the resulting data had significant limitations.

When the researchers went to the jurisdictions, they often found the superintendents in charge of Indigenous affairs claiming that imperative data are either not available or inconsistent. Due to the lack of quality data, the report stated there was no concrete evidence for the success of the educational service. The absence of longitudinal and/or accurate data from the superintendents led researchers to gather cross-sectional data. Also, the Indigenous participants in the study may not have understood the questions being asked, given the language barrier between the researchers and tribes. Furthermore, the ability to speak in English may have led researchers to collect data from only English speakers, which would impact measurement validity. There are no specific details on the measures used in the surveys, so it is difficult to understand the limitations in the measurement validity of the study. The limited sampling decreases the external validity of the study. In other words, implications and policy changes resulting from this research may not hold or apply to all the tribes located within the United States. Nonetheless, the report demonstrates how prominent the Meriam Report was in Indigenous policy and, generally, how influential national datasets can be on Indigenous policy. Shifting from educational data in the late 1920s to 2011, national data are still imperative to policy but still continue to have substantial limitations as did the Meriam Report.

National Indian Education Study

The purpose of the 2011 National Indian Education Study (NIES) was to describe the condition of and support the improvement of education for Indigenous students in the United States (NCES, 2012). The National Center for Education Statistics conducts the study through the National Assessment of Educational Progress (NAEP). NAEP provides data on the fourth- and eighth-grade Indigenous academic performance in math, reading, and educational experiences. NAEP also collects data on the condition of Indigenous education through teacher and administrator questionnaires.

The sampling for NIES was in tandem with the sampling of the 2011 NAEP assessments. The sampled students included 10,900 fourth-graders and 8,300 eighth-graders assessed in NAEP reading or math. Researchers administered questionnaires to 20,500 Indigenous students, approximately 7,600 participating Indigenous students' reading and math teachers, and approximately 3,900 administrators. The questionnaire measured five separate categories related to increasing Indigenous academic achievement and examining the role of language and culture in increasing achievement. These five categories include (NCES, 2012)

> 1. the extent to which Indigenous culture and language are part of the curriculum; 2. Availability of school resources for improving Indigenous student achievement; 3. How assessment information is used by schools with Indigenous student populations; 4. Involvement of Indigenous tribes, groups, or villages with the schools; and 5. How Indigenous students, teachers, and schools feel about education. (p. 52)

The study indicates the samples are representative of Indigenous students in the United States and allows for comparisons between Bureau of Indian Education (BIE) schools and Indigenous low- and high-density public schools.

Findings from the assessments indicated average reading and math scores for both fourth- and eighth-grade students were not different from prior years. Compared to non-Natives, Indigenous fourth-graders scored 19 points lower on a scale ranging from zero to 500, and eighth-grade Indigenous students scored 13 points lower in their reading comprehension on average. Although the comparisons were not statistically significant, Indigenous fourth-grade students scored 16 points lower, and Indigenous eighth-graders scored 19 points lower than non-Native students on the math assessment. The findings indicated students from BIE schools had greater knowledge of Indigenous history than Indigenous students in public schools with low populations of Indigenous students. There were also higher percentages of teachers in BIE schools than in high-density or low-density Indigenous public schools. Teachers also indicated they learned by working and living in an Indigenous community. The results also indicate almost two thirds of the sample of eighth-graders reported they have not talked to a school counselor about academic plans. From school administrators' responses, the findings show more community members share traditions and culture for eighth-graders in BIE schools than any of the other schools included in the sample.

The NIES contains a representative sample of Indigenous students in the United States. However, researchers based the sample on the school determination of Indigenous students, meaning that in some cases, schools excluded some Indigenous students from the study based on the school's knowledge of the student's ethnicity (NCES, 2012). The schools' determining Indigenous status may give researchers difficulties identifying meaningful relationships. If Indigenous students are not correctly identified, the external validity of the study decreases. Furthermore, the data in this dataset are specific to questions about fourth- and eighth-grade reading and math performance and may not control for variables that influence reading or math.

Summary

The Meriam Report and the NIES provide evidence of historical and contemporary disparities in educational achievement, but more importantly they illustrate the difficulties researching Indigenous education because they are based in whiteness. Moreover, the history of documented educational achievement differences may be inaccurate given the limitations of the datasets used to sample and measure Indigenous educational experiences. They may only partially, or not at all, reflect Indigenous reality or experience because of statistical limitations. For these reasons, researchers need to continue to develop and collect data in different manners that are more representative of the Indigenous experience in postsecondary education that has not been invaded by whiteness. However, these studies at a federal level offer an opportunity to measure Indigenous values at a national level alongside values placed on Indigenous people through assimilation practices.

Whiteness as Endemic to Indigenous People

Whiteness was ingrained through the boarding school era and the federal legislation such as the Indian relocation act to move Indigenous people to cities for trade jobs. Braboy (2005) spoke to this process when he stated,

> The colonization has been so complete that even many American Indians fail to recognize that we are taking up colonialist ideas when we fail to express ourselves in ways that may challenge dominant society's ideas about who and what we are supposed to be. (p. 431)

Even as Indigenous people, if we fail to recognize the ways in which colonization and whiteness have infiltrated our communities, we will continue to rely on data that express values that are outside of Indigenous communities. Due to the infiltration by which colonization and whiteness have come to our community, we must as Indigenous people seek ways to create sustainable education systems using Indigenous perspectives.

Windchief (2018) examined these concepts and stated that if we as educators intend to use education to preserve a sustainable quality life for Indigenous students, then we must build educational values that are culturally sustaining. There is a particularly powerful metaphor presented by a student in looking at Indigenous education: "The student understands graduate education to be like horses taken from the enemy" (p. 81). Horses were used to provide for family, and there is honor in providing for family. Horses were also something that Indigenous people in North America adopted as a means for battle. Education is something that we can also take and use to provide a better life for family, but the education has to be made our own. In that Indigenous values are represented and measured.

Lopez (2020) talked about measuring Indigenous educational outcomes through the values of the community using Indigenous quantitative methodologies. In essence, Indigenous quantitative methodologies seek to use quantitative research from an Indigenous perspective for community purposes (Lopez, 2021; Walter & Andersen, 2013). When basing educational outcomes in the Indigenous communities we are able to address some of the whiteness that continues to dominate the values that we measure Indigenous students against. Having quantitative outcomes based on the values of the community additionally help the historical understanding, knowledge, policies, and practices that colleges and universities use to interact with Indigenous people, especially as most universities have struggles or have had difficulties working in Indigenous communities.

Researchers don't have to look far for examples of misuse. One such case is the misuse of blood samples that an Arizona State University faculty member had from a tribe. The faculty member examined the blood samples outside the scope of their proposed diabetes project, and the misuse led to an out-of-court settlement for testing the blood for research. The ASU faculty member tested the blood for schizophrenia, ethnic migration, and population inbreeding, all taboo topics in Havasupai culture (Garrison, 2013). Colonization and whiteness have empowered such problematic scholars in academia, that there is entitlement to examining Indigenous folks against topics looking to demonstrate the superiority of whiteness. In reality, these values allowed this researcher to misuse blood samples and explore topics that are not of Indigenous values, solely to demonstrate the ways in which Indigenous people should exist according to whiteness. Additionally, we can find more recent struggles, such as that at the University of Arizona.

On October 3, 2019, 15 undergraduate students, myself (Felisia), and two other graduate student instructors were engaged in a Native Student Outreach Access and Resiliency (SOAR) outreach activity, outside of the University of Arizona's (UA) Old Main building. The students, who primarily identify as Native, were writing letters to family and community members encouraging the pursuit of postsecondary education and the possibility of UA enrollment. As the students were discussing their letters, the UA president approached the group and attempted to make a connection but instead offered a microaggression. After the uncomfortable exchange, he concluded the conversation by pushing back on recommendations to examine university systems and structures that deter and resist Indigenous student success. Varying in differing levels of critical consciousness, a few undergraduates expressed feelings of anger while others described feelings of disappointment. The president later apologized and made a commitment to return to the class to offer an apology. In the months that followed, Native SOAR leaders experienced macroaggression. Whiteness permeates higher education, creating hostile places for Indigenous people, partly because the institutions of higher education have never respected Indigenous values. If they did, we would be measuring them in quantitative research.

Implications and Conclusion

There are two main implications that we see from this work. First there is a need for Indigenous data sovereignty. Second, more funding is needed for Indigenous initiatives to bring awareness to university campuses that reside on Indigenous land. Carroll et al. (2019) defined *Indigenous data sovereignty* as "the right and capacity of tribes to develop data collection processes and analysis to influence the collection of data by external entities" (p. 3). The collection and analysis of data ensure many beneficial components of diverting from whiteness that have permeated Indigenous communities through colonization. Indigenous data sovereignty allows Indigenous people to control the data collected and encourages the collection of data based on the values of the community. Indigenous communities could then measure outcomes based on their own values as opposed to the values imposed by non-Indigenous people. Furthermore, there would be control over which data are available for public consumption, allowing tribes to be in charge of their narrative as a tribal community.

Additionally, by researchers in higher education utilizing Indigenous data sovereignty, they will be able to address the historically marginalized ways of knowing that are suppressed by whiteness on college campuses.

Some of those include the erasure by which Indigenous students are seen as a monolithic group (Shotton et al., 2013) and the lack of educational outcomes based on the values of the community (see Lopez, 2020, 2021).

Second, many of the problems that we see facing Indigenous communities in higher education could be avoided by funding Indigenous initiatives. There is unconscious bias that exists in everyone, and often folks in higher education are not aware of those biases in the case of the administration. With more funding, especially for Indigenous personnel, campuses can benefit from training to avoid these scenarios and correct any past wrongdoings. Awareness is an issue we see with many non-Indigenous folks. It's obvious in how there is a lack of Indigenous values being measured in data and even more obvious in the micro/macroaggressions that Indigenous students experience on campus.

In this chapter we explored how whiteness privileges white perspectives that have (a) caused researchers to measure Indigenous people from values other than our own and (b) been assimilated to the point of we as Indigenous people not even knowing we are assimilated. In order to move toward the future that dismantles these notions of whiteness that are problematic to Indigenous communities, we must consider supporting Indigenous data sovereignty and funding Indigenous initiatives.

References

Brayboy. (2005). Toward a tribal critical race theory in education. *The Urban Review, 37*(5), 425–446. https://doi.org/10.1007/s11256-005-0018-y

Carmen, A. (2006). *Recruiting Native American college students: "Why don't they just show up from their high schools like other students do?"* [Unpublished doctoral thesis]. University of Oregon.

Carroll, S. R., Rodriguez-Lonebear, D., and Martinez, A. (2019). Indigenous data governance: Strategies from United States Native Nations. *Data Science Journal, 18*(1), 31. https://doi.org/10.5334/dsj-2019-031

Garrison, N. A. (2013). Genomic justice for Native Americans: Impact of the Havasupai case on genetic research. *Science, Technology, & Human Values, 38*(2), 201–223.

Huffman, T. E. (2008). *American Indian higher educational experiences: Cultural visions and personal journeys.* Peter Lang.

Indian Affairs. (2021). *Who we are.* http://www.bia.gov/WhoWeAre/index.htm

Indian Reorganization Act of 1934, Pub. L. No. 73-383, 48 Stat. 984 (1934). https://iowaculture.gov/history/education/educator-resources/primary-source-sets/new-deal/indian-reorganization-act-1934

Lopez, J. D. (2020). Indigenous data collection: Addressing limitations in Native American samples. *Journal of College Student Development, 61*(6), 750–764. https://doi.org/10.1353/csd.2020.0073

Lopez, J. D. (2021). Research and evaluation in Indigenous communities. In J. Tippeconic & M. J. Tippeconic-Fox (Eds.), *On Indian ground: The Southwest* (pp. 177–189). Information Age.

Meriam, L. (1928). *The problem of Indian administration; report of a survey made at the request of Hubert Work, secretary of the interior, and submitted to him, February 21, 1928.* Johns Hopkins Press.

National Center for Education Statistics. (2012). *National Indian education study 2011* (NCES 2012-466). Institute of Education Sciences, U.S. Department of Education.

Pavel, D. M., & Padilla, R. V. (1993). American Indian and Alaska Native postsecondary departure: An example of assessing a mainstream model using national longitudinal data. *Journal of American Indian Education, 32*(2), 1.

Shotton, H. J. (2020). Beyond reservations: Exploring diverse backgrounds and tribal citizenship among Native college students. In R. T. Teranishi, B. M. D. Nguyen, C. M. Alcantar, & E. R. Curammeng (Eds.), *Measuring race: Why disaggregating data matters for addressing educational inequality* (pp. 119–130). Teachers College Record.

Shotton, H. J., Lowe, S. C., & Waterman, S. J. (Eds.). (2013). *Beyond the asterisk: Understanding Native students in higher education.* Stylus.

Shotton, H., Oosahwe, E., & Cintrón, R. (2007). Stories of success: Experiences of American Indian students in a peer-mentoring retention program. *The Review of Higher Education, 31*(1), 81–107.

Smith, L. T. (2021). Decolonizing methodologies: Research and Indigenous peoples (3rd ed.). Zed Books.

Tachine, A., & Lopez, J. D. (2020). Native Americans in higher education. In M. David & M. Amey (Eds.), *The SAGE Encyclopedia of higher education.* SAGE.

Walter, M., & Andersen, C. (2013). *Indigenous statistics: A quantitative research methodology.* Left Coast Press.

Waterman, S. J. (2007). A complex path to Haudenosaunee degree completion. *Journal of Education, 46*(1), 20–40.

Windchief, S. (2018). Stealing horses: Indigenous student metaphors for success in graduate education. In R. S. Minthorn & H. J. Shotton (Eds.), *Reclaiming Indigenous research in higher education* (pp. 76–87). Rutgers University Press.

14

STARTING FROM THE MARGINS

Reflections on Challenging Whiteness in Higher Education

Zak Foste and Melvin A. Whitehead

As in the old days of racial segregation where black folks learned to "wear the mask," many of us pretend to be comfortable in the face of whiteness only to turn our backs and give expression to intense levels of discomfort. Especially talked about is the representation of whiteness as terrorizing.

—hooks, 1992, p. 341

Bell hooks (1992) opened her seminal essay "Representing Whiteness in the Black Imagination" with the reminder that "black folks, from slavery on, shared in conversations with one another 'special' knowledge of whiteness gleaned from close scrutiny of white people" (p. 338). Her words speak to the unique power and value of Black people's experiential knowledge concerning whiteness and its violence—a knowledge that, as the opening passage indicates, is often born from terror. hooks's assertion about the special knowledge Black people have about whiteness is a significant departure from the dominant arc of critical whiteness scholarship, which Leonardo (2013) had argued could be understood as a white-dominant discourse that has muted People of Color's voices in critical analyses of whiteness. To be clear, studying whiteness from white vantage points is not inherently counterproductive. Indeed, white people *should* dialogue with one another about whiteness; critical analyses of whiteness from white vantage points are necessary for both revealing the complicit ways through which white people perpetuate white supremacy and engaging white people in disrupting it. *And* we concur with hooks's (1990) conceptualization of the margins as a place of radical resistance and argue that Black, Indigenous, and People of

Color's (BIPOC's) knowledge about and lived experiences under the terror of whiteness is critically necessary for not only fully analyzing the contours of whiteness but for disrupting it. In this concluding chapter, we use hooks's (1990) conceptualization of the margins as a framework to imagine directions for critical whiteness praxis in higher education.

Interrogate How Whiteness Intersects With Other Oppressive Systems

Although critical analyses of whiteness understandably foreground systems perpetuating *racialized* oppression, BIPOC's lives have never been singularly structured around race. Indeed, Feminists of Color have long spoken about how sexism, imperialism, classism, capitalism, and homophobia intersect with white supremacy to create the conditions affecting immigrant, poor, working-class, and lesbian Women of Color's lives (Beal, 1970; Collins, 1991; Crenshaw, 1989, 1991; hooks, 1981; Lorde, 1984; Moraga & Anzaldúa, 1983). Whiteness, then, could be understood to structure oppressions targeting People of Color (through these intersections), rather than as just rhetoric that structures white supremacy. Positioning whiteness in this way allows educators to retain an analytic focus on the totality and complexity of People of Color's lives and demands that we think intersectionally and expansively about how we disrupt whiteness in our work. Such an approach involves continuously (a) developing our own understandings of the multiple and interlocking forms of oppression affecting BIPOC students, faculty, and staff; (b) developing our own understandings of how these systems are each connected to one another and to white supremacy; and (c) applying our evolving understandings of whiteness *and* its connections to multiple forms of oppression to the ongoing work of locating and disrupting these systems in our policies and practices (see Lange et al., chapter 8, this volume).

Developing our own understandings of the interlocking forms of oppression affecting Students of Color must both include *and* move beyond racism, sexism, and classism to include all oppressions targeting specific BIPOC communities. These include anti-Blackness (which structurally positions Black people in an antagonistic relationship with humanity; Dumas, 2016), misogynoir (anti-Black racist misogyny targeting Black women; Bailey & Trudy, 2018), transmisogynoir (the intersection of anti-Blackness, misogyny, and transphobia that targets Black trans women; Preston, 2020), settler colonialism (an ongoing project/structure that remakes land and bodies into property; Tuck & Yang, 2012), anti-Asian racism and model minority rhetoric (Museus & Park, 2015), and racist nativism (which privileges the association between nativeness and whiteness; Huber et al., 2008).

Not only must we continuously develop our own understandings of each of these systems, but also how each is connected to one another and to white supremacy. Here, we underscore the necessity of not lumping all racisms together, while also understanding that they are interconnected.

For example, educators must understand how connections between white supremacy, settler colonialism, and racist nativism shape dominant racialized perceptions of who is "native" and who is not, how these dominant perceptions are shaped by power (vis-à-vis whiteness), and how these perceptions are enacted and maintained through policies that erase and harm Indigenous peoples and Immigrants of Color (and those perceived as such).

Finally, taking intersectional approaches to disrupting whiteness means continuously applying our evolving understandings of whiteness *and* its connections to multiple forms of oppression to the ongoing work of locating and disrupting these systems in our practice. For example, MacDonald's (2019) work calls us to be diligent in interrogating how education settings act as sites of settler silencing targeting Indigenous students, and how whiteness enables that silencing. Using the example of settler colonialism and its connections to whiteness, MacDonald's (2019) work suggests that intersectional approaches to disrupting whiteness can involve asking, (a) How are indigenous identities and cultures constructed on campus (e.g., through curricula and cocurricular programming)?, (b) How do these constructions align with the interests of the institution?, and (c) How do these constructions privilege (white) settler ways of being, behaving, and knowing? This set of questions serves as one example of the types of questions we should be asking about our practices and institutional policies to locate and disrupt whiteness.

Interrogate How Diversity Rhetoric Masks Racial Harm and Reproduces the Normative Center of Whiteness

Language of diversity and inclusion permeates college and university campuses. Yet, as Bell and Hartmann (2007) noted, language of diversity requires us to consider the question, "Different from what?" (p. 908). Such a question requires deeper reflection on how diversity language "rests on a white normative perspective. This perspective starts from the dominance of white worldviews and sees the culture, experiences, and indeed *lives*, of people of color only as they relate to or interact with the white world" (Bell & Hartmann, 2007, p. 907). In order to challenge the deeply embedded nature of whiteness within institutions of higher education, we encourage faculty, staff, and administrators to consider the consequences of uncritically adopting diversity language in ways that recenter the normative status of whiteness. Here we briefly highlight three possible consequences as they relate to the reproduction of whiteness.

First, institutionalized diversity language in higher education rarely comes with corresponding attention to deep structural inequities. In turn, programs and policies grounded in diversity rhetoric may obstruct, rather than facilitate, meaningful institutional transformation. Diversity language tends to center celebratory approaches to difference, emphasize campus unity, and highlight the benefits that come from learning across difference (Berrey, 2011; Marvasti & McKinney, 2011; Moses & Chang, 2006; Warikoo, 2016). The normative center of whiteness is left untouched. In a study Zak (Foste, 2019) conducted on white college students and their relationship to whiteness, it became apparent that a majority of students internalized institutional narratives of diversity and inclusion. That is, the very presence of diversity language and symbols throughout campus produced a misguided sense of campus harmony (Foste, 2019). Further, and perhaps most troubling, Students of Color who protested the racist climate of the institution were seen as an imposition to the university. If, as the thinking went, the university is constantly talking about and promoting diversity, what are they protesting? The language of diversity internalized by so many of these white students failed to offer any critical literacy that could name and address deeply ingrained structural inequities related to access, belonging, retention, and representation. Further, and perhaps most troubling, diversity rhetoric without a corresponding structural critique delegitimizes the critiques of Student Activists of Color who labor to change campus structures and policies (Linder et al., 2019). In a similar fashion, in his study of white college students' racial meaning making, Melvin found that some white students justified claims that their institution was "diverse" by juxtaposing the racial makeup against their predominantly white precollege communities (Whitehead, 2021). In short, diversity rhetoric produces a very particular institutional narrative that is at odds with the racial status quo. Or, as sociologist James Thomas (2020) noted, we would be wise to question the types of stories we tell about our institution and what such stories accomplish.

Second, diversity language functions in such a way that it often further affirms and accelerates white racial ignorance. As Corces-Zimmerman and Guida explained in chapter 4, racial ignorance refers to an active form of not knowing, a refusal to know the racial world as experienced by People of Color. Prior scholarship has illustrated that white parents do not explicitly speak to their children about race and racism, instead opting to endorse color-evasive parenting strategies (Hagerman, 2020; Underhill, 2018; Vittrup, 2018). Megan Underhill's (2018) research on white parenting strategies during the racial unrest in Ferguson, Missouri, highlighted how white parents sought to preserve the innocence of their children by evading discussions about racism and white supremacy. Higher education is uniquely positioned to challenge white students to rethink their relationship to whiteness, enlarge their racial consciousness, and develop a historical and structural racial literacy. Programs and policies grounded in diversity rhetoric rarely accomplish such goals. Although such efforts are grounded in a belief that students are rarely exposed to racial difference prior to college, this claim is typically only true for white college students who, because of the pervasive nature of whiteness, often live racially insulated lives. As such, these approaches often ask that Students of Color share their culture, experiences, and worldviews for the consumption of, although unspoken, white students. Whiteness remains the normative center while Students of Color are understood as ethnic and diverse commodities beneficial to the white student experience.

Finally, and related to our previous point, programs, policies, and practices grounded in diversity rhetoric often frame Students of Color as consumable commodities meant for the enrichment of white students. Thus, rather than improve the material conditions of Students of Color, these practices often produce what Nancy Leong (2013) described as *racial capitalism*. In essence, Students of Color represent significant capital to white students who seek a distant affiliation with difference to signal particular virtuous qualities. Such events repeatedly play out in environments such as study abroad, service-learning programs, and residential life—all of which purport to "expose students to difference."

Implement and Continuously Engage in Transformative Interventions

In naming the terror of whiteness, hooks (1992) evoked the significant role of trauma in understanding Black people's experiences living under it. Given the trauma and violence of whiteness, we must develop practices that go beyond intellectual exercises, checklists of action items, and one-off workshops; we must center healing to address the embodied experiences of carrying this trauma. For BIPOC, healing can mean unearthing the extent to which we[1] have internalized whiteness and its detrimental impacts on our psyche, stress, and sense of self; prioritizing self-love; counterstorytelling as a method of talking back to deficit-based frameworks rooted in whiteness; and resisting the forces that attempt to seduce us into forgetting our own power and who we are holistically in mind, body, and spirit (Dillard, 2012).

Although white people's racialization precludes experiencing racialized trauma in the ways BIPOC do, we concur with others who have articulated the spiritual severances from humanity (broadly) and from People of Color (in particular) that whiteness demands from white people, as well as the ways through which whiteness distorts white people's sense of who they are and masks their roles in maintaining white supremacy (Baldwin, 1998; Jackson, 2011; Smith, 1963; Thompson & Watson, 2016; Whitehead, 2021). We argue these detrimental spiritual and psychological impacts of whiteness on white people should also be addressed through ongoing transformative interventions that promote healing. For example, as an antidote to the trauma of whiteness, Thompson and Watson (2016) called for the cultivation of a "critical white double-consciousness"—a resistant subjectivity that

> demands a fuller, multi-voiced narrative of the past and present, which it then utilizes for honest self-reflection and accountability. It seeks out multiracial, multiethnic interactions as an antidote to the monologues of whiteness, and learns the twin disciplines of silence and close listening as antiracist praxis. It commits itself to remaining a fully present and vocal witness in the face of white lies, denial, and aggression. (p. 249)

Others have called for additional healing practices that could also facilitate the deep work of cultivating a critical white double-consciousness. Love (2020), for example, suggested therapy and counseling for white educators to help with processing the emotions that can arise through engaging in antiracist work. Others have recognized the necessity of healing for everyone (inclusive of racial identities) through somatic approaches (e.g., Menakem, 2017) and reflective exercises (e.g., Saad, 2020; Singh, 2019) that can help educators unlearn the racial messages we have internalized and identify the trauma that racism has created.

Beyond individual healing from the spiritual, emotional, psychological, and physical violence of whiteness, higher education professionals must also take up the task of transforming institutions through broader policies and practices that also center healing. We must recognize whiteness as a pervasive and permanent reality that harms BIPOC within higher education while continuously working to create liberatory spaces. Here again, ways of knowing born from the racialized margins are instructive, as BIPOC know better than anyone else what heals, nourishes, affirms, and sustains Communities of Color. For example, Mustaffa (2021) defined *Black lifemaking* as the collective processes of "what Black people think, do, and create to value their own lives, to define their own humanity" (p. 77). Mustaffa's (2017, 2021) work documented both the centuries-long history and contemporary examples of

Black lifemaking in U.S. education, which has included Black people's persistent pursuit of education as a pursuit of freedom, acts of resistance to racial injustice, and creation of counterspaces that allow Black people to be more whole. Mustaffa (2021) argued that retaining a focus on what Black people do to value our/their own lives is a useful alternative to questions that, for example, focus on Black people's alleged under- or hyper-achievement or how Black people respond to anti-Black realities.

We use Mustaffa's theorizing work on Black lifemaking as a launching point for thinking about the lifemaking practices within various BIPOC communities. Educators should identify and scale up these practices if we hope to cultivate liberatory microclimates within institutions of higher education and root higher education practices in what Communities of Color need. To be clear, white people shoulder a unique and primary responsibility for disrupting whiteness, as this work is not the burden of BIPOC to clean up. At the same time, we take up hooks's (1990) explication of the margins as a radical location of resistance, creativity, power, and possibility to suggest that the lifemaking practices in which BIPOC engage are critically important and informative for racial justice praxis.

Question How Supposedly Race-Neutral Policies Often Reproduce the Racial Status Quo

A central theme of this book has been that whiteness is institutionalized within our colleges and universities. Although it is important to address racist ideas, attitudes, and beliefs, such work is insufficient without also attending to the structures and policies that reinforce and reproduce the racial status quo. One such way that whiteness is institutionalized and sustained is via supposedly race-neutral policies that reproduce racial hierarchies. Wilson Okello's writing on promotion and tenure (chapter 6, this volume) as well as Beatty and Garcia's chapter on sorority and fraternity life (chapter 9, this volume) both illuminate how supposedly race-neutral practices privilege white interests while further marginalizing People of Color in higher education. Put otherwise, in both instances, supposedly race-neutral policies become a vehicle for the production and maintenance of whiteness.

A few years ago Zak (Foste, 2021) conducted a study examining the dynamics of race, whiteness, and student life in on-campus housing. Although he entered the study interested in interactions across differences within the halls, he ended up focusing a great deal of his energy on how supposedly race-neutral housing policies produced inequitable access to university housing. At one institution, for instance, undergraduate students selected their housing option based on the order in which they put down a nonrefundable housing deposit (Foste, 2021). This process, combined with the stark differences in pricing for newer residence halls, produced a highly stratified on-campus housing population. White, affluent students who had the resources to put down a deposit early and could similarly afford the additional $1,000 a year in housing costs, ended up in the premier, state-of-the-art residence hall. One Staff Member of Color described the building as the "Vermont of residence halls" (Foste, 2021, p. 177), given the high concentration of white people in the building. Conversely, Students of Color tended to be concentrated in older, outdated buildings often referred to as the "hood" or the "ghetto."

At another institution in the same study, university officials created a unique housing option for registered student organizations. The community was called "The Neighborhood" (pseudonym) and was located on the edge of campus behind a secure gate. The Neighborhood featured a number of housing options that resembled small houses with green space and common, shared outdoor areas among the houses. Although the university marketed the space to all registered student organizations, all but two houses at the time were occupied by historically white fraternities and sororities. Numerous Black students shared with Zak during his time on campus that the space felt completely off limits to them and that they simply would not feel comfortable there. The irony was not lost on one particular Black woman student who pointedly noted her frustration with the fact that a part of her campus felt completely off limits to her, despite the fact that she was a member of the institution. Rather than interrupt precollege patterns of racial segregation, many of these housing practices reproduced them. These examples serve as a useful reminder for faculty, staff, and administrators to consider the racialized impact of supposedly race-neutral policies on Communities of Color.

Trouble Individual and Institutional Desires for White Innocence

Eddie Glaude (2020) described how James Baldwin experienced

> "a kind of retrospective terror." The terror was not rooted in a fear for his safety or a fear of dying at the hands of racist bigots. Instead, what shook Baldwin at his core was a "realization of the nature of the heathen." The white southerner had to lie *continuously* to himself in order to justify his world. (p. 49)

Baldwin spoke to the tensions between the moral evil of a society grounded in white supremacy and the simultaneous need and desire for individual white people to see and think of themselves as good and virtuous. Because racism is largely understood as an individual character flaw to be avoided, desires to be seen and understood as morally good and not racist are strong among white individuals and the institutions they inhabit (Applebaum, 2010; Foste, 2020; Sullivan, 2014). Desires for white racial innocence are nothing new; rather, they are a central means by which whiteness remains so pervasive (Glaude, 2020; Morrison, 1992; Yancy, 2018). Here we wish to emphasize the series of contradictions and tensions associated with white desires for racial innocence, declarations of support for racial equity, and the reality that historically white colleges and universities still serve white interests.

In chapter 5 Lee and colleagues pointedly note how such desires for racial innocence obstruct meaningful institutional transformation in postsecondary education. In effect, preoccupations with racial innocence and goodness function to disassociate individual white people and institutions from the racial structure and its consequences. In a study Melvin conducted on white college students' racial meaning making, he documented how white innocence was maintained vis-à-vis historical amnesia, or an intentional forgetting of racial violence (Whitehead, 2021). For instance, he documented how a preoccupation with white racial innocence produces "an emotional detachment from both Black people and concern for Black life" (p. 320). These processes play out across campus. When presidents, provosts, and deans quickly proclaim that the latest racist theme party or act of racist expression on campus is at odds with the very ethos of the campus culture, such statements reflect a deep investment in (white) racial innocence. These statements locate racist actions as anomalies that are incongruent with institutional values, rather than consider the contexts and conditions that make such behaviors possible in the first place. Desires for racial innocence allow for a type of epistemic violence that dismisses the lived experiences of BIPOC communities with racist violence. As Yancy (2018) explained, "I bear witness to Black pain and suffering because the deniers are out there. For we are told that what we know in our very bodies to be true isn't credible, which is a different kind of violence, the epistemic kind" (p. 47). Desires for racial innocence were on full display in the days following the murder of George Floyd in the summer of 2020. Presidents and chancellors across the United States released statements in the wake of rising racial unrest, yet much of this rhetoric again reflected a certainty in the goodness of the university itself. For instance, the President of Bradley University released a statement that read, in part:

> The vandalism and violence that have taken place in our community over the past few days are an outcry against the systemic racism that continues to plague our country. At a time when we should be together to fight

> against a global pandemic, we are fighting each other instead. It is especially critical during this challenging time that we reaffirm our value of creating an inclusive community. Open dialogue, empathy, understanding, tolerance and kindness are needed now, more than ever. Please join me in reaffirming our commitment to an inclusive environment, an environment where we do not tolerate violence based on perceived differences but instead embrace our diversity as one of our greatest strengths. This is at the heart of who we are as an institution. (Bradley University, 2020, paras. 2–3)

The statement was met by significant pushback among the students of Bradley, in part because of the president's rhetoric focusing on "vandalism and violence." Yet we would also note how the statement presupposes that Bradley somehow stands outside of the anti-Black ideologies at the heart of protests across the United States in the summer of 2020. Rather than acknowledge how Bradley officials might reflect on anti-Black racism on campus; the experiences of Black students, faculty, and staff; or what the university might learn in this historical moment, the president instead opted to highlight the inherent goodness of the university via its commitment to an "inclusive environment." We are left to consider what alternative messages the president might have sent the Bradley community had he not been primarily concerned with the goodness and innocence of the institution itself.

Similar desires for innocence play out in classroom contexts (see Walker & Patton, chapter 7, this volume). Prior scholarship on discussions of race in college classrooms have illustrated how white students often expect Students of Color to absolve them of racial guilt (Levine-Rasky, 2016). Scholars have described such processes as a form of racial confession, where white students perform a sense of remorse in the presence of their Peers of Color (Applebaum, 2010; Levine-Rasky, 2016). The problem is not so much the affective response to learning about race and racism in and of itself, but instead the assumption that such a response will be met with care, compassion, and forgiveness by Students of Color. The assumption is that BIPOC students sitting in the room will respond in such a way that the emotional response in class has a particular payoff. It will reassure the white student of their inherent goodness and insist that they stand outside of historical, political, and social contexts that privilege whiteness. In our own experience we have also seen supposedly racially progressive white students use content knowledge on race and racism to distance themselves from other whites. In this sense, white students intellectualize matters of race and racism (Watt, 2007) in order to disassociate themselves from peers who simply "do not get it."

It is unsurprising that white desires for racial innocence are so strong. In order to combat such desires, we encourage white individuals to start from a place of complicity (Applebaum, 2010). Starting from a place of complicity highlights how individual white people are embedded within racist structures that inherently benefit white interests. Barbara Applebaum (2010) has written extensively on notions of white complicity and emphasized that the approach is less concerned with self-transformation toward a "good white" and instead might promote a vigilance about how one is wrapped up in a system of white supremacy. In short, starting from a place of complicity highlights how by virtue of benefiting from white racial privilege, individual white people (and by extension white institutions) contribute to the maintenance and reproduction of the racial status quo. White people cannot simply stand outside of these systems. Applebaum offered three questions central to what she describes as white privilege pedagogy:

> How do white people reproduce and maintain racist practices even when, and especially when, they believe themselves to be morally good? How do these practices function to protect their white moral innocence? What allows whites to see themselves as a part of the solution and to deny they are a part of the problem? (p. 180)

We believe these questions are instructive for white people in higher education and might challenge the tendency to center white goodness and self-transformation at the expense of systemic change.

Move Beyond Whiteness as Invisible

Throughout this book contributors have challenged us to think about how whiteness operates as the normative, universal marker of human experience (see, for instance, Irwin, chapter 3, this volume). Indeed, we believe naming the universal and normative nature of whiteness is essential in efforts to render its consequences more visible for critique. At the same time, we wish to offer caution about how faculty, staff, and administrators take up the whiteness-as-invisible stance (Whitehead et al., 2021). First, we urge caution in blanket statements that insist whiteness is invisible. Such statements further dismiss the lived experiences of so many People of Color for whom whiteness is anything but invisible (hooks, 1992; Patton & Haynes, 2020). As bell hooks (1992) explained, whiteness operates at times as a form of terror in the Black imagination. That is, whiteness is quite familiar because People of Color navigate it in everyday life. From classrooms and student group work to faculty meetings and cocurricular activities, whiteness rears its ugly head. Thus, we want to offer this reminder that universal claims that whiteness is invisible dismiss the knowledge People of Color hold about racism and white supremacy.

Second, while the assumed invisibility of whiteness to white people has been a central hallmark of what Bonilla-Silva (2013) aptly described as the era of color-blindness,[2] our current political and historical moment calls into question the primacy of this framework. Color-evasive racial ideologies represented a particular racial worldview that endorsed a postracial society and diminished the role of race as a central factor in access to wealth, opportunity, employment, education, and so forth. In a post–Civil Rights era, success or failure was solely the result of individual achievement and efforts. Racism was downplayed and white people were not assumed to have a racial identity. Yet recent events, culminating in the election of Donald Trump and the ripple effects of his ascendancy to the presidency, call into question the extent to which whiteness is irrelevant to white people as a marker of identity. Of course, whiteness has always been significant to white people, who often chose a racial identification of white in order to have some form of superiority over Black people with whom they shared common class struggles (Roeidger, 1991).

Notwithstanding, dominant racial discourses have often been predicated on the notion that white people, in an era of color-evasiveness, do not identify with a racial group. Yet, among a significant portion of white Americans, whiteness is publicly embraced as a racial identity similar to Blackness or Indigeneity (Leonardo, 2020). This public embrace has often been fueled via claims to freedom of speech and a belief that white people are victims in an increasingly multicultural society (Whitehead et al., 2021). Embrick et al. (2020) described this process as *whitelash*, or "individual, institutional, and/or structural countermeasures against the dismantling of white supremacy or actions, real or imagined, that seek to remedy existing racial inequities" (p. 203). Similarly, Leonardo has argued for a shift in thinking from color-blindness to post-color-blindness in order to name the ways in which whiteness is increasingly taken up by individual white people as an aggrieved identity. Faculty, staff, and administrators would be wise to incorporate such language into broader policies, practices, and approaches to race, racism, and institutional climates. Higher education has long been a venue in which white aggrievement and backlash have played out—be it in opposition to ethnic studies course, renderings of history that are not congruent with white illusions of the past, contestations over admissions and race-conscious policies, or perceived censorship and limiting of free speech

(Whitehead et al., 2021). If institutions of higher education are going to challenge the foundation of white supremacy in university life, it is absolutely necessary that individuals have the language to name the problem as it exists. Accounting for whitelash, post-color-blindness, and the public embrace of whiteness by a segment of the white population is thus incredibly necessary. In doing so we might make sense of matters both internal (i.e., racist events that produce hostile climates for Students of Color, tensions between free speech and safety) and external (i.e., state legislature hostility to telling the truth about our racial history) to our campus.

Conclusion

In this chapter we have drawn on hooks's (1992) notion of whiteness as a form of terror and the corresponding need to begin our analysis from the margins. The recommendations offered here to advance a critical whiteness praxis are not exhaustive and will certainly depend in part on local contexts and circumstances. Yet we do believe that starting from the margins, rather than the center, honors the voices of BIPOC communities who know quite well the inner workings of whiteness and offers potential pathways forward to disrupt deeply ingrained patterns of white supremacy on our campuses.

Notes

1. As a Black person, it was important for me (Melvin) to use *we* and *us* in this paragraph, so as not to remove myself from the trauma whiteness enacts upon BIPOC.

2. Language of *color-blindness*, which has been used extensively in scholarship on race and racism, has been critiqued as a form of ableism. Annamma et al. (2017) advocated for language of color-evasiveness to capture such a racial ideology. As such, while we introduce Bonilla-Silva's notion of color-blindness, in the rest of the chapter we use language of color-evasiveness (Annamma et al., 2017).

References

Annamma, S. A., Jackson, D. D., & Morrison, D. (2017). Conceptualizing color-evasiveness: Using dis/ability critical race theory to expand a color-blind racial ideology in education and society. *Race Ethnicity and Education*, *20*(2), 147–162. https://doi.org/10.1080/13613324.2016.1248837

Applebaum, B. (2010). *Being white, being good: White complicity, white moral responsibility, and social justice pedagogy.* Lexington Books.

Bailey, M., & Trudy. (2018). On misogynoir: Citation, erasure, and plagiarism. *Feminist Media Studies, 18*(4), 762–768. https://doi.org/10.1080/14680777.2018.1447395

Baldwin, J. (1998). *Baldwin: Collected essays*. Library of America.

Beal, F. (1970). Double jeopardy: To be Black and female. In Third World Women's Alliance (Ed.), *Black women's manifesto* [Pamphlet] (pp. 19–34). Third World Women's Alliance.

Bell, J. M., & Hartmann, D. (2007). Diversity in everyday discourse: The cultural ambiguities and consequences of "happy talk." *American Sociological Review, 72*(6), 895–914. https://doi.org/10.1177%2F000312240707200603

Berrey, E. C. (2011). Why diversity became orthodox in higher education, and how it changed the meaning of race on campus. *Critical Sociology, 37*(5), 573–596. https://doi.org/10.1177%2F0896920510380069

Bonilla-Silva, E. (2013). *Racism without racists: Color-blind racism and the persistence of racial inequality in the United States* (4th ed.). Rowman & Littlefield.

Bradley University. (2020). Bradley University statement regarding racial tensions and violence. https://www.bradley.edu/offices/communications/pr/releases/article.dot?id=48f8cef6-8b03-449d-9162-3325e71a5629&fbclid=IwAR1D-SpRE2XvgvyK3xKwxzzVip-ud4GIUqMUoAjO1W1RykruNrp_g0JWufjs#.Yhzxgqzed4k.link

Collins, P. H. (1991). *Black feminist thought: Knowledge, consciousness, and the politics of empowerment*. Routledge.

Crenshaw, K. W. (1989). Demarginalizing the intersection of race and sex: A Black feminist critique of antidiscrimination doctrine, feminist theory, and antiracist politics. *University of Chicago Legal Forum, 1989*(1), 139–167.

Crenshaw, K. W. (1991). Mapping the margins: Intersectionality, identity politics, and violence against women of color. *Stanford Law Review, 43*(6), 1241–1299.

Dillard, C. B. (2012). *Learning to (re)member the things we've learned to forget: Endarkened feminisms, spirituality, and the sacred nature of research and teaching*. Peter Lang.

Dumas, M. J. (2016). Against the dark: Antiblackness in education policy and discourse. *Theory Into Practice, 55*(1), 11–19. https://doi.org/10.1080/00405841.2016.1116852

Embrick, D. G., Carter, J. S., Lippard, C., & Thakore, B. K. (2020). Capitalism, racism, and Trumpism: Whitelash and the politics of oppression. *Fast Capitalism, 17*(1), 203–224. https://doi.org/10.32855/fcapital.202001.012

Foste, Z. (2019). Reproducing whiteness: How white students justify the campus racial status quo. *Journal of Student Affairs Research and Practice, 56*(3), 241–253. https://doi.org/10.1080/19496591.2019.1576530

Foste, Z. (2020). The enlightenment narrative: White student leaders' preoccupation with racial innocence. *Journal of Diversity in Higher Education, 13*(1), 33–43. https://doi.org/10.1037/dhe0000113

Foste, Z. (2021). "Oh, that's the white dorm": The racialization of university housing and the policing of racial boundaries. *Journal of College Student Development, 62*(2), 169–185. https://doi.org/10.1353/csd.2021.0015

Glaude, E. (2020). *Begin again: James Baldwin's America and its urgent lessons for our own.* Penguin.

Hagerman, M. A. (2020). Racial ideology and white youth: From middle childhood to adolescence. *Sociology of Race and Ethnicity, 6*(3), 319–332. https://doi.org/10.1177%2F2332649219853309

hooks, b. (1981). *Ain't I a woman?: Black women and feminism.* South End Press.

hooks, b. (1990). *Yearning: Race, gender, and cultural studies.* South End Press.

hooks, b. (1992). Representing whiteness in the Black imagination. In L. Grossberg, C. Nelson, & P. Treichler (Eds.), *Cultural studies* (pp. 338–346). Routledge.

Huber, L. P., Lopez, C. B., Malagon, M. C., Velez, V., & Solorzano, D. G. (2008). Getting beyond the "symptom," acknowledging the "disease": Theorizing racist nativism. *Contemporary Justice Review, 11*(1), 39–51. https://doi.org/10.1080/10282580701850397

Jackson, T. A. (2011). Which interests are served by the principle of interest convergence?: Whiteness, collective trauma, and the case for anti-racism. *Race, Ethnicity and Education, 14*(4), 439–459. https://doi.org/10.1080/13613324.2010.548375

Leonardo, Z. (2013). *Race frameworks: A multidimensional theory of racism and education.* Teachers College Press.

Leonardo, Z. (2020). The Trump presidency, post-colorblindness, and the reconstruction of public race speech. In O. K. Obasagie (Ed.), *Trumpism and its discontents* (pp. 18–55). Berkeley Public Policy Press.

Leong, N. (2013). Racial capitalism. *Harvard Law Review, 126*(8), 2151–2226.

Levine-Rasky, C. (2016). *Whiteness fractured.* Routledge.

Linder, C., Quaye, S. J., Stewart, T. J., Okello, W. K., & Roberts, R. E. (2019). "The whole weight of the world on my shoulders": Power, identity, and student activism. *Journal of College Student Development, 60*(5), 527–542. http://doi.org/10.1353/csd.2019.0048.

Lorde, A. 1984. *Sister outsider: Essays and speeches.* Crossing Press.

Love, B. L. (2020, February 6). White teachers need anti-racist therapy. *Education Week.* https://www.edweek.org/teaching-learning/opinion-white-teachers-need-anti-racist-therapy/2020/02

MacDonald, L. (2019). "The same as everyone else": How academically successful Indigenous secondary school students respond to a hidden curriculum of settler silencing. *Whiteness and Education, 4*(1), 38–52. https://doi.org/10.1080/23793406.2019.1626758

Marvasti, A. B., & McKinney, K. D. (2011). Does diversity mean assimilation? *Critical Sociology, 37*(5), 631–650. https://doi.org/10.1177%2F0896920510380071

Menakem, R. (2017). *My grandmother's hands: Racialized trauma and the pathway to mending our hearts and bodies.* Central Recovery Press.

Moraga, C., & Anzaldúa, G. (1983). *This bridge called my back: Writings by radical Women of Color.* Kitchen Table—Women of Color Press.

Morrison, T. (1992). *Playing in the dark: Whiteness and the literary imagination.* Harvard University Press.

Moses, M. S., & Chang, M. J. (2006). Toward a deeper understanding of the diversity rationale. *Educational Researcher, 35*(1), 6–11. https://doi.org/10.3102%2F0013189X035001006

Museus, S. D., & Park, J. J. (2015). The continuing significance of racism in the lives of Asian American college students. *Journal of College Student Development, 56*(6), 551–569. http://doi.org/10.1353/csd.2015.0059

Mustaffa, J. B. (2017). Mapping violence, naming life: A history of anti-Black oppression in the higher education system. *International Journal of Qualitative Studies in Education, 30*(8), 711–727. https://doi.org/10.1080/09518398.2017.1350299

Mustaffa, J. B. (2021). Can we write about Black life?: Refusing the unquenchable thirst for Black death in education. *The Journal of Educational Foundations, 34*(1), 68–84.

Patton, L. D., & Haynes, C. (2020). Dear white people: Reimagining whiteness in the struggle for racial equity. *Change: The Magazine of Higher Learning, 52*(2), 41–45. https://doi.org/10.1080/00091383.2020.1732775

Preston, A. M. (2020, September 9). The anatomy of transmisogynoir. *Harper's BAZAAR*. https://www.harpersbazaar.com/culture/features/a33614214/ashlee-marie-preston-transmisogynoir-essay/

Roediger, D. R. (1991). *The wages of whiteness: Race and the making of the American working class*. Verso.

Saad, L. F. (2020). *Me and white supremacy: Combat racism, change the world, and become a good ancestor*. Sourcebooks.

Singh, A. A. (2019). *The racial healing handbook: Practical activities to help you challenge privilege, confront systemic racism, and engage in collective healing*. New Harbinger Publications.

Smith, L. (1963). *Killers of the dream*. Anchor Books.

Sullivan, S. (2014). *Good white people: The problem with middle-class white anti-racism*. SUNY Press.

Thomas, J. M. (2020). *Diversity regimes: Why talk is not enough to fix racial inequality at universities*. Rutgers University Press.

Thompson, B., & Watson, V. (2016). Theorizing white racial trauma and its remedies. In S. Middleton, D. Roediger, & D. Shaffer (Eds.), *The constructions of whiteness: An interdisciplinary analysis of race formation and the meaning of a white identity* (pp. 234–255). University Press of Mississippi.

Tuck, E., & Yang, K. W. (2012). Decolonization is not a metaphor. *Decolonization: Indigeneity, Education & Society, 1*(1), 1–40.

Underhill, M. R. (2018). Parenting during Ferguson: Making sense of white parents' silence. *Ethnic and Racial Studies, 41*(11), 1934–1951. https://doi.org/10.1080/01419870.2017.1375132

Vittrup, B. (2018). Color blind or color conscious? White American mothers' approaches to racial socialization. *Journal of Family Issues, 39*(3), 668–692. http://doi.org/10.1177/0192513X16676858

Warikoo, N. K. (2016). *The diversity bargain*. University of Chicago Press.

Watt, S. K. (2007). Difficult dialogues, privilege and social justice: Uses of the privileged identity exploration (PIE) model in student affairs practice. *College Student Affairs Journal, 26*(2), 114–126.

Whitehead, M. A. (2021). Whiteness, anti-Blackness, and trauma: A grounded theory of white racial meaning-making. *Journal of College Student Development, 62*(3), 310–326. https://doi.org/10.1353/csd.2021.0027

Whitehead, M. A., Foste, Z., Duran, A., Tevis, T., & Cabrera, N. L. (2021). Disrupting the big lie: Higher education and whitelash in a post/colorblind era. *Education Sciences, 11*, 486. https://doi.org/10.3390/educsci11090486

Yancy, G. (2018). *Backlash: What happens when we talk honestly about racism in America.* Rowman & Littlefield.

EDITORS AND CONTRIBUTORS

Editors

Zak Foste is an assistant professor of higher education administration at the University of Kansas. His research critically explores whiteness in American higher education. This work examines both how whiteness functions to underwrite racially hostile and unwelcoming campus climates for Students of Color and the ways in which white college students understand their relationship to race and whiteness. His most recent work has examined how whiteness structures students' experiences in campus residence halls and community service-learning programs. Foste received his bachelor's degree in sociology and political science from Western Illinois University, his master's degree in student affairs in higher education from Miami University, and his PhD in higher education and student affairs from The Ohio State University.

Tenisha L. Tevis is an assistant professor of adult and higher education at Oregon State University. She earned her PhD in educational theory and policy studies with a cognate in higher education from The Pennsylvania State University, and a bachelor's degree and master's degrees in sociology from California State University, Sacramento. As a praxis scholar, her research attempts to disrupt dominant ideologies and biased institutional practices in two substantive and intersecting areas: students' transition to college—exploring how marginalized students continue to be disenfranchised by inequitable practices, and the confluence of leadership and identity in higher education—understanding how leadership practices contribute to patterns of inequality and exclusion. Her most recent work includes a systematic literature review focused on the college access literature to better inform college advising for Black high school students, and a study on the paradoxical identity of white women postsecondary administrators.

Contributors

Ellie Ash-Bala is a doctoral student at Colorado State University. Her research focuses on whiteness, white ally development, and racism in higher education.

Cameron C. Beatty (he/him) is an assistant professor in the Educational Leadership and Policy Studies Department at Florida State University. Beatty teaches courses in the undergraduate leadership studies program and the higher education graduate program, as well as conducts research with the Leadership Learning Research Center. Beatty's research foci include exploring the intersections of gender and race in leadership education, leadership development of Students of Color on historically white college campuses, and understanding experiences of racial battle fatigue for Black and Latinx students. In 2019, Beatty coedited a monograph titled *Critical Considerations for Race, Ethnicity and Culture for Fraternity and Sorority Life* (Wiley). He is a scholar passionate about deconstructing race, systemic racism, and hegemonic masculinity in postsecondary education environments.

James Black serves as director of resource management for academic affairs at Bloomsburg University. T/He/y is a PhD candidate in the Higher Education Leadership program at Colorado State University, researching how administrative discourse reproduces white supremacy in higher education.

Chris Corces-Zimmerman is a scholar-practitioner working at San Jose State University. Corces-Zimmerman's scholarship centers an unapologetic critique of whiteness and white supremacy in higher education, primarily focused on challenging structural and institutional manifestations of whiteness. His work is indebted to and influenced by the legacy of critical thought created by past and present generations of Black, brown, and Indigenous leaders from within and beyond the academy. His contribution in this volume is deeply influenced by and in service to the extraordinary work of the late Charles Mills, whose theorization of the "Racial Contract" is foundational to any understanding of whiteness.

Natasha Croom is associate dean of the graduate school and associate professor of higher education and student affairs in the College of Education at Clemson University. As a critical race feminist scholar-practitioner, Croom identifies and disrupts systemic oppression that manifests within and is reinforced by higher education. She centers womyn of color in analyses of institutional barriers to thriving and success in higher education environments. Through her praxis, Croom strives to work in and with communities to support the creation of practices and policies constructed from equity-based ideologies.

Antonio Duran (he/him) is an assistant professor of higher education at Florida International University. His research interests include using critical and poststructural frameworks to complicate the study of college student identity, experiences, and success. As a scholar, Duran is deeply committed to reimagining educational institutions to center those most minoritized in society.

Meg E. Evans (they) currently serves as the director of education and the interim executive director for a small, justice-based educational nonprofit in Atlanta. Prior to serving in this role, Evans worked within student affairs divisions at the University of Georgia, Carnegie Mellon University, Guilford College, and Warren Wilson College. Evans holds a BA from Warren Wilson College, an MS from Duquesne University, and a PhD from UGA where their research focused on student, staff, and faculty activism/advocacy/resistance. Prior to working in student affairs, Evans worked as a middle school teacher, emergency medical technician, and a nurses' assistant and played professional football for the Pittsburgh Passion.

Crystal E. Garcia (she/her), PhD, is assistant professor of educational administration at the University of Nebraska-Lincoln. Her research critically examines the mechanisms by which racially minoritized college students experience campus environments. Garcia is a 2021–2023 ACPA Emerging Scholar-Designee and was awarded the 2020 NASPA Latinx/a/o Knowledge Community Outstanding Faculty Award, the 2018 AERA Hispanic Research Issues SIG Dissertation of the Year Award, and the 2018 ACPA Burns B. Crookston Doctoral Research Award. She currently serves as a member of the editorial boards for the *Journal of College Student Development*, the *Journal of Student Affairs Research and Practice*, and the *College Student Affairs Journal*.

Tonia Guida is an assistant professor of instruction in the diversity, equity, and inclusion concentration in the College of Natural Sciences at UT-Austin. She has over 7 years of experience working in student support programs, study abroad, and teaching intergroup dialogue. Her research agenda entails theorizing around whiteness, space, and gender in higher education and developing more racially and socially just campus environments. Guida earned her doctorate in social science comparative education with a concentration in race and ethnicity from the University of California, Los Angeles (UCLA).

Bryan K. Hotchkins is an assistant professor of higher education in the Department of Educational Psychology and Leadership at Texas Tech University in Lubbock. A critical race pedagogue, Hotchkins studies how people of African descent navigate the geographies of racism while experiencing racial trauma as leaders, based on organizational climate, context, and culture. Hotchkins continues his How to Reverse Racism training program to teach people how to actualize antiracism across practices, policies, and programs. His new book *My Black is Exhausted: Forever in Pursuit of a Racist-Free World Where Hashtags Don't Exist* (Think Positionality Books) debuted in the fall of 2021. Hotchkins earned his doctorate in educational leadership and policy from the University of Utah.

Lauren N. Irwin (she/hers) is a PhD student in the University of Iowa's Higher Education and Student Affairs program and a research assistant with the Center for Research on Undergraduate Education. Irwin completed her bachelor's at UCLA and earned a master's at Michigan State University. Prior to pursuing her PhD, Irwin created and ran a campus-wide leadership education program and taught InterGroup Dialogues at California Polytechnic State University in San Luis Obispo, California. Irwin's research critically examines racism and whiteness, with a particular focus on cocurricular contexts (e.g., leadership education, service-learning) in higher education.

Romeo Jackson (they/them) is from the southside of Chicago and the grandchild of Gracie Lee Fowler. They are a queer, nonbinary femme, and a Black descendant of the estimated 11 million Africans who were kidnapped and sold into enslavement. Currently, Jackson serves as the political education coordinator at Black Youth Project 100 and is a PhD student at Colorado State University in the Higher Education Leadership program.

Alex C. Lange (they/them) is an assistant professor of higher education at Colorado State University. Their scholarship explores transgender students' college experiences, identity-based student activism, and LGBTQ history in education. Prior to being a faculty member, Lange worked within LGBTQ+ campus- and community-based work, intercultural engagement, leadership education, and alumni relations.

Douglass H. Lee is a doctoral student at Colorado State University. His research focuses on the experiences of Asian American college students. He currently serves as a research fellow with the Campaign for College Opportunity.

Jameson D. Lopez is an enrolled member of the Quechan tribe located in Fort Yuma, California. He currently serves as an assistant professor in the Center for the Study of Higher Education at the University of Arizona. He studies Native American higher education using Indigenous statistics. Additionally he has expertise in the limitations of collecting and applying quantitative results to Indigenous populations. He carries unique experiences to his research that include a 2010 deployment to Iraq as a platoon leader where he received a bronze star medal for actions in a combat zone.

Wilson Kwamogi Okello, PhD, (he/him/his) is an assistant professor of higher education in the Department of Educational Leadership at the University of North Carolina Wilmington. Deploying critical and creative qualitative approaches, Okello is an interdisciplinary scholar who draws on theories of Blackness and Black feminist theories to think about knowledge production and identity development, particularly, the relationship between history, the body, and epistemology, in and beyond educational spaces. He is also concerned with how theories of Blackness and Black feminist theories inform and reconfigure understandings of racialized stress and trauma, masculinities, curricula, and pedagogies.

Moira L. Ozias is assistant professor in the Center for the Study of Higher Education at the University of Arizona. Her research focuses on equity in higher education practice, especially investigating white women's racism and processes for creating educational spaces and curricula that resist racism and settler colonialism. She uses critical whiteness, gender, and affect theories to understand how college experiences support and resist white women's affective and spatial investments in white supremacy. Ozias worked for over 15 years in higher administration before moving into faculty roles. She has also served as director of research and scholarship for ACPA–College Student Educators International (2019–2022).

Penny A. Pasque (she/her) is professor in educational studies/higher education and student affairs, director of qualitative methods, and director of the QualLab in the Office of Research, Innovation and Collaboration (ORIC) in the College of Education and Human Ecology at The Ohio State University. In addition, she is editor of the *Review of Higher Education* (with Thomas F. Nelson Laird), which is considered one of the leading journals in the field. Her research addresses complexities in qualitative inquiry, in/equities in higher education, and dis/connections between higher education and society. Pasque's research has appeared in over 100 journal articles and books.

Lori D. Patton, PhD, is department chair of Educational Studies and professor of higher education and student affairs at The Ohio State University. Her scholarship focuses on critical race theory, campus diversity initiatives, Black women and girls in education, and college student development. She coedited *Critical Perspectives on Black Women and College Success* (Routledge, 2016) and has authored numerous journal articles, book chapters, and other academic publications. She has received national awards for her scholarship, including being ranked among the top 200 educators in the United States. She is a frequently sought expert on various education topics.

OiYan A. Poon is an associate professor affiliate at Colorado State University. Her research focuses on the racial politics and discourses of college access, admissions, affirmative action, race, racism, and Asian Americans.

Felisia J. Tagaban (Diné/Tlingit/Filipina) is a 2nd-year doctoral student in the Educational Policy Studies and Practice Department at the University of Arizona (UA). Tagaban holds bachelor of arts (creative writing) and master of arts (higher education) degrees from the University of Arizona. Currently, Tagaban serves as a student relations coordinator for UA Admissions and the College of Education, in partnership with Sunnyside Unified School District. Tagaban is working to establish and support educational pathways for Indigenous SUSD students, while advocating for systemic and structural change at both institutions.

Kenyona N. Walker, PhD, is a senior project manager at The Ohio State University. Her research focuses on the unique experiences and educational needs of Black women and girls. She is a cofounder of the Racial Equity, Diversity, and Inclusion (REDI) movement at the Center on Education and Training for Employment at The Ohio State University. As a lecturer, she frequently taught a graduate-level Urban Issues in Education course. Walker is a sought-after racial justice educational consultant and presenter for a variety of educational institutions.

Anton Ward-Zanotto is a PhD candidate in the Colorado State University Higher Education Leadership program and assistant dean of students at Seattle University. Zanotto completed a bachelor's degree in business and a bachelor's degree in political science at Santa Clara University and earned a master's in higher education and student affairs at Indiana University, Bloomington. Zanotto's research works to understand and critiques the ways that institutional policies act as manifestations of white power in higher education.

Erin Weston is the director of the First-Year Experience at Georgia College. She has 20 years of experience in higher education administration and is committed to advancing equity and justice in academia. She is a 2021 graduate of the University of Georgia College Student Affairs Administration PhD program. Her dissertation focused on increasing antiracist activism among white college students.

Melvin A. Whitehead is an assistant professor of student affairs administration at Binghamton University. He received his PhD in Education from the University of Georgia. His current research uses qualitative methodologies and critical frameworks to examine connections between whiteness and anti-Blackness in U.S. higher education. His work focuses on how white college students make meaning of race and whiteness and how those processes connect to the campus experiences of Black college students at historically white institutions. Previously, Whitehead worked as a librarian at a community college and engaged in research examining the campus experiences of LGBTQ+ community college students.

Brittany M. Williams is an assistant professor of higher education at St. Cloud State University. A national award-winning writer and speaker, her research explores issues of career development, social class, and health disparities in and relating to college environments. Black women and girls serve as her primary point for scholarly inquiry. Williams had the distinct pleasure of serving as Teach for America's inaugural Writer in Residence and was a 2020–2021 American Association for University Women American Fellow for her work on pay inequality in student affairs and higher education. She is a proud product of Atlanta Public Schools.

INDEX

academic achievement, measurement of, 247
academic advisors, 140–141
activists, student, labeling of, 193
administration, 34–35, 139–145, 248–249, 264
affect, whiteness as, 34–35
Afro-futurism, 215
Afro-pessimism, 215, 216
answerability, questions for, 38–40
anti-Asian racism, 257
anti-Asian violence, 1
anti-Blackness, 54–56, 213–215, 257. *See also* Blackness
anti-Blackness literature, 212–218
anti-Black racism, 206–208, 213, 214, 218–219
apologies, 175
Arbery, Ahmaud, 1, 135, 182, 224
Arch Society (University of Georgia), 196
Arizona State University, 252
Asian American people, 27
assignments, 145–146, 148
Auburn University, 98
awareness status of WREM, 234

Baldwin, James, 70, 75, 87, 103, 106, 150, 263–264
Baylor University, 98, 194
behaviors, student, 194–195
belongingness, 55, 147
bias training, 144
Black, Indigenous, People of Color (BIPOC)
  chilly campus climate to, 194
  code-switching by, 190–191
  dehumanization of, 22, 35
  discussions regarding, 106
  emotional responses of, 265
  experiential knowledge of, 256–257
  exploitation of, 31
  healing for, 260
  within higher education, 102–103
  leadership roles of, 190, 191
  muting of, 256
  oppression to, 257
  racial categories of, 51
  Robert's Rules of Order against, 195
  strategies and opportunities for, 197–198
  student government for, 193
  visibility gap of, 188
  whiteness effects on, 2, 257, 266–267
  whiteness proximity and acclimation to, 190–192
  whiteness resistance by, 29–30
  white supremacy effects to, 23–25
  writings of, 26–27
  See also Black people/students; Black women; Indigenous people/students; Students of Color
the Black concept, 115–116
Black culture center (BCC), 139–140
Black exceptionalism, 129
Black faculty, 123–126
Black Justice League (BJL) (Princeton University), 100, 101
Black lifemaking, 261–262
Black Lives Matter movement, 212–213, 217
Blackness, 117, 118, 208. *See also* anti-Blackness

Black people/students
  academic advisors and, 140–141
  belonging for, 147
  bodies of, 118, 215
  dehumanization of, 22, 35
  exclusion of, 147
  experiential knowledge of, 256
  within higher education, 102–103
  history of, 117
  racial experiences of, 224
  reform for, 99
  within residence halls, 140
  trans, 158–159
  unbelonging of, 55
  as unwelcome, 141
  violence against, 98, 106–107, 135, 224, 264–265
  whiteness effects on, 6
  white racial frames and, 127
Black women, 137–145, 146, 191, 215
blood, misuse example of, 252
Boggs, Grace Lee, 107
Boren, David, 90–91, 99
boundaries, by whiteness, 6
bound liberation, 236
Braasch, Sara, 54
Bradley University, 264–265
breathing, concept of, 115, 116, 131–132
Brick House, 141–142
Brochu, Breonna, 140
Brown v. Board of Education, 93–94, 97
Bucknell College, 98
Bureau of Indian Education (BIE) schools, 250

campus ecology framework, 181–182
campus housing, policies within, 262–263
chilly campus climate, 194
chokehold concept, 121–122, 127
citations, use of, 131
Clark, Kenneth B., 146
Clark, Mamie Phipps, 146
classrooms, whiteness and inclusion within, 145, 147, 148
codes of white culture, 210–211
code-switching, 190–191
cognitive dissonance, 79–80
Collected Rules and Regulations (University of Missouri), 123–124, 125
colonialism, settler, 51, 119, 251–253, 257
Colorado State University, 54
color-blindness, 267, 268n2
color-evasiveness, 52, 71
complicity, white, 266
consensual hallucination, 74
Cooper, Amy, 1
Cooper, Christian, 1
COVID-19 pandemic, 137–138
critical discourse analysis (CDA), 122, 123–126, 127–128, 129–131
critical race theory (CRT), 93
critical white double-consciousness, 261
critical whiteness praxis, 9–11, 22, 26–28, 36
critical whiteness studies (CWS), 3, 93–94, 96–98, 156–159, 226
culturally based sororities and fraternities (CBSFs), 172, 176–177, 178, 179–180
culture of forgetfulness, 74

Davis, Jefferson, 48
Dear White Administrators, 139–145
Dear White Faculty, 145–149
Dear White People, 137–139
deconstructing whiteness status of WREM, 235–236
denial status of WREM, 234–235
discourse, whiteness as, 30–31, 52, 209
dispositions, of whiteness, 209
disruption, politics of, 36–41
diversity
  efforts regarding, 61
  exposure to, 141

language regarding, 259–260
over justice, 85–86
racial harm masking and, 258–260
within sorority and fraternity life (SFL), 182
diversity, equity, and inclusion (DEI), 103, 104–105
diversity statements, 104–105
diversity training program, 90–91
Du Bois, W. E. B., 48, 226

Eisgruber, Christopher, 101
emotionality, white ignorance and, 97
Enlightenment, 117
epistemic asphyxiation, 116, 122–123, 131–132
epistemic violence, 120, 121–122, 217
epistemology, 72
epistemology of ignorance, 71, 73–74
equity, learning programs toward, 105–106
explicit bias training, 144

faculty
assignments from, 145–146
Black women as, 142–143
Dear White Faculty, 145–149
feeling and affect role of, 34–35
hiring process of, 57
inclusion policies by, 148
of Indigenous education, 248–249
name pronunciation by, 148–149
professional development of, 144
race role regarding, 124–125
racial engagement role of, 239
feeling, whiteness as, 34–35
Feminists of Color, 257
Ferguson, Missouri, 260
film-based resources, 146
Floyd, George, 1, 98, 106, 115, 135, 182, 224, 264–265
Foucault, Michel, 116

Garner, Eric, 115
Gray, Lloyd and Thomas, 6
Grinnell College, 98

happy talk path, 182
Harris, Paul, 116–117, 126–128
Harris, Taylor, 127
Hercules, 96
HESA graduate programs, inequities within, 56
heteronormativity, 156–157
higher education
anti-Blackness literature within, 212–218
anti-Blackness within, 54–56
anti-Black racism within, 206–208
diversity efforts within, 61, 85–86, 259
facilities naming within, 55
hiring process within, 57, 83–84
history of, 49–50
Indigenous perspective erasure within, 245–254
leadership demographics within, 24
policing within, 54–55, 99
post-color-blindness of, 267–268
racial climate within, 79
racism incident responses within, 82–83
settler colonialism within, 55–56
slavery and, 215
white cultural spaces within, 83–84
white innocence within, 92–93, 98–102
whiteness protection within, 56–58
white normativity within, 53–61
white racial ignorance within, 77–86
as white spaces, 54–55
white supremacy within, 102–106, 211
See also specific institutions
hiring, within higher education, 57, 83–84

historical amnesia, 79
Historically White Colleges and Universities (HWCUs), 2, 21–22. *See also specific institutions*
historically white sorority and fraternity (HWSF), 172, 176–177, 178, 179. *See also* sorority and fraternity life (SFL)
homonormativity, 156–157, 159
horses, significance of, 252
housing, campus, policies within, 262–263
Hydra, 96

identity, whiteness as, 29
ideology, whiteness as, 30, 52
imperialism, 246
implicit bias training, 144
Indigenous data sovereignty, 253–254
Indigenous people/students
  Bureau of Indian Education (BIE) schools for, 250
  dehumanization of, 35
  demographics of, 246
  educational outcomes measurement of, 252
  within higher education, 102–103
  horse significance to, 252
  Indigenous data sovereignty and, 253–254
  Meriam Report and, 248–249, 251
  National Assessment of Educational Progress (NAEP), 249–250
  National Indian Education Study (NIES) and, 249–250, 251
  Native Student Outreach Access and Resiliency (SOAR), 253
  perspective erasure of, 245–254
  values measurement of, 247–251
  whiteness and, 251–253
  writings of, 27
intellectual alibis, white, 34
interactional theory of whiteness, 35–36
interest convergence, 27, 236
interpretive filter, of whiteness, 209, 225
interviews, white supremacy effects on, 24
inverted epistemology, 71–72, 73

Jefferson, Thomas, 117
Jones, Nikole Hannah, 6
justice, diversity over, 85–86

Kanoute, Omou, 54
knapsack metaphor, 25
knowledge, legitimate, 58–60
knowledge, template for, 119–120

labeling, within leadership, 192–193
Latinx people, 27, 214
leadership
  of Black, Indigenous, People of Color (BIPOC), 190, 191
  of Black women, 142–143, 191
  within higher education, 24
  labeling within, 192–193
  within predominantly white institutions (PWIs), 192
  strategies and opportunities for, 197–198
  student behavior within, 194–195
  student leadership organizations, 188–190, 191, 194–198
  whiteness within, 192, 195–196
learning programs, toward equity, 105–106
legitimate knowledge, 58–60
Leigh, Simone, 141–142
LGBTQ
  center staffing and budgeting for, 164–167
  exclusion of, 156–157
  homonormativity and, 156–157, 159
  National Coming Out Day (NCOD) and, 162–163
  programming regarding, 162–164

resources for, 155, 160
Safe Zone training and, 160–162
Transgender Day of Remembrance (TDOR) and, 163
transnormativity and, 157–159
white innocence and, 159
whiteness and, 163–164
liberation, praxis and, 9
light, metaphor of, 117
literature, 146, 212–218
logic of elimination, 119
Lorde, Audre, 115

margins concept, 256–257
McDade, Tony, 224
membership, within sorority and fraternity life (SFL), 174–175
Meriam Report, 248–249, 251
microaggression, 253
misogynoir, 257
Multicultural Greek Council (MGC), 172, 175, 176, 177
multicultural student government, 193

names, correct pronunciation of, 148–149
National Assessment of Educational Progress (NAEP), 249–250
National Coming Out Day (NCOD), 162–163
National Indian Education Study (NIES), 249–251
National Panhellenic Conference (NPC), 172, 174, 176, 177, 180
National Pan-Hellenic Council (NPHC), 172, 175, 176, 177
Native American students, 6
Native Student Outreach Access and Resiliency (SOAR), 253
nescient whiteness, 233–234
norms, whiteness within, 119
North American Interfraternity Conference (NIC), 172, 176, 177, 180

Obama, Michelle, 139
oppression, 33–34, 236, 257–258
the Other, destruction of, 116

pants pocket metaphor, 25
parenting, strategies regarding, 259–260
Pennsylvania State University, 141–142
People of Color. *See* Black, Indigenous, People of Color (BIPOC)
Plessy v. Ferguson, 94
policies, 2, 262–263
policing, 54–55, 99, 135
politics of disruption, 36–41
positivism, 59
post-color-blindness, 267–268
praxis, 9
predominantly white institutions (PWIs), 189–190, 192, 197–198
Princeton University, 98, 99–102
privilege
cultural dimension of, 210
intergenerational, 33–34
structural dimension of, 217–218
white, 25, 49, 77, 96, 208, 210–211, 212
professional development, 144
property, whiteness as, 33–34, 118–120, 127, 175
protests, 205

queer and trans people of color (QTPOC), 162–164, 166

race, 21, 50–51, 58, 59, 71–72. *See also specific races*
racial capitalism, 260
racial cognizance, 234
racial comfort, 57
racial contract, 31–33, 71, 73
racial development, 225–228
racial hierarchy, 58
racialization, 50

racial justice ideas and actions status of
  WREM, 236
racial privilege, 209
racial victimhood, white, 237
racism
  actions against, 100–101
  administrative response to, 142
  anti-Black, 206–208
  cultural dimension of, 206–207
  defined, 206, 227
  denial of, 234–235
  disruption of, 236
  downplay of, 267
  examples of, 92, 173, 224
  faculty within, 124–125
  within historically white sorority and fraternity (HWSF) communities, 172–173
  history ignorance regarding, 31
  ideological dimension of, 206
  incident responses to, 82–83
  individualization of, 81
  within literature, 213
  reproduction of, 60
  structural dimension of, 206, 207
  as systemic, 81–83
  whiteness *versus,* 206, 219
  White women response within, 56–57
racist nativism, 257
reciprocity, 120, 121
reflexivity questions, 47
residence halls, 140, 262–263
response-ability, 38–40
reverse racism, 77
rioting, 205
Robert's Rules of Order, 195
Rowe, Chennel, 140

Safe Zone training, 155, 160–162
segregation, 94–95
self-reflection, 238–239
separate but equal doctrine, 94
settler colonialism, 51, 55–56, 119, 214–215, 251–253, 257
Sigma Alpha Epsilon (SAE) fraternity (University of Oklahoma), 90–91, 99
1619 Project, 2, 144
Siyonbola, Lolade, 54
slavery, 21, 128–131, 148, 215
Smith College, 54
socialization, 219, 234
social location, of whiteness, 209
socially induced ignorance, 73
solipsism, 194
sorority and fraternity life (SFL)
  acknowledgment within, 181–183
  change recommendations within, 180
  deconstruction within, 183
  demographics of, 178
  diversity within, 182
  grade reporting policies within, 176
  implications for practice within, 181–183
  languages and practices within, 175–176
  membership within, 174–175
  overview of, 172
  questions regarding, 183–184
  recruitment within, 176
  resource allocation within, 176–177
  whiteness within, 173
  white normativity within, 173–178
  white racial ignorance within, 178–180
  See also historically white sorority and fraternity (HWSF)
sorority recruitment, 176
staff, for LGBTQ centers, 164–167
structure, whiteness as, 52
student activists, labeling of, 193
student affairs programs, 56, 215
student leadership organizations, 188–190, 191, 194–198

Students of Color
bicultural actions of, 59
community-oriented work of, 60
within HESA graduate programs, 56
racial capitalism of, 260
within sororities and fraternities, 175
university experience of, 2
white racial ignorance and, 182
See also Black, Indigenous, People of Color (BIPOC)
Supreme Court, 93–94, 97
systemic whiteness, 81–83, 208–212. *See also* whiteness

Tatum, Beverly Daniel, 146
Taylor, Breonna, 1, 135, 182, 224
template, for knowledge production, 119–120
tenure, 123–126
testimonial smothering, 121
transformative paradigm, 230
Transgender Day of Remembrance (TDOR), 163
transmisogynoir, 257
transnormativity, 157–159
trauma, 260
Trump, Donald, 101–102

unbelonging, 55
unconscious beliefs of white superiority status of WREM, 237
"Unite the Right" rally, 24
University of Alabama, 174, 193
University of Arizona, 252–253
University of Florida, 193
University of Georgia, 173, 196
University of Kansas, 193
University of Michigan, 155
University of Minnesota, 155
University of Missouri, 116–117, 123–126
University of North Carolina Chapel Hill, 6
University of Oklahoma, 6, 90–92, 99
University of Richmond, 194
University of Tennessee, Knoxville, 194
University of Virginia, 116–117
U.S. Capitol Building, 205

victimhood, white racial, 237
violence
anti-Asian, 1
against Blacks, 98, 106–107, 135, 224, 264–265
epistemic, 120, 121–122, 217
of whiteness, 51, 260

Washington, D. C., 205
wealth, racial gap regarding, 78–79
Wheatley, John and Susanna, 128–129, 130
Wheatley, Phillis, 117, 128–131
white complicity, 266
white cultural spaces, 83–84
white fragility, 96
white habitus, 227, 234
white ignorance, 97, 226–227
white imaginary, 118
white immunity, 25, 96
white innocence
analytic lens of, 93–102
as cloak, 159
critical whiteness studies (CWS) and, 96–98
defined, 92, 93–94, 103
desires for, 263–266
disruption of, 95
example of, 92
framework for, 95
function of, 97–98
in higher education, 92–93, 98–102
maintenance of, 264
overview of, 107
relinquishing, 102–106
white institutional presence, 53–60, 196–197

white intellectual alibis, 34
whitelash, 267
white liberalism, 235
whiteness
  acclamation to, 190–192
  acknowledgment of, 181–183
  awareness of, 234
  benefits of, 147
  as Black impediment, 118
  Black incapacity for, 123–131
  boundaries of, 6
  chokehold of, 122
  in the classrooms, 145
  construction of, 51, 227
  as controlling mechanism, 130
  cultural dimension of, 210–211
  deconstruction of, 183, 235–236
  default of, 207
  defined, 3, 24, 26, 165, 173, 225, 233
  as discourse, 30–31, 52
  disruption of, 36–41
  effects of, 5–6
  employment decisions and, 123–126
  enormity of, 1
  entitlement within, 2
  as epistemic violence, 120, 121–122
  as feeling and affect, 34–35
  function of, 6
  homonormativity and, 156–157
  ideological dimension, 209–210
  as ideology, 30, 52
  immunity of, 33
  incident responses to, 82–83
  Indigenous people and, 251–253
  institutionalization of, 262–263
  as interactional and interlocking, 35–36
  interpretive filter of, 209, 225
  interrupting, 161–162, 164, 165–166
  invisibility of, 71–72, 96, 174, 266–268
  within leadership, 192, 195–196
  nascient, 233–234
  as normal, 83–85
  normative nature of, 49
  oppressive system intersection with, 257–258
  overview of, 50–53, 208–212
  as property, 33–34, 118–120, 127, 175
  protection of, 56–58
  proximity to, 190–192
  as racial contract, 31–33
  racism *versus,* 206, 219
  research regarding, 3–4
  resistance to, 29–30
  Safe Zone training and, 160–161
  structural dimension of, 211–212
  systemic, 81–83, 208–212
  tarrying with, 28
  as terror form, 266–267, 268
  transnormativity and, 158
  trauma of, 260–261
  understanding, 29–36
  as universalized, 9
  violence of, 51, 260
  from white supremacy, 212
  working through, 226
"whiteness as a container" concept, 36, 41n1
whiteness-as-invisible analytic, 7
white normality, 96, 189–192, 259
white normative center, 182
white normativity
  acknowledgment of, 181–183
  boundary defining within, 118–119
  deconstruction of, 183
  disrupting, 177–178
  in higher education, 53–61
  legitimate knowledge and, 58–60
  overview of, 50–53
  reproduction of, 52–53, 165
  settler colonialism and, 55–56
  within sorority and fraternity life (SFL), 173–178
white parenting, 259–260

white privilege, 25, 49, 77, 96, 208, 210–211, 212
white queer and trans innocence, 159
white racial engagement model (WREM)
  awareness status within, 233–234
  deconstructing whiteness status within, 235–236
  defined, 225
  denial status within, 234–235
  development of, 230–231
  nescient whiteness, 233–234
  overview of, 240
  in practice, 238–240
  racial justice ideals and actions status within, 236
  self-reflection through, 238–239
  status descriptions within, 231–238
  unconscious beliefs of white superiority status within, 237
  white liberalism status within, 235
  white supremacist ideals and actions status within, 237–238
white racial frame, 30, 121, 127
white racial ignorance
  as agentic, 75–77
  challenging, 80–81
  within higher education, 77–86
  manifestations of, 77–86
  overview of, 73–77, 87
  reinforcement of, 182
  as safeguard to privilege, 76
  as socially sanctioned, 75–77
  within sorority and fraternity life (SFL), 178–180
white racial norm maintenance, 192–197
white racial propriospect, 228
white racial victimhood, 237
white solipsism, 194
White students, 57, 74, 77, 79, 189–190, 191, 225–228
white supremacy
  defined, 23, 26, 225
  disruption of, 236
  harms of, 22
  within higher education, 102–106, 211
  ideals and action status within, 237–238
  ideology of, 210
  individualization of, 81
  overview of, 245
  promotion of, 24
  relinquishing, 102–106
  understanding, 29–36
  whiteness from, 212
  white racial ignorance and, 76
White women, 56–57
Wilson, Woodrow, 100–101
women of color, 26
Woodson, Ashley, 116–117, 123–126

Yale University, 54

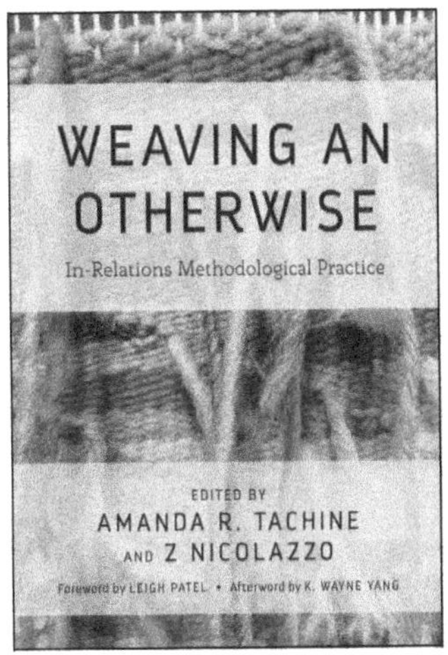

Weaving an Otherwise

In-Relations Methodological Practice

Edited by Amanda R. Tachine and Z Nicolazzo

Foreword by Leigh Patel

Afterword by K. Wayne Yang

Who (and what) are you bearing witness to (and for) through your research? When you witness, what claims are you making about who and what matters? What does your research forget, and does it do it on purpose?

This book reconceptualizes qualitative research as an in-relations process, one that is centered on, fully concerned with, and lifts up those who have been and continue to be dispossessed, harmed, dehumanized, suffered, and erased because of white supremacy, settler colonialism, or other hegemonic world views.

It prompts scholars to make connections between themselves as "researchers" and affect, ancestors, community, family and kinship, space and place, and the more than human beings with whom they are always already in community.

What are the modes and ways of knowing through which we approach our research? How can the practice of research bring us closer to the peoples, places, more than human beings, histories, presents, and futures in which we are embedded and connected to? If we are the instruments of our research, then how must we be attentive to all of the affects and relations that make us who we are and what will become? These questions animate *Weaving an Otherwise*, providing a wellspring from which we think about our interconnections to the past, present, and future possibilities of research.

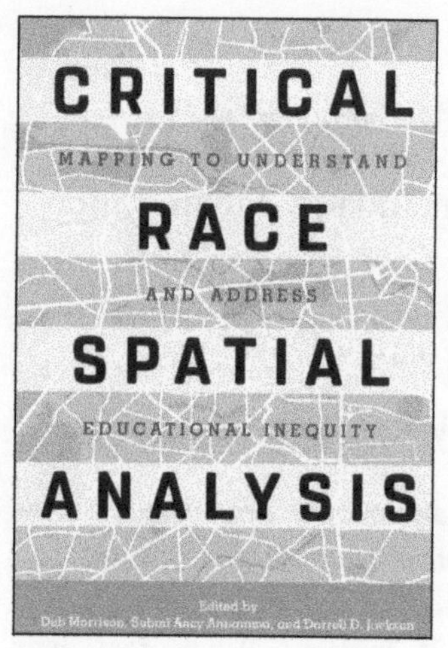

Critical Race Spatial Analysis

Mapping to Understand and Address Educational Inequity

Edited by Deb Morrison, Subini Ancy Annamma, and Darrell D. Jackson

How does space illuminate educational inequity?

Where and how can spatial analysis be used to disrupt educational inequity?

Which tools are most appropriate for the spatial analysis of educational equity?

This book addresses these questions and explores the use of critical spatial analysis to uncover the dimensions of entrenched and systemic racial inequities in educational settings and identify ways to redress them.

The contributors to this book—some of whom are pioneering scholars of critical race spatial analysis theory and methodology—demonstrate the application of the theory and tools applied to specific locales, and in doing so illustrate how this spatial and temporal lens enriches traditional approaches to research.

"The editors and chapter authors of *Critical Race Spatial Analysis* have taken it upon themselves to embark upon a bold challenge: to fulfill the interdisciplinary charge of critical race theory. For now and into the distant future, their work stands as testament to the commitment to grapple with the layers of race, space, and school. In the long road toward justice, I am overly grateful to my comrades for producing this seminal volume."—***David Stovall**, Professor of Educational Policy Studies and African-American Studies, University of Illinois at Chicago*

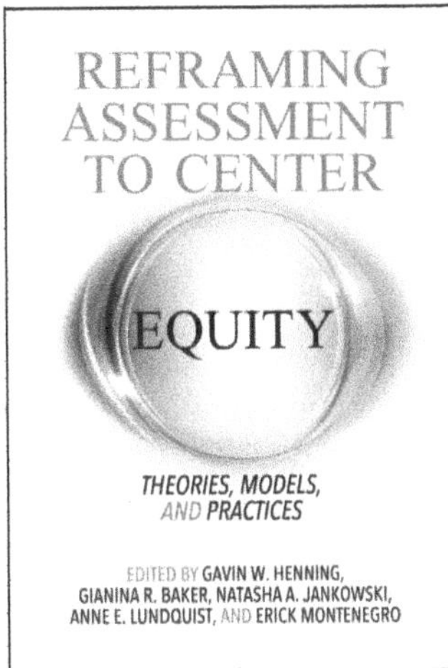

Reframing Assessment to Center Equity

Theories, Models, and Practices

Edited by Gavin W. Henning, Gianina R. Baker, Natasha A. Jankowski, Anne E. Lundquist, and Erick Montenegro

"Assessment practitioners are change agents. The very design of assessing for learning implies that what is learned from the process will create a need for change and improvement. But what if the assessment work is not fair and equitable? What if we unintentionally create or continue a system that works against fairness and inclusivity? *Reframing Assessment to Center Equity* is foundational to how we think about assessment as a tool for positive and responsible change."—***Catherine M. Wehlburg****, Provost and VPAA at Athens State University*

This book makes the case for assessment of student learning as a vehicle for equity in higher education. The book proceeds through a framework of "why, what, how, and now what." The opening chapters present the case for infusing equity into assessment, arguing that assessment professionals can and should be activists in advancing equity, given the historic and systemic use of assessment as an impediment to the educational access and attainment of historically marginalized populations.

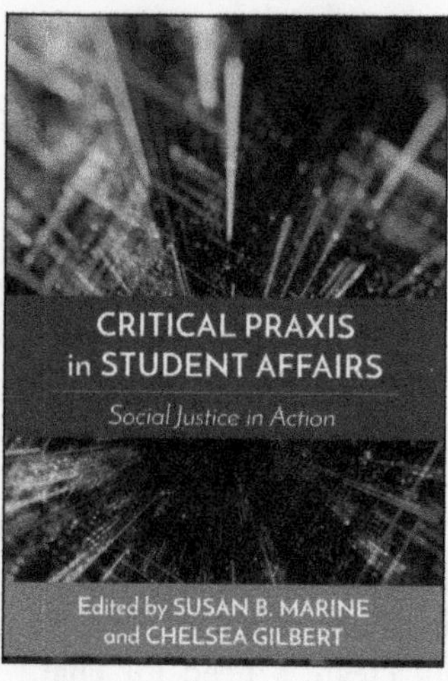

Critical Praxis in Student Affairs

Social Justice in Action

Edited by Susan B. Marine and Chelsea Gilbert

Student affairs work—like higher education—is fundamentally about change. Principally, the change work performed by student affairs practitioners is about supporting the growth and development of individual students and student groups. Increasingly, that work has called for practitioners to become more active in working to change higher education so that it lives up to its radically democratic, inclusive ideals. This means adopting new strategies to transform student affairs staff, students, and institutions, and drawing on insights from critical, liberatory theories. This text represents an effort to describe and document these practices of intentionally centering critical theories.

The first section of this text examines the ways that critically minded practitioners lead through equitable, liberatory frameworks, offering important models for reimagining the future of higher education. In the second section, the editors take up thinking and acting to support the development of critical consciousness in students, providing examples of programs, initiatives, and student support offices that center social justice in their work and foster a critical lens through their interactions with students. In their conclusion, the editors provide a model for critical praxis, offering enduring strategies for practitioners seeking to incorporate critical, socially just praxis into their everyday work and defining areas for future research and praxis, including identifying strategies for effective assessment of critical praxis and modalities for "scaling up" the work for maximal impact.

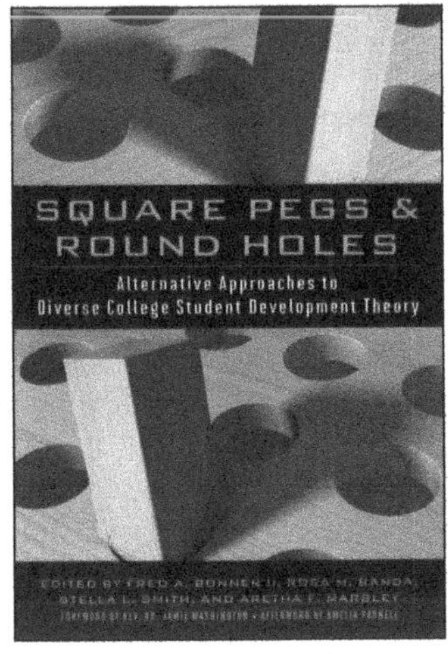

Square Pegs & Round Holes

Alternative Approaches to Diverse College Students Development Theory

Edited by Fred A. Bonner II, Rosa M. Banda, Stella L. Smith, and Aretha F. Marbley

Foreword by Jamie Washington

Afterword by Amelia Parnell

"*Square Pegs and Round Holes* is an important asset to the field of higher education and student affairs. Uniquely centering critical race theory as the organizing frame for alternative student development models and perspectives presented, the book empowers practitioners and faculty with updated tools for understanding the intersectional, contextualized, and diverse identities of today's college students. While this book thoughtfully critiques the shortcomings of traditional theories, it does not reject them entirely. Rather, it builds new space for emerging voices that tell a more complete story about the complexity of student experiences and identities."—***Alexa Wesley****, Associate Director for Research and Policy, NASPA, Student Affairs Administrators in Higher Education*

Developing alternative student development frameworks and models, this groundbreaking book provides student affairs practitioners, as well as faculty, with illuminating perspectives and viable approaches for understanding the development of today's diverse student populations, and for building the foundation for their academic success and self-authorship.

With the increasing number of adult working students, minoritized, multiracial, LGTBQ, and first-generation students, this book offers readers vital insights into—and ways to interrogate—existing practice, and develop relevant responses to the needs of these populations.

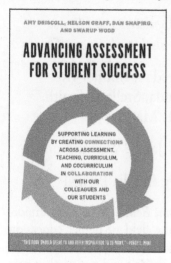